Journal of the British Academy, **5**, 1–35. DOI https://doi.org/10.5871/jba/005.001
Posted 18 January 2017.

Penal power in America: Forms, functions and foundations

British Academy Law Lecture
read 7 June 2016

DAVID GARLAND
Fellow of the Academy

Abstract: In this article I discuss the exercise of penal power in contemporary America with a view to explaining its historical causes, its contemporary forms and functions, and its social foundations. I argue that the leading characteristic of American penality today is not degradation, retribution, racial caste-making, or neoliberal discipline but instead the imposition of penal controls. The remainder of the article develops some hypotheses about the social and political roots of that distinctive form of punishment. Re-connecting penal controls with patterns of crime and violence, I highlight the deficits of social control and social capital that set America off from comparable nations and I trace the sources of these deficits to the structure and operation of certain American institutions as well as the limited capacities and patterned dispositions of the American state.

Keywords: penality, political economy, criminal violence, social control, social deficits, state capacity, penal control, mass penal control.

How should we understand the extraordinary deployment of penal power that operates in the US today? That is the question I address in this article. I will approach it primarily as a research question, though it also has implications for criminal justice reform—a subject that is high on America's political agenda at the present time.

Most of the existing research on this question is historical in nature, tracing the build-up of punishment from the 1970s to 2010. And most of it focuses on America's very high rates of imprisonment or what has come to be known as 'mass incarceration'. But here I want to address comparative as well as historical questions, and to consider other forms of penal power as well as incarceration. I want to ask why America is an international outlier on virtually every dimension of criminal punishment, and to reflect on what this might tell us about the relationship of penal power to other forms of social control and state action. The analysis I present is schematic, but I hope that a provisional and somewhat provocative outline will be of interest nevertheless.

The comparative scholarship on penal policy is still at an early stage of development, but the most promising work associates cross-national differences in punishment with differences in levels of inequality (Wilkinson & Pickett 2009); differences in welfare state regimes (Cavadino & Dignan 2005); and differences in types of political economy or 'varieties of capitalism' (Lacey 2007; Lacey & Soskice 2017).[1]

It seems to me that these macro-social analyses point us in the right direction and I attempt to build on them in what follows. But they are primarily accounts of correlations and covariance, and each grows vague when it comes to specifying the mechanisms and processes that link the macro-structures they discuss with the phenomena of crime and punishment.[2] One of the contributions I make here is to say a little more about these linkages—some of which become more apparent when we attend to the details of historical research on processes of penal change and social and economic transitions. And whereas each of these analyses associates penal policies with the social–structural contexts in which they develop, I also focus on the problem-solving work that penal systems endeavour to do, and particularly their relationship to changing patterns of crime and violence.

The explanatory framework I develop seeks, *first*, to reconnect America's extraordinary use of penal power with its distinctive levels of criminal violence and social problems, particularly those problems associated with social disorganisation and cumulative disadvantage, such as drug addiction, untreated mental illness, homelessness, domestic violence, family breakdown, suicide, low birth weight, infant mortality, child poverty, and so on; *second,* to trace how these patterns of crime and punishment—and more generally the social problems and state responses characteristic of the United States—have been structured over time by distinctive forms of government and political economy; and, *third,* to highlight the crucial role played by processes of informal social control—and by what I call 'social control deficits'—in linking social and economic structures with the phenomena of crime and punishment. The aim of this framework is thus to connect penal policy with overarching structures of political economy but also with underlying patterns of violence, crime, and insecurity.

[1] Other important contributions include: Whitman (2003); Sutton (2004); Lappi-Seppälä (2008); Pratt & Ericksson (2013) and the essays in Reitz (2017).

[2] Recent work by Lacey & Soskice (2015; 2017) has begun to address this question of causal mechanisms with greater specificity.

ESTABLISHING THE PHENOMENON: AMERICA'S DISTINCTIVE USE OF PENAL POWER

I begin by specifying the thing to be explained: America's distinctive deployment of penal power. There are at least six separate dimensions on which American punishment is 'exceptional' or, as I would prefer to say, an *outlier* when viewed in a comparative perspective.[3]

(i) *Imprisonment rates:* The per capita imprisonment rate of America as a whole is more than eight times higher than the Western European average (Walmsley 2016). And although there is great internal variation, the mildest US states have incarceration rates that are higher than the harshest of the Western European nations and higher than all but one of the Eastern European countries (Lappi-Seppälä 2008).

(ii) *Penal supervision:* America's use of correctional supervision is five times greater than the European average. It is also much more conditional and control-oriented. Probation and parole in the US today are not primarily forms of social assistance or social work: they are modes of constraint and control (Simon 19993; Rhine & Taxman 2017; Van Zyl Smit & Corda 2017).

(iii) *Monetary penalties*—criminal fines and reparations—are used much less frequently in the US than in other Western jurisdictions (O'Malley 2009). Fines are deployed against corporations and traffic violators, but very rarely against individual felons and even misdemeanors are mostly dealt with by jail and probation rather than fines (Kohler Hausmann 2014; 2105).[4] Moreover, when fines are used by criminal courts today, they are mostly 'add-on' sanctions, tagged onto a sentence of probation or jail—rather than stand-alone punishments.

(iv) *Extreme penalties:* Thirty-one American states and the federal government still have the death penalty on their penal codes; there are currently some 2,900 death-sentenced offenders on death row; and ten or twelve states still carry out executions with some regularity. By contrast, no European nation any longer retains the death penalty (Garland 2010). More importantly—and again, quite distinctively, all fifty states and the federal government now sentence offenders to imprisonment for terms of Life Without Possibility of Parole (LWOP)—another extreme sentence that

[3] Many analysts talk of the 'exceptional' nature of American crime and punishment—see the contributions to Reitz (2107)—but as I argue in Garland (2010; 2017) this is not the most helpful way to frame the issues. On the US as an 'Outlier Nation' see Karabel & Laurison (2011). I also avoid the common tendency to describe US penality as comparatively 'punitive'—because it seems to me that this term begs a number of questions; including the question of how patterns of punishment relate to underlying patterns of crime. US penal practice is certainly degrading and harsh, perhaps distinctively so, but I will suggest that this is less the effect of a harsh culture (Whitman 2003) and more the outcome of a demand for maximum penal control in a context of minimalist public funding.

[4] In 2004 less than 1 per cent of federal felony cases resulted in a fine (O'Malley 2009).

is not permitted to nations that are signatories of the European Convention on Human Rights. Currently there are approximately 50,000 American prison inmates sentenced to spend the whole of their natural lives in custody with no prospect of early release (Nellis 2013).

(v) *Sentence lengths* and *time served in prison* are much longer in the US than elsewhere. Lappi-Seppälä (2008; 2017) estimates that sentences of American courts are, on average, between three and four times longer than in Western Europe. And the likelihood of a custodial sentence following a criminal conviction is very much higher in the US than elsewhere (Subramanian & Shames 2013).

(vi) Finally, there are *collateral consequences*—by which I mean the imposition of disqualifications, exclusions, banishment, deportation, and public criminal records as a consequence of a criminal conviction. These penal consequences are much more extensive and much more enduring in the US than elsewhere (Jacobs 2015; Demleitner 2017). There are thousands of such provisions, many of them imposed by local administrative laws and regulations (Travis 2002; Mauer & Chesney-Lind 2002).[5] And though recent scholarship and advocacy have begun to bring them to public attention (Manza & Uggens 2006; Alexander 2010; Lerman & Weaver 2014), most of these measures are low-visibility restrictions, largely unknown to the general public.

These then, are six dimensions along which American penality currently[6] exhibits a distinctive, outlier status when compared with other Western nations.[7] Readers will notice that I do not include in this list the over-representation of African-Americans and people of colour in the correctional population—a feature of American penality that is of great moral and political significance and that many regard as a defining characteristic of the system (Alexander 2010; Cole 1999; Loury 2008). I choose to omit this because it seems to me that this characteristic is neither distinctive to the US

[5] According to the American Bar Association's National Inventory, there are 44,500 statutes in the US that impose collateral consequences.

[6] An absence of reliable data prevents us from knowing whether the US was an outlier in these respects over the long term. I believe we should be skeptical of the standard claim that, before 1975, US incarceration rates used to be close to the Western European norm, running at about 160 per 100,000, since that number excludes the jail population and neglects to mention that for much of the 20th century Southern states used modes of punishment—convict leasing, chain gangs, and prison farms—that were not enumerated as imprisonment.

[7] There are other contrasts that go in the same direction. American prison regimes appear to be harsher than elsewhere in the developed world, with high levels of violence and frequent resort to force and isolation (Whitman 2003). Rehabilitation, education, and treatment seem to be more available in other nations than in the US (Subramanian & Shames 2013). And the emerging practice of imposing administrative costs and 'pay-to-stay' charges on offenders and their families is more extensive in the US than elsewhere (Gottschalk 2015). That American police kill civilians at a much higher rate than occurs elsewhere in the liberal democratic world is another mark of America's distinctive form of criminal justice (Karabel 2015).

nor exceptional in its extent. Other nations also exhibit massive ethnic and racial disparities in punishment. In Australia, for example, Aboriginal people are 2.5 per cent of the general population and 27 per cent of prison inmates.[8] Similarly, there is evidence that the incarceration rates for ethnic minorities in Canada[9] and in England and Wales[10], exceed that of the US.[11] Moreover, the meaning of 'over-representation' in this context deserves more careful consideration since the most appropriate denominator is not the number of people in the general population—the figure conventionally used—but rather the number of offenders in each demographic group (Pease 1994).

AMERICAN PENALITY AS A HISTORICAL INDIVIDUAL

There is, then, good reason to believe that the US currently deploys a quite distinctive apparatus of comparatively severe punishments; a penality that is, as compared to other nations, an outlier on several important dimensions. How might we explain these characteristics?

One preliminary problem for this inquiry is that there is no such thing as 'America' when it comes to the deployment of penal power (Garland 2010; Zimring 2017). Criminal punishments are separately imposed by the fifty states, the federal government, and by thousands of local jurisdictions—and there is great variation across these different entities.

So how can one analyse the overall pattern? How can we talk sensibly about American penality while acknowledging its internally differentiated character?

I suggest we deal with this issue by conceptualising contemporary American punishment as a 'historical individual' in the sense that Max Weber gave to the term. Weber defines a historical individual—modern capitalism, for example—as 'a complex of elements associated in historical reality which we unite into a conceptual whole from the standpoint of their cultural significance' (Weber 2002; 2011). Adopting Weber's approach allows us to talk about American penality as a single, culturally meaningful complex, thereby uniting for analytical purposes an entity that we acknowledge to be legally and geographically differentiated. In contemporary culture and politics, America's penal system has become a meaningful topic of discussion and

[8] http://copylinemagazine.com/2015/01/28/race-justice-news-racial-disparities-in-uk-and-australian-prisons-exceeds-those-in-u-s/

[9] http://www.sentencingproject.org/news/race-justice-news-native-americans-in-the-justice-system/

[10] https://www.theguardian.com/society/2010/oct/11/black-prison-population-increase-england

[11] France does not permit ethnic or racial classification of prison inmates, but ethnographers report a massive over-representation in prison of migrants and citizens of North African descent (Fassin 2016).

debate—its existence as a significant cultural object—and it falls to social scientists to analyse that object and explain its conditions of existence.

Having invoked the spirit of Max Weber, I want also to recall some of the methodological lessons that he taught: lessons that are especially pertinent to our topic but are often forgotten by commentators.

First: Distinguish originating causes from subsequent functioning. Explanations of historical emergence are not the same as explanations of contemporary reproduction. The meaning and effects of any practice or institution tend to change over time, so we should resist the temptation to project today's understandings back onto the past. That mass incarceration has come to operate as a mode of racial stratification (Western 2006; Alexander 2010) or of governing neoliberal insecurity (Wacquant 2009a) does not mean that it was developed with these purposes in mind.

Policy changes regularly generate consequences that were not originally anticipated. If we want to assert, for example, that the racial disparities associated with the War on Drugs were anticipated and intended by the architects of that policy, we will need to adduce the relevant historical evidence—one cannot simply point to the effects and infer the intention.

We should also observe what happens when unanticipated consequences *do* become apparent. Consequences that are unintended at Time 1 may become apparent at Time 2; at which point a choice to continue the practice is, in effect, a choice to embrace these consequences. So if an inquiry into the emergence of mass incarceration produces a story of adverse unintended consequences, we should proceed to ask 'why was this phenomenon tolerated once these unintended effects became apparent?'

Second: Avoid retrospective projection. There was no plan to build mass incarceration; no campaign to mount a decades-long march through the state and federal legislatures.[12] Multiple, diverse processes, dispersed in time and space, produced the differentiated assemblage of penal practices and institutions that currently exists. The supposed unity and coherence of 'mass incarceration' is largely a function of having given it a collective name and viewing it as a single problem.

Third: Specify mechanisms! A full explanation must describe how empirically identifiable actors and actions gave rise to causal processes and produced patterned outcomes. If our claim is that a particular level of inequality, or welfare state regime, or variety of capitalism gives rise to a specific set of criminal justice outcomes, we have to capture that process at the level of individual action and organisational process.

[12] It is true that there were frequent campaigns to persuade state legislatures across the nation to adopt specific policies—e.g. victim rights, or Three Strikes laws—and organisations such as the American Legislative Exchange Counsel played a key role in this. My point is that there was no overall campaign linking all the reforms of the thirty-year, nationwide, transformation that produced the present.

Fourth: Interpretive accounts must be adequate to the level of meaning. Analyses of penal change or of penal functioning should provide an account of the meanings that key actors attached to their actions, bearing in mind that the same event or undertaking may have different meanings to the various actors involved. An analysis that claims that mass incarceration is a functional mode of governing neoliberal insecurity (Wacquant 2009), or of recreating racial subordination (Alexander 2010), must show the forms of meaningful action that produce these outcomes and should account for any discrepancy between what was meant, what was done, and what outcomes eventuated.

Fifth: Distinguish functional uses from dysfunctional effects. An institution that is useful for some groups may be damaging for others; and practices producing net benefits in the short term may produce net costs at a later point (cf. Merton 1996). Functional explanations of mass incarceration (e.g. Wacquant 2009a) should specify how that institution does and does not serve the interests of definite social groups over specified time periods and provide supporting evidence for these claims.

Sixth: Adopt a dispassionate, value-neutral approach. The question of punishment is highly salient in American politics today and its value-laden character makes it all the more difficult to avoid biased premises and partisan interpretations. Committed scholarship that deals with politically charged subjects may be inclined to overlook inconvenient facts or draw back from unwelcome conclusions, thereby failing to reflect the moral and political complexity of the phenomenon in question.

With these considerations in mind, we can embark on our analysis, beginning with a descriptive account and then proceeding to explanation.

THE NEW IMPERATIVE: PENAL CONTROL

In setting out our descriptive account, a strategic place to start is with a focus on differences and commonalities. As I noted above, American penality is a complex assemblage of laws, policies, and practices that has emerged, piecemeal, over the last forty years. Far from being the realisation of some national plan, it is the cumulative result of multiple contributing causes; operating at the local, state, and federal levels; prompted by different events and considerations; involving diverse political actors and coalitions; and enacted in thousands of laws, policies, and enforcement practices.[13] But despite this multiplicity and variation, it is a remarkable fact that for forty consecutive years, all fifty states and the federal government have moved more or less

[13] I draw here on the 'new generation' sociological scholarship that focuses on state-level penal history and emphasises this variation and contingency: for an excellent overview, see Campbell & Schoenfeld (2013).

continuously in the same expansionist direction (Zimring 2010; Wagner 2014). And, even more remarkably, I would suggest, there is a common thread that runs throughout this vast range of historical moments, political contexts, and penal laws—a fundamental principle that links together these diverse reforms and provides an operational logic that underpins the whole penal apparatus in its day-to-day routines. This common principle is not something vague and generic such as 'law and order', 'harsh justice', or 'tough on crime' but instead a specific form of penal power that I will call 'penal control.'

Criminal punishment comes in several distinct forms, as the ideal type classification set out in Table 1 illustrates.[14] Penal afflictions, penal levies, penal controls, and penal assistance are distinct forms of punishment, each of them commonly found in penal history and still in widespread use today.[15] What is striking is that, in recent decades, American criminal justice has come to rely overwhelmingly on only one of them—punishment as penal control—in contrast to the contemporary penal systems of other Western nations where penal levies and penal assistance are much more prominent.

Table 1: Forms of punishment.

Penal Afflictions	Capital punishments; corporal punishments; maiming; public shaming; stigmatising, etc.
Penal Levies	Fines; deductions; prelevements; restitution; compensation; damages; forfeiture; community service; public works, etc.
Penal Controls	Imprisonment; confinement; supervision; exclusion; banishment; incapacitation; disqualification, etc.
Penal Assistance	Correctional treatment; restorative work; mediation; drug therapy; remedial education; counselling; job training, etc.

Penal control is, I believe, the fundamental principle and basic imperative that runs throughout this whole historical period and across this vast institutional landscape. (The degrading, cheap-and-mean aspects of American penal institutions—as described by Whitman (2003) or Lynch (2009)—are, I believe, a secondary characteristic: the result of an under-funded penal state tasked by a tax-averse, anti-government electorate with imposing control on the cheap.) If we review the list of distinctive features I set out above, no fewer than five of them describe how American

[14] Specific penal sanctions may combine one or more of these modal characteristics: e.g. a criminal record or a branding can function as an afflictive stigma as well as an incapacitating control; a probation or custodial order may provide assistance as well as control, and so on.

[15] Afflictive forms of punishment have declined in the modern Western world, though they were a core feature of pre-modern punishment and are still common in many parts of the world (Geltner 2014; Garland 2010).

criminal justice imposes more extensive forms of control (extreme penalties, frequency and length of prison confinement, frequency and length of correctional supervision, extent and duration of collateral consequences, etc) while the sixth concerns America's reluctance to use monetary penalties—penal levies that, whatever their other advantages, and however much they are utilised elsewhere, impose little in the way of penal control.[16]

The leading characteristic of the American penal landscape today is not harshness (Whitman 2003), or racism (Alexander 2010), or neoliberalism (Wacquant 2009a). Its basic imperative is the imposition of penal control—an imperative that is now embodied in penal codes, in the culture of enforcement, and in the legal provisions (such as mandatory penalties and 'truth-in-sentencing' legislation) that limit the discretion of penal actors and oblige them to impose effective and long-lasting penal controls on criminal offenders.[17] And if we focus on this fundamental principle we will be able to glimpse some important affinities (another Weberian concept) that link America's distinctive penality with two distinctive features of the American state and American society—a set of linkages that will, in turn, point us to the underlying causal processes driving the recent development of American penality.

The first of these features is the weakness of social organisation, social integration, and informal social control that affects so many of America's cities and above all its poorest communities of colour.[18] These structural weaknesses—I will term them 'social deficits'—have been produced over time by the operation of relatively untrammelled market forces; overlaid by the continuing legacies of racial division, disadvantage, and segregation (Kerner Commission 1968/2016; Krivo *et al.* 2009; Omi & Winant 2014); and reproduced by economic and social disinvestment—much of

[16] The death penalty is typically enacted and imposed in America today as an expressive, retributive gesture and a symbol of tough-on-crime politics (Garland 2010). But it delivers the ultimate form of penal control—even when, as is usually the case, death sentences are commuted to sentences of life imprisonment without parole. Collateral consequences are mostly forms of exclusion, restriction, and incapacitation. Disenfranchisement is an important exception, but it dates from an earlier time and the current trend is for these political disabilities to be repealed. Welfare benefit ineligibilities are a mixed case: exclusion from public housing is framed as public safety for other residents, but there are elements of cost-saving punishment and deterrence here too. The fact that these collateral consequences are not well publicised—they are sometimes described as 'invisible punishments' (Travis 2002)—suggests that deterrence is not their main aim.

[17] Public suspicion and distrust extend beyond offenders to include the soft-on-crime officials who might turn them loose or fail to lock them up. As I note below, the sentencing revolution was as much about controlling judges and parole boards as it was about controlling criminals.

[18] Social deficits in the US are by no means restricted to urban communities and minority groups. Most people below the poverty line live in rural areas, and there are more poor whites than blacks or Hispanics. But many poor blacks live in segregated urban neighbourhoods with high concentrations of poverty and disadvantage—a fact that multiplies the detrimental effects of poverty and generates higher levels of disorder and disorganisation (Denton & Massey 1998).

which was a consequence of government policies (Wilson 2011). Social deficits are the result of processes of cultural adaptation, accommodation, and coping that link structural circumstances with collective behaviours and give rise, over time, to high rates of criminal violence, social problems, and other forms of social dislocation (Wilson 1997; 2011; 2012; Sampson 2012; Sharkey 2013).

These structural conditions are also associated with low levels of trust—which also have consequences for crime and punishment. Distrust of others and distrust of government are dimensions of America's low levels of solidarity that have been shown to be positively associated with high levels of violence (LaFree 1998; Roth 2012; for comparative evidence on levels of trust and crime rates, see Karstedt & LaFree 2006). And it seems likely that America's emphasis on penal control expresses an underlying distrust of others: above all, anyone convicted of a criminal offence and any criminal justice professional who might release dangerous offenders rather than protect the public.

The second characteristic associated with the extensive use of penal control is the comparatively limited control capacities and dispositions of the American state. The American state has long been distinctive in its relative emphasis on market-freedoms rather than social protections—an orientation that distinguishes it from comparable states elsewhere and has had the effect of limiting its capacity (and its disposition) to deal with problems of social disorganisation other than by penal means.[19] When American state actors—at federal, state, or local level—decide to address a specific social problem (such as drug abuse, criminal violence, homelessness, or mental illness) they have fewer positive, effective means at their disposal than do nations with more developed and more extensive social states.[20] The result is that American criminal justice is frequently charged with tasks—such as care and control of the mentally ill, the drug addicted, and the homeless—that other nations allocate to social service agencies. And on those occasions where non-penal approaches have been tried—e.g. public health approaches to drug abuse in New York in the early 1960s or social welfare approaches to crime control during the federal 'war on poverty'—these initiatives have foundered for lack of experience, support, and resources (Fortner 2015; Kohler-Hausmann 2015; Hinton 2016). Before long, these more positive efforts were judged to have been ill-conceived failures and political opinion quickly reverted to the default of a penal approach.

[19] America's welfare state regime can be classified as a market-protecting liberal regime and is thus grouped together with other liberal regimes such as those of Australia, Canada and New Zealand. But within that classification, the US is, on most measures, at the extreme end of the distribution. On the distinctive characteristics of the US state and its penal power, see Garland (2010; 2013).

[20] This is not to deny that there is a plethora of local programmes and initiatives in most American jurisdictions. The point is that the comparative weakness of the American welfare state's social provision for lower income groups ensures government exerts less positive, pro-social influence over individuals, families, and communities.

Sentencing reform and the build-up of penal control

If we review the historical processes that produced today's penal apparatus, we observe control issues continually taking prominence and shaping the direction of penal change.[21] Of course the historical record is by no means univocal, and there is considerable disagreement about why American punishments became so much more severe after 1975. But there is very little disagreement about *how* this happened, or about the *proximate* causes that brought the current system into existence (Garland 2013). These proximate causes were: (i) changes in sentencing law and practice; (ii) changes in back-end 'resentencing'—i.e. parole, remission, and pardons; and (iii) changes in prosecution practice (Tonry 2016; Pfaff 2017).

The following pages describe how these legal changes emerged and how, over time and in a variety of ways, they expressed an overweening concern with public safety and a singular commitment to penal control as the appropriate response.

PHASE 1: SENTENCING REFORM

The long-term upwards movement of America's prison and jail populations began in the 1970s with a Sentencing Reform movement that, in retrospect, can be seen as the first phase in a thirty-year, multi-phase sentencing law revolution. Prior to 1975, most states (and the federal system) adopted an 'indeterminate sentencing' model, the chief aim of which was to individualise the treatment of offenders, rehabilitating where possible and incapacitating where necessary (Reitz 2012). The sentence imposed by the court was a provisional, indeterminate one stipulating an open-ended term of custody (e.g. 'one year to life') to be served in a state penitentiary (or a 'correctional institution' as prisons came to be known). A parole board would later recalibrate the court's sentence in light of the offender's risk profile and response to treatment—with the consequence that most offenders were released early after serving only a fraction of their sentences. 'Good time' laws allowed additional reductions as rewards for compliant behavior (Jacobs 1992).

These arrangements eventually attracted widespread criticism. Indeterminate sentencing robbed punishments of certainty and reduced their deterrent value; discretionary release opened the way to arbitrariness; and 'individuation' was a recipe

[21] That increased penal control is the recurring outcome of so many different political processes in so many different settings strongly suggests that it is a functional response to a generalised problem. For the classic version of this argument, see Karl Polanyi's account of the re-assertion of social protections in the laissez-faire era (Polanyi 1944).

for unfairness and inequality. When research suggested that correctional treatment did little to reduce recidivism, the writing was on the wall (Garland 2001; 2016).

The sentencing law reforms passed between 1975 and 1984 were a reaction to these problems. Their chief aim was to establish standards that would constrain discretion, minimise disparities, and subject sentencing powers to legal regulation. The new ideal was the 'determinate' sentences, proportionate to the offence, not tailored to the offender. Many states (and the federal government) abolished parole, enacted sentencing guidelines, and established sentencing commissions to oversee their new systems.

The legislative activity of the 1970s and early 1980s transformed the politics of sentencing. Instead of being administered by experts behind the scenes, questions of sentencing now became political questions, discussed in newspaper editorials and debated on the floors of legislative chambers. To the on-looking public, the revelation that most felons were released much earlier than the sentence length imposed by the court appeared less as a sensible way of motivating rehabilitation and more as a scandalous leniency. In a political climate increasingly dominated by 'law and order', the liberal aims that initiated the reform movement gave way to more conservative goals. Tough-on-crime conservatives joined liberals in demanding an end to sentencing discretion, not because they worried about discrimination but because they distrusted criminal justice personnel and wanted to prevent them jeopardising public safety by releasing dangerous felons. The legislative drive, from this point onwards, was not to enhance sentencing equity but instead to mandate penalties that would protect the public. Such was the political concern to guarantee effective penal control that it soon overcame the judicial opposition to mandatory sentencing and eventually dissolved the discretionary powers of penal officials.

American sentencing turned on its axis. By the 1960s, indeterminate sentencing had been more firmly established in the US than anywhere else (Pifferi 2016) and American courts imposed very lengthy sentences that were altogether unknown in other nations—the idea being to make a deterrent show of harshness, safe in the knowledge that the court's sentence would later be reduced by parole and good time. Thirty years later, very lengthy sentences were still being imposed, but now they meant what they said. As Tonry (2016) observes, the old practice of announcing high—but effectively meaningless—maximum sentences helps explain why US prison terms are now so much longer than those imposed elsewhere.

PHASE 2: THE WAR ON DRUGS

The impact of the 'War on Drugs' is one of the most discussed and least understood issues in current debates about the build-up of American penality. The phrase itself (which dates from remarks by President Nixon in the early 1970s—see Hinton (2016)) refers to the nationwide movement to criminalise the possession and sale of banned substances, imposing harsh, often mandatory, penalties—such as New York State's Rockefeller Drug Law of 1973 or the federal Anti-Drug Abuse laws of 1984, 1986, and 1988—backed up by vigorous enforcement at the local level.

Many commentators regard this wave of legislation as the primary cause of mass incarceration and its racial consequences, pointing to the fact that a majority of federal prisoners are serving time for drug offences, and to the marked racial disparities that characterise drug law enforcement (Alexander 2010; Hinton 2016). But while critics are right to deplore the drug war's harsh racial effects it is important to observe that the policy aims originally motivating these efforts were rather more complex and, for my purposes, rather more revealing.

The Rockefeller Drug Laws, to take an important example, emerged following a series of failed efforts to deal with the crime and disorder generated by widespread heroin use in neighbourhoods like Harlem in New York City (Fortner 2015; Kohler-Hausmann 2015). In response to community demands for action to alleviate these problems, New York authorities initially put in place a public health, penal–welfare approach, providing non-penal treatment to addicts and reserving criminal penalties for 'pushers'. When these efforts—which were under-resourced and poorly implemented—did little to reduce the problem, Governor Nelson Rockefeller shifted to a markedly penal approach, enacting harsh mandatory penalties for possession as well as for sale. Rockefeller's decision was no doubt a political one, shaped by his presidential ambitions and his wish to be seen as a 'law and order' conservative. But it is striking that his tough approach attracted vocal support from African-American community leaders (Fortner 2015)—just as the Federal Anti-Drug Abuse Acts of the mid-1980s would garner strong support from the Congressional Black Caucus (Forman f.c.). Whatever its subsequent history, the War on Drugs was initially viewed by some of its proponents as a necessary, good faith effort to relieve poor urban communities of the blight of street drugs and the neighbourhood crime and violence associated with them.[22]

[22] Miller (2016) and Forman (f.c.) point out that community activists generally called for an 'all of the above' approach to the drug problems in their neighbourhoods—favouring social and public health remedies as well as law enforcement ones. But when the former failed to materialise, or to appear effective, many lent their support to increased policing and penal control.

As a crime-control tactic, this focus on drug offences offered several advantages. To prosecute crimes of violence, the authorities must typically rely on the willingness of witnesses to come forward and a showing of criminal intent on the part of the accused—both of which can be hard to obtain. The laws prohibiting drug possession and sale created offences that were easier to prove and that could be proactively enforced by police stops and 'buy and bust' methods.[23] They thereby provided a new and potentially more effective means of apprehending and convicting violent offenders, gang leaders, organised criminals, and 'drug czars'—and their penalty scales were calibrated accordingly. This was why, for at least some of its supporters—above all for prosecutors and police—the War on Drugs was a proxy war, a set of crime-control measures directed not at recreational drug users but at violent criminals (Stuntz 2013; Lynch 2016).

An additional motivation—perhaps the most significant one in the long term—derived from the fact that a focus on drug control provided the federal government with a plausible basis for becoming more directly involved in crime control at a time when crime was becoming a problem of urgent concern to large numbers of voters. Historically, American criminal justice had been a matter for state and local government and the US Constitution placed strict limits on the extent to which federal authorities could involve themselves in the business of crime-control. But with crime growing in political salience, national politicians looked for ways to involve themselves more actively and thereby reap some of the political rewards of responding to public concerns (Gottschalk 2006; Stuntz 2013, Hinton 2016). This involvement initially took the form of establishing federal agencies such as the Law Enforcement Assistance Agency to coordinate or fund local law enforcement. But the criminalisation of drugs opened up a new and more direct form of federal involvement since illegal drugs could be deemed a form of 'interstate commerce'—a domain over which the federal government did have jurisdiction. Waging a war on drugs was, for the federal government, a means of circumventing constitutional limitations, expanding its law enforcement apparatus (Hinton 2016), and engaging the politics of law and order at the national level.

From the 1980s on, Congress passed anti-drug abuse laws and federal prosecutors, federal courts, and federal penitentiaries began to enforce them with increasing vigour. But ultimately the War on Drugs would mostly be fought by local police and county prosecutors, so federal authorities also took steps to incentivise action at this level, providing generous subsidies for local drug-law enforcement and enacting forfeiture statutes that allowed local law enforcement to retain the proceeds of drug crime

[23] See Dubber (2005) on possession offences as a means of relaxing evidentiary burdens for the prosecution.

investigations.[24] Over time, these incentives would produce a massive enforcement over-reach. A drug war supposedly aimed at serious violent offenders would eventually sweep up masses of petty offenders and low-level street dealers and sentence them to prison terms that bore little relation to their culpability or to any threat they might pose to the public (Tonry 2016; Hinton 2016; Lynch 2016).

PHASE 3: THE WAR ON CRIME

The most notorious phase of recent sentencing history is the 'law and order' period that ran from the mid-1980s to the mid-1990s, with the US Congress encouraging, subsidising, and emulating the states in the pursuit of 'tough on crime' policies (Garland 2001). These policies aimed to ensure public safety, express public anger, and satisfy victims by increasing the certainty and severity of penalties. The lesson of Willie Horton in the 1988 presidential race (Anderson 1995) had been well learned: henceforth there were to be no dangerous offenders let loose on the public and no politicians seen as soft on crime.

To secure these goals, legislators took near-total charge of punishment, stipulating in advance the precise penalty to be imposed; depriving judges, parole boards, and prison officials of sentencing discretion; and empowering hard-charging prosecutors who could be relied upon to be aggressive in locking-up 'bad guys' (Lynch 2016). In a flurry of legislative activity, states across the nation passed mandatory minimum sentences (targeting drug offences, sex crime, and gun crime); Three-Strikes laws (which could send third-time felons to prison for life); Truth-in-Sentencing laws (which gave the states federal subsidies for prisons in return for guarantees that state prisoners would not be given early release); and Life Without Parole sentences (Tonry 2016). Tight legal controls were thus imposed upon sentencers and penal officials who were mandated to impose extensive penal controls on offenders and inmates.

In this context, the working practices of probation and parole offices were transformed, with a new emphasis on risk management, revocation, and the re-imprisonment of supervisees who failed to meet the conditions of their licences.[25] By 2000, 34 per cent of all prison admissions resulted from parole revocations rather than new crimes. In some states the figure was higher than 50 per cent. Correctional

[24] The 1984 Comprehensive Crime Control Act permitted local law enforcement to seize as much as 90 per cent of cash and property from accused drug dealers (Hinton 2016: 312)

[25] As Simon (1993) points out in an analysis that connects penal policy with the wider political economy, the difficulty of securing employment or housing for ex-felons in the wake of deindustrialisation and reduced social support created insurmountable problems for a parole system dedicated to assistance and resettlement.

supervision had transformed itself from a form of social assistance to a mode of penal control.

Meanwhile, prosecutors became the most powerful actors in the system, and many used the leverage provided by mandatory sentences and sentence enhancements to pile on charges, obtain guilty pleas, and elicit information about other offenders and offences (Lynch 2016; Pfaff 2017). In the 1970s, approximately 66 per cent of cases resulted in a plea bargain. By the 1990s the figure was more than 95 per cent (Wright 2012). Without this mass production of guilty pleas—and the effective end of due process and trial by jury that it entailed—mass incarceration would not be sustainable.

In this recalibrated system, the cumulative effect of prior convictions took on a new meaning. Because a subsequent offence could result in a mandatory prison sentence that was two or three times longer than the sentence for the first offence, prior convictions operated as multipliers. And given the number of people who pass through the system, and their high rates of recidivism, criminal justice became a self-sustaining growth machine. The system also exhibited the sociological law of cumulative disadvantage—groups such as young black men who received a disproportionate level of criminal justice early in their lives would subsequently receive enhanced sentences and be disproportionately subject to imprisonment.

The eventual impact of these laws—which would continue to authorise draconian sentences long after crime and violence rates steeply declined[26]—was to double the size of an already swollen prison population and project this population far into the future. As for individual offenders, the new sentencing norms meant that vast numbers of people were sentenced to terms of confinement that were measured not in months and years but in 'decades and lifetimes' (Tonry 2016).

Instead of adjudicating the blame-worthiness of individuals and punishing them accordingly, the new system was designed to sequester and incapacitate masses of offenders for lengthy periods of time. Over time, the principle of proportionality disappeared—particularly in respect of drug offences (now punished as severely as violent crime) and criminal history enhancements (which increased an offender's sentence by multiples of two, three, or even four). So did any concern with parsimony or the liberty interests of convicted offenders (Tonry 2016). America's penal system became profoundly illiberal and unequal. Convicted offenders came to be seen as too risky to circulate in public and altogether undeserving of 8th Amendment protections. America's system of criminal justice became a system of criminal control (Garland 2001).

[26] The post-1990 pattern of crime rate declines coinciding with prison rate increases is often presented as evidence that the two are unconnected. Such an interpretation ignores the effect of time lags and stored-up consequences.

Today, after two decades of declining rates of crime and violence, it is difficult to appreciate the climate of opinion that produced draconian measures such as the Violent Crime Control and Law Enforcement Act of 1994—and politicians associated with these laws are now being made to pay a price. But it is important to recall, along with all the populism, racism, and opportunism of political officials, that homicide levels and public concern about violent crime were, in these years, at an all-time high (Enns 2016).[27] Even a system as illiberal, unequal, and oppressively racialised as American criminal justice was not entirely devoid of genuine public purpose and community-safety motivations as it emerged over time. Over the forty years during which American sentencing was caught up in an ongoing revolution, a multiplicity of separate projects, plans, and purposes unfolded. In the process, the conservative politics of the war on crime came to displace the liberal politics of sentencing reform and to overlay the community politics of public safety, with the result that an imperative of penal control came to dominate the entire system. The criminal justice system that exists today is the result of complex interactions rather than the realisation of an overall plan or a single set of motivations. But, for all this dispersion and conflict, an emergent principle has continually been asserted and supported: the imperative of penal control.

SOCIAL AND POLITICAL CAUSES

These shifts in law, policy, and practice—each of them increasing the extent, the intensity, and the certainty of penal control—were the proximate causes that together created the penal system that exists today. But what were the broader forces that moved law and policy in this direction and that created a penal system that is much more extreme than that in any comparable nation? And why did this diversity of causal processes give rise to the monotonous demand for more penal control? This, it seems to me, must be a distinctively American story. In the years after 1980, other Western nations also experienced increased crime, disruptive social change, economic insecurity, and neoliberal politics. Many became more punitive, more restrictive, decreasing welfare and increasing prison. But none matched the extent or intensity of American penality (Walmsley 2016; Lappi-Seppälä 2008; Tonry 2009). So why has the US been more prone to the use of penal control than has any other nation in the developed world? In the remainder of this article, I discuss four theories of historical change—each of which offers a different causal narrative for understanding American

[27] As Kleiman (2016) observes, in 1994, the nation's homicide figures topped 23,000 for the fourth year in a row, and no one could know that this number was about to decline and to keep on decreasing for the next twenty years. Today the annual number of homicides is around 14,000.

penality and the forces that brought it about.[28] Building on these accounts – and developing significant points of disagreement—I conclude by sketching an alternative framework for the study of American penality.

(i) Mass incarceration as racial subordination

The most provocative and widely read account of contemporary American punishment is *The New Jim Crow: Mass Incarceration in the Age of Colorblindness* (2010) by legal scholar and civil rights activist Michelle Alexander. Alexander argues that mass incarceration, together with the multiple disqualifications imposed on felons, amounts to a new racial caste system that consigns poor black men to a second-class citizenship, barring them from government housing, welfare benefits, and political participation, permitting their discriminatory treatment in employment, and ensuring that masses of them will cycle in and out of prison.

According to Alexander, this system emerged in the wake of the civil rights movement as a means of restoring blacks to a subordinate social status similar to the one that operated in the Jim Crow South. Because explicit race controls were outlawed by civil rights reforms and are expressly prohibited in today's political culture, the New Jim Crow is premised not on race but on a supposedly 'colour-blind' criminality. But Alexander insists that contemporary law enforcement and, above all, the 'War on Drugs' are thoroughly racialised, operating in ways that target poor, minority youth and ensuring that mass incarceration and its disabilities exclude millions of African Americans from participation in American democracy.

The New Jim Crow is a work of real political importance. More than any other intervention, it can be credited with putting the problem of mass incarceration on the American political agenda, and (together with Black Lives Matter) initiating a growing social movement that now presses for criminal justice reform. And Alexander is clearly right to deplore the racial disparities generated by the War on Drugs and accurate in describing the overall effect of disfranchisement, disqualification, and discrimination as a form of second-class citizenship for former felons, one third of whom are black. In light of America's history, a diminished citizenship status disproportionately occupied by blacks inevitably takes on the appearance of a racial caste system.

However, as others (Forman 2012) have pointed out, around 40 per cent of prison inmates are white, which means that millions of white people are also condemned to

[28] Despite differing emphases, these four accounts overlap at many points, with each pointing to some or all of the following: a rightward shift in the American electorate, a backlash against civil rights, rising public concern about street crime and disorder, the fusion of crime and race issues forged by the Republican Party's southern strategy, the rise of 'law-and-order' politics, and the mobilisation of cross-party support for tough-on-crime measures.

this second-class citizenship. Indeed, if federal and state authorities were to release all of their black prison inmates tomorrow, the US would still have the largest prison population and rate of incarceration in the world—which means that a racial explanation leaves much of America's distinctive penality unexplained. American criminal justice is undoubtedly racially skewed in its operations and effects but not to the extent that Alexander claims, and not primarily for the reasons that she alleges.

Alexander presents her indictment with the forensic skill of a first-class litigator, so it is no surprise that she cites the War on Drugs as her leading example of racialised punishment. As many commentators have observed, survey evidence suggests that blacks and whites consume (and perhaps sell) illicit drugs at about the same rates, but law enforcement focuses much more on blacks; and people of colour are disproportionately imprisoned for drug offences. Little wonder then, that the War on Drugs is Exhibit A in Alexander's critique.

But the problem with this analysis is that the unequal racial justice that occurs in respect of drugs is not so evident in regard to other offences. When it comes to violent crime, for example, blacks (that is to say poor black males) have a disproportionately high level of involvement in offending—and their rates of punishment are not significantly different from their rates of crime (FBI 2013; Western 2006). And this matters, because most prisoners in America's prisons are serving time not for drug offences but for violent crimes.[29]

Nor was the War on Drugs unrelated to the problem of criminal violence. Recall that in the 1970s and 1980s, communities of colour and their political representatives were deeply concerned about drug-related crime and violence in their neighbourhoods, which is why they called for tough punishments and supported legislation such as the Rockefeller Drug laws of 1973 and the Federal Anti-Drug Abuse Acts of 1986 and 1988 (Fortner 2015; Forman 2012). As we have seen, the War on Drugs was, at least in part, a 'proxy war' strategy for apprehending and convicting violent offenders by other means. Its origins—and much of its original support—lay not in an attempt to suppress recreational drug use but in an effort to address the associated problem of violent street crime. Even the notoriously 'racist' sentencing disparity between crack cocaine possession and powder cocaine possession can be understood (though not justified) in these terms. 'Crack' is cocaine packaged for the poor. And when it took hold in poor communities it generated an enormous amount of street crime and violence. In contrast, the consumption of powder cocaine by Wall Street reprobates and affluent drug users generated very little visible violent crime. Crack was more severely

[29] 52 per cent of state prisoners are currently incarcerated for crimes of violence. Only in the federal prison system—which houses about 10 per cent of American prisoners—do drug offenders form a majority of those incarcerated (BJS 2013).

punished not because it was associated with blacks but because—rightly or wrongly—it was perceived to be associated with waves of crime and violence.

Contra *The New Jim Crow,* the creation of a racial caste can best be understood not as deliberate policy of racial subordination but instead as the unintended but foreseeable result of overreaching law enforcement operating in a class- and racially-stratified environment—a result that was long tolerated because there were no organised political forces advocating for poor black men (Stuntz 2001) and, it must be said, because the lives of these individuals are not highly valued by policymakers, politicians, and the American public. It was the established hierarchies of race and class—together with the differential levels of violence and worklessness that these hierarchies fostered—that ensured that penal power concentrated its effects on poor communities of colour: a story of class overlaid by race, not of race alone. The fact that, in contrast to black high-school dropouts, college-educated blacks are less likely to be imprisoned today than they were in the 1970s (Western 2006) provides further support for this interpretation.

The fact that the racial and class effects of penal policy have been tolerated and reproduced long after they came to light tells us a great deal about America's power structure and the value placed on the lives and liberties of poor black people. Penal controls are always imposed by one group on another, and in 1990s America, the crime fears of suburbanites and the white middle class counted for much more than the lives of young black men and the welfare of their families and communities. Only with the emergence of Black Lives Matter in 2013 has this situation been publicly contested in an organised way.

A final point: segregated areas of concentrated poverty were the worst affected by drugs, crime, and violence—meaning that they were the locus of victimisation and calls for action but also that they were communities where many violent offenders lived and which attracted tough enforcement, stop and frisk, buy and bust, etc. This, in turn, produced a disproportionate number of black arrestees and convicted, imprisoned offenders. These racial disparities thus made their way into criminal justice (where they were subsequently amplified by the multiplier effects of 'prior convictions') because of concerns about crime and its control, not by dint of racism as such. And this is important politically as well as analytically, since it points to the need to address the structural racism of economic and social organisation rather than assume that the problem is primarily one of discrimination by police and penal officials. Established hierarchies, social divisions, power structures, and biases will shape how any social policy is implemented—even when the policy is colour-blind, race-neutral, or race-sensitive. But the racial disparities that are produced by law enforcement and criminal justice are not the foundation of the problem. These processes build on and amplify racially disparate patterns of criminal involvement and criminal vulnerability—

disparate patterns that are a product of structures of economic and social exclusion and of intergenerational transmission of cumulative disadvantage.

(ii) American penality as neoliberal governance

Sociologist Loïc Wacquant argues a different but equally provocative thesis in his book, *Punishing the Poor: the Neoliberal Government of Social Insecurity* (2009a).[30] Wacquant's thesis is that America's expanded penal system is a means of reinforcing America's increasingly precarious labour market and controlling the disruptive social fallout of the austerity and insecurity now faced by working people and, above all, by poor, unskilled, black males.

According to Wacquant, prison growth is an unspoken but strategically integral element of the neoliberal policies that have dominated US politics since the late 1970s. On this account, America's prison system expanded to contain a surplus population thrown out of work by deindustrialisation and deprived of social support by the roll-back of the Keynesian welfare state. In this socioeconomic context, the threat of imprisonment operates—alongside scaled-back and increasingly conditional welfare benefits—as a means of pressurising individuals to accept low-wage work. Like the Poor Law and the workhouse before it, today's system of imprisonment operates as a 'less eligible' adjunct to the labour market. Its message is: accept the terms of employment or become subject to welfare discipline and penal control (see also Soss *et al.* 2011). Wacquant argues that the build-up of the penal system is an integral part of neoliberal strategy and not a pragmatic response to crime rates or criminal victimisation. There is, he insists, a 'crime–incarceration disconnect' (Wacquant 2009b: 144). According to Wacquant, 'the level of incarceration in a given society bears no relation to its crime rate' (2009b: 158)—and any attempt to link the two is mere ideology.[31]

Wacquant is right to insist that labour-market insecurity, intensified by segregation and concentrated poverty, provides a structural context that helps explain the massive imprisonment of poor, black, working-age males. (These same structures also determine the educational careers, health outcomes, family formation, alcohol and drug use, and rates of violence of the groups in question.) And he is right to insist that neoliberal economic and social policies, including the 'welfare reforms' of the 1990s, have served to reinforce rather than alleviate these effects. But on closer inspection, it seems clear that America's welfare state has changed rather less than Wacquant claims: as Shannon (2013) points out, working-age, able-bodied males never had a 'social

[30] See also, *Prisons of Poverty* (Wacquant 2009b) which contains many of the same arguments.
[31] '... the discourses that seek to connect crime and punishment in America have no validity other than ideological' (Wacquant 2009b: 159).

right to assistance' and it is women and children, not young men, who have felt the main impact of the 1996 Act.

Similarly, Wacquant's claim that prison expansion was a neoliberal strategy, intended to pre-empt the disruption that its economic policies would bring in its wake, remains an unsupported—and ultimately implausible—assertion for which he supplies no persuasive evidence. Although one might claim that mass incarceration has come to operate as a functional support for neoliberal policies by warehousing a surplus labour population and penalising illegal alternatives to low-waged work, there is no evidence that any neoliberal thinker ever strategised in this way or proposed any such policy of punishment.[32] And given that neoliberals generally oppose the build-up of the state apparatus and state power, and might be expected to propose less expensive means of propping up their labour-market regime, Wacquant's explanation looks like the kind of post-hoc functionalism that Weber warned against.[33] A more likely explanation is that the problem of crime—itself structured by free-market inequalities and social neglect—gave rise to popular demands for tougher punishment which, in turn, disproportionately affected the dispossessed and illegally employed inner-city black males. The association between neoliberalism and increased punishment is better viewed as an emergent outcome, not a precipitating cause or intention. And rather than see the build-up of penal controls as a pre-emptive strategy in anticipation of the 'social fallout' that neoliberalism might produce, it seems more likely that these controls were developed in response to the high-crime environment and public safety concerns that characterised the 1980s and 1990s (Garland 2001).

Wacquant is also fundamentally mistaken when he insists that there is a 'disconnect' between crime rates and punishment rates—a position that he argues most expressly and emphatically but which is also embraced by writers such as Tonry (2009), Alexander (2010), Mauer (2006), and Hinton (2016) who say much the same thing. Support for this 'disconnect' thesis is summoned up by pointing out that punishment and crime did not change in lockstep; that American imprisonment rates continued to increase during the 1990s even as crime rates fell; and that many other countries experienced crime rate rises but none of them reacted by creating mass incarceration; *ergo*, they say, there is no causal connection.[34] But these arguments are

[32] The explicitly neoliberal critique of mass incarceration and excessive correctional expenditure by the group 'Right on Crime' tends to support the view that a massive and increasingly expensive penal state was no part of any neoliberal agenda (Gottschalk 2014).

[33] The mistake is to assume that right-wing parties and their signature policies are 'neoliberal' when in fact these parties are coalitions and their policies are an eclectic, contradictory mix. See Garland (2001) on the coalitions between neoliberals and neoconservatives with roots in the Republican Party in the US and in Britain's Conservative Party, and the importance of that distinction for understanding penal policy.

[34] For an alternative view, see Western (2016), who argues that crime rates and penal rates are *not* unrelated though they do not change together in lockstep. 'Punishment is not determined by crime, but crime

largely specious. Policy effects typically take a considerable time to occur, since processes of problem definition, political mobilisation, legislative enactment, and implementation often unfold over years or decades, creating a temporal gap between the problem and the response. American property crime rose steeply from the 1960s to the 1980s, as did violence and homicide, which did not peak until the early 1990s. Throughout that period and beyond, the American public came to regard crime as one of the most serious problems facing the nation, and political representatives scrambled to put new laws and policy responses in place (Garland 2001; Flamm 2005; Enns 2016). That rising imprisonment rates lagged behind rising crime rates and continued to increase even as crime rates showed a sustained decline is evidence of these temporal processes (and of the stored-up consequences I described above) not proof of a 'crime–incarceration disconnect'.

The relationship between crime rates and penal policies is an empirical issue that will vary across time and space, but our approach to this empirical question will be shaped by theoretical assumptions. A founding principle of the sociology of punishment (Garland 1990) is that penal phenomena are not to be understood as a simple reaction or response to crime, but instead have their own dynamics and determinations. Punishment is a social institution not an automatic reaction or a mechanical response. But to assert this principle is not to assert that penal policies are unrelated to crime rates, crime perceptions, crime fears, and theories of crime causation and crime control. Crime affects punishment insofar as it produces a volume effect (changes in the number of case processed) or a policy effect (changes in penal tactics or strategy intended to respond to perceived crime problems). When the latter effect occurs, it generally does so slowly and in a mediated fashion. Real or perceived changes in crime rates or in the nature of crime affect policy to the extent that they generate shifts in public or professional opinion that subsequently gain political traction, legal enactment, and practical enforcement. The relationship is a complex, mediated one—but a significant one nevertheless.

As for the comparative claim that other nations experienced crime rate rises without resorting to mass incarceration, we need to bear in mind two facts. One is that, in most such nations, imprisonment rates did rise in the wake of crime rate rises, even if these increases were modest by comparison with the US (Walmsley 2016; Miller 2016).[35] The second, and more important, is that crime problems in the US are quite

and violence are ripe with the potential for punishment because they occur in the context of social policy failure and poverty.'

[35] According to Lappi-Seppälä (2008), differences in prison rates across Western European nations are not correlated with differences in crime rates across these nations. I think this finding makes sense: penal policy is relatively autonomous of crime rates and nations with similar levels of crime may develop rather different penal policies. But it does not follow that penal policy is never driven by crime rates and by

different from those typically experienced by the nations of Western Europe. As Zimring and Hawkins (1997) pointed out years ago, and as Miller (2015, 2016) Roth (2017) and Gallo *et al.* (2017) have recently reminded us, America has extraordinarily high rates of homicide and these comparatively high rates increased dramatically between the 1960s and the early 1990s. High levels of life-threatening violence change how people react to crime. The salience of crime, the fear of crime, and the public demand for forceful crime-control are liable to be much greater where the crime mix is weighted towards lethal violence and—to remind ourselves of another salient difference—where guns are routinely present in the background of social life.

For many communities in the US—and above all for poor, black, urban communities—crime is not a social nuisance or a quality of life issue: it is an existential threat. No other developed nation has homicide levels that are remotely comparable to those in the US, even following twenty years of falling US murder rates. Consequently, fear of crime in America—where homicide is a leading cause of death for young males, and *the* leading cause for black males aged fifteen to thirty-four—is not the equivalent of the crime fears that affect more peaceable societies.

I don't know why so many serious commentators deny that penal policies are, to some degree, shaped by crime levels and by the public perceptions and sentiments that form around them. But I suspect the reason is ideological. I suspect they believe that explanations that foreground crime and violence, or view penal policy as a policy response to crime and violence, are inherently 'conservative' and ought to be avoided lest they appear to provide a justification for mass incarceration. Better, these commentators assume, to insist that penal policy is purely political, or racial, or neoliberal and to subject it to a political critique, leaving the difficult problems of crime and violence out of the discussion. But if this is the rationale for such a position, it is fundamentally misconceived. There is nothing intrinsically conservative about pointing to underlying problems of crime and victimisation. Nor does it depoliticise penality to insist that, however much politics and ideology shape penal laws and their enforcement, at its core penal policy involves some attempt to contain, control, and otherwise discourage crime.

Interpersonal violence is a product of social and economic structures, mediated by patterns of social control and cultural adaptation, and enacted in specific social situations by particular individuals. It is a patterned phenomenon, not a random one, and those most prone to violence are disproportionately drawn from highly disadvantaged circumstances. To recognise that certain communities exhibit very high rates of

associated public fears, resentments, and political mobilisations. And where rates of serious crime are on an altogether different scale—as is the case with US violence rates—one would expect penal policy also to operate at a different level.

violence is *not* to blame their residents—and certainly *not* to link race and violence.[36] It is to call attention to a major social problem that is (in the US) disproportionately experienced by communities of colour, a problem that is intimately linked to the problem of mass incarceration, and that ought also to be made a priority for remedial governmental action. The poor, urban communities of colour that experience the most incarceration are the same communities most affected by street crime and criminal violence. Far from disconnecting penal policy from the crime problem we need to bracket these together and trace their genesis back to larger structures of political economy and state action.[37]

Alexander and Wacquant may well be right in their account of the functional effects of mass incarceration, but neither is correct in their causal accounts of its emergence. Racism and neoliberalism should be viewed not as primary motivating causes but instead as structural contexts in which *both* crime problems *and* penal policies emerge, are given meaning, and produce effects.

(iii) Crime control as a recipe for governing

In his book, *Governing Through Crime: How the War on Crime Transformed American Democracy and created a Culture of Fear* (2007) socio-legal scholar Jonathan Simon offers a third—and more explicitly political—explanation for America's expansive penality. Simon describes how law-and-order politics became an attractive option for elected officials, and especially for state governors, in a post-1970s era when economic transformations made it much more difficult for elected officials to distribute New Deal-style social provision benefits to constituents in return for political support. Simon argues that the newfound appeal of a 'war-on-crime' and a victim-centred politics prompted vote-seeking politicians to use crime control—and its associated rhetoric and techniques—as an all-purpose template for governance in areas as diverse as education, housing, workplace relations, and family policy. American penality, on this account, is the outcome of a default political strategy of 'governing through

[36] Black crime typically occurs at elevated rates only where black disadvantage is layered and concentrated. Where these socio-economic effects are removed, offending rates for blacks are no higher than for other groups. White rates of crime and violence are also elevated in the US compared to elsewhere, and are also concentrated in areas of social and economic deprivation. And of course most crime and violence is intra-racial (Sampson & Wilson 2005).

[37] I should stress that poverty and unemployment do not directly cause crime or violence—and anti-social behaviours are plentiful among the rich and privileged (Hagan 2010). But concentrated poverty and social exclusion undermine the strength of a group's collective efficacy (Sampson 2012) and lead to failures of socialisation and social control in families, schools, labour markets, and communities—which in turn give rise to crime. Socialisation, social control, social integration are all made more difficult by the stress of chronically scarce resources.

crime' and Simon's book documents the extent to which penal control recipes have, since the 1980s, become pervasive throughout American society.

I regard this thesis as largely correct in its descriptive claims but it leaves an important causal question unanswered. Simon is persuasive when he describes crime control as a prominent theme in recent state and federal government and he is similarly convincing when he points out that the demise of the New Deal settlement has meant that American politicians are now less able to win support by distributing social and economic benefits to their constituents (Fraser & Gerstle 1990). But what his analysis does not explain is why the decline of the earlier political quid pro quo led to the emergence of the current one. Why this new formula and not some other?

We need to ask *why* crime control recipes have become so central to American political action and so appealing to American popular audiences. What are the circumstances prompting demands for penal-style controls, not just in criminal justice but also in schools, city planning, shopping malls, public housing, and workplaces? And why is penal control—rather than other more pro-social interventions—the default response of American governments to every symptom of deviance and disorder? The answer, it seems to me, must point to the social control deficits that I have described above—deficits that grew worse in the period Simon describes, just as other pro-social forms of state action came to be politically discredited, retrenched, and restricted (Garland 2001; Fraser & Gerstle 1990: Hinton 2016).

(iv) Social change, social control, and social order

The final narrative I want to discuss is developed in *The Culture of Control: Crime and Social Order in Contemporary Society* (Garland 2001) a study of changing US and UK crime-control policies and their social causes. In that book I argue that structural transformations in social ecology—brought about in the mid-20th century by economic growth, social emancipation, and consumer capitalism—generated not just new freedoms, opportunities, and affluence but also a new set of risks and problems. Chief among these problems was increased rates of crime and violence, a widespread phenomenon that gave rise to 'high-crime societies' and their associated cultural and political characteristics. I then traced how, from the mid-1970s onward, various actors within the state and civil society reacted to these new risks, producing, inter alia, a reactionary 'culture of control' with consequences for social and penal policy as well as for the conduct of everyday life. The decline of penal-welfarism, the rise of penal populism, the shift to a risk-averse criminal justice, the expansion of private security, and the emergence of mass imprisonment were all, or so I argued, concomitants of these late modern socio-economic transformations and the political and cultural adaptations that followed in their wake.

The Culture of Control is not a comparative study and it nowhere addresses the question of why America is an outlier in its use of penal power. But the book does deal with the interaction between changes at the level of social and economic structures, and changes in patterns of informal social control and state action. And it does highlight the role that criminal violence—and associated public fears, resentments, and political mobilisations—played in articulating these socio-economic developments and channeling a series of social and political responses to them. *The Culture of Control* argues that the effect of the economic and social changes of the post-war decades was to deplete existing social controls and to generate new risks, new crime opportunities, and higher levels of crime and violence. Over time, the collective experience of crime and insecurity prompted a patterned response, both in state agencies and in civil society—a response that I described as a new 'culture of control'. It seems to me that this same analytical framework—linking economic and social structures to patterns of crime and punishment *via* an analysis of (formal and informal) social control—can be put to work for our present purposes. In other words, the framework I developed for historical purposes in *The Culture of Control* can be reworked as a basis for thinking comparatively about American penality, highlighting the connections between America's penal practices, its political, economic, and social structures, its patterns of informal social control, and the problems and policies to which these give rise.[38]

SOCIAL STRUCTURE, SOCIAL ORGANISATION, AND SOCIAL PROBLEMS

It is an established social science finding that high levels of crime, violence, and other social dislocations are associated with low levels of social capital, social integration and informal social control (Sampson, 1987; Sampson *et al.* 1997; Sampson & Wilson 2005; Morenoff *et al.* 2001; McCarthy 2002). And a series of comparative research studies strongly suggests that social capital, social integration, and informal social control—in families, schools, communities, and neighbourhoods—are on average less developed and more unequally distributed in the US than in comparable nations; with areas of concentrated poverty and cumulative disadvantage in American cities exhibiting very serious levels of disorganisation and endemic social problems (Messner & Rosenfeld 1997; Avendano & Kawachi 2014; Darroch *et al.* 2001; Banks *et al.* 2010;

[38] Because it focused on parallel developments in the US and the UK, rather than contrasts between them, Garland (2001) said little about the role of America's distinctive political system in shaping penal policy. For a detailed discussion of that issue, see Garland (2010).

Singh & Kogan 2007; Williams & Collins 2001).[39] America's 'social control deficits'—which are preponderantly though by no means exclusively experienced by communities of colour[40]—exist for reasons that are historical and institutional, among which are the following: (i) long-term legacies of slavery, segregation, and discrimination (Wilson 2011); (ii) an extraordinary political commitment to free markets and private sector solutions (Garland 2016); and (iii) the under-development of a social state, especially as it affects the urban poor and people of colour (Katz 2013). In the past, programmes associated with the New Deal and the Great Society worked to reduce these problems, and succeeded to some extent (Jencks 2015). But since the rise to dominance of neoliberalism in the 1980s, American social and economic policies have mainly worked to reproduce these characteristics rather than alleviate them.

Social and economic structures provide the settings in which civil society institutions such as families, schools, churches, and communities undertake the ongoing work of socialisation and social control, so it is hardly surprising that the chronic stresses imposed by these structures on certain sections of the population result in failures of social control and the emergence of social problems. These social and economic structures also provide the contexts in which governmental action is undertaken, so it is also no surprise that American welfare policies are designed to support and reinforce market relations and to de-emphasise social interventions that provide social and economic protections to those who are ill-served by market processes. There is, in other words, a series of linkages that ties together America's political economy, governmental processes, high levels of crime, and extraordinary levels of punishment. And this, it seems to me, is how we should frame the question of America's extraordinary use of penal power.

CONCLUSION

I have argued that we should think of American punishment not primarily as a form of retribution, or racial oppression, or neoliberal governance but as a specific form of penal power that emphasises control above everything else. Despite diverse local concerns and motivating circumstances, the sentencing revolution of the last forty

[39] This finding does not necessarily confound the traditional Tocquevillian view of the US as a society with a weak state and a strongly associational civil society. Such strengths do exist, even if they have been diminished in recent decades—see Putnam (2010). The point is that America's very high levels of inequality, together with minimalist state protections for poor communities and families, gives rise to communities that exhibit very high levels of disorganisation and dysfunction.

[40] Several recent studies have observed that sections of America's white working class have recently been experiencing serious problems of disorganisation and dysfunction: see Chen (2016).

years has amounted to one long, cumulative process of extending, deepening, and guaranteeing penal control. American criminal justice has abandoned retributive fundamentals such as 'proportion' and liberal principles such as 'parsimony' (Stuntz 2013; Tonry 2016). The penalties that follow on a repeat offence have nothing to do with retributive proportion and everything to do with imposing control. The sentences handed down to drug or sex offenders have little to do with culpability and everything to do with perceptions of dangerousness and disorder. And each element of America's sentencing revolution expresses distrust of government, fear of dangerous criminals, and a public safety imperative demanding the incapacitation and control of anyone convicted of a crime.

American criminal justice today is best understood not as a system of criminal punishment but as a system of penal control—a large-scale network of intensive, long-acting constraints and controls. Concerns about public safety and the need to impose control are explicitly and repeatedly stated in public discourse and in the political arguments that were made to justify these penal measures.[41] In the 1980s and 1990s, representations of popular sentiment repeatedly revolved around questions of public safety and the need to protect innocent people from violent crime. Politicians presented their proposals not as harsh punishments or wild vengeance but as guaranteed, long-lasting, thoroughgoing controls. Prison works! Three Strikes and You're Out! Life Without Prospect of Parole. Mandatory Sentences. Truth in Sentencing. The slogans say it loud and clear (Garland 2001). So too do today's leading reform proposals, nearly all of which take care to preserve the imperative of penal control by targeting non-violent, non-repeat, non-sexual offenders (Gottschalk 2014).

American criminal justice is distinctively committed to what we might call 'mass penal control' because, as compared to other developed nations, American society exhibits an institutionalised pattern of social control deficits and because the American state is disposed to respond to these problems by means of penal control rather than by other means. The tragedy is that these penal control measures do little to address the underlying problems of social disorganisation, even if they do succeed in curbing crime rates to some extent. Indeed, in these more fundamental respects, penal control is counterproductive, especially when exercised on a massive scale. It destroys human and social capital; it dis-integrates and excludes (Lynch & Sabol 2004; Moore 1996; Clear & Rose 1998; Rose & Clear 1998; Western *et al.* 2004). The penal controls of the state, exercised on a massive scale, work to undermine society's capacity for social control, not to build that vital capacity.

[41] As Foucault (2015) notes, we need not deploy hermeneutics or deep analysis in order to identify strategic considerations: the aims of political actors can generally be read on the surface of their statements and in the substance of what is said.

Acknowledgements
This is an expanded version of the 2016 British Academy Law Lecture delivered on 7 June 2016. I am grateful to Hugh Collins who chaired the lecture, Michael Meranze, Jim Jacobs, Janet Carsten, and an anonymous referee for their comments, and to the Filomen D'Agostino and Max E. Greenberg Research Fund of NYU School for its support.

REFERENCES

Alexander, M. (2010) *The New Jim Crow: Mass Incarceration in the Age of Colorblindness* (New York, The New Press).

Anderson, D. (1995) *Crime and the Politics of Hysteria: How the Willie Horton Story Changed American Criminal Justice* (New York, Crown).

Avendano, M. & Kawachi, I. (2014), 'Why do Americans Have a Shorter Life Expectancy and Worse Health than Do People in Other High-income Countries?', *Annual Review of Public Health*, 35: 307–25. https://doi.org/10.1146/annurev-publhealth-032013-182411

Banks, J., Berkman, J. F., Smith, J. P., Avendano, M. & Glymour, M. (2010), 'Do Cross-country Variations in Social Integration and Social Interactions Explain Differences in Life Expectancy in Industrialised Countries?', in E. Crimmins (ed.) *International Differences in Mortality at Older Ages* (Washington, DC, National Academy of Sciences), 210–67.

Bureau of Justice Statistics (2013) *Correctional Populations in the United States.* http://www.bjs.gov/index.cfm?ty=pbdetail&iid=4843

Campbell, M. & Schoenfeld, H. (2013), 'The Transformation of America's Penal Order: A Historicized Political Sociology of Punishment', *American Journal of Sociology*, 118: 1375–423. https://doi.org/10.1086/669506

Cavadino, M. & Dignan, J. (2005) *Penal Systems: A Comparative Approach* (London, Sage).

Chen, V. (2016), 'All Hollowed Out: The Lonely Poverty of America's White Working Class' *The Atlantic*, 16 January. http://www.theatlantic.com/business/archive/2016/01/white-working-class-poverty/424341/

Clear, T. & Rose, D. (1998), 'Social Capital and Crime: Explaining the Unintended Consequences of Incarceration' *Criminology*, 36: 441–79.

Cole, D. (1999) *No Equal Justice: Race and Class in the American Criminal Justice System* (New York, The New Press).

Darroch, J., Singh, S., Frost, J. & the study team (2001), 'Differences in Teenage Pregnancy Rates Among Five Developed Countries', *Family Planning Perspectives*, 33: 244–50. https://doi.org/10.2307/3030191

Demleitner, N. (2017), 'Collateral Sanctions as a Tool of Exclusion and "Re-exit"', in K. Reitz (ed.) *American Exceptionalism in Crime and Punishment* (New York, Oxford University Press).

Denton, N. & Massey, D. (1998) *American Apartheid: Segregation and the Making of the Underclass* (Cambridge, MA, Harvard University Press).

Dubber, M. (2005), 'The Possession Paradigm', in A. Duff & S. Green (eds) *Defining Crimes: Essays on the Special Part of the Criminal Law* (Oxford, Oxford University Press), 91–119. https://doi.org/10.1093/acprof:oso/9780199269228.003.0005

Enns, P. (2016) *Incarceration Nation: How America Became the Most Punitive Democracy in the World* (New York, Cambridge University Press). https://doi.org/10.1017/CBO9781316471029

Fassin, D. (2016), 'The Will to Punish' *Tanner Lectures,* delivered University of California at Berkeley, March 2016. http://tannerlectures.berkeley.edu/2015-2016-lecture-fassin/

FBI, Federal Bureau of Investigation (2013) *Crime in the United States 2013* Table 43. https://www.fbi.gov/about-us/cjis/ucr/crime-in-the-u.s/2013/crime-in-the-u.s.-2013/tables/table-43

Flamm, M. (2005) *Law and Order: Street Crime, Civil Unrest and the Crisis of Liberalism in the 1960s* (New York, Columbia University Press).

Forman, J. (2012), 'Racial Critiques of Mass Incarceration: Beyond the New Jim Crow', *NYU Law Review*, 87: 101–46

Fortner, M. (2015) *Silent Black Majority: The Rockefeller Drug Laws and the Politics of Punishment* (Cambridge MA, Harvard University Press). https://doi.org/10.4159/9780674496088

Foucault, M. (2015) *The Punitive Society: Lectures at the College de France 1972–1973*, ed. B. Harcourt (London, Palgrave Macmillan).

Fraser, S. & Gerstle, G. (eds) (1990) *The Rise and Fall of the New Deal Order* (Princeton, NJ, Princeton University Press).

Gallo, Z., Lacey, N. & Soskice, D. (2017), 'Comparing Serious Violent Crime in the US and England Wales', in K. Reitz (ed.) *American Exceptionalism in Crime and Punishment* (New York, Oxford University Press).

Garland, D. (1990) *Punishment and Modern Society: A Study in Social Theory* (Oxford, Oxford University Press). https://doi.org/10.7208/chicago/9780226922508.001.0001

Garland, D. (2001) *The Culture of Control: Crime and Social Order in Contemporary Society* (Oxford, Oxford University Press).

Garland, D. (2010) *Peculiar Institution: America's Death Penalty in an Age of Abolition* (Cambridge, MA, Harvard University Press).

Garland, D. (2013), 'Penality and the Penal State', *Criminology*, 51: 475–517. https://doi.org/10.1111/1745-9125.12015

Garland, D. (2016), 'Land of the Unfree', *Times Literary Supplement*, 25 July.

Garland, D. (2017), 'The Concept of American Exceptionalism and the Case of Capital Punishment', in K. Reitz (ed.) *American Exceptionalism in Crime and Punishment* (New York, Oxford University Press).

Geltner, G. (2014) *Flogging Others: Corporal Punishment and Cultural Identity from Antiquity to the Present* (Amsterdam, Amsterdam University Press).

Gottschalk, M. (2006) *The Prison and the Gallows: The Politics of Mass Incarceration in America* (New York, Cambridge University Press). https://doi.org/10.1017/CBO9780511791093

Gottschalk, M. (2015) *Caught: The Prison State and the Lockdown of American Politic*s (Princeton, NJ, Princeton University Press). https://doi.org/10.1515/9781400852147

Hagan, J. (2010) *Who are the Criminals? The Politics of Crime Policy* (Princeton, NJ, Princeton University Press).

Hinton, E. (2016) *From the War on Poverty to the War on Crime: The Making of Mass Incarceration in America* (Cambridge MA, Harvard University Press).

Jacobs, J. B. (1982), 'Sentencing by Prison Personnel: Good Time', *UCLA Law Review*, 30: 216–70

Jacobs, J. B. (2015) *The Eternal Criminal Record* (Cambridge, MA, Harvard University Press). https://doi.org/10.4159/harvard.9780674735842

Jencks, C. (2015), 'The War on Poverty: Was it Lost?', *New York Review of Books*, 2 April.

Karabel, J. (2015), 'The Other Capital Punishment', *Huffington Post*, 9 February.

Karabel, J. & Laurison, D. (2011), 'Outlier Nation? American Exceptionalism and Societal Wellbeing', IRLE working paper, University of California at Berkeley.

Karstedt, S. & LaFree, G. (2006) 'Democracy, Crime and Justice', *The Annals of the American Academy of Political and Social Science*, 605: 6–23. https://doi.org/10.1177/0002716206288230

Katz, M. (2013) *The Undeserving Poor: America's Enduring Confrontation with Poverty*, 2nd edn (New York, Oxford University Press).

Kerner Commission (1968/2016) *Report of the National Advisory Commission on Civil Disorders* (Princeton, NJ, Princeton University Press).

Kleiman, M. (2016) op ed on the 1994 Crime Act. http://washingtonmonthly.com/2016/02/17/the-current-crime-debate-isnt-doing-hillary-justice/

Kohler Hausmann, I. (2014), 'Managerial Justice and Mass Misdemeanors', *Stanford Law Review*, 66: 611–93.

Kohler Hausmann, I. (2015), 'Misdemeanor Justice: Control Without Conviction', *American Journal of Sociology*, 119: 351–94. https://doi.org/10.1086/674743

Kohler-Hausmann, J. (2015), 'Guns and Butter: The Welfare State, the Carceral State and the Politics of Exclusion in the Postwar United States', *The Journal of American History*, 102: 87–99. https://doi.org/10.1093/jahist/jav239

Krivo, L., Peterson, R. & Kuhl, D. (2009), 'Segregation, Racial Structure, and Neighborhood Violent Crime', *American Journal of Sociology*, 114: 1765–802. https://doi.org/10.1086/597285

Lacey, N. (2007) *The Prisoners' Dilemma: Political Economy and Punishment in Contemporary Democracies* (Cambridge, Cambridge University Press).

Lacey, N. & Soskice, D. (2015), 'Crime, Punishment and Segregation in the United States: The Paradox of Local Democracy', *Punishment & Society*, 17: 454–81. https://doi.org/10.1177/1462474515604042

Lacey, N. & Soskice, D. (2017), 'American Exceptionalism in Crime, Punishment and Disadvantage', in K. Reitz (ed.) *American Exceptionalism in Crime and Punishment* (New York, Oxford University Press).

LaFree, G. (1998) *Losing Legitimacy: Street Crime and the Decline of Social Institutions in America* (Boulder, CO, Westview Press).

Lappi-Seppälä, T. (2008), 'Trust, Welfare and Political Culture: Explaining Differences in National Penal Policies', in M. Tonry (ed.) *Crime and Justice, Volume 37* (Chicago, IL, Chicago University Press), 313–87. https://doi.org/10.1086/525028

Lappi-Seppälä, T. (2017), 'American Penal Exceptionalism in Comparative Perspective', in K. Reitz (ed.) *American Exceptionalism in Crime and Punishment* (New York, Oxford University Press).

Lerman, A. & Weaver, V. (2014) *Arresting Citizenship: The Democratic Consequences of American Crime Control* (Chicago, IL, University of Chicago Press). https://doi.org/10.7208/chicago/9780226137971.001.0001

Loury, G. (2008) *Race, Incarceration and American Values* (Cambridge, MA, MIT Press).

Lynch, J. & Sabol, W. (2004), 'Assessing the Effects of Mass Incarceration on Informal Social Control in Communities', *Criminology and Public Policy*, 3: 267–94. https://doi.org/10.1111/j.1745-9133.2004.tb00042.x

Lynch, M. (2009) *Sunbelt Justice: Arizona and the Transformation of American Punishment* (Palo Alto, CA, Stanford University Press).

Lynch, M. (2016) *Hard Bargains: The Coercive Power of Drug Laws in Federal Court* (New York, Russell Sage Foundation).

Manza, J. & Uggens, C. (2006) *Locked Out: Felon Disenfranchisement and American Democracy* (New York, Oxford University Press). https://doi.org/10.1093/acprof:oso/9780195149326.001.0001

Mauer, M. (2006) *Race to Incarcerate Revised edition* (New York: The New Press).

Mauer, M. & Chesney-Lind, M. (eds) (2002) *Invisible Punishment: The Collateral Consequences of Mass Imprisonment* (New York, The New Press).

McCarthy, B. (2002), 'New Economics of Sociological Criminology', *Annual Review of Sociology*, 28: 417–42. https://doi.org/10.1146/annurev.soc.28.110601.140752

Merton, R. K. (1996) *On Social Structure and Science* (Chicago, IL, University of Chicago Press).

Messner, S. & Rosenfeld, R. (2007) *Crime and the American Dream* 4th edn (Monterey, CA, Wadsworth).

Miller, L. (2015), 'What's Violence Got to Do With It? Inequality, Punishment and State Failure in American Politics', *Punishment and Society*, 17: 184–210. https://doi.org/10.1177/1462474515577153

Miller, L. (2016) *The Myth of Mob Rule: Violent Crime and Democratic Politics* (New York, Oxford University Press). https://doi.org/10.1093/acprof:oso/9780190228705.001.0001

Moore, J. (1996) 'Bearing the Burden: How Incarceration Policies Weaken Inner-city Communities', *The Unintended Consequences of Incarceration* (New York, Vera Institute), 73–5.

Morenoff, J., Sampson, R. & Raudenbush, S. (2001), 'Neighborhood Inequality, Collective Efficacy and the Spatial Dynamics of Urban Violence', *Criminology*, 39: 517–60. https://doi.org/10.1111/j.1745-9125.2001.tb00932.x

Nellis, A. (2013) *Life Goes On: The Historic Rise of Life Sentences in America* (Washington, DC, The Sentencing Project).

O'Malley, P. (2009) *The Currency of Justice: Fines and Damages in Consumer Societies* (London, Routledge).

Omi, M. & Winant, H. (2014) *Racial Formation in the United States* 3rd edn (New York, Routledge).

Pease, K. (1994), 'Cross-national Imprisonment Rates: Limitations of Method and 5 Possible Conclusions', *British Journal of Criminology*, 34: 116–30.

Pfaff, J. (2017) *Locked In: The True Causes of Mass Incarceration—And How to Achieve Real Reform* (New York, Basic Books).

Pifferi, M. (2016) *Reinventing Punishment: A Comparative History of Criminology and Penology* (Oxford, Oxford University Press). https://doi.org/10.1093/acprof:oso/9780198743217.001.0001

Polanyi, K. (1944) *The Great Transformation: The Political and Economic Origins of our Time* (New York, Beacon Press).

Pratt, J. & Eriksson, A. (2013) *Contrasts in Punishment: An Explanation of Anglophone Excess and Nordic Exceptionalism* (London, Routledge).

Putnam, R. (2010) *Bowling Alone: The Collapse and Revival of American Community* (New York, Simon and Schuster).

Rhine, E. & Taxman, F. (2017), 'American Exceptionalism in Community Service', in K. Reitz (ed.) *American Exceptionalism in Crime and Punishment* (New York, Oxford University Press).

Reitz, K. (2012) 'The Traditional Indeterminate Sentencing Model', in J. Petersilia & K. Reitz (eds) *The Oxford Handbook of Sentencing and Corrections* (New York, Oxford University Press). https://doi.org/10.1093/oxfordhb/9780199730148.013.0011

Reitz, K. (ed.) (2017) *American Exceptionalism in Crime and Punishment* (New York, Oxford University Press).

Rose, D. & Clear, T. (1998), 'Incarceration, Social Capital and Crime: Implications for Social Disorganization Theory', *Criminology*, 36: 441–80. https://doi.org/10.1111/j.1745-9125.1998.tb01255.x

Roth, R. (2012) *American Homicide* (Cambridge, MA, Belknap Press).

Roth, R. (2017), 'How Exceptional is the History of Violence and Criminal Justice in the United States', in K. Reitz (ed.) *American Exceptionalism in Crime and Punishment* (New York, Oxford University Press).

Sampson, R. (1987), 'Urban Black Violence: The Effects of Male Joblessness and Family Disruption', *American Journal of Sociology*, 93: 348–83. https://doi.org/10.1086/228748

Sampson, R. (2012) *Great American City: Chicago and the Enduring Neighborhood Effect* (Chicago, IL, University of Chicago Press). https://doi.org/10.7208/chicago/9780226733883.001.0001

Sampson, R. & Wilson, W. J. (2005), 'Toward a Theory of Race, Crime and Urban Inequality', in S. Gabbidon & H. Greene (eds) *Race, Crime and Justice: A Reader* (New York, Routledge), 37–56.

Sampson, R., Raudenbush, S. & Earls, F. (1997), 'Neighborhoods and Violent Crime: A Multilevel Study of Collective Efficacy', *Science*, 277: 918–24. https://doi.org/10.1126/science.277.5328.918

Shannon, S. K. S. (2013), 'Does the Right Hand Know What the Left Hand is Doing? General Assistance Welfare, Crime and Punishment in the United States', Ph.D. dissertation, University of Minnesota.

Sharkey, P. (2013) *Stuck in Place: Urban Neighborhoods and the End of Progress towards Racial Equality* (Chicago, IL, University of Chicago Press). https://doi.org/10.7208/chicago/9780226924267.001.0001

Simon, J. (2007) *Governing Through Crime: How the War on Crime Transformed American Democracy* (New York, Oxford University Press).

Simon, J. (1997) *Poor Discipline: Parole and the Social Control of the Underclass* (Chicago, IL, University of Chicago Press).

Singh, G. & Kogan, M. (2007), 'Persistent Socioeconomic Disparities in Infant, Neonatal, and Postnatal Mortality Rates in the United States, 1969–2001', *Pediatrics*, 119: 928–39. https://doi.org/10.1542/peds.2005-2181

Soss, J., Fording, R. & Schram, S. (2011) *Disciplining the Poor: Neoliberal Paternalism and the Persistent Power of Race* (Chicago, IL, University of Chicago Press). https://doi.org/10.7208/chicago/9780226768786.001.0001

Stuntz, W. (2001), 'The Pathological Politics of Criminal Law', *Michigan Law Review*, 100: 505–600. https://doi.org/10.2307/1290411

Stuntz, W. (2013) *The Collapse of American Criminal Justice* (Cambridge, MA, Harvard University Press).

Subramanian, R. & Shames A. (2013) *Sentencing and Prison Practice in Germany and the Netherlands* (New York, Vera Institute).

Sutton, J. (2004) 'The Political Economy of Imprisonment in Affluent Western Democracies, 1960–1990', *American Sociological Review* 69: 170–189. https://doi.org/10.1177/000312240406900202

Tonry, M. (2009), 'Explanations of American Punishment Policies: A National History', *Punishment & Society*, 11: 377–94. https://doi.org/10.1177/1462474509334609

Tonry, M. (2016) *Sentencing Fragments* (New York, Oxford University Press).

Travis, J. (2002), 'Invisible Punishment: An Instrument of Social Exclusion', in M. Mauer & M. Chesney-Lind (eds) *Invisible Punishment: The Collateral Consequences of Mass Imprisonment* (New York, The New Press), 1–36.

Van Zyl Smit, D. & Corda, A. (2017), 'American Exceptionalism in Parole Release and Supervision', in K. Reitz (ed.) *American Exceptionalism in Crime and Punishment* (New York, Oxford University Press).

Wacquant, L. (2009) *Punishing the Poor: The Neoliberal Governance of Social Insecurity* (Durham, NC, Duke University Press). https://doi.org/10.1215/9780822392255

Wacquant, L. (2009a) *Prisons of Poverty* expanded edn (Minneapolis, MN, University of Minnesota Press).

Wagner, P. (2014), 'Tracking Prison Growth in Fifty States', Prison Policy Initiative. http://www.prisonpolicy.org/reports/overtime.html

Walmsley, R. (2016) *World Prison Population List* 11th edn (London, Institute for Criminal Policy Research).

Weber, M (2002) *The Protestant Ethic and the Spirit of Capitalism* (New York, Penguin).

Weber, M (2011) *Methodology of the Social Sciences* (New Brunswick, NJ, Transaction Publishers).

Western, B (2006) *Punishment and Inequality in America* (New York, Russell Sage Foundation).

Western, B. (2016), 'Response to Didier Fassin', Tanner lectures audiotape, University of California at Berkeley. http://tannerlectures.berkeley.edu/2015-2016-lecture-fassin/

Western, B., Weiman, D. & Patillo, M. (eds) (2004) *The Impacts of Incarceration on Families and Communities* (New York, Russell Sage Foundation).

Whitman, J. Q. (2003) *Harsh Justice: The Growing Divergence between America and Europe* (New York, Oxford University Press).

Wilkinson, R. & Pickett, K. (2009) *The Spirit Level: Why Greater Equality Makes Societies Stronger* (London, Bloomsbury).

Williams, D & Collins, C. (2001), 'Racial Residential Segregation: A Fundamental Cause of Racial Disparities in Health', *Public Health Reports*, 116: 404–16. https://doi.org/10.1016/S0033-3549(04)50068-7

Wilson, W. J. (1997) *When Work Disappears: The World of the New Working Poor* (New York, W. W. Norton).

Wilson, W. J. (2011), 'Being Poor, Black and American: The Impact of Political, Economic and Cultural Forces', *American Educator*, Spring: 10–23.

Wilson, W. J. (2012) *The Truly Disadvantaged* 2nd edn (Chicago, IL, University of Chicago Press). https://doi.org/10.7208/chicago/9780226924656.001.0001

Wright, R. (2012), 'Charging and Plea Bargaining as Forms of Sentencing Discretion', in J. Petersilia & K. Reitz (eds) *The Oxford Handbook of Sentencing and Corrections* (New York, Oxford University Press), 247–69. https://doi.org/10.1093/oxfordhb/9780199730148.013.0010

Zimring, F. (2010), 'The Scale of Imprisonment in the United States', *Journal of Criminal Law and Criminology*, 100: 1225–45.

Zimring, F. (2017) 'American Exceptionalism or Fifty Different Countries?', in K. Reitz (ed.) *American Exceptionalism in Crime and Punishment* (New York, Oxford University Press).

Zimring, F. & Hawkins, G. (1997) *Crime is not the Problem: Lethal Violence in America* (New York, Oxford University Press).

Note on the Author: David Garland FBA, FRSE, FAAAS is Arthur T. Vanderbilt Professor of Law and Professor of Sociology at New York University. He is the author of several books on the history and sociology of punishment, including *Punishment and Modern Society* (OUP 1990), *The Culture of Control* (OUP 2001), and *Peculiar Institution: America's Death Penalty in an Age of Abolition* (OUP 2010). His most recent book is *The Welfare State: A Very Short Introduction* (OUP 2016).
david.garland@nyu.edu

To cite the article: David Garland (2017), 'Penal power in America: Forms, functions and foundations', *Journal of the British Academy*, 5: 1–35.
DOI https://doi.org/10.85871/jba/005.1

Journal of the British Academy (ISSN 2052–7217) is published by
The British Academy—the national academy for the humanities and social sciences.
10–11 Carlton House Terrace, London, SW1Y 5AH
www.britishacademy.ac.uk

Journal of the British Academy, **5**, 37–59. DOI https://doi.org/10.5871/jba/005.037

Stages of papal law

Raleigh Lecture on History
read 1 November 2016

DAVID L. D'AVRAY
Fellow of the British Academy

Abstract: Papal law is known from the late 4th century (Siricius). There was demand for decretals and they were collected in private collections from the 5th century on. Charlemagne's *Admonitio generalis* made papal legislation even better known and the Pseudo-Isidorian collections brought genuine decretals also to the wide audience that these partly forged collections reached. The papal reforms from the 11th century on gave rise to a new burst of papal decretals, and collections of them, culminating in the *Liber Extra* of 1234. The Council of Trent opened a new phase. The 'Congregation of the Council', set up to apply Trent's non-dogmatic decrees, became a new source of papal law. Finally, in 1917, nearly a millennium and a half of papal law was codified by Cardinal Gasparri within two covers. Papal law was to a great extent 'demand-driven', which requires explanation. The theory proposed here is that Catholic Christianity was composed of a multitude of subsystems, not planned centrally and each with an evolving life of its own. Subsystems frequently interfered with the life of other subsystems, creating new entanglements. This constantly renewed complexity had the function (though not the purpose) of creating and recreating demand for papal law to sort out the entanglements between subsystems. For various reasons other religious systems have not generated the same demand: because the state plays a 'papal' role, or because the units are small, discrete and simple, or thanks to a clear simple blueprint, or because of conservatism combined with a tolerance of some inconsistency. It is difficult to find a religious system with the same complexity problems combined with a strong sense that the whole needed to remain united without internal contradictions.

Keywords: Siricius, Pseudo-Isidoran collections, Gratian, decretals, *Liber Extra*, Apostolic Penitentiary, Congregation of the Council, other early modern papal law, Gasparri, complexity, Trent.

FIRST PART: DESCRIPTIVE SURVEY

This paper aims to help explain the evolution of papal law over a millennium and a half,[1] but it will help if I first survey the main changes to be explained. The natural starting point is 385, the date of what is generally reckoned to be the first papal decretal, sent by Pope Siricius to Himerius of Tarragona.[2] Imitation of the style of Roman imperial rescripts mark it out from previous papal letters. The answers to the bishop's questions are meant to be widely applicable, for Siricius asks him to pass them on to others. This was seven years after the battle of Adrianople (378), which arguably started the chain reaction leading to the collapse of the Roman Empire in the West.

The difficult political and military situation is relevant to the origins of papal law. Church law for the whole empire was already a familiar concept thanks to the Council of Nicaea (325), which did a lot more than lay down dogma. Nicaea made laws, especially about the clergy and ritual, which set a pattern for papal law. Full Western participation in a general council like Nicaea depended on imperial infrastructure, which was becoming shaky in the West by the late 4th century. The desire for general church law remained, and the baton was passed to the papacy.

The 4th-century decretal of Siricius was followed by a burst of papal legislation from the early 5th century on.[3] The pattern of the first decretal was repeated: bishops sent questions to the pope, who replied with the evident intention that the answers should apply outside the diocese in question. The process was demand-led. Popes could not make anyone ask for rulings and were in no position to enforce them. There is a lot of repetition in these 5th-century rulings, but we must remember that initially there were no canon law collections.

Early collections of canon law

It was not long before they appeared.[4] The first in the West was probably put together by African bishops early in the 5th century. It would have consisted of conciliar decisions. Smaller collections were compiled in the first half of the 5th century and these included papal decretals too. Around about 500 CE three major collections of papal

[1] Gaudemet (1994) is a rare attempt to survey the *longue durée* history of canon law. Some key arguments about the period up to 1200 developed here are anticipated in brilliant compressed pages by Duggan (2008: especially 201–11).

[2] Zechiel-Eckes (2013); Hornung (2011); Jaffé & Herbers *et al.* (2016: no. 605, 112).

[3] Jasper & Fuhrmann (2001: 7–87).

[4] Kéry (1999: 1–86), gives a brief introduction to and bibliography on the main collections, including those mentioned below.

(with conciliar) collections were compiled: the Frisingensis (so called because of its Freising provenance), the Quesnelliana (called after the early modern scholar who first edited it), and the Dionysiana, after Dionysius Exiguus, the monk to whom we also owe the current AD or CE dating. The Dionysiana had a great future ahead of it. The papal decretals were organised pope by pope, with thematic headings within sections for a given pope.

Thematic organisation of whole collections was the next stage. In these collections papal decretals and conciliar canons were grouped together under subject headings. The so called *Vetus Gallica*[5] and the collection of Cresconius[6] are the two best studied thematic collections of the early Middle Ages.

Chronological collections continued to be copied. An updated version of Dionysius Exiguus's collection was compiled before 774 and given to Charlemagne.[7] Charlemagne himself incorporated papal decretal decisions in his widely diffused *General Admonition*.[8] Without perhaps intending it, he was thus providing propaganda for the idea of papal law.

Pseudo-Isidore

Some decades later the idea of papal law was given a new impetus by the compilation (when and by whom are fiercely disputed) of the so-called false or Pseudo-Isidorian decretals. The investigation of the genesis of these collections has been an intensely active area of research recently and interpretation is still in flux.[9] Here suffice it to say three things. Firstly, the 'false decretals' include a fairly comprehensive collection of the earliest genuine papal decretals. Secondly, genuine decretals evidently provided a model for forged decretals, even if the latter took the forgers' agenda further than the genuine one could (by emphasising the rights of bishops below the level of the arch-bishops, the so-called metropolitans who commanded other bishops, and also by stressing papal authority, because it out-trumped the authority of metropolitans). Thirdly, the Pseudo-Isidorian version of genuine early decretals was copied very widely indeed, thus further familiarising the educated clergy of the West with the idea of papal law.

[5] Mordek (1975).
[6] Zechiel-Eckes (1992).
[7] Kéry (1999: 13–14).
[8] Mordek *et al.* (2013).
[9] Ubl & Ziemann (2015); Harder (2014); Patzold (2015).

Burchard of Worms

Pseudo-Isidore was a combination of (genuine and fake) papal decretals and conciliar canons, and in this respect it shared the structure of the Dionysiana and the other very early collections. It also grouped the decretals by successive pontificates. The other kind of structure, thematic, was adopted by a massively successful collection produced around 1000 AD by Burchard of Worms.[10] This differed from Pseudo-Isidore in another respect: it contained a lot of material that came neither from councils nor from popes: passages from authoritative theologians like St Augustine, and content from the strange genre of 'Penitentials' that had originated in Ireland and spread over the Continent, to the disapproval of some.

Papal reform collections

In the later 11th century a new kind of canon law compilation appears: the agenda-driven collections of the papal reform movement. This first attacked the purchase of episcopal office and marriage or concubinage by clerics from subdeacon up, then extended the reform agenda to combatting rituals which made religious office seem dependent on secular rulers.[11] Genuine and forged papal decretals were important in these collections, which can be regarded as weapons in a propaganda war.

Ivo of Chartres and the age of Gratian

Pro-papal but too comprehensive to be predominantly propagandist were the canon law compilations of Ivo of Chartres (*c.* 1100).[12] While incorporating the programme of the Gregorian Reform, they followed the same broad pattern as the pre-Reform Burchard of Worms: viz., thematic arrangement and a mixture of papal decretals, conciliar canons, extracts from authoritative theologians, and penitential material. The same may be said of Gratian's *Decretum*[13] (mid-12th-century, 'published' in at least two 'editions'),[14] which nonetheless marks a turning point, in that it is clearly designed as an academic teaching tool. An inspired innovation was a technique of analysis through quite complex narratives, from each of which not just one but a series of problematic cases were hung. The *Decretum*'s succes was rapid. It attracted learned marginal glosses from early on. These are a written deposit corresponding to

[10] An excellent guide is Hoffman & Pokorny (1991).
[11] See e.g. Cushing (1998); Gilchrist (1973).
[12] See e.g. Rolker (2010).
[13] Friedberg (1922a).
[14] Winroth (2000): which sparked lively controversy.

oral teaching at what would become universities. Clerics trained with the help of the *Decretum* had plenty of employment opportunities in the new network of professionally staffed ecclesiastical courts, which took over from the previous system of more informal judgements by individual bishops and synods of bishops. In this world Gratian's *Decretum* took on a quasi-official status.

Decretals after Gratian

Gratian's *Decretum* did not provide all the answers to the flood of legal problems that flowed towards the papal court. There are strong structural analogies with the early age of papal decretals, but the old decretals were designed for a very different society, a point to which I will return. Still, history repeated itself and bishops wrote to popes with questions. Moreover, concrete cases increasingly came to the papacy on appeal. When new points of law arose from these cases, popes were effectively making case law, as judges do under the common law system.

Papal case law and replies to bishops' questionnaires were collected by papal judges delegate. The judge delegate system was the papal way of coping with the massive demand for justice—and for justice handed down by the highest possible authority. The Roman Curia could not begin to cope with demand, but delegation of ad hoc papal authority to local men solved the problem. Collections of papal case law, compiled or acquired, must have helped them make decisions.

Thus collections of post-Gratian decretals were soon in circulation (a process analogous to the creation of the first Western canon law collections in the 5th century). They became more formal and comprehensive. Finally an official compilation, the *Liber Extra*, known to canon law historians as 'X', was promulgated by Pope Gregory IX, in 1234. This was followed by further papal compilations: the *Sext*, promulgated by Boniface VIII in 1298, then a couple of others.[15] These solved technical legal problems and dealt with high-profile controversies, but on the whole they lack the human interest of the many cases involving individuals' problems that one finds in the *Liber Extra.* This is probably because a case law adequate for the medieval world had gradually fallen into place, so that most remaining problems were either recondite or ideological.[16]

Even before the *Liber Extra* the judge delegate system had been rationalised. How to select local judges who would be impartial had been a problem. It was largely solved by Innocent III, who devised a technical mechanism that would enable defendants to challenge judges they did not trust at the last stage before a letter of

[15] Friedberg (1922b).

[16] On the foregoing see Hartmann & Pennington (2008).

appointment went out from the papal court. This would have the effect of encouraging litigants to agree on judges before the request for judge delegates was copied at some cost by a papal *scriptor*: rather a brilliant system that enabled popes to be universal judges with minimal administrative expenses. Specialists in papal 'diplomatic' know that it could also be streamlined from the litigant's point of view. (Diplomatic is the subdiscipline of history that focuses on the genres, genesis, setting in life and legal force of documents.)

Contrasts with papal law in late Antiquity

It will be apparent that while the new age of papal law bears surprising similarities to the first age of papal law in late Antiquity, there are major differences. In the first age of papal law most problems were brought to the pope by bishops. This process is also characteristic of the 12th century (as noted above, Anne Duggan drew attention to the parallel[17]), but alongside it we have appeals from individuals and organisations. No doubt the dramas of the Gregorian Reform and the success of the First Crusade put the possibility of appeal to the pope before the minds of more people than in the 5th century. The high profile of the papacy on the European stage may also have affected the way in which bishops applied papal law.

How bishops applied papal law in late Antiquity and the early Middle Ages is hard to judge, but we may hazard a guess that they allowed themselves a degree of freedom. It has been argued that Byzantine canon law was just part of a set of 'tools for constructing and effecting justice'[18]. Even early papal canon law tended to be more precise, nearer to the formality of modern legal systems, but at point of application there was not much control over the bishops' decision making. The enhancement of papal prestige by the Reform and the successful crusade may have made bishops pay more attention to the letter of papal law when judging cases.

Furthermore, the administration of papal justice was increasingly controlled by academically trained canon lawyers, and this made a difference. The reference books they used, above all those of Ivo of Chartres and Gratian, aimed for internal consistency. A Byzantine bishop or even an early medieval Western bishop was free to act according to the principle of 'economy', which might allow general rules to be quietly overlooked in a tricky individual case. Clerics trained at Bologna would be less happy with inconsistency.

Clerics trained at Bologna and in similar centres had power. Increasingly, they ran local ecclesiastical courts. As episcopal administration expanded its scope and became

[17] See note 1.
[18] Wagschal (2015: 7).

more complex, delegation was essential. Legally trained clerics were natural people for a bishop to employ, for the same reason that employers today like graduates. Conversely, the academically trained could hope for benefices to support them while they worked in ecclesiastical legal administration. Lay patronage was not abolished, but it was diminished, and new criteria for appointments had to be found. Academic achievement was one. Academic achievement in the study of law might indeed lie behind a bishop's own appointment. His training would not be forgotten when he applied papal law. But even a bishop with a different background would know that the legally trained clerics around him would expect him to operate within canon law.

The inquisition

Canon law was less effective in regulating the practice on the ground of the medieval inquisition, something that should be easier for us to understand after the failure of the robust American legal system to control imprisonment without trial and torture. The medieval papal inquisition[19] (quite distinct from the Spanish Inquisition of later times) is a special case of papal delegation, in that inquisitors received delegated powers to investigate heresy. In this period there was no 'head office' or anything like that, and it has been argued that there was not really an institution at all in the Middle Ages, only a large number of discrete inquisitors and their staffs. The 'Black Legend' of the inquisition has a solid basis in fact. Awareness of the similar methods of secular government in parts of Europe at the time, as well as of the measures taken by modern liberal democracies panicked by terrorism, should relativise our indignation, but not our admiration for those religious dissidents who held on to sincere convictions.

The Rota

For cases closer to modern corporate law, a new high court evolved in the 14th century, the Rota. High-value property disputes between ecclesiastical bodies, say an episcopal see and a monastery, might come to the Rota. It does not appear to have dealt with marriage cases, as the modern Roman Rota does, and its records are short on human interest. Nonetheless, the interest of its procedures as a surprisingly efficient system of dispute resolution has been highlighted in a recent study by Kirsi Salonen.[20]

[19] See Biller *et al.* (2011) for texts illustrating the way the inquisition worked and an up-to-date bibliography; also, out of a vast bibliography, Arnold (2001).
[20] Salonen (2016).

The Apostolic Penitentiary and Counter-Reformation reforms

All this constituted what was called the 'external forum', alongside which grew up another kind of law, that of the 'internal forum': that is, the confessional. By the mid-13th century, if not before, a system of at least annual confession was in place. For some grave sins only the pope could grant absolution, and an institution grew up at the centre to deal with all the cases.[21] Salaried papal 'penitentiaries' heard confessions and granted absolutions. The penitentiary could also change penances imposed at a lower level when the penitent felt that he or she could not cope.

The Apostolic Penitentiary also dealt with enormous numbers of cases that did not really belong to the 'internal forum' at all: namely, dispensations. A dispensation from the penitentiary, say to marry within the forbidden degrees of kinship, cost a lot less than via other routes, though costs seem to have spiralled towards the end of the medieval period.[22] It may be noted en passant that it was a feature of papal government that there were often several possible ways to get a result from it: or, to put it another way, the division of competencies between different governmental organs was not always clear. These dispensation cases are at the opposite extreme to the Roman Rota's so far as human interest is concerned. A whole social history of the late Middle Ages was recently written by Arnold Esch from this evidence alone.[23]

The 'external forum' competence of the Apostolic Penitentiary was in principle taken away from it in the course of the reform of papal government that followed the Reformation. Absolutions for grave sins were now at the centre of its activity, though dispensations for the internal forum, e.g. for a marriage which could not be made public for some reason or another, remained within its remit.[24] (After the Council of Trent a marriage was invalid if not conducted by the parish priest, and such marriages would in the nature of the case be public—usually. But not necessarily. There might be reasons to keep a marriage secret. In Manzoni's *I Promessi Sposi* a lascivious lord is determined to prevent a young woman on whom he has his eye from getting married, but the marriage could have gone ahead in secret if the priest had not been terrorised. If one adds to such a scenario the need for a routine dispensation for the marriage, then it could be obtained from the penitentiary through the confessor. This would be an 'internal forum' dispensation.)

It should be said that the penitentiary's (inadequately studied) early modern records reveal prima facie that it continued to carry out some external forum business,

[21] From a rich recent literature: Salonen & Schmugge (2009); Schmugge *et al.* (1996). A study of the institution's whole medieval history, on the basis of formularies, is being prepared by Arnaud Fossier.
[22] Müller (2004).
[23] Esch (2014).
[24] Müller (2014: 273–4).

mostly marriage dispensations, but much less than in the medieval period: what may have happened is that the penitentiary continued to do the substantive work on the less contentious 'external forum' marriage dispensations, and to get the fees, while the actual correspondence was conducted by the papal chancery.[25] The new-style penitentiary made no charge whatsoever for internal forum business.[26]

The early modern registers of the penitentiary seem much less interesting than the medieval registers, so far as one can judge without detailed study. To compensate, other records of the early modern penitentiary offer new insights into the inner side of Counter-Reformation Catholicism. Research on these records has hardly begun.

The Congregations

The shake-up of papal government in the Counter-Reformation was seismographic. One of the outcomes was replacement of government by conclave—something like a cabinet of cardinals—with government by 'congregations', which were committees of cardinals with specific competencies. The same cardinals could of course belong to a number of congregations. The most famous of these is the Holy Office or inquisition. By this time the inquisition truly was an institution, and its competence extended well beyond heresy narrowly defined. It dealt, for instance, with abuse of the confessional for sexual ends, and some devotional practices.

The decisions made by congregations should be classed as papal law. They can be found in the learned footnotes of the 1917 Codex,[27] which recorded them as precedents. Probably the most important of these congregations from the point of view of papal law was the Congregation of the Council.

The Congregation of the Council

Scholars have only quite recently become aware of the astonishing richness of the Congregation of the Council archive, which is within the Archivio Segreto Vaticano.[28] No shortage of human interest there. A woman self-denounces herself for heretical witchcraft. Absolution by a bishop is required but neither she nor the bishop can easily travel to the same place.[29] A pious laymen takes minor clerical orders though he has been married twice, which offended the symbolism of the clerical state for reasons

[25] De Luca (1683: Disc. XII: 5–6, p. 86).

[26] Plettenberg (1693: 187); MS Penitenzieria Apostolica Archive APA, Miscellanea Mangiono: 36.

[27] *Codex Iuris Canonici* (1917). Scholars should be warned that there is a version without the source apparatus.

[28] For a bibliography on the Congregation of the Council up to circa 2009 see d'Avray (2010: 195–6).

[29] Archivio Segreto Vaticano Congr. Concil. (Sess.) 58 fo. 405^{r}.

that cannot be quickly summarised. That one was passed by the Cardinals of the Congregation right up to the pope.[30] Now a group of scholars is working on this archive, led by a young Italian based at the Max Planck Institut für Rechtsgeschichte in Frankfurt, Dr Benedetta Albani.

This congregation was making law. The decisions were not supposed to be published, though that changed in the 18th century. Throughout its history, however, records of its decisions were kept for internal reference, so that consistent answers could be returned to similar questions. The records that survive record all the reasoning behind the decisions. Though the Congregation of the Council stood to the side of the 'normal' canon law system, the experts it consulted had classical canon law at their fingertips (theology too) and their expert opinions for or against a decision were backed up by long lists of authorities.

Other early modern papal law

The Congregation of the Council is now being intensively studied, though that is a development of the last few years. The penitentiary archive has been the focus of much research since it was opened in 1983. Other papal records for the early modern period have been available since the 19th century yet are still hardly studied. To a medievalist, the uncertainty surrounding the systems of the early modern papacy is astounding. I know of no study explaining which organ of government generated which series of documents, nor what those series of documents contained. They contain among other things a lot of papal law in action. The judge delegate system continued in this period in a slightly different form.

The Codex

The foregoing summarises the situation more or less up to 1917, when the Catholic Church emulated secular states in producing a 'Code'.[31] Leaving aside Antiquity, where Justinian's code was the model, Prussia had got in first in the later 18th century, followed by the Code Napoleon, then at some distance by the *Bürgerliches Gesetzbuch* for Germany, and similar codes for other countries. The papal code was largely the work of a Cardinal Gasparri, who made a remarkable attempt explicitly to base it on earlier papal law.[32] As noted above, the footnotes of the *Codex Iuris Canonici* contain materials for the whole history set out sketchily above.

[30] Archivio Segreto Vaticano *Congr. Concilio 58 (Sess.), displaced fo. 288*^{r}–301^{v}.
[31] *Codex Iuris Canonici* (1917) (Rome).
[32] Gasparri & Seredi (1923–39).

SECOND PART: INTERPRETATION

The foregoing has been almost exclusively descriptive, though it was necessary in that it would be hard to find the narrative in a connected form elsewhere. The remainder of this paper will be more argumentative and interpretative. Nothing I have said so far explains how papal law has exercised so much influence or lasted so long. That does need explanation. More particularly, we need to explain why an authority that lacked the sinews of a state was able to orchestrate a centralised system of law.

Contrast with Islamic law

Contrast with the history of Islamic law sharpens the question. Early Islamic law had a distinctly papal character. The caliph was a source of authoritative law, though he was obviously subordinate to the Koran just as the pope was to the Bible. Interpreting the law when no unambiguous answer was forthcoming from Koran or Bible was precisely where a central authority came in. This aspect of the early caliphate was brilliantly brought out in the *God's Caliph* by the late Patricia Crone and Martin Hinds.[33] This quasi-papal role was more or less air-brushed out of Islamic history by later legal developments. From the 9th century of the Common Era onwards control of law was taken over by the learned men, trained at Madrasas. Of course, they did not always agree. Four major schools of Sunni law emerged,[34] not to mention Shi-ite jurisprudence.[35] While there was a lot of hostility between Shi-ite and Sunni Islam, the different Sunni schools of law coexisted more or less peacefully, like different schools of academic thought. Within each school, a consensus of lawyers settled major questions, and when new questions arose they could be dealt with on a case-by-case basis, without binding case law.

Could this have happened to canon law?

Could this have happened to canon law in the West? The question is not so absurd as it might seem. Think of the most successful textbook of all, Gratian's *Decretum*. Here papal decretals and even conciliar decisions rub shoulders with texts whose authority status is much more like that of Islamic muftis. The same may be said of Ivo of Chartres and Burchard of Worms before Gratian. But the papal element was by that time if not predominant, at least prominent—for reasons to be explained—in a way

[33] Crone & Hinds (2003).
[34] Melchert (1997); Hallaq (2005).
[35] Halm (2004).

that pronouncements by caliphs never were in lawbooks. Crone and Hinds had to excavate the caliph's role as religious lawgiver from under layers of later law. The very prominence of papal decretals is precisely what requires explanation.

Comparative complexity

Part of the explanation is comparative complexity.[36] The clerical and ritual systems of of late Roman Christianity were complex and evolving. As ritual systems like baptism and penance evolved, decisions about the direction they should take had to be faced. Furthermore, incompatibilities between different systems created a desire for a sort of help-desk. The modern world of fast-developing softwares is not a bad metaphor. Even within the same university, software changes in one part of the overall information system can create incompatibilities with other parts. My suggestion is that the ritual and clerical systems of Islam were simpler than those of 4th and 5th-century Christianity.

Perhaps an overall comparison between the two religions in terms of relative complexity is impossible. Islam has all the complexity of states, because in principle there is no separation of Islam and the state. The rituals around the Kaaba stone at Mecca, and the rules of ritual washing, also involve symbolic complexity. Leaving those aside, though, there are some sharp contrasts. Islam has no priesthood—only men learned in the law capable of preaching and leading congregations. In this respect Islam resembles much Evangelical Protestantism, in which (baptism aside) the ritual tends to be less complex than in Catholic or Orthodox Christianity, and ministers are not thought to possess special ritual powers. They need to have studied theology and to be able to preach and lead, but any special 'charismatic' gifts are regarded as resulting from their personal relation with God, not from their ordination.

In Latin Christianity, furthermore, complexity was not of a static sort. Not only were there many imperfectly coordinated subsystems: these subsystems were often in a state of flux, so that new incompatibilities with other subsystems easily arose.

The function of complexity

At this point, perhaps rashly, a general explanation for the genesis and long survival of papal law is proposed: that the function of evolving complexity was enhancement of papal legal authority. This draws on a very old-fashioned kind of social theory:

[36] The debt of my ideas about complexity to Niklas Luhmann will be evident. Out of his vast oeuvre, see especially Luhmann (1987) and Luhmann (2009).

classical functionalism.[37] Functionalism in a nutshell is the idea that features of a practice or a whole society can ensure its durability even if that is not the conscious purpose. The practice reinforces a given social order which in turn supports the practice. Examples: vaccination creates reverence for the state, which is enabled to go on taxing and vaccinating; racialism ensures that workers do not unite against bosses, so that economic systems do not change. (The latter example shows that functionalism can take a Marxist form.) Other examples are Peter Brown's interpretation of late Antique holymen as social mediators,[38] Karl Leyser's functionalist interpretations of Ottonian sacral kingship,[39] and Jack Goody's explanation of the medieval Church's consanguinity rules as functioning to increase ecclesiastical property holdings.[40] Without subscribing to all of these theories, it seems to me that functionalism still has a lot going for it.

So my thesis is: the function of complexity was papal law. It would be absurd to say that it is the *aim* of complexity to bolster papal power, but that has been the effect, and there is a causal loop by which the papacy's role in resolving incompatibilities enables the subsystems to continue their own autopoiesis, self-making, and thus create new incompatibilities that the papacy had to sort out, like an information systems help-desk dealing with problems created by software innovation that is initially incompatible with existing systems.

This line of explanation also works in a rather obvious way for states, and also for religious systems incorporated in states, as most religious systems in history have in fact been: think of Ancient Near-Eastern monarchies, the Greek polis, and the pagan Roman Empire; also of Classical China, Hindu kingdoms, Islamic states, Byzantium, and early modern Protestant states in Germany and Scandinavia. In such systems, the king or prince or city government plays the papal role of resolving problems arising from complexity.

Other types of religion

In many religious systems such problems do not arise or not to the same degree. We noted above that Islam and Evangelical Protestantism have less complexity to deal with so far as the clergy and ritual are concerned. Furthermore, a congregational model has proved successful. It is a very simple type of religious social system: a congregation/synagogue/mosque, with a pastor/rabbi/imam; a set of people who advise

[37] For a summary of two powerful presentations of functionalism, by Mary Douglas and Gerry Cohen, see d'Avray (2010: 95).
[38] Brown (1971).
[39] Leyser (1989: e.g. 85–6, 102).
[40] Goody (1983).

him and make a lot of decisions; and some well-integrated groups such as the choir, prayer circles, and caritative groups. This solves many of the problems of complexity. Congregational units of this kind are relatively uncomplicated per se, and the life of the few and simple subsystems is not far from the control of the pastor and the movers and shakers of the local community. If the community is divided on doctrine or ritual, it can split into two communities of a similar sort. The community can join a federation of similar communities for collective purposes (supporting institutions to train the clergy, pension funds), but if it does not like the way that federation is going, it can split off and join a different one. Yet another model is represented by Methodism: there was from the start a coherent plan, incorporating well-integrated subsystems. John Wesley's plan was so well conceived that it has continued to work.

Papal christianity differs at least in degree from all of the above in that it consisted of a multitude of heterogeneous subsystems which the papacy never planned, and which had volatile lives of their own, so that the 'environments' of subsystems were constantly changing as other subsystems evolved. Here it differs in degree from Greek and Russian Orthodox Christianity, even though these are also highly complex and ritualised. A strong tendency to conservatism in doctrine and ritual, and the desire to preserve what has been in place since the 8th century or so, mitigate the problems that arise as subsystems evolve and interfere with each other. The principle of 'economy' means that there is not too much anxiety over whether a decision in one complex case is compatible with decisions in other cases. In late Antiquity, Eastern Christianity was still very fluid, but, in the East the emperor could play the quasi-papal role. In the West a multiplicity of Christian subsystems were evolving and changing each other's environment, even while the wider society around them was in flux, as the empire fell apart.

The complex clerical structure of late Antique Christianity

The Christianity of late Antiquity had a highly complex clerical structure, one laid out in the first surviving decretal and many others over the ensuing century. There were many stages on the path to becoming a priest, marked out by taboos: physical disability was a bar, so was marriage to a widow or two marriages by the candidate; the move to the higher stages, deacon, subdeacon or priest, was marked by taking on celibacy, though within marriage and in the nature of the case usually after children. This highly structured clerical elite was, from the 4th century on, confronted by a quite different elite, that of the monks, and the relationship between these two elites was problematic ever afterwards. Do bishops control monastic property? Can they keep a *cathedra* in a monastic church? What happens when monks become priests? How much independence of a bishop can a monastery enjoy in its internal life? Then, as time goes by: how do the governmental systems of international orders like the Franciscans relate to the hierarchy of bishops? Later still, when orders are founded on a diocesan level: what happens when they spill over into other dioceses? In the Latin American missions, Jesuit missionaries get permission to grant marriage dispensations to native American converts, when indigenous customs make the forbidden degrees rules too onerous. But what if the native American lives in a region long converted, and how 'Indian' do you have to be by descent to be eligible for a dispensation? As one problem is solved, another arises.

The ritual structure of late Antique Christianity

Then there was the ritual structure: baptism, penance, the eucharist, exorcism. These rituals interacted in complex ways. There is a complex symbolic system behind the social development of marriage in the Middle Ages, and also behind the strange rules barring twice-married men from becoming clerics. Similarly with baptism. Now, in each case, the life of the subsystem leads to open questions demanding a response. Can marriages of the unbaptised be dissolved? If a man was married when pagan, then widowed, then baptised, then remarried, then became a cleric, is he barred by the 'bigamia' rules from becoming a bishop? Can an unconsummated but valid marriage be dissolved by divorce, given its symbolic imperfection?

Ritual, heresy, doctrine

Complex problems arose from the interaction of ritual systems with the system for reintegrating heretics in the church. Is a baptism conducted by Novatians or Calvinists valid? Defining heresy is itself a problem, in a way rather different from in Islam. In Islam we find a plethera of sects, but the differences between them are seldom doctrinal. In the case of the Shia–Sunni split, it is originally a difference about whether the caliph has to be from the Prophet's family or just the best man for the job. Other differences are not so much doctrinal as like differences between Jews, viz., how and how far the sacred law must be observed to the letter. In the Christianity of late Antiquity good minds were exercised by questions about how one could have different persons in one God, or two natures in one person, and how free will and predestination could be intellectually reconciled. Individual Islamic thinkers would evolve intellectual systems of tremendous sophistication, but there is a lot less obligatory dogma than in late Antique Christianity. Doctrine was only a small part of papal law which was mostly concerned with the clergy and ritual, but still doctrinal complexities did intersect with the systems of papal law, in that some papal decretals regulating doctrine-related problems were included in canon law collections.

The papacy, bishops, and complexity

The church of Rome had a deep-rooted sense that its bishop inherited the authority of St Peter. This belief was by no means generally shared, but it made popes ready to lay down the law when asked to resolve difficulties. Bishops must in fact have been the principle consumers of papal law. Only they had the power to enforce it, and, directly, only on their clergy. The clergy of a diocese depended on the bishop for legitimacy, so had to accept his authority, and bishops wanted rules to help them govern and administer their clergy. This papal law also affected the laity insofar as marriage was included within its scope. Even here it would not have been enforceable. It would, however, have been enforceable on the married clergy.

A question of quantity

The complexities that bishops had to deal with involved so much recourse to the papacy that decretals were too large an element in Church law to be ignored. Direct comparison with early caliphal law is hard because the latter has survived so patchily, but one may make an educated guess that caliphs were not so often called upon to resolve incompatibilities between subsystems, so that God's caliphs made fewer rulings than Peter's successors.

Bishops continued to need canon law collections to guide their direction of the clerical communities around them, to judge by the large number of surviving canon law manuscripts. Charlemagne's adoption of a papally updated version of the Dionysiana ensured wider diffusion. Above all, the enormous quantitative success of the Pseudo-Isidorian collections ensured that papal decretals could not be ignored as part of canon law. This quantitative prominence made a difference as it prevented papal law from being overgrown by the other kinds of texts that Burchard, Ivo and Gratian included in their compilations. Decretals from late Antiquity were still readily available in the 11th and 12th centuries.

Old law in a new society

Big changes in the system's environment help explain its later evolution. Evidently, society had changed radically around these durable decretals. This includes clerical society. A parish system of single parish priests serving village churches was gradually taking the place of larger communities of clerics around the bishop or a big baptismal church. In these isolated parishes, celibacy within marriage was not a practical proposition, if only because there were no other wives to disapprove if one of their number got pregnant. Furthermore, the laity were involved in church appointments at all levels.

Parish churches were usually founded and funded by landowners who did not relinquish control of them. The late Antique system of election of bishops by the 'clergy and people' hardly made sense after the decline of the ancient city. Bishops and abbots had acquired huge properties and the local government authority that went with them in this period. It was natural, in the absence of any other clear rules, that rulers would take over the task of appointing them, a handy governmental technique given that bishops unlike secular nobles were not succeeded by legitimate sons who might not be easy to control. The tension between law readily available in old papal decretals and the actual state of affairs may have been one of the causes of the Gregorian Reform. The gap between theory and practice would make men who took religious law seriously want change. To restore the old law would hardly do, however, in that it was made for a different society.

New papal law for a new environment

Thus it was natural that a new burst of decretal making should follow. The practice was there in old collections for everyone to see. The deviation of society from the law found in them was equally evident. But circumstances had changed so much that custom-built decretals, combined with papally led councils, were required to create a law that actually worked. Lay control of parishes was not abolished, but modified to save the symbolic superiority of the bishop. A new law was needed for the new kind of celibacy—living altogether without a wife, not simply stopping sex before promotion to deacon. To make the rule work, sons of priests were banned from becoming priests. But this soon came to seem too harsh. So a dispensation law developed, allowing exceptions for worthy candidates.

A recurrent pattern: creating collections

Different though the new canon law was, the recurrence of a pattern from late Antiquity needs to be noted. The complexity of the religious system, or systems, created demand for decretals, which were eventually numerous enough to constitute a complexity problem themselves. In late Antiquity, decretal collections were created by people like Dionysius Exiguus and Cresconius to bring some order to the mass of decretals. Exactly the same thing happened in the decades around 1200. A mass of individual decretals was unmanageable by the judges and courts who used them as case law, so private collections were compiled to bring order to the chaos: a sequence of them, until finally the papacy issued an official one, the *Liber Extra.* This collection and the subsequent papal updates were a system for dealing with the complexities arising from the decretal system, itself an attempt to deal with the complexities of the many systems in the Latin Church. By the end of John XXII's reign, 1334, the objective of creating a relatively orderly and coherent legal system had been achieved: the Rota could deal with the remaining and increasingly recondite problems that continued to arise.

The pattern is repeated after Trent

The mass of legislation passed by the Council of Trent disrupted that relative stability.[41] It now stood alongside the existing corpus of canon law. This presented a complexity problem of a whole new order. How to integrate the Tridentine legislation with the existing corpus of canon law? The *Liber Extra* and subsequent updates all followed the same structure. Tridentine legislation did not map easily onto that structure. How to force the new wine into old bottles? A legal genius like Raymond of Peñaforte, who had compiled the *Liber Extra* promulgated in 1234, or Gasparri, who would compile the Codex of 1917, might have attempted it, but in the later 16th century the papacy had other priorities. Even had there been such a genius and if a new corpus had been created, what a field day for the professional lawyers in public courts!

We have seen that another answer was found: the Congregation of the Council. It dealt with questions arising from the legislation of Trent, and, increasingly, with non-dogmatic questions generally. It was not at odds with the classical canon law, however, for decisions by the congregation tended to be based on exhaustive reflection on the traditional canon law, together with theology and of course with Trent. Canon law experts shaped the council's decisions. We do not know much about the staff of the congregation before the 19th century, but we may guess that young legal eagles did the work. Certainly canon law experts gave impressively learned advice for internal consumption by the congregation. Advice from canon lawyers ensured consistency with the classical corpus, while internal records ensured consistency with early decisions of the council. It its way, it was an efficient system, though not transparent in its original workings.

In the 18th century it became more transparent in that its decisions were published on a regular basis. Of course that had advantages, but it must also have aggravated the problem of the religious legal system's complexity. Who could keep intellectual control in the public domain of the stream of decisions? In the 19th century there were attempts: multivolume alphabetical thematic collections by Pallottini[42] and Zamboni,[43]

[41] Richter & Schulte (1853).
[42] Pallottini (1868–93).
[43] Zamboni (1812–16).

were produced and made available for consultation alongside the enormous corpus of classical canon law.

But once again, a system for managing the complexity of multiple religious subsystems had itself become enormously complicated. Once again, the solution adopted was an orderly compilation. It was more ambitious than any previous Catholic compilation in that it endeavoured to synthesise the classical canon law with the decisions of the Congregation of the Council and the decrees of other congregations. This time, though, secular states provided a model: the *Code Civile des Français* of 1804, the *Bürgerliches Gesetzbuch* which became law in Germany in 1900. The 1917 Codex follows in this tradition.

CONCLUSION

F. W. Maitland said that 'the medieval Church was a state',[44] and that holds good for the post-medieval church, in that the legal aspects of a state have recognisable counterparts in papal government after the Middle Ages too. A key difference, though, is that state power can draw on physical force. Popes did have armies as rulers of the papal states, but they were third or fourth rate in geopolitical terms. Popes also tried to direct crusades, but for funding and forces they relied on the consent of people over whom they had no material power. There were some 'spiritual' means of enforcement (though not for failure to sign up for a crusade): the power of excommunication and interdict. In the heyday of papal monarchy these spiritual sanctions counted for a lot. Though, equally, they were often ignored. They would have been altogether ineffective had a lot of people not been prepared to treat them with respect: if not those against whom the sanctions were aimed, then those around them who could exert social pressure. Yet these sanctions are hardly comparable with the threat of imprisonment and death at the disposal of political rulers in the period covered—and in all periods. Furthermore, even those physical threats are not perhaps enough to explain why people obeyed and obey state governments. Fear of consequences is only one reason for obeying a pope or a state government. There is also a demand for what government can give. For states and the papacy share this: both preside over a multitude of systems that they did not plan or create. Both state power and papal power have met a demand from below—for dispute resolution, obviously, but also, less obviously, for the management of complexity. In the case of papal law, that demand is best explained by features of the religious system it regulated: namely the fact that it was more complicated than most religious systems not run by 'real' state governments, because

[44] Maitland (1898: 100).

of the large number of uncoordinated subsystems it incorporated. Walter Ullmann devoted much intellectual energy to showing that popes had a plan of world government from late Antiquity and progressively realised it until it provoked a reaction in the 13th century.[45] A subsequent generation has tended to reject such a top-down model, without providing a satisfactory substitute. I would propose that the papacy as a system was 'passively ambitious': seldom taking the initiative, usually happy enough to respond to demand. What neither Ullmann nor his critics have sufficiently explained is why there was so much demand for papal law. That is the problem on which I have focused and my answer in a nutshell is: because of the special complexities of Latin Christianity—a strong thesis that should give rise to plenty of healthy dissent.

Acknowledgements
Thanks are due to students on the 'Popes, Law and Religious', 'Popes and Caliphs', and 'Social Systems in Religious History' courses at UCL, to the Bloomsbury Sacred Law group, especially Sami Zubaida, Werner Menski and John Sabapathy, and also Benedetta Albani, Danica Summerlin and Julia Walworth

REFERENCES

Manuscripts

Archivio Segreto Vaticano, Vatican City: *Congr. Concilio 58 (Sess.)*.
Penitenzieria Apostolica, Rome: APA, Miscellanea Mangiono.

Printed sources

Arnold, J. (2001) *Inquisition and Power: Catharism and the Confessing Subject in Medieval Languedoc* (Philadelphia, PA, University of Pennsylvania Press). https://doi.org/10.9783/9780812201161

Biller, P., Bruschi, C. & Sneddon, S. (2011) *Inquisitors and Heretics in Thirteenth-century Languedoc. Edition and Translation of Toulouse Inquisition Depositions 1273–1282* (Leiden, Brill).

Brown, P. (1971), 'The Rise of the Holy Man', *The Journal of Roman Studies*, 61: 80–10. https://doi.org/10.2307/300008

Codex Iuris Canonici (1917) (Rome).

Crone, P. & Hinds, M. (2003) *God's Caliph. Religious Authority in the First Centuries of Islam* (Cambridge, Cambridge University Press).

Cushing, K. G. (1998) *Papacy and Law in the Gregorian Revolution. The Canonistic Work of Anselm of Lucca* (Oxford, Clarendon Press). https://doi.org/10.1093/acprof:oso/9780198207245.001.0001

d'Avray, D. L. (2010) *Rationalities in History. A Weberian Essay in Comparison* (Cambridge, Cambridge University Press). https://doi.org/10.1017/CBO9780511762758

De Luca, J. B. (1683) *Relatio Curae Romanae* (Cologne, Arnoldus Metternich).

[45] Ullman (1970).

Duggan, A. (2008), '*De consultationibus*: The Role of Episcopal Consultation in the Shaping of Canon Law in the Twelfth Century', in B. C. Brasington & K. G. Cushing *Bishops, Texts and the Use of Canon Law around 1100. Essays in Honour of Martin Brett* (Aldershot, Ashgate), 191–214.

Esch, A. (2014) *Die Lebenswelt des europäischen Spätmittelalters. Kleine Schicksale selbst erzählt in Schreiben an den Papst* (Munich, C. H. Beck).

Friedberg, A. (1922a) *Corpus Iuris Canonici*, I, *Decretum Magistri Gratiani* (Leipzig, Tauchnitz).

Friedberg, A. (1922b) *Corpus Iuris Canonici*, II, *Decretalium Collectiones* (Leipzig, Tauchnitz).

Gasparri, P. & Seredi, J. (1923–39) *Codicis iuris canonici fontes* (Vatican City).

Gaudemet, J. (1994) Église *et cité: histoire du droit canonique* (Paris, Éditions du Cerf).

Gilchrist, J. T. (1973) *Diversorum patrum sententie sive Collectio in LXXIV titulos digesta* Monumenta Iuris Canonici Series B: Corpus Collectionum, I (Vatican City, Biblioteca Apostolica Vaticana).

Goody, J., (1983) *The Development of the Family and Marriage in Europe* (Cambridge, Cambridge University Press). https://doi.org/10.1017/CBO9780511607752

Hallaq, W. B. (2005) *The Origins and Evolution of Islamic Law* (Cambridge, Cambridge University Press).

Halm, H. (2004) *Shi'ism,* 2nd edn (Edinburgh, Edinburgh University Press).

Harder, C. (2014) *Pseudoisidor und das Papsttum. Function und Bedeutung des apostolischen Stuhls in den pseudoisidorischen Fälschungen* (Cologne, Böhlau Verlag).

Hartmann, W. & Pennington, K. (2008) *The History of Medieval Canon Law in the Classical Period, 1140–1234. From Gratian to the Decretals of Pope Gregory IX* (Washington, DC, The Catholic University of America Press).

Hoffmann, H. & Pokorny, K. (1991), *Das Dekret des Bischofs Burchard von Worms. Textstufen – Frühe Verbreitung – Vorlagen* Monumenta Germaniae Historica Hilfsmittel 12 (Munich).

Hornung, C. (2011) *Directa ad decessorem. Ein kirchenhistorisch-philologischer Kommentar zur ersten Dekretale des Siricius von Rom* Jahrbuch für Antike und Christentum, Ergänzungsband Kleine Reihe, 8 (Münster, Aschendorff Verlag).

Jaffé, P. & Herbers, N., *et al.,* (2016) *Regesta Pontificum Romanorum ab condita ecclesia ad annum post Christum natum MCXCVIII),* 3rd edn, *I (a S. Petro usque ad A. DCIV)* (Göttingen, Vandenhoeck & Ruprecht).

Jasper, D. & Fuhrmann, H. (2001) *Papal Letters in the Early Middle Ages* (Washington, DC, The Catholic University of America Press).

Kéry, L. (1999) *Canonical Collections of the Early Middle Ages (ca. 400–1140). A Bibliographical Guide to the Manuscripts and Literature* (Washington, DC, The Catholic University of America Press).

Leyser, K., (1989) *Rule and Conflict in an Early Medieval Society. Ottonian Saxony* (Oxford, Basil Blackwell).

Luhmann, N. (1987) *Soziale Systeme* (Frankfurt am Main, Suhrkamp).

Luhmann, N. (2009), 'Soziologie als Theorie sozialer Systeme', in *Soziologische Aufklärung,* 1 *Aufsätze zur Theorie sozialer Systeme* (Wiesbaden, VS Verlag für Sozialwissenschaften), 143–72.

Maitland, F. W. (1898) *Roman Canon Law in the Church of England* (London, Methuen).

Melchert, C. (1997) *The Formation of the Sunni Schools of Law, 9th–10th Centuries C.E.* (Leiden, Brill).

Mordek, H. (1975), *Kirchenrecht und Reform im Frankenreich. Die Collectio Vetus Gallica, die* älteste *systematische Kanonessamlung des fränkischen Gallien. Studien und Edition* 2 vols., Beiträge zur Geschichte und Quellenkunde des Mittelalters, I (Berlin, Walter de Gruyter). https://doi.org/10.1515/9783110831900

Mordek, H., Zechiel-Eckes, K. & Glatthaar, M. (2013) *Die Admonitio generalis Karls des Großen* Monumenta Germaniae Historica Fontes Iuris Germanici Antiqui in usum scholarum separatim editi xvi (Wiesbaden, Harrassowitz Verlag).

Müller, W. (2004), 'The Price of Papal Pardon—New Fifteenth-century Evidence', in A. Meyer, C. Rendtel & M. Wittmer-Butsch (eds) *Päpste, Pilger, Pönitentiarie. Festchrift für Ludwig Schmugge zum 65. Geburtstag* (Tübingen, Max Niemeyer Verlag), 457–81.

Pallottini, S. (1868–93) *Collectio omnium conclusionum et resolutionum quae in causis propositis apud Sacram Congregationem Cardinalium S. Concilii Tridentini interpretum prodierunt ab eius institutione anno MDLXIV ad MCCCCLX* 17 vols. (Rome: Typis S. Congregationis de propaganda fide 1868–1884).

Patzold, S. (2015) *Gefälschtes Recht aus dem Frühmittelalter. Untersuchungen zur Herstellung und* Überlieferung *der pseudoisidorischen Dekretalen* (Heidelberg, Universitätsverlag Winter).

Plettenberg, H. (1693) *Notitia Congregationum et Tribunalium Curiae Romanae* (Hildesheim).

Richter, A. & Schulte, F. (1853) *Canones et Decreta Concilii Tridentini* (Leipzig, Tauchnitz).

Rolker, C. (2010) *Canon Law and the Letters of Ivo of Chartres* (Cambridge, Cambridge University Press). https://doi.org/10.1017/CBO9780511674709

Salonen, K. (2016) *Papal Justice in the Late Middle Ages. The Sacra Romana Rota* (London, Routledge).

Salonen, K. & Schmugge, L., (2009) *A Sip from the 'Well of Grace'. Medieval Texts from the Apostolic Penitentiary* (Washington, DC, The Catholic University of America Press).

Schmugge, L., Hersperger, P. & Wiggenhauser, B. (1996) *Die Supplikenregister der päpstlichen Pönitentiarie aus der Zeit Pius' II. (1458–1464)* (Tübingen, Max Niemeyer Verlag).

Ubl, K. & Ziemann, D. (eds) (2015) *Fälschung als Mittel der Politik. Pseudoisidor im Licht der neuen Forschung. Gedenkschrift für Klaus Zechiel-Eckes* (Wiesbaden, Harrawowitz Verlag).

Ullmann, W. (1970) *The Growth of Papal Government in the Middle Ages. A Study in the Ideological Relation of Clerical to Lay Power* (London, Methuen).

Wagschal, D. (2015) *Law and Legality in the Greek East. The Byzantine Canonical Tradition* (Oxford, Oxford University Press), 381–3.

Winroth, A. (2000) *The Making of Gratian's* Decretum (Cambridge, Cambridge University Press). https://doi.org/10.1017/CBO9780511496639

Zamboni, J. F. (1812–16) *Collectio declarationum Sacrae Congregationis Cardinalium Sacri Concilii Tridentini interpretum*, 8 vols (Vienna).

Zechiel-Eckes, K. (1992) *Die Concordia canonum des Cresconius. Studien und Edition*, 2 vols., Freiburger Beiträge zur mittelalterlichen Geschichte, 5 (Frankfurt am Main, Peter Lang).

Zechiel-Eckes, K. (2013) *Die erste Dekretale. Der Brief Papst Siricius' an Bischof Himerius von Tarragona vom Jahr 385 (JK 255)* MGH Studien und Texte, 55 (Hannover).

Note on the Author: Professor David d'Avray obtained a BA from Cambridge in 1973 an MA in 1977 and a DPhil from Oxford in 1977. He has been Professor of History at University College London since 1996; previously he was a Lecturer 1977–93 and Reader, 1993–6. He became a Fellow of the British Academy in 2005. His latest publications are: *Papacy, Monarchy and Marriage* (CUP, 2015) and *Dissolving Royal Marriages: A Documentary History, 860–1600* (CUP, 2014).
ucradav@ucl.ac.uk

To cite the article: David d'Avray (2017), 'Stages of Papal Law', *Journal of the British Academy*, 5: 37–59.
DOI https://doi.org/10.85871/jba/005.37

Journal of the British Academy (ISSN 2052–7217) is published by
The British Academy—the national academy for the humanities and social sciences.
10–11 Carlton House Terrace, London, SW1Y 5AH
www.britishacademy.ac.uk

Journal of the British Academy, **5**, 61–89. DOI https://doi.org/10.5871/jba/005.061
Posted 21 March 2017.

Whatever happened to lifelong learning? And does it matter?

Sir John Cass's Foundation Lecture
read 14 September 2016

JOHN BYNNER
UCL Institute of Education

Abstract: While adult education has a long history in Britain going back to the Workers Education Association of the 19th century, the term 'lifelong learning' does not extend much further back than the 1970s. The paper considers the accelerating technological changes that lay behind the idea of cradle to grave learning in a global context and the life-enhancing and economic returns to be expected. The longitudinal British birth cohort studies that have charted people's changing lives since the Second World War display the benefits to be gained from learning. A policy shift is revealed towards dominance of the 'economic' over the 'wider' (social and well-being) learning goals and from analysis of basic skills data a trajectory of disadvantage and growing 'learning divide'. What halted lifelong learning's progress? Where does the programme go next?

Keywords: lifelong learning, wider benefits, basic skills, longitudinal, adult education, trajectory.

The title of this paper is intentionally provocative, implying something valuable has gone that should continue to be here. The reason for approaching the topic of lifelong learning this way is to show that after a slow start, the era of lifelong learning, and the crucial role of adult education within it, has truly arrived. And as I hope to show, in the digital age their relevance to sustaining a cohesive, healthy and prosperous society could hardly be stronger.

The paper starts with a brief overview of the development of the idea of lifelong learning in which the focus is particularly on the British story. What historical context gave birth to it and what are its achievements to date? I then turn to what seems like a significant disjunction in lifelong learning's inevitable upwards path: the move towards a narrowing of curricula based on work-related skills enhancement as opposed to the broader *life-wide* capabilities approach. The reasons for this switch are then considered, why at least temporarily, progress might have stalled, and then why such a reversal should be a matter for concern.

The empirical part of the argument relies on research in a 15-year programme carried out using data from the 1958 and 1970 *British Birth Cohort Studies.* These two studies are from the internationally renowned longitudinal series of cohort studies starting respectively in 1946, 1958, 1970, 1992/1993 (county of Avon) and 2000. With the exception of the 1946 study, which took a one-third sample for follow-up, and the 'Avon longitudinal study of parents and children (ALSPAC)', which began during pregnancy, each study is derived from a representative sample of over 16,000 individuals in the specified birth year and followed up subsequently through their lives.[1] Data were also collected for one third of the 1958 cohort members' children when the cohort mother or father had reached age 33 and for half of the 1970 cohort members' children when the cohort mother or father had reached age 34 [2].

The two selected studies lend themselves particularly well to understanding the role and progress of lifelong learning in individual lives, each collecting data on experience in the intersecting domains of life—family, community, education, employment, health and so on—as the developing individual passes through them on the route to adulthood. The life-course perspective first formulated by Glen Elder in his study of US children and families living through the 1930s, *Children of the Great Depression*, offers a widely accepted conceptual framework for the individual development observed—(Elder 1974/1999; Heinz 1991; Schoon 2006; Blossfeld *et al.* 2014). The life-course 'trajectories', including that of lifelong learning starting from birth, are shaped in accordance with four principles:

human agency (i.e. individual adaptation to the social, economic and physical environment),
linked lives (i.e. social relations),
timing of events (i.e. intersection of age, period and cohort),
location in space and time (i.e. geography, history, culture, and social structure).

Guided by this framework, the paper draws on research, using the 1958 and 1970 cohort studies data. The work was located in two government-funded research centres in what is now the Department of Social Sciences in UCL Institute of Education: 'Wider Benefits of Learning (WBL)' and 'National Research and Development Centre

[1] Data collection for the 1958 cohort began at birth followed by ages 7, 11, 16, 23, 33, 37, 42, 44 (biomedical survey), 46, 50, 55, 60, and for the 1970 birth cohort at birth followed by ages 5, 10, 16, 21, 26, 10, 34, 38, 42, 46. Both studies have maintained active samples of over 10,000 responding individuals. Full details of the two studies are available at http://www.cls.ioe.ac.uk/

[2] Because of the significantly later child bearing of the more recent 1970 cohort, to achieve comparable numbers of children for the two cohorts, it was necessary to expand the 1970 cohort member parents sample to 50% compared with the 1958 study's 33%.

for Adult Literacy and Numeracy (NRDC)'. The first of these centres was established following the publication of the Government White Paper the *Learning Age* (Blunkett 1998), making the case for a 'modern' approach to lifelong learning. The second arose from the 'Skills for Life' policy that followed in 1999, the Moser Committee's report (1999) *A Fresh Start*, devoted to improving adult literacy and numeracy—one of the 1997 newly elected Blair Government's top seven policy priorities.

As will be clear from this brief synopsis, the birth cohort studies' long reach in relation to individual development from childhood through to adulthood makes them a particularly powerful tool for understanding the role of lifelong learning in the UK life course—as a simple example shows (Bynner & Parsons 2009). Using data from the 1958 birth cohort study, we analyse the extent to which individual differences in literacy and numeracy scores, as measured by the scores' 'variance' at different ages, was predictable and consequently in principle 'explainable' from prior circumstances and experience, including educational attainment. Literacy acquisition was measured by simple literacy tests for adults, covering reading comprehension and spelling at different levels of difficulty. Similarly, for numeracy, tests were used involving simple calculations and numerical understanding of such concepts as percentages. We find rapidly rising percentages of variance explained up to age 10 and a levelling off at around 40% by age 34—larger for literacy (42%) than for numeracy (35%).

Notably, although 40% of the variance in adult literacy and numeracy scores was predictable from what we know about the cohort members' lives up to age 34, when the most recent assessment was made, even taking account of measurement error and missing variables, a significant proportion of the remaining variance (60%) cannot be explained away in these terms. Learning goes on outside formal educational institutions in a variety of contexts, such as the family, the community and the workplace and through the exercise of individual agency by means of self-instruction, much of it through adulthood. The message is that in understanding basic skills inequalities[3], even at the age of 34, there is much known and much still to be explained in terms of individual, largely unpredictable, experience. Both formal and informal methods of learning are the means of acquiring each skill—the foundation of lifelong learning.

DEVELOPMENT OF LIFELONG LEARNING

Although lifelong learning is a cradle to grave phenomenon, its foundations, as generally understood, lie in post-compulsory part-time adult education (Hodgson 2000). But

[3] The variance of a set of scores reflects a rank order of individual differences, an indicator of basic skills inequality.

what characterises such adult education's goals and practice? A good place to start is Winston Churchill speaking in 1954:

> There is, perhaps, no branch of our vast educational system which should more attract within its particular sphere the aid and encouragement of the State than adult education. How many must there be in Britain after the disturbance of two destructive wars, who thirst in later life to learn about the humanities, the history of their country, the philosophies of the human race, and the arts and letters which sustain and are borne forward by the ever-conquering English language? ... The appetite of adults to be shown the foundations and processes of thought will never be denied by a British Administration cherishing the continuity of our Island life. (Ministry of Education 1954: 95–6)

Now, a young adult student interviewed in 2005:

> The lecturer helps coordinate the group. They're like the pinpoint, the pivot the balance, the centre they are in the middle. So you start off by learning—the lecturer throwing an idea at them—and then by the end of two years, the lecturer is no longer so pivotal because the group has gained all the information he or she can give them. All of a sudden the questions start flowing among the group. It's amazing that everybody has so many different ideas and you learn not to be so biased, to be more objective, not to take things personally. (Schuller *et al.* 2004:175)

Finally, a leading commentator on adult education, Alan Tuckett writing in *The Guardian* newspaper in 2007:

> A distinguished Maori educationalist recently told me he was impressed by the way colleges in the UK help people to learn how to do things. He was, though, puzzled by the things that they didn't teach: how to be a good family member; how to relate to your community; what stories to tell your children. With an education like this, he wondered, 'who would want to come to your funeral?' The question stuck in my mind as I was reading the Leitch review, with its ambitious targets for making the UK economy more competitive. (Tuckett 2007)

These extracts supply something of the substance and scope of adult learning, expressing complementary facets of the learning experience that could apply at any age and at any time. There is imparting of knowledge, understanding, skills and cultural continuity; there is the dynamics of the effective adult classroom comprising the expert with knowledge to impart and adults interacting over their desire to learn and use it. In contrast, there is the beginnings of critique in the questioning of whether curriculum content, in this case vocational skills directed exclusively at employment, is not missing out on some of the other components of education that the truly educated individual needs to have. The importance of skills in the economy is undeniable, but the broader societal context of well-being has a central place as well.

So what transformed the optimism about the value of adult education in Churchill's day, into a global mission to transform the human life course into a continual educational experience? Adult education has a long history going back to the work of Toynbee Hall founded at the end of the 19th century; the establishment in 1903 of the Workers Educational Association; and the post-First World War boost from the Adult Education Committee Report produced by the Ministry of Reconstruction (1919). But the idea of cradle to grave lifelong learning is of much more recent origin, coinciding with the technological transformation of industry and the labour market upheavals of the late 1970s and 1980s. UNESCO was the first major international organisation to put the concept of what was then referred to as *lifelong education* on the map with Edgar Faure's 1972 report *Learning to Be*, also coining the term 'Learning Society'. In the report's words:

> Tomorrow's education must form a co-ordinated totality in which all sectors of society are structurally integrated. It will be universalized and continual. From the point of view of individual people, it will be total and creative, and consequently individualised and self-directed. It will be the bulwark and the driving force in culture, as well as in promoting professional activity. This movement is irresistible and irreversible. It is the cultural revolution of our time. (Faure 1972: 164)

Closer to the language of present priorities, but still couched in the idealism of the time, was Harold Wilson's speech in 1964 devoted eight years earlier to the 'White Heat of Science' and the technological revolution occurring as a result of it. He made the telling point that: 'Our way of life is likely to be more fundamentally transformed in the next several decades than in the previous one thousand years' (Wilson 1964).

The manifestation of Wilson's vision came, though not in quite the totally positive terms he saw it, in the transformation of industry through the 1970s and early 1980s brought about by information and communications technology (ICT) and the *globalisation* that came in its wake. That is to say, the skills underpinning industrial production were increasingly becoming obsolete and the increasingly ICT-driven components of distribution, consumption and the finance behind them were now operating globally (Ashton & Bynner 2011: 122–47). The consequence for most Western countries was losing out competitively to the long-term planning and cheaper production methods and manpower of competitors across the world, especially in the Far East; though the full implications of these changes were barely recognised much before the 1990s.

The main response was the establishment in 1974 of the Manpower Services Commission with the brief of building the workforce that the labour market was going to need in responding to the replacement of traditional industries, such as coalmining and shipbuilding, and the massive expansion of service industry. There was increasing talk of creating a 'knowledge economy' underpinned by lifelong learning. The human cost, as set out later by such writers as Charles Handy (*The Future of Work*) (1984), Aronowitz and Di Fazio (*The Jobless Future*) (1994) and Jeremy Rifkin (*The End of Work*) (1995), pointed to a steady decline in employment as the need for men and women in manufacturing and much of service industry dried up through digitalisation and, prospectively, robotics. Jeremy Rifkin's third industrial revolution—already adopted as a blueprint by the European Union—predicts not only this latter feature but the 'internet of everything' ranging from energy to warfare (Rifkin 1995; 1998). His *Biotech Century* sets out an even more transformational vision of 'new life forms', a 'second genesis' and 'eugenic civilisation', with implications for every area of human existence. The point to make is that, whether proved right or wrong in any particular predicted instance, technological change in what is now becoming the *digital age* is already far ahead of expectation.

Apart from the newly established MSC, innovative adult education was also on the agenda through the establishment of such path-breaking institutions as the *Open University* in 1969 (over 200,000 adult students). The OU offered not only second-chance higher education, but by deploying an advanced distance teaching model—comprising television, radio and more recently, digital technology, coupled with summer schools—set new curriculum standards for further and higher education generally. In parallel, through the establishment of the 'new universities' (24 in the 1960s alone), there was a major expansion across the country of university extramural studies programmes. Outside the formal system, other institutions emerged a bit later such as the *University of the Third Age*[4] established in the UK in the early 1980s (following a 1973 start in France) and catering for the learning of thousands of adults classed as 'no longer in full-time employment'. The core structural feature is a nationwide network of self-managing learning cooperatives comprising 36,000 courses for 350,000 adult learners in 2015.

At the same time the traditional systems for face-to-face adult learning came into their own. The Inner London Education Authority (1965–90), for example, offered, through the 1970s and 1980s, a network of provision, 'Education for the Whole Community', via a mix of polytechnics (five in all), further education colleges and adult education institutes for different learning purposes (Jupp 2010). By the end of its life in 1990, ILEA was laying on 20,000 classes with 240,000 enrolments—14% of the non-vocational adult education in England and Wales for 5% of the population, in which adult education was described as the 'jewel in the crown' (Tuckett 1998). Although there had been traditional separation between the provision and location of vocational and non-vocational courses, the barrier became increasingly more permeable,

[4] http://u3a.org.uk/

spearheaded by the highly successful 'Access Courses', supplying a bridge from early school leaving to higher education (Tuckett 2015). The popular worldwide idea of 'Learning Cities' as concentrations of learning resources linked globally and promoted widely by UNESCO (2015),[5] was epitomised by London through the 1990s.

More widely, as Leisha Fullick (2010) records, the National Institute of Adult and Continuing Education (NIACE)—established in 1998 and brilliantly led to become a major national institution by Alan Tuckett—not only pursued the permeability goal on a national scale but internationally. NIACE also supplied the steering, monitoring and policy development framework (e.g. the National Adult Learning Surveys) for ensuring coherence of the whole system, together with the consultative machinery for those who worked and studied through it.[6]

The 1988 Education Reform Act and the 1992 (DFES) Further and Higher Education Act changed irrevocably these arrangements with the incorporation by central government of first the polytechnics and then the further education colleges—to be followed in London's case by the winding up of ILEA in 1990. The adult education institutes were mostly taken over by the colleges, with funding only of non-qualification-bearing provision remaining as the responsibility of the local authorities—now designated as 'clients' of the colleges and other third sector and private providers.

DIGITAL REVOLUTION

In his forward to *The Learning Age* consultative 'Green Paper', David Blunkett (1998) updated Churchill's and Wilson's visions, laying the foundations for the second stage of technological transformation in Britain: the 'digital revolution'. Blunkett also brought more centre stage the economic drivers of the educational change to follow, signalling where a key tension in further education planning had lain from the 1973 Russell Report on Adult Education onwards (DES 1973) and to which I return—the competing claims of skills for the *economy* versus *learning for individual and community well-being.* In Blunkett's memorable words:

> We stand on the brink of a new age. Familiar certainties and old ways of doing things are disappearing. Jobs are changing and with them the skills needed for the world of tomorrow. In our hearts we know we have no choice but to prepare for this new age in which the key to success will be the education, knowledge and skills of our people.

[5] http://uil.unesco.org/lifelong-learning/learning-cities

[6] The collection of Alan Tuckett's influential *Times Higher Education* commentaries is reproduced in Nash (2014).

> To achieve stable and sustainable growth, we will need a well-educated well-equipped and adaptable labour force. To cope with rapid change, we must ensure that people can return to learning throughout their lives, we cannot rely on a small elite. We will need creativity, enterprise and scholarship for all our people …
>
> Learning enables people to play a full part in the community and strengthens the family, the neighbourhood and consequently the nation. It helps us to fulfil our potential and open doors to a love of music, art and literature. That is why we value learning for its own sake and are encouraging adults to enter and re-enter learning at every point of their lives as parents at work and as citizens. (Blunkett 1998: 2–3)

Added to the priority of 'developing a well-equipped and adaptable labour force', towards the end of the 1990s growing concern was directed towards the phenomenon of demographic shift. Increased immigration brought attention to cultural assimilation and English as a foreign language, issues in which gender and class inequalities also played a central part. In addition, the rapidly extending lifespan was producing an ageing population in which a third of working life could now be spent in retirement. Here was another open door for lifelong, or even more appropriately for this age group, life-wide learning!

The Learning Age was published following the appearance in 1997 of three key reports reflecting something of a culmination of the golden age of lifelong learning programmes preceding it and also the first signs of major policy shifts: Dearing on further and higher education (Dearing 1997); Kennedy on disadvantaged access to further education (Kennedy 1997); Fryer on continuing education and lifelong learning (Fryer 1997). The Moser Report (1999), *A Fresh Start*, concerned with upgrading adult basic skills, followed, leading to the 'Skills for Life' policy that began in 2001. All heralded, in varying degrees, not only a changing lifelong learning agenda in favour of economic priorities but new means of resourcing it, including, in the case of Dearing, recommending for the first time, the charging of fees for undergraduate higher education.

However, change was not all in one direction. Another major milestone, developing further the theme of UNESCO's *Learning to Be* (Faure 1972), was the inspirational report, *The Treasure Within*, presented in the fifth UNESCO (CONFINTEA) adult education conference in Hamburg (1997) by ex-president of the European Union, Jacque Delors (1996). The paper set out the mission of lifelong learning for contemporary times and the means of achieving it. The UNESCO Institute of Lifelong Learning was established in Hamburg and a programme of work began, including the four-yearly series of Global Reports on Adult Learning and Education (GRALE) (UNESCO 1997) to review progress in its development across the world (Schuller 2016).

As Delors (1996: 11–12) had said in describing what he now called 'life-wide' as well as 'lifelong' learning:

> An indispensable asset to attain ideals of peace, freedom and social justice ... one of the principle means available to foster a deeper and more harmonious form of human development and thereby to reduce poverty, exclusion, ignorance, oppression and war. ... While education is an ongoing process of improving knowledge and skills it is also perhaps primarily an exceptional means of bringing about personal development and building relationships among individuals, groups and nations.

He proposed four 'pillars' of lifelong learning:

> *learning to know,* (knowledge and understanding),
> *learning to do* (skills and capabilities),
> *learning to live together* (social cohesion),
> *learning to be* (self-realisation and fulfilment). (Delors 1996)

Coupled with the Faure Report's idea of untapped human capability, i.e. *'learning to be'*, (Faure 1972), this four-way structure was directed at strengthening the twin well-being goals of advanced democratic societies: social cohesion and eliminating demographically defined educational inequality—in contemporary UK parlance the 'skills gap'. As Helena Kennedy's famous maxim from her report on further education, *Learning Works*, puts it: 'If at first you don't succeed ... you don't succeed' (Kennedy 1997: 21).

The mission also confronts paradoxically the other form of inequality and perhaps the major challenge to be faced in the new era—usually referred to as the 'Matthew effect', as Stanovitch (1986: 381) describes it in relation to learning to read: 'The richer you are the more you get. The poorer you are the poorer you become.' A striking example comes from the NRDC Report *Illuminating Disadvantage* (Parsons & Bynner 2007) in the form of the distribution across literacy levels from below the age 16 school leaving standard (Level 2)[7] of three key features of achievement in the modern economy: full-time employment, work-based training, and using a computer at work. The likelihood of being in employment rose substantially with literacy level, with the gradient for women steeper than for men; work-based training, though relatively rare, was most common among those with the best literacy. But the most striking relationship was for using a computer at work: 83% of women and 78% of men at literacy Level 1 or above did so compared with 37% of women and 23% of men at pre-qualification standard Entry Level 2 or below. The task of lifelong learning policy is not only to support ever-more of it but to reverse what can be its polarising effects.

[7] Educational attainment age 16 leaving standards—basic skills assessment equivalence. Level 2, General Certificate of Secondary Education (GCSE) grades A–C; Level 1, GCSE grades D–G; No certification other than basic skills assessment: Entry Level 3; Entry Level 2; Entry Level 1.

THE NEW AGENDA

The Delors pillars have a distinctly different feel about them from those that underpin most adult and continuing education today. In fact, the EU 'Memorandum on Lifelong Learning' prepared for the Lisbon conference of ministers (EC 2000) and the policy conclusions drawn from it (European Council of Ministers, 2000), though recognising the twin aims of economic returns and social inclusion, already gave major emphasis to the former. Organisation for Economic Co-operation and Development (OECD) reports in this period — for example, *Lifelong Learning for All* (OECD 1996) —also tended to be exclusively devoted to the economic value of lifelong learning, with a special focus on improvement of basic skills for economic development. The top priority for OECD was the worldwide problem of illiteracy involving 95 million people of whom over 60% were women.

As signalled in the report by NIACE as the UK contribution to the sixth CONFINTIA conference in Belém Brazil, 2009 (McNair & Quintero-Re 2008), the period following 1998 was one of further retrenchment, with the shift in government interest away from the life-wide conception towards vocational programmes. A major influence was the 2005 Leitch Report, 'Skills in the UK' (Leitch 2006), which reported that one third of adults did not have the equivalent of a basic school leaving qualification (5 GCSE grades A–C). Almost half (17 million) had difficulty with numbers and one seventh (5 million) were not functionally literate. Deficiencies were also evident in technical and intermediate skills, which is where another national requirement needed subsequently to be met. Completion of a course at one level should be followed by one at a higher level to mark 'progress'. That is to say, no diversions to explore other curriculum options on the way were allowable free of cost, effectively ruling out the defining feature of life-wide learning.

The Leitch Report and others from OECD (e.g. OECD 2013)—the last as recent as 2016—placed the UK on the bottom rank of European and OECD league tables for skills and work-based training (OECD 2016). The solution Leitch offered was a national commitment to raise skills levels to the point where the UK would become a 'world leader in skills'. The shift was further driven by government intent, of whatever political complexion, to strengthen the distinction between the public and the private benefits of education. The former were identified with the skills that the nation needed, as defined principally by employers—most obviously the basic skills (literacy and numeracy) up to Level 2 (GCSE grade A–C equivalent). The others were primarily, if not exclusively, of personal value by either boosting personal earnings, as in the case of higher education, or simply engaging in out of non-vocational personal interest.

As Alan Johnson, successor to David Blunkett as Minister of Education famously said in 2006 promoting the skills agenda:

> We need plumbers, less Pilates; to subsidize precision engineering not over-subsidized flower arranging, except of course where flower arranging is necessary for a vocational purpose! …Tai chi may be hugely valuable to people studying it, but it's of little value to the economy. There must be a fairer apportionment between those who gain from education and those who pay for it—state, employer or individual. Surveys show that adults agree they should pay more for courses where they can. [8]

The introduction of fees for higher education in September 1998 was soon accompanied by increased charges on commercial lines for non-vocational adult education courses.

As another response to Leitch in 2006 the 'Train to Gain'[9] scheme was launched, which enabled employers to seek government support for training. This pushed the responsibly for deciding what state-funded skills were going to be needed onto employers, with learning brokers interfacing between them and the local providers. In many cases the employers approached were already buying the courses they needed or were providing them 'in-house'. Hence, as Alan Tuckett (2015) points out, the scheme was effectively draining learning resources from one section of the population, disadvantaged adults, to another section, employees, who were already getting them.

At the same time, as local authority budgets were continually being squeezed, the adult education sector was becoming more impoverished. The winding up in 2011 of the 'Lifelong Learning Sector Skills Council' may be seen as a further signal of AE's downgrading. In fact, with the economic shocks arising from further technological transformation, interspersed with periodic recessions and the collapse of the banking system in 2007/8, sustaining the wider range of (non-vocational) learning outcomes from health to civic participation, as we shall see, could not have been more important.

Participation

With the massive promotion of lifelong learning since the launch of *The Learning Age* and the idea that every member of the labour force needed to gain or upgrade their qualifications to obtain, or sustain, employment in any kind of job, we might have expected the numbers signing up for part-time courses to be continually expanding. In opening the January 2016 House of Lords debate devoted to adult learning, Baroness Sharp reports evidence telling the opposite story.[10] Open University recruitment had been steadily dropping from 260,000 in 2009/10 to 187,000 in 2013/14. In universities

[8] Speech, delivered at the first *Quality Improvement Agency* conference on 7 June 2006 at the Birmingham International Conference Centre.

[9] Funded by the Department for Education and Skills and delivered by the Learning and Skills Council https://www.skillsforlifenetwork.com/article/train-gain-employer-training-scheme/1689

[10] *Hansard* 28 January 2016.

more widely 2 million part-time adult learners had been lost since 2007. Since the fees increase for university degree courses, while full-time undergraduate numbers had increased, part-time student numbers had decreased by 58%. Moreover, over the same period, adult participation in further education was down from 50% to 15%, a drop of over 500,000 aged 24 or more. This was paralleled by a fall in the adult skills budget of 35%. NIACE annual adult learning surveys show much the same pattern of declining participation in non-award-bearing part-time courses from a peak in 2010.

In view of the many ways in which part-time adult education supplies the foundations for extended learning through adulthood that the economy is said to need, the retreat from it is therefore significant. The collapse coincides with a number of shifts in bipartisan government policy towards adult education including:

- making students bear the costs of adult education rather than the state;
- prioritising the Leitch skills agenda against the wider mission of, for example, NIACE;
- raising the price of engaging in non-award-bearing courses coupled with ever-rising university fees for both full-time and part-time study;
- restricting support for students taking award-bearing courses below degree level if not demonstrating progression in qualification terms.

All these factors add up to a powerful disincentive for adults to sign up for learning, as critics had been arguing for some time on a number of fronts (see, for example, Coffield 1999; Tight 1998; Field 2005).

Rising costs

Where does the boundary between the private and public value of adult learning lie? There were good grounds from cohort study analysis to believe that achieving the Moser targets of 10% improvement in literacy and numeracy scores by 2012 would produce substantial financial returns to government. A collaborative study shared between the Wider Benefits of Learning, the Centre for Economics of Education and the Institute of Fiscal Studies was able to demonstrate, from modelling 1958 and 1970 birth cohort study data, potential gains of £2.54 billion for numeracy and £0.44 billion for Literacy (Bynner *et al.* 2001). But what claims could be made of such returns from non-vocational adult education courses?

Award-bearing courses below university level, even if signifying progression above the level of basic skills, are no longer available free of charge. The rising cost to students of part-time adult education courses, at one time no more than 15% of provision costs or free, is a reflection of the policy thinking that depends on distinguishing what is seen as a public benefit from a private one. In a penetrating analysis of the issues involved,

Smethurst (1995) identifies three types of skill. The first is of clear value to the state, such as the Level 2 skills (GCSE A–C equivalent) that supply the entry requirement for a wide range of jobs. The second is what he calls 'merit skills' that have only indirect vocational value such as team working, willingness to learn and so on; while the third, which it is difficult to prove exists, comprises skills that benefit nobody but the individual who has them, such as the much-derided Pilates and flower arranging. Smethurst rejects the distinction in public value terms because it ignores the worth of *externalities*, such as improvements in health and well-being contributing to social cohesion, reduction in working hours lost and so on, to which all learning contributes. As we shall see, the work of the Wider Benefits of Learning research centre has been critically important in demonstrating the public value of such forms of learning.

Skills agenda

Other criticism was directed at the principles leading to the post-2006 Leitch strategy. As writers such as John Field (2005) argue, there was downgrading of social cohesion and well-being goals in favour of economic priorities. The Leitch committee was wedded to the view that the country's economic problems arise from individuals lacking the skills to make a productive contribution to the economy, as reflected in the report's general emphasis on vocational education at the expense of non-vocational courses.

This whole approach had already been challenged by such writers as Frank Coffield (1999; 2010; 2012) director of the Economic and Social Research Council's 'Learning Society' research programme (1994–2001). Coffield argued that vocational (work-based) skills presented at whatever level of education as the means to employability and productivity, without jobs to deploy them in, have dubious labour market or motivational value. As NRDC research shows, even performance on the essential adult basic skill courses was much enhanced when embedded in a vocationally relevant and employment-integrated programme rather than as stand-alone provision (Casey *et al.* 2006). To quote the late David Raffe, 'Education for education's sake is a defensible concept, but training for training's sake is a contradiction in terms' (Raffe 1985: 92).

Form and content of adult education

With the skills agenda of target setting and tightly controlled progression rules on which funding for award-bearing courses is based, there is disregard for the style, quality and relational value of adult part-time courses. Such attributes not only have intrinsic worth in the development of generic ('soft') skills but can be the main attraction for adults engaging in them. The most powerful corrective, however, comes from NIACE with the report of their commission on lifelong learning authored by Tom Schuller and the late David Watson (Schuller & Watson 2009). Economic value specifically described as 'Prosperity, Employment and Work', is only one of the nine themes of the report to which the report's needs-based programme for lifelong learning relate. What follows in the list is first: 'Changing Demography and Social Structure', then 'Wellbeing and Happiness'; 'Migration and Communities' follow. Social inclusion and inequality issues are addressed through 'Technological Change', 'Poverty Reduction', 'Citizenship and Belonging' and 'Crime and Social Exclusion'. 'Sustainable Development', on which the rest depend, makes up the list.

A ten-point policy implementation framework is also offered, at the centre of which is an argument for the rebalancing of the financial resources allocated to lifelong learning across the whole lifespan[11] towards the adult population in terms of a four-stage model:

1. up to 25 years (from 86% to 80%),
2. 25 to 50 years (from 11% to 15%),
3. 50 to 75 years (from 2.5% to 4%),
4. 75 + years (from 0.5% to 1%).

The proposed redistribution would nearly double proportionately the allocation of financial resources to the third and fourth lifelong learning stage from its current (dwindling) 3%. Other proposals include accreditation of prior learning and a credit transfer system for recognising achievement across the whole system.

THE PROPER PLACE FOR SKILLS

So where should skills fit into the new lifelong learning agenda? Defining the term 'skill' and distinguishing it from other overlapping constructs is problematic, as economist Francis Green argues in his book devoted to the subject. He settles on 'personal qualities that can produce value at work' (Green 2013: 9–25), thus focusing on the economic benefit end of the returns to education spectrum. For the purpose here of locating skills in life-wide learning, the scope needs to be broader, embracing the other domains of life besides the economic as a simple four-level model suggests.

[11] £54.8 billion in 2007/8 of which £25.5 billion was state provision.

1. At the first (input) level there are the different kinds of courses available: formal (linked to certification), non-formal (without certification), and informal (day-to-day learning in the family, the community and the workplace).
2. At the next level are the broad outcomes of the learning: knowledge, understanding and skills. Skills, however, take different forms depending on the learning's purpose:

   Basic skills (comprising, literacy, numeracy, oracy and most recently digital competence) supply the foundations of subsequent skills development in all life-course domains.

   Generic work-related skills (such as teamwork, leadership and creativity), depending on application context, supply the key components of adult functioning in the family, the community and increasingly the workplace.

   Work-based skills (ranging from plumbing to dentistry), in large part acquired in the workplace are not generally transferable from one work situation to the next.

   The three types of skill are acquired in different learning contexts, with the basic skills as a given for all of them. Further associated spin-offs from the learning involved in acquiring the skills may include values and identity shifts as well as behavioural change. At every stage, learning the skill is likely to motivate further learning.
3. The common thread of all these outcomes occurs at the next level, *capability*, or as development economist Amartya Sen (1992) defines it, 'freedom to achieve wellbeing'.
4. In Sen's terms, capability drives the outcomes of learning in education, the labour market and the community, supplying the potential through which effective functioning and consequently well-being, the *fourth level,* will be achieved. In other words, skills and the goals to which they are directed in the capability approach are bound to the context in which they will be exercised and the freedom to gain them.

The retreat from life-wide learning thus needs to be resisted because it underpins the decline of the means of acquiring capability that the coming population of adults are going to need. In summary, the tensions that need to be resolved are between:

- World-class skills (Leitch) versus Freedom to achieve well-being (Sen)
- Education as a positional good versus Education as a democratic right
- Education for the economy versus Education for democracy

Clearly both elements of each tension are in play when any given education policy is to be decided. What matters is that any one of each pair does not run roughshod over the other one or, in the opposite scenario through shifting priorities, disappears without trace. Two issues alluded to earlier therefore arise here: (1) the role of adult learning in matching the broadest range of individual and community needs—i.e. the '*wider benefits of learning*' (Schuller 2004: 3–11); (2) the role of learning in resisting social exclusion and widening inequality—i.e. reversing the '*trajectory of disadvantage*' (Bynner 2007; Parsons & Bynner 2007: 10, 78–81) in which, in Peter Blossfeld and colleagues' words, 'structures of inequality are enshrined' (Kilpi-Jakonen *et al.* 2014: 7–12).

The wider benefits of learning

To assemble the evidence I turn first to analysis of the non-economic returns to learning in the 1958 cohort study gained between the ages of 33 to 42 (Feinstein *et al.* 2003; Bynner & Hammond 2004).[12] Over this age period, 58% of all cohort members, for whom data had been collected at both age points, had taken part in one or more courses offered through further education colleges, community provision or at work. Women were in the majority for leisure courses and courses leading to qualifications (academic and vocational). Men were in the majority for work-related, generally short, courses, which accounted for 58% of the total. The returns were in terms of the percentage of total change over the period in the whole sample that could be attributed to the learning engaged in, taking account of other factors such as prior educational attainment and social background that could also have influenced them.

The results pointed to improvements in psychological and physical well-being from taking two or more courses over the nine-year period assessed: smoking declined; exercise increased. For other well-being outcomes, though the learning effect was not statistically significant at the level set,[13] the same positive tendency was evident, including reduced drinking and resistance to and exit from, depression. Life satisfaction showed the interesting result of an average decline for the sample as a whole that was significantly less among adult learners. Life satisfaction was also the only effect that differed significantly for men and women, with more men than women likely to have remained satisfied.

The Social Cohesion benefits were even more evident from the cohort data, as reflected in the larger learning effect sizes: race tolerance increased; association

[12] Carried out for the Wider Benefits of Learning Research Centre, Institute of Education, London.

[13] Probability $P < .05$ level (i.e. odds of more than 20 to 1 against a chance result). The statistical change estimates were based on sample sizes averaging 9,000 for all change outcomes except giving up smoking, voting in 1997 having abstained in 1987 and recovery from depression. For smoking and voting the sample sizes reduced to between 2,000 and 3,000, demanding a larger change in outcome to achieve statistical significance at the same probability level as for the other outcomes, $P<.05$—and even more so for depression recovery where the sample size reduced to 616.

memberships expanded; political interest and participation in elections increased (voted in 1997 having abstained in 1987); while political cynicism and authoritarian attitudes declined. Moreover, these effects varied across the different kinds of learning context. Leisure courses showed positive effects for all but one of the six outcomes, political cynicism, and academic courses for all but association memberships. Work-based and vocational courses showed statistically significant improvement only for race tolerance (up) and authoritarian attitudes (down). The overall results were much the same for men and women.

Apart from the quantitative analysis, case studies were also conducted of the learning experiences and outcomes for individual learners. The complexity of the relation between the learning and the social context in which it takes place is illustrated by the case of a Pakistani young woman. As a first-generation English speaker in her immigrant family she was the key family resource for communicating with the wider society. She married and had children and in the course of her interactions with the local infants' school started helping out with the reception class. She then did basic skills courses, finally graduating to teaching assistant. Her learning career moved on to a certificate in child care taken at the local college, increasing her involvement with fellow students and the wider community. Further learning and a job followed. Apart from the positive effects of her educational achievement, another less anticipated outcome was a weakening of bonds within the family as the time and the resources she had always supplied were eroded. Finding her own identity outside the family had clearly been at the expense of one part of her identity within it.

What emerges from this example is a picture of learning leading to life changes, which themselves lead to positive outcomes while moderated in some cases by problematic consequences. More learning may follow and further life-course changes and benefits and the establishment of a learning career. There may sometimes be conflicting pressures between work and family, where additional support is needed to alleviate feelings of identity conflict and, in some cases depression, and to maintain the sense of progress and fulfilment. Such experiences and reactions may be present in any adult learning pathway (Raffe 2003), but are completely disregarded in progression rules, thus risking the halting of a learning career before it has properly begun. Courses need to be seen as learning resources rather than shackles if they are to meet the full spectrum of learning needs that adults have.

Such findings thus point to significant gains from participation in adult education classes in a number of government priority areas, ranging from physical and psychological well-being to civic engagement and social cohesion. Moreover, the latter appear to be most strongly boosted by leisure classes, the traditional staple of adult education provision.

Trajectory of disadvantage

> Something like one adult in five in this country is not functionally literate and far more people have problems with numeracy. This is a shocking situation and a sad reflection on past decades of schooling. It is one of the reasons for relatively low productivity in our economy, and it cramps the lives of millions of people. We owe it to them to remedy at public expense the shortcomings of the past. To do so should be a priority for Government, and for all those, in the business world or elsewhere, who can help. (Moser Report 1999: 8)

As part of the age-34 follow-up survey in the 1970 cohort study, a data module funded by the Moser-inspired 'Skills for Life' programme was devoted to basic skills, including a literacy and numeracy assessment. The aim was to build on a programme of earlier work for the Basics Skills Agency on identifying difficulties with achieving literacy and numeracy proficiency and to profile individuals with them in terms of origins and consequences at different stages of their lives (Bynner & Parsons 2005; Parsons & Bynner 2007; Bynner 2010).

Poor basic skills in adulthood were typically associated with a disadvantaged family background and poor educational progress early on in a school career that teachers, though often aware of the problem, had achieved little success in correcting. The general lack of interest in and engagement with adult education among this group contributed further to what Sargent *et al.* (1997) describe as the '*learning divide*'[14] and the challenge of bringing about its reversal.

These problems were accentuated in the more recent (1970) cohort where literacy and numeracy competence and subsequently digital skills were becoming increasingly mandatory for employability, independent of the qualification level reached (Bynner 1997; 2004). It was possible to identify a '*trajectory of disadvantage*' (Parsons & Bynner, 2007: 78–81), whereby in accordance with the 'Kennedy maxim' and the 'Matthew effect', the gap between those performing adequately on literacy and numeracy tasks and those unable to do them, steadily widened throughout the school career and subsequently.

As children, cohort members in the lowest adult basic skills category showed from an early age all the signs of such a developing trajectory. Even by the age of five those whose skills were poor as adults, revealed a poor grasp of the visual motor skills that supply crucial preparation for later literacy learning. It was not surprising that these children entering primary school would start falling behind the others, not least because it was clear from teachers' reports that their parents had very little idea how to support their children educationally.

[14] The widening gap in learning participation between the socioeconomically advantaged and disadvantaged population.

It is understandable that these parents soon became resigned to the fact that, despite high hopes for their children when they first entered school, the experience of failure would continue to build disappointment coupled with loss of interest. Their children rapidly fell behind, many failing to learn to read or gain the rudiments of numeracy. However, although many of the poorly skilled adults had spent time in remedial classes, over half of those with literacy problems and two thirds with numeracy problems in adulthood had not been identified by teachers as having difficulties when they were children.

The consequence was that the whole educational career through primary and secondary school could be stunted, becoming little more than a route to early leaving and restricted opportunities in the labour market. At age 34 in 2004, the full effect of poverty in childhood was revealed, not only in the constraints on everyday living that this experience reflected, but in many cases also in the reinforcement of the transmission within families of poor educational achievement and lack of preparation for learning from one generation to the next.

Those whose literacy and numeracy skills were poor as adults typically had children whose measured skills were also poor—a pattern repeated from the parents of the cohort members to the cohort members themselves. The relationship across the generations was substantially stronger for literacy than for numeracy, as revealed by the steeper gradient of children's scores for the former. Notably these relationships were sustained when the cohort members' highest qualification was controlled. Hence the vicious circle of downward mobility and poor performance was continually being reproduced. Such a circle underlines the importance of family learning programmes to help parents and their children bridge the gap together. As we shall see in the final section, it also underlines the importance of investment in adult education in a life-course scenario based on provision matched to need and embedded in a truly motivating teaching context. Because of parents' desire to help their children, family learning programmes provide such a context and are generally effective (Brooks *et al.* 1996; 1997).

The poor acquisition of the basic skills in childhood carried through to a chequered educational career, followed by poor progress in the labour market. At age 30 in 2004 adults with Entry Level basic skills[15] were more likely than others with higher level skills to be unemployed, and when they were in jobs, were far less likely to receive any work-based training. But perhaps the most striking result was revealed by the lack of a key learning resource in modern adult life—access to the internet.

[15] Below the level of GCSE grade G.

Digital divide

The expectation of exposure to computers and the internet is growing, especially as children enter school. Lack of family access to digital technology and the digital skills to go with it are therefore becoming key indicators of disadvantage, as reported, for example, by the Oxford Internet Institute (Helsper 2008). Data from the 1970 cohort study at age 34 showed such a 'digital divide' between groups defined at the different adult literacy levels [16]: 62% of age-34 adults (men and women equally) at Entry Level 2 or below had *no* access to the internet, compared with 20% of those at Level 1 and above. Moreover, 48% of men and 40% of women in the former group had no computer at home and 16% of men and 17% of women never used one. Not only were those Entry Level 2 adults failing to participate in the now digitalised learning society, but those with families were likely to be similarly passing this disadvantage to their children.

As an extension to the Skills for Life programme, a comparative study between London and Portland, Oregon modelled the way the relationships worked between literacy proficiency, computer use and employment for disadvantaged adults in the two areas, and produced surprises (Bynner *et al.* 2010). This was at the time of a booming labour market in London and a depressed labour market in Portland. The disadvantaged adult learners in Portland were ahead of their counterparts in England with respect to their use of computers. This exposure was related to employability for men and women in Portland, but only for the women in London, many of whom were returning to employment after child bearing. For men in London, progression in employment rather than getting a job was associated with computer use. Counter-intuitively, the direction of causation implied that improved digital competence boosted literacy proficiency rather than the other way round: that is, the influence of exercising digital competence on literacy proficiency, usually at work, exceeded the influence of literacy proficiency on digital competence.

CONCLUSION

The work of the Wider Benefits of Learning Centre and the National Research and Development Centre for Adult Literacy demonstrates the value of longitudinal research in gaining understanding of lifelong learners' needs and offer pointers to the means of meeting them. The formidable obstacles that many adults face in engaging with learning underline the continual need for support to bring about the 'turning

[16] Educational attainment age 16 leaving standards: Level 2, General Certificate of Secondary Education (GCSE) grades A–C; Level 1, GCSE grades D–G; Entry Level 3; Entry Level 2; Entry Level 1.

points' in individual lives that can establish a learning career. The life-course conception embraces the shaping influences on the process including:

- policy and practice operating at different times and in different places in which consistency to aid perseverance is at a premium;
- social relations, in different interactional settings, the home, the family, the workplace and the community, which aid rather than inhibit learning;
- the timing of critical experiences and events that foster rather than obstruct learning;
- motivational learning contexts that stimulate individual agency and drive the critical steps towards success rather than stand-alone provision detached from everyday experience at home and in the workplace.

This may be seen as the point where the programme set out in NIACE's *Learning Through Life* through the 'nine themes' shows the way. Long-term entitlement to life-wide adult learning needs to be a policy priority. As Smethurst (1992) shows, it is a mistake, in relying on cost–benefit kinds of consideration of skills acquisition, to focus on the *economic* outcome alone as there is a need to recognise externalities. That is to say, policy needs to embrace, as well, learning effects that impact on economic returns indirectly. It is important, therefore, to focus attention on equity in access to opportunity and the means of realising it across the range of capabilities that are enhanced through it. Every individual should have the right to enhance their learning potential as the means of boosting not only their own capabilities but that of the succeeding generations to whom these capabilities are transferred. This principle applies not only in relation to prioritising the Leitch-defined core skills but to the wider range of learning opportunities and their outcomes where motivation may be fostered and a learning career begun.

The cohort study analyses help identify the *wider benefits* to be gained from adult learning and the *trajectory of disadvantage* that restricts access to them among those who start off from the lowest educational base. Literacy and numeracy, and increasingly ICT competence, supply the foundations of the capability that is needed. The rising incidence of depression, which has increased in the more recent cohort (Ferri *et al.* 2003) is only one of many poor well-being indicators that adult learning can help to ameliorate as general practitioners are already coming to recognise through the growing use of 'social prescribing'.[17]

As futurologists like Jeremy Rifkin (1995) tell us, society is faced with an ever-contracting pool of employment for an ever-widening section of the population

[17] http://www.ageconcernyorkshireandhumber.org.uk/uploads/files/Social%20Prescribing%20Report%20new.pdf

resigned to zero-hour contracts and short-term jobs or no jobs at all and increasingly called the '*precariat*' (Standing 2011). The provision of lifelong and life-wide learning opportunities in this critical area of basic skills and capability development therefore merits the highest priority. The disregard of the skills agenda for the wider context of learning and the multiple benefits to be obtained from both its inputs and outputs therefore needs to be resisted.

The challenge is to create learning conditions in which motivation is triggered and social relations are strong. Family learning devoted to literacy development provides one of the most effective examples in which the motivation of adults comes from the desire to help their children while enhancing their own skills in the process. The model involves additional literacy and numeracy teaching provided for parents and primary schoolchildren learning together (Brooks *et al.* 1996; 1997). Further examples come from embedding basic skills provision in routine tasks in motivating contexts such as vocational training courses (Casey *et al.* 2006) or other less obvious venues such as antenatal classes, for example (Bynner & Parsons 2005).

The golden days of adult education, when all courses available to adults were seen as valuable in their own right and virtually free of charge if individuals wanted to undertake them, are unlikely to be restored in the foreseeable future. Though many countries such as the Nordic five still hold to this principle that education in whatever form it takes should be available to all citizens as a democratic right, the general trend under austerity-driven policy thinking is towards marketisation of post-compulsory education rather than offering it as a public good. Moocs (Massive Open Online Courses) are another free or very cheap option relying exclusively on digital rather than face-to-face instruction. But the evidence of very low certification rates, widely quoted as 7% on average, suggests that the early hopes for them may well evaporate.[18]

What is indisputable is that, as society transforms digitally at an accelerating rate, a wide range of capabilities is critical to adult functioning, individually, in the family, the community and the workplace. The argument here is that lifelong learning in the broadest sense underpins not only the capabilities of the individual who gains them but contributes to the well-being of all. Without it, as the NIACE surveys show (Tuckett & Aldridge 2010), from an earlier peak in 2010 there are strong signs of what Sargent *et al.* (1997) described as a growing learning divide [19].

Such initiatives as learning cities with rural as well as urban catchment areas, as promoted by UNESCO (2015), is one way of realising such a goal and cities are places where the resources for learning, such as libraries and educational institutions and the

[18] http://er.educause.edu/articles/2014/12/mooc-completion-and-retention-in-the-context-of-student-intent

[19] The widening gap in learning participation between the socioeconomically advantaged and disadvantaged population.

expert teachers to deploy them, can in principle be fairly easily consolidated, that is serving as *learning hubs*. But in Britain the idea extends further than this. The incorporation into state provision of vocational education through further education colleges and what were polytechnics, leaving a residue of adult education with local authorities and the voluntary sector, cuts across the principles of localism—institutional networks, local engagement, and progression—horizontally as well as vertically. This is the message of the Delors Report and the NIACE review. All providers from national down to local level, need to supply the core of a restored system of all-embracing lifelong learning provision.

But these forms of lifelong learning provision should not be seen in isolation. Employment itself is often inadvertently the other major provider, or should be, as Lorna Unwin and Alison Fuller (2003; Unwin 2010) argue, particularly for young people entering their first jobs. The workplace is a core source of learning and raising the status of this function as in Germany and Scandinavia, for example, should be seen as an inevitable development for the digital age. Trade unions with 23,000 learning representatives across the whole country are another source of such educational infrastructure, together with charitable foundations directly concerned with particular groups, ranging from ethnicity to disability. Prison education, rather than being used for filling the gaps in time-serving in a shattered occupational career, should be a central part of the rehabilitation (Schuller & Watson 2009). Coupled with such a development, the continuing collection of monitoring data (the NIACE surveys) and longitudinal data of the cohort studies kind, becomes the critical counterpart of provision in assessing and gaining understanding of lifelong learning's effects.

Overall the picture has both discouraging and encouraging aspects for the importance of adult learning and is why '*Whatever Happened to Lifelong Learning*' matters. Clearly the significance of early-life factors could lead to the conclusion that investment in the skills of the next generation, rather than the current adult one, is likely to produce the best pay-off (e.g. Choudry & Fitzsimmons 2016). However, our analysis clearly indicates in two ways that this approach would be an over-simplification.

First, certain influences emerge as significant in boosting basic skills through post-16 experience, especially exposure to ICT provision as originating in the University for Industry at its peak and often run in local libraries, such as 'Learn Direct'.[20] Secondly, although age-34 basic skills are predictable from the demographic, experience and achievement variables included in the analysis presented at the beginning of this paper, over 60% of the inequality between people in relation to these skills measures could not be predicted and consequently 'explained' in terms of them.

[20] Set up in 1998 in response to the 'Learning Age' http://www.leeds.ac.uk/educol/documents/000000654.htm

Individual life-course patterns of the kind revealed qualitatively through biographical analysis, as in the case study reported, can point to the combinations of salient experiences that give rise to 'turning points'.

In the case of literacy and numeracy acquisition, as David Mallows and Jennifer Litster (2016) argue, drawing on Steve Reder's work on motivating disadvantaged adult learners (Reder 1994) repeated and sustained practice integrated into everyday activity in the workplace, at home and in the community offers the best prospects of success. Their example of basic skills education for new recruits to the British Army (Mallows & Litster 2016: 22) is just one of many where all the ingredients of an effective programme can be put in place.

Thus given the right learning opportunities, adequate learning provision and support in the right form at the right time and, crucially, a realisable goal to motivate the desire to 'transform' or 'sustain' (under threat) the quality of life (Schuller *et al.* 2004, 24–9), the prospect of acquiring, at any stage of life, the basic skills and the capabilities to follow is always attainable. Finally, the intergenerational continuities in basic skills transfer make the point that enhancing parents' basic skills can be the critical factor in raising the educational level of their children—the foundation of capability in the next generation.

There is a long way to go before Britain achieves the levels of equality of educational outcomes as achieved, for example, in Scandinavian countries, and they themselves are always trying to improve them. Moreover, the nature of inequality has itself shifted in industrial countries—including the most economically successful like Germany—towards polarisation between 'insiders' with secure employment prospects and 'outsiders', who have failed to get on the employment ladder for demographic or educational reasons (Blossfeld in press). Such young people are subsequently 'scarred' in the eyes of employers because of their perceived lack of qualifications and continuing work experience: that is, they are short of the 'human capital' on which employability is considered to depend.

Nevertheless, the goal of bridging irreversibly the *learning divide* is realisable given the recognition of *lifelong* and *life-wide* learning as the means of achieving it. Apart from individual fulfilment, society will always benefit from the resulting contribution to the enhanced quality of life, social cohesion and productivity that learning brings. It is therefore still a matter of 'never too early never too late' but reconfigured now for the digital world.

Acknowledgements

I could not have attempted this paper without the much valued help of Alan Tuckett (Emeritus Professor, University of Wolverhampton) and Tom Schuller (Emeritus Professor, UCL Institute of Education) who in memorable conversations directed me to the key papers in the history and latest developments in lifelong learning. The empirical findings reported were drawn from the work in the 15-year joint programme of cohort study research on basic skills conducted with my colleague Samantha Parsons to whom I am indebted, as well as to colleagues in the IoE's research centre for the Wider Benefits of Learning. My thanks also go to the Sir John Cass's Foundation who funded the lecture in the series from which this paper was derived and to the British Academy for hosting it.

REFERENCES

Aronowitz, S. & Di Fazio, W. (1994) *The Jobless Future* (Minneapolis, MN, University of Minnesota Press).

Ashton, D. & Bynner, J. (2011), 'Labour Market, Employment and Skills', in M. E. J. Wadsworth & J. Bynner (eds) *A Companion to Life Course Studies: The Social and Historical Context of the British Birth Cohort Studies* (London, Routledge).

Blossfeld, P. (in press), 'Labour Market Entry Before and After the Financial Crisis in Germany: Duration of Labour Market Entry, Quality of First Job, and Fixed-term Employment', in I. Schoon & J. Bynner (eds) *Young People's Development and the Great Recession: Uncertain Transitions and Precarious Futures* (Cambridge, Cambridge University Press).

Blossfeld, H.-P., Kilpi-Jakonen, E., Vono de Vilhena, D., Buchholz, S. & Friedrich, O. (eds) (2014) *Adult Learning in Modern Societies: Patterns and Consequences of Participation from a Life Course Perspective*, Edu LIFE Lifelong Series.Vol.1. (Cheltenham, Edward Elgar).

Blunkett, D. (1998), Preface to *The Learning Age: A Renaissance for a New Britain* (London, HMSO).

Brooks, G., Gorman, T. P., Harman, J., Hutchison, D. & Wilkin, A. (1996) *Family Literacy Works: The NFER Evaluation of the Basic Skills Agency's Family Literacy Demonstration Programmes* (London, Basic Skills Agency).

Brooks, G., Gorman, T. P., Harman, J., Hutchison, D., Kinder, K., Moor, H. & Wilkin, A. (1997) *Family Literacy Lasts: The NFER Follow-up Study of the Basic Skills Agency's Demonstration Programmes* (London, Basic Skills Agency).

Bynner, J. (1997), 'Basic Skills in Adolescents' Occupational Preparation', *Career Development Quarterly*, 45: 305–21. https://doi.org/10.1002/j.2161-0045.1997.tb00536.x

Bynner, J. (2004), 'Literacy, Numeracy and Employability: Evidence from the British Birth Cohort Studies', *Literacy and Numeracy Studies*, 13: 31–48.

Bynner, J. (2007), 'A Trajectory of Disadvantage', *Reflect*, 9: 13–15.

Bynner, J. (2010), 'Lifelong Learning, the Life Course and Longitudinal Study', in J. Derick, U. Howard, J. Field, S. Meyer, E. N. von Rein & T. Schuller (eds) *Remaking Adult Learning* (London, Institute of Education Press), 56–64.

Bynner, J. & Hammond, C. (2004), 'The Benefits of Adult Learning: Quantitative Insights', in T. Schuller, J. Preston, C. Hammond, A. Brassett-Grundy & J. Bynner (eds) *The Benefits of Learning: The Impact of Education on Health, Family Life and Social Capital* (London, Routledge), 161–78.

Bynner, J. & Parsons, S. (2005) *New Light on Literacy and Numeracy*, NRDC Report (London, Institute of Education).

Bynner, J. & Parsons, S. (2009), 'Insights into Basic Skills from a UK Longitudinal Study', in S. Reder & J. Bynner (eds) *Tracking Adult Literacy and Numeracy Skills; Findings from Longitudinal Research* (New York, Routledge), 27–58.

Bynner, J., Mcintosh, S., Vignoles, A., Dearden, L., Reed, H. & Van Reenen, J. (2001) *Improving Adult Basic Skills: Benefits to the Individual and to Society*, DfEE Research Report RR251 (London, HMSO).

Bynner, J., Reder., S., Parsons, S. & Strawn, C. (2010) *The Three Divides: The Digital Divide and its Relation to Basic Skills and Employment in Portland, USA and London, England*, NRDC Report (London, Institute of Education).

Casey, H., Cara, O., Eldred, J., Grief, S., Hodge, R., Ivanic, R, Jupp, T, Lopez, D. & McNeil, B. (2006), *"You wouldn't expect a maths teacher to teach plastering…" Embedding Literacy, Language and Numeracy in Post-16 Vocational Programmes – The Impact on Learning and Achievement*. NRDC Report (London, Institute of Education).

Choudry, H. & Fitzsimmons, P. (2016) *The Cost of Late Intervention: EIF Analysis, 2016* (London, Early Intervention Foundation).

Coffield, F. (1999), 'Breaking the Consensus: Lifelong Learning as Social Control', *British Educational Research Journal*, 25: 479–99. https://doi.org/10.1080/0141192990250405

Coffield, F. D. (2000), 'Introduction: A Critical Analysis of the Concept of a Learning Society', in F. Coffield (ed.) *Differing Visions of a Learning Society*, (Bristol, Polity Press), 1–38.

Coffield, F. (2012), 'Why the McKinsey Reports will not Improve School Systems', *Journal of Education Policy*, 17: 131–49. https://doi.org/10.1080/02680939.2011.623243

Dearing, R. (1997), *Higher Education in the Learning Society*, (Dearing Report), National Committee of Inquiry into Higher Education (London, HMSO).

Delors, J. (1996), *Learning: The Treasure Within* (Paris, UNESCO).

DES (Department of Education and Science) (1973) *Adult Education* (Russell Report), (London, HMSO).

EC (European Commission) (2000), 'A Memorandum on Lifelong Learning', Commission Staff Working Paper (Brussels, European Commission).

Elder, G. H. Jr. (1974/99) *Children of the Great Depression: Social Change in Life Experience* (Boulder, CO, Westview Press).

European Council of Ministers (2000), Lisbon European Council March 2000: Presidency Conclusions. http://www.europarl.europa.eu/summits/lis1_en.htm

Faure, E., Herrera, F., Kaddoura, A.-K., Lopes, H., Petrovsky, A. V., Rahnema, M., Champion Ward, F. (1972) *Learning to Be: The World of Education Today and Tomorrow* (Paris, UNESCO).

Feinstein, L., Hammond, C., Woods, L., Preston, J. & Bynner, J. (2003) *The Contribution of Adult Learning to Health and Social Capital*, Wider Benefits of Learning Centre Report (London, Institute of Education).

Ferri, E., Bynner, J. & Wadsworth, M. E. (eds), (2003) *Changing Britain, Changing Lives: Three Generations at the Turn of the Century*, Bedford Way Papers (London, Institute of Education).

Field. J. (2005) *Social Capital and Lifelong Learning* (Bristol, Policy Press). https://doi.org/10.1332/policypress/9781861346551.001.0001

Fryer, R. H. (1997) *Learning for the 21st Century: First Report of the National Advisory Group for Continuing Education and Lifelong Learning* (Fryer Report) (Sheffield, National Advisory Group for Continuing Education and Lifelong Learning).

Fullick, L. (2010), 'NIACE Policy, Politics and Campaigning 1988–2008', in J. Derick, U. Howard, J. Field, S. Meyer, E. N. von Rein & T. Schuller (eds) *Remaking Adult Learning* (London, Institute of Education Press), 201–14.

Green, F. (2013) *Skills and Skilled Work* (Oxford, Oxford University Press).

Handy, C. (1984) *The Future of Work* (Oxford, Blackwell).

Heinz, W. R. (1991), 'Status Passages, Social Risks and the Life Course', in W. R. Heinz (ed.) *Theoretical Advances in Life Course Research* (Weinheim, Deutscher Studien Verlag), 9–22.

Helsper, E. J. (2008) *Digital Literacy: Different Cultures Different Understandings*, International Digital Literacy Conference (Uxbridge, Brunel University).

Hodgson, A. (2000) *Policies, Politics, and the Future of Lifelong Learning* (London, Kogan Page).

Jupp, T. (2010), 'Innovation and Change in the Inner London Education Authority', in J. Derick, U. Howard, J. Field, S. Meyer, E. N. von Rein & T. Schuller (eds) *Remaking Adult Learning* (London, Institute of Education Press), 187–200.

Kennedy, H. (1997) *Learning Works: Widening Participation in Further Education*, (Kennedy Report) (Coventry, Further Education Funding Council).

Kilpi-Jakonen, E., Buchholtz, S., Dammrich, P. M & Blossfeld, H.-P. (2014), 'Adult Learning, Labour Market Outcomes and Social Inequalities in Modern Societies', in H.-P. Blossfeld, E. Kilpi-Jakonen, D. Vono de Vilhena, S. Buchholz & O. Friedrich (eds) *Adult Learning in Modern Societies: Patterns and Consequences of Participation from a Life Course Perspective*, Edu LIFE Lifelong Series.Vol.1. (Cheltenham, Edward Elgar), 3–28.

Leitch Report (2006) *Leitch Review of Skills: Prosperity in the Global Economy—World Class Skills Final Report* (Norwich, The Stationery Office).

McNair, S. & Quintero-Re, L. (2008) *CONFINTEA VI: United Kingdom National Report on the Development and State of the Art of Adult Learning and Education (ALE)* (Leicester, National Institute of Adult Continuing Education).

Mallows, D. & Litster, J. (2016) *How Can We Motivate Adults to Engage in Literacy and Numeracy Learning?*, Future of Skills & Lifelong Learning Evidence Review (London, Government Office for Science Foresight).

Ministry of Education (1954) *The Organisation and Finance of Adult Education in England and Wales* (Ashby Report) (London, HMSO).

Ministry of Reconstruction, Board of Adult Education (1919) *Final Report* (London, HMSO).

Moser Report (1999) *A Fresh Start: Improving Literacy and Numeracy* (Sudbury, Suffolk, Department for Education and Employment).

Nash, I. (2014) *Seriously Useless Learning: The Collected TES Writings of Alan Tuckett.* (Leicester, National Institute of Adult Continuing Education).

OECD (1996) *Lifelong Learning for All* (Paris, OECD).

OECD (2013) *OECD Skills Outlook 2013: First Results from the Survey of Adult Skills* (Paris, OECD).

OECD (2016) *Building Skills for All: Review of England: Policy Insights from the Survey of Adult Skills by the Organisation for Economic Co-operation and Development (OECD)* (Paris, OECD).

Parsons, S. & Bynner, J. (2007) *Illuminating Disadvantage: Profiling the Experiences of Adults with Entry Level Literacy or Numeracy over the Life Course*, NRDC Research Report (London, Institute of Education).

Raffe, D. (1985), 'Post-compulsory Education and Training Initiatives in Scotland: A Personal View', *Youth Studies Australia*, 4: 85–94. http://acys.info/resources/ysa/volume-4/youth-studies-australia-v4-n3-august-1985/

Raffe, D. (2003), 'Pathways Linking Education and Work: A Review of Concepts, Research and Policy Debates', *Journal of Youth Studies*, 6: 3–20. https://doi.org/10.1080/1367626032000068136

Reder, S. (1994), 'Practice–Engagement Theory: A Sociocultural Approach across Languages and Cultures', in B. Ferman, R.-M. Webber & A. G. Ramirez (eds) *Literacy Across Languages and Cultures* (New York, State University of New York Press), Chapter 2.

Rifkin, J. (1995) *The End of Work*, (New York, Putnam).

Rifkin, J. (1998) *Biotech Century* (New York, Putnam).

Sargant, N., Field, J., Francis, H. Schuller, T. & Tuckett, A. (1997) *The Learning Divide* (Leicester, National Institute of Adult Continuing Education).

Schoon, I. (2006) *Risk and Resilience. Adaptations in Changing Times* (Cambridge, Cambridge University Press). https://doi.org/10.1017/CBO9780511490132

Schuller, T. (2004), 'Studying Benefits', in T. Schuller, J. Preston, C. Hammond, A. Brassett-Grundy & J. Bynner (eds.) *The Benefits of Learning: The Impact of Education on Health, Family Life and Social Capital* (London, Routledge Falmer), Chapter 1.

Schuller, T. (ed.) (2016) *Global Report on Adult Learning and Education (GRALE 3)* (Paris, UNESCO).

Schuller, T. & Watson, D. (2009) *Learning Through Life: Inquiry into the Future for Lifelong Learning* (Leicester, National Institute of Adult Continuing Education).

Schuller, T., Preston, J., Hammond, C., Brassett-Grundy, A. & Bynner, J. (2004) *The Benefits of Learning: The Impact of Education on Health, Family Life and Social Capital* (London, Routledge Falmer).

Sen, A. (1992), *Inequality Re-examined* (Cambridge, MA, Harvard University Press).

Smethurst, R. (1995), 'Education: A Public or Private good?', *RSA Journal*, 143: 33–45.

Standing, G. (2011) *The Precariat: The New Dangerous Class* (London, Bloomsbury Academy).

Stanovich, K. E. (1986), 'Matthew Effects in Reading: Some Consequences of Individual Differences in the Acquisition of Literacy', *Reading Research Quarterly*, 22: 360–407. https://doi.org/10.1598/RRQ.21.4.1

Tight, M. (1998), 'Education, Education, Education! The Vision of Lifelong Learning in the Kennedy, Dearing and Fryer Reports', *Oxford Review of Education*, 24: 473–85. https://doi.org/10.1080/0305498980240404

Tuckett, A. (1998) *The Jewel in the Crown: Adult Education in Inner London* (London: Inner London Education Authority).

Tuckett, A, (2007), 'Leitch Cannot Disguise the Death of Lifelong Learning', *The Guardian*, 2 January 2007.

Tuckett, A. (2015), 'Jesus and History and Thunder and Lightning', Inaugural Professorial Lecture, University of Wolverhampton, October.

Tuckett, A. & Aldridge, F. (2010) *A Change for the Better: The NIACE Survey on Adult Participation in Learning 2010* (Leicester, National Institute of Adult Continuing Education).

UNESCO (1997) *The Hamburg Declaration and Agenda for the Future,* Fifth International Conference on Adult Education 14–18 July (CONFINTEA V) (Paris, UNESCO).

UNESCO (2015), UNESCO Global Network of Learning Cities: Guiding Documents (Hamburg, UNESCO Institute of Lifelong Learning).

Unwin, L. (2010), 'Making Jobs Bigger for Better Learning: Connecting Policies for Lifelong Learning to Workplace Improvement', in J. Derick, U. Howard, J. Field, S. Meyer, E. N. von Rein & T. Schuller (eds) *Remaking Adult Learning* (London, Institute of Education Press), 153–62.

Unwin, L. & Fuller, A. (2003) *Expanding Learning in the Workplace* (Leicester, National Institute of Adult Continuing Education).

Wilson, H. (1964) *Purpose in Politics: Selected Speeches by Rt. Hon. Harold Wilson*. (London, Weidenfeld and Nicolson).

Note on the Author: John Bynner is Emeritus Professor of Social Sciences in Education at the London UCL Institute of Education and until retirement in 2004 was Director of the Centre for Longitudinal Studies, the Wider Benefits of Learning Research Centre and founder Director of the National Research and Development Centre for Adult Literacy and Numeracy. He is Executive Editor of the international journal *Longitudinal and Life Course Studies*. His principal research interest is the contemporary life course. Recent relevant publications include *A Companion to Life Course Studies* (with Michael Wadsworth) (Routledge, 2011), *Journey to a Life-course*

Perspective in Developmental Science (Routledge, 2014), *The Institutionalization of Life Course Studies* (Springer, 2016).
J.bynner@ucl.ac.uk

To cite the article: John Bynner (2017), 'Whatever happened to lifelong learning? And does it matter?', *Journal of the British Academy*, 5: 61–89.
DOI https://doi.org/10.85871/jba/005.61

Journal of the British Academy (ISSN 2052–7217) is published by
The British Academy—the national academy for the humanities and social sciences.
10–11 Carlton House Terrace, London, SW1Y 5AH
www.britishacademy.ac.uk

Journal of the British Academy, **5**, 91–124. DOI https://doi.org/10.5871/jba/005.091
Posted 4 May 2017.

The UK's changing party system: The prospects for a party realignment at Westminster

Lecture in Politics and Government
to be read on 4 July 2017

DAVID SANDERS
Fellow of the Academy

Abstract: The paper examines the main changes in the UK party system that have occurred in recent decades. It focuses on the decline of party identification and class-based voting, and the unintended consequences of decisions made by political elites. It analyses the fragmentation of contemporary UK political opinion and describes the emergence of a new set of 'political tribes' that cut across old left–right party loyalties, taking particular note of the growth of Authoritarian Populism sentiment. It concludes that a major realignment of the UK party system is already underway and that the changes set in train by past elite decisions and changing public perceptions are likely to continue.

Keywords: party systems, party fragmentation, party identification, class-based voting, Authoritarian Populism.

Party systems—and support for the parties that comprise them—develop and evolve in response to three broad sets of factors: electoral rules; the actions and decisions of political elites; and the political beliefs, attitudes and preferences of mass publics. The evolution of the UK's party system since 1945 reflects the tension between the strong constraining impact of electoral rules and deep-seated, long-term changes in public opinion. Declining party identification and increasing popular disillusion with Labour and the Conservatives have weakened what, for the two main governing parties, were the 'virtuous circle' effects of First-Past-the-Post (FPTP) elections. These long-term changes have stimulated movement towards a multiparty system—although, as UKIP's experience in the 2015 general election showed, FPTP can still reassert its virtuous (or in this case, vicious) circle effects. This paper reviews the factors that have underpinned the UK's changing party systems over the last six decades. It argues that, partly as a result of recent decisions by Labour and Conservative elites, UK public opinion is now ripe for a party-system realignment. With the Conservatives divided over Europe and human rights, and Labour divided over immigration and whether the party should be primarily a party of government or a protest movement, an important opportunity has opened up for a resurgence of the liberal political centre. The key issue is whether or not sufficient politicians from the centrist factions of Labour and the Conservatives possess the will and courage to develop it.

Part 1 of this paper reviews the conventional wisdom about the relationship between electoral rules and patterns of party competition. *Duverger's Law* (Duverger 1954) has undoubtedly acted as a constraint on the development of parties that could challenge the post-war dominance of Labour and the Conservatives. However, it is also the case that the UK's party system (or more correctly, party systems if we consider local government and the devolved assemblies in Scotland, Northern Ireland and Wales, as well as the Westminster parliament) has become increasingly fragmented since 1945. Part 2 briefly documents this increasing fragmentation. It outlines the decline of the Westminster two-party vote since the 1950s; the increasing number of local councils where no single party has overall control, especially after 2000; and the clear multiparty systems (encouraged by electoral rules that include a proportional component in terms of regional lists) that have characterised each of the UK's devolved assemblies since 1998. The section also examines the increasing disproportionality between parties' vote shares and seat shares in the Westminster parliament, a phenomenon that has grown as the vote shares of the two major parties have declined.

Part 3 examines the main factors that have contributed to the increasing party fragmentation at Westminster. It differentiates between explanatory factors that are capable of being measured systematically, in terms of both their extent and their impact on fragmentation, and those that are not. Among the 'unmeasurable factors' are the long-term decline in deference towards received wisdom and elite judgement; the rise of new regional, ethnic and religious identities; increased media criticism (including social media criticism) of conventional politics and politicians; and the unintended consequences of elite decisions. Key among the measurable factors are the long-term decline in party identification and the gradual weakening of class-based voting. The final section considers the prospects for a new realignment of the Westminster party system. It analyses recently collected survey data which show that Authoritarian Populist attitudes are widespread among the UK mass public. Cluster analysis suggests that there are now four distinct 'political tribes' among UK voters, defined in terms of their left–right positions and their attitudes towards Europe, immigration, human rights and Britain's foreign policy role in the world. A new centre party could make a strong electoral appeal to a large proportion of two of these tribes, acting as a bulwark against the otherwise likely election of future Authoritarian Populist governments at Westminster.

FIRST-PAST-THE-POST (FPTP) VERSUS INCREASING PARTY FRAGMENTATION, 1945–2016

The UK has always had a rather more complex party structure than the simple two- or two-and-a-half party system typically used by comparative political analysts to characterise the Westminster parliament. Many towns and cities in Great Britain have evolved local party systems, particularly since 1945, which look very different from the classic Conservative/Labour/Liberal (Democrat) Westminster model. Northern Ireland has had its own distinctive system, variously instituted, since the 1920s. And since devolution in the late 1990s, Scotland and Wales have developed entirely new systems that have in turn evolved in different ways over time. This said, Duverger's conclusions about the impact of FPTP or plurality electoral rules on party competition have proved a useful way of explaining why the Conservatives and Labour have maintained their electoral dominance for most of the post-war period—and of explaining why third parties without a clear regional base have found it extraordinarily difficult to make an electoral breakthrough.

The core of Duverger's analysis is very straightforward: plurality voting, over time, encourages competition between two broad-based, catch-all parties, making it difficult for third parties to challenge the two-party status quo. On occasion, of course, a minor party might be able to sustain itself under FPTP (especially if it could make some sort of local or regional appeal) or one of the two parties might even (temporarily) achieve the status of a 'dominant party'. However, for the two major parties under FPTP, a 'virtuous circle' calculus of voting and activism tends to operate—which for any challenger party, by implication, acts as a vicious circle. Voters and political activists learn, either in advance or through experience, that third-party votes and activism tend to be wasted in terms of gaining parliamentary seats. Both voters and would-be activists accordingly gravitate towards one or other of the two major parties, even if this involves voting tactically for a lesser evil or, for the activist, 'compromising' with the dominant values of the party he or she has decided to join. This gravitation effect in turn squeezes the third-party vote, which encourages the sense after an election that third-party voting and activism have been wasteful—thus reinforcing the FPTP virtuous/vicious circle. The counterpoint to plurality voting rules, of course, is Proportional Representation (PR) in its various forms. In Duverger's view, PR encourages multiparty competition, since under PR there are fewer (if any) wasted votes or wasted activism. This enables 'sincere' voting (that is, genuine first-preference voting) to predominate and ensures that the public's preferences—however fragmented they might be—can be reasonably accurately translated into parliamentary seats. For Duverger, it is no accident (as subsequent studies have repeatedly shown) that plurality systems exhibit the highest disparities between parties' vote shares and parliamentary seat shares and that these disparities are associated (other things being equal) with higher levels of dissatisfaction with democracy.

Plurality electoral rules, of course, do not mean there is no serious challenge to existing parties. Irish nationalists made a successful challenge to the dominant Conservative and Liberal parties in the first two decades of the 20th century, resulting in Irish independence in 1922. And Labour successfully supplanted the Liberal Party in the decade or so after the First World War. The logic of the FPTP virtuous circle soon reasserted itself, however. The Liberals received only 7 per cent of the popular vote in the 1931 general election—a position from which they did not really start to recover until 1974. Yet it is clear that over the last 40 years or so, the Conservative/Labour two-party system at Westminster has transmuted into a form of 'unbalanced multipartism'—involving the Conservatives, Labour, Liberal Democrats, Scottish National Party (SNP) and Plaid Cymru (PC)—even though the electoral rules have not changed. Electoral rules do not determine party competition, though they do constrain it in different ways. Regionally focused or national parties can clearly prosper under FPTP, but those parties which lack either a clear regional/national base (like the SNP and PC and to a lesser extent the Liberal Democrats) or a class demographic (like the Conservatives and Labour, at least in the past) find that their support, even if it is considerable, can be spread so thinly as to deliver no real electoral payoff. UKIP's experience in the 2015 general election, with 12 per cent of the popular vote and only one parliamentary seat to show for it, is a clear testimony to the dangers of 'no distinctive demographic'. All this said, the experiences of the devolved assemblies in Scotland, Wales and Northern Ireland clearly support the Duverger thesis that the introduction of a substantial PR component in the electoral process strongly encourages multipartism: since their inception, all the newly devolved assemblies (as demonstrated in the next section) have been characterised by multiparty competition.

THE FRAGMENTATION OF WESTMINSTER, DEVOLVED ASSEMBLY AND LOCAL COUNCIL VOTING IN HISTORICAL PERSPECTIVE

The timescales over which changes in party competition can usefully be analysed vary according to the different levels of governance. For Westminster elections, the earliest reference point is generally considered to be 1832, when the UK's modern party system, focusing on competition between Conservatives and Liberals, was initiated. For the devolved assemblies, the simplest start date is the first set of post-devolution elections—1998 in Northern Ireland and 1999 in Scotland and Wales.[1] For local elections, the position is complicated by the significant changes in local authority boundaries and designations that have been introduced, particularly since 1945. The most consistent basis for an over-time comparison is to consider the electoral position in the UK's major cities (excluding London, which has had a variety of distinctive arrangements) since 1945. The discussion here focuses initially on the *vote* shares obtained by the various parties, turning then to discuss the relationship between *vote* shares and *seat* shares in the national, Westminster context.

Westminster

Figure 1 reports the changes in party vote shares for the Westminster parliament between 1832 and 2015. Until 1910, support for the Conservatives and Liberals was overwhelming, with very low levels of support for 'Other' parties. From 1918 to 1931 there was a period of transition in which Labour replaced the Liberals as one of the two 'major' parties able to benefit from the FPTP virtuous circle. From the mid-1950s, there was a gradual decline in the combined Labour and Conservative share of the vote, with a concomitant rise in support for the Liberals (Liberal Democrats) and 'Other'.[2] By 2015, the constraining effects of FPTP had loosened sufficiently for roughly a third of the electorate to decide to vote for parties other than Labour and the Conservatives. Support for UKIP (at 12.5 per cent) was part of the explanation for the loosening. However, as Figure 2 shows, another part of the story was the success of nationalist parties in Wales and Scotland. Plaid Cymru and the Scottish National Party started to attract very small percentages of Welsh and Scottish votes, respectively, in Westminster elections in 1931—but by 2015 this had grown to a 12 per cent share for PC in Wales and a massive 50 per cent SNP share in the wake of the 2014 Scottish independence referendum.

[1] It should be stressed, of course, that the fragmentation of party politics in each of the devolved regional assemblies did not begin in the late 1990s. Scotland, Wales and Northern Ireland had already shown evidence of divergent patterns of party politics, to varying degrees, in the preceding decades—which was partly why devolution was considered to be necessary in the first place. In this sense, the introduction of partial proportional representation in the devolved assemblies after 1998/99 was by no means the sole reason for the relatively high levels of party fragmentation that have characterised them since their inception.

[2] As Annex 1 shows, if we look at long-term opinion poll evidence, support for the governing party fell gradually but consistently from the late 1940s through to 2016, regardless of which party was in power. A simple trend function suggests that governing parties in the 2010s were on average 15 percentage points less popular than their counterparts in the late 1940s and early 1950s.

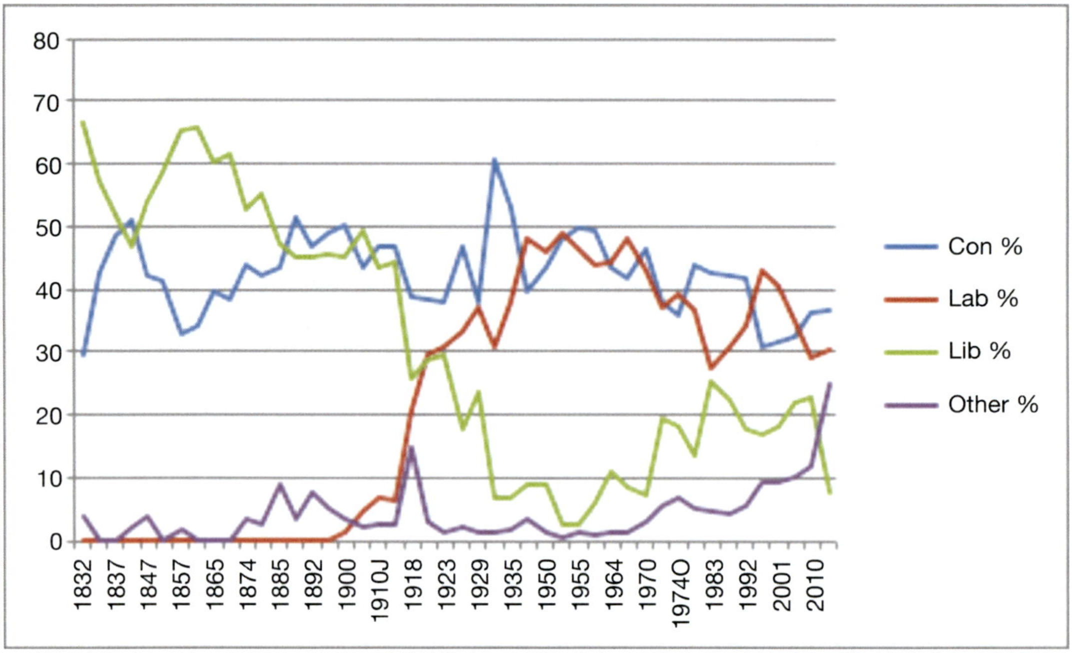

Figure 1. Conservative, Labour, Liberal (Democrat) and Other Parties' vote shares in general elections, 1832–2015.
Source: Butler & Butler (2011) and, for 2015, www.bbc.co.uk/news/election/2015/results.

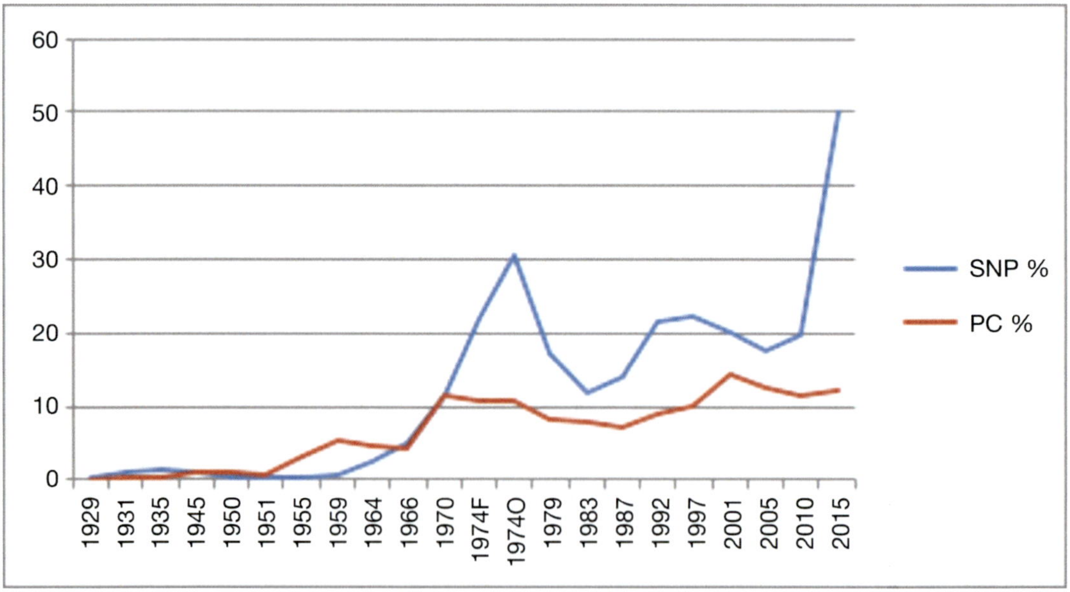

Figure 2. Scottish National Party (SNP) vote share in Scotland and Plaid Cymru (PC) vote share in Wales in UK general elections, 1929–2016.
Source: see Figure 1.

Devolved assemblies

Figures 3–5 show the changing vote share patterns for the three UK devolved assemblies after 1998. In all three cases, given that roughly half the seats were awarded on the basis of parties' vote shares for regional lists, votes were from the outset relatively evenly distributed across four or more parties. The devolved assemblies, in short, have consistently been characterised by multiparty systems. In Scotland in 1999, as Figure 3 shows, Labour, the SNP, the Conservatives, Liberal Democrats and even 'Others' secured substantial shares of the vote. This pattern continued through 2003 and 2007, though by 2011 the SNP had achieved a clear dominance, which was reinforced even more strongly in 2016. An analogous position is described in Figure 4, which presents equivalent data for Wales. In 1999, four parties obtained substantial votes shares, though Labour and Plaid Cymru were in a sufficiently strong position to suggest that a two-party system could develop. In fact, by 2003, PC had lost support to such an extent that Labour was clearly the dominant party, a position that it broadly maintained through to 2016. The growth of UKIP, however, meant that by 2016 votes for the Welsh Assembly were distributed across five parties—each with Assembly representation. Finally, Figure 5 summarises the position in Northern

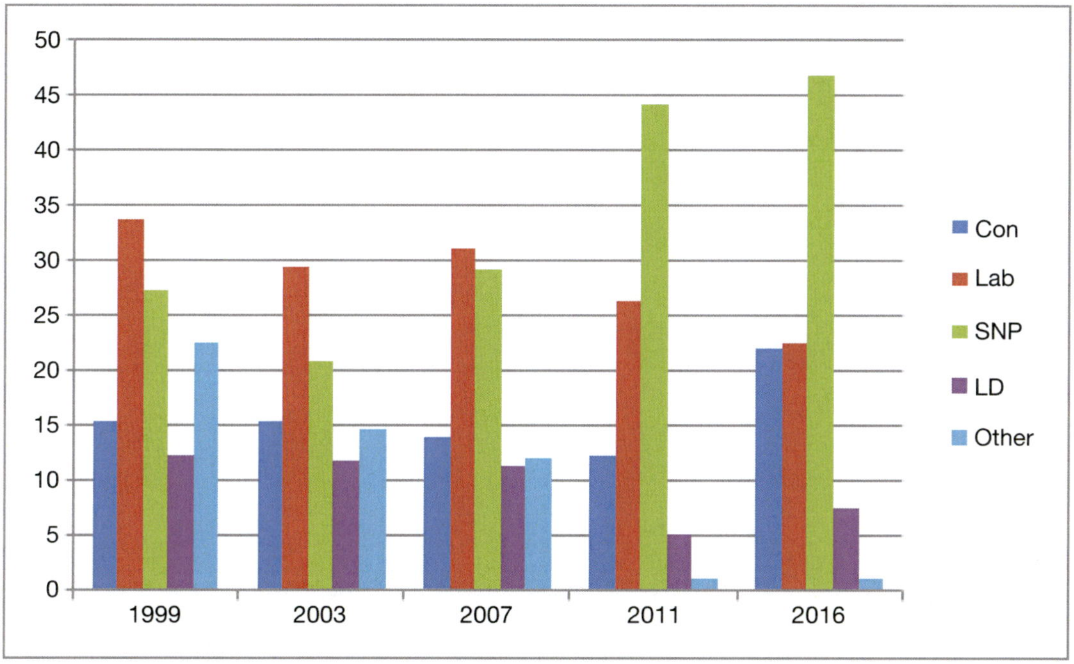

Figure 3. Party vote shares (List Vote) in Scottish Parliament elections, 1999–2016.
Source: https://en.wikipedia.org/wiki/Scottish_Parliament_election

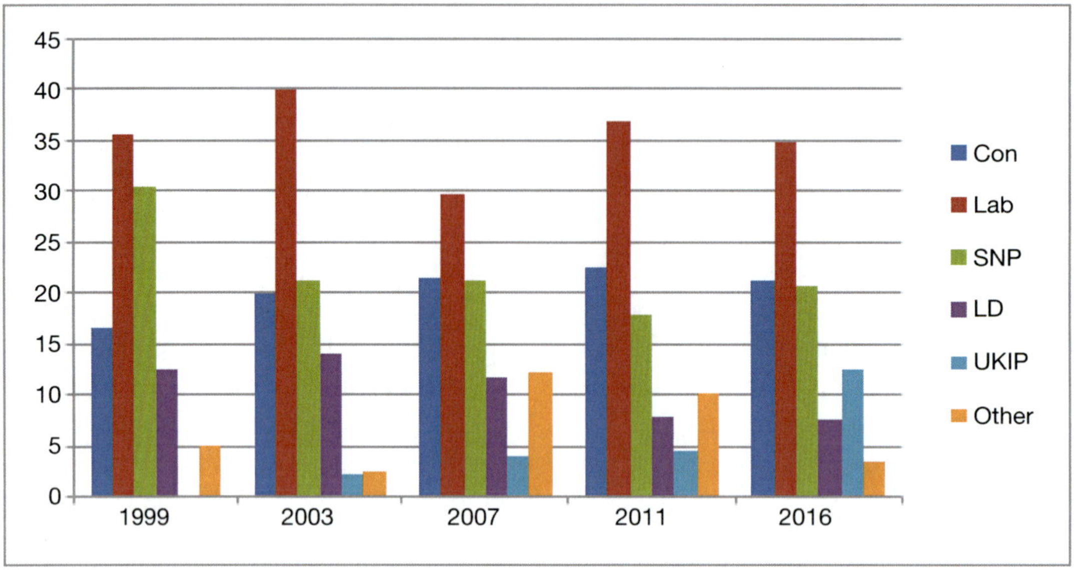

Figure 4. Party vote shares (List Vote) in Welsh Assembly elections, 1999–2016.
Source: https://en.wikipedia.org/wiki/National_Assembly_for_Wales_election

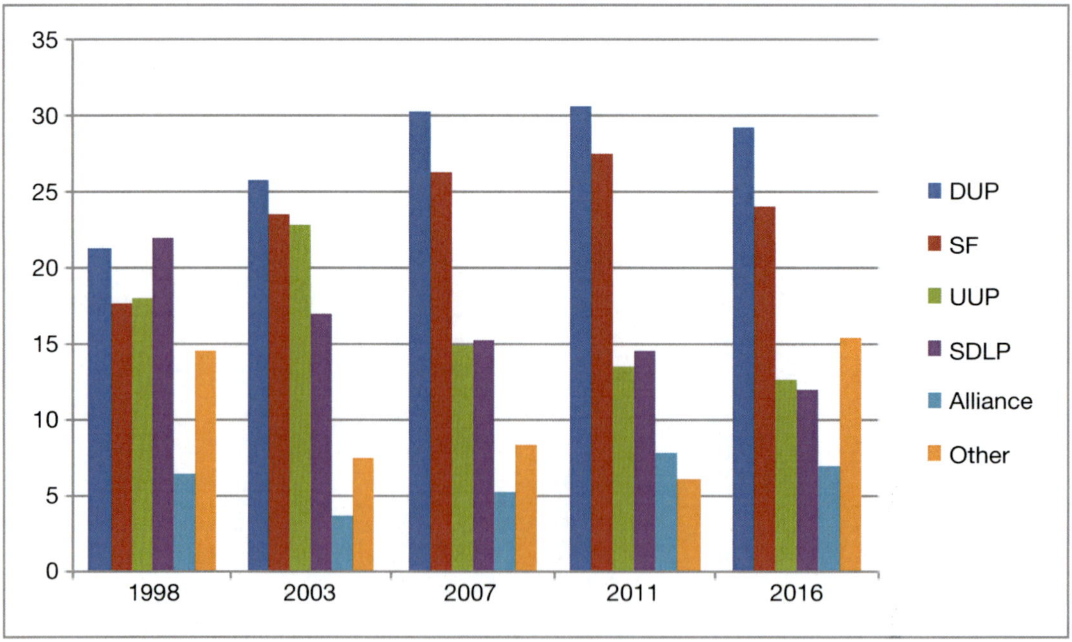

Figure 5. Party vote shares (List Vote) in Northern Ireland Assembly elections, 1998–2016.
Source: https://en.wikipedia.org/wiki/Elections_in_Northern_Ireland

Ireland Assembly elections since 1998. From the beginning, voting for the NI Assembly followed a very clear multiparty vote pattern, with votes distributed across five parties plus 'Others'. By 2007, this had transmuted into a system in which, though still involving substantial voting for multiple parties, the Democratic Unionist Party (DUP) and Sinn Fein had established themselves as the two dominant parties—though on only one occasion (the DUP in 2011) did either of them secure over 30 per cent of the popular (list) vote.

Local councils

As an illustration of the changing levels of fragmentation in UK local authority voting, Figure 6 reports the year-by-year variations in the number of major UK city councils (out of a total of 22 councils whose boundaries and status remained broadly stable over the 1945–2016 period) in which there was No Overall Control (NOC) by a single party or formal coalition of parties. The NOC characterisation is obviously an imperfect measure of voting fragmentation, but it does give a general indication of the extent to which the Conservative and Labour parties fail to perform effectively in local elections: a higher incidence of NOC, in short, reflects a higher level of local vote

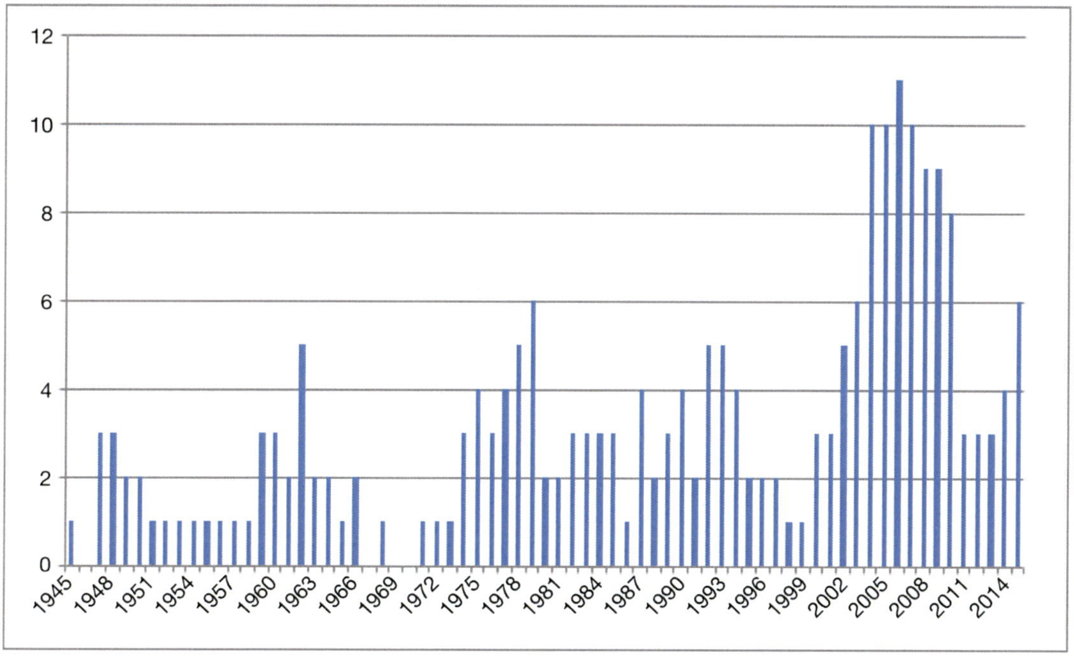

Figure 6. Number of major UK cities with No Overall Control, 1945–2016 ($N = 22$).
Source: See Figure 1. I am grateful to Colin Rallings and Michael Thrasher of the Elections Centre, University of Plymouth who supplied the data for the period 2010–15.

fragmentation. Viewed in this light, Figure 6 shows that NOC is by no means a new phenomenon. Its incidence grew slowly in the 1970s and 1980s and increased markedly after 2000, with half of the 22 councils in the sample group experiencing NOC in 2006. As with Westminster voting, a constant set of electoral rules based on FPTP, is capable of producing some degree of voting fragmentation, notwithstanding Duverger's Law.

Vote shares, seat shares and disproportionality

The evidence reported in Figures 1–6 shows that *voting fragmentation* has been a feature of UK representative democracy to varying degrees both over time and at the three levels reviewed. Party systems, however, are defined not just by *voting* patterns in any one series of elections, but also by the *distribution of seats* that result from the way votes are cast. As noted earlier, FPTP is less likely than electoral rules based on some form of Proportional Representation accurately to translate vote shares into seat shares. Typically, FPTP gives the winning party a parliamentary majority to govern only at the cost of depriving 'minor' parties of a 'fair' share of parliamentary seats. Analysts have devised a number of different measures of vote share/seat share disproportionality. Most measures focus on the idea of the Effective Number of Parties.[3] For any given parliament, this Effective Number can be calculated for the distributions of both vote shares and seat shares: the gap between the two is one way of summarising any vote/seat disproportionality.[4] Figure 7 shows the gap between the Effective Number of Parties (ENP) in terms of votes and seats at *Westminster* since 1900. Since 1918, the ENP in terms of votes has been higher than the ENP in terms of seats. The gap narrowed briefly in the early 1950s, but since then it has been growing progressively so that by 2015 electors votes were spread across 3.9 Effective Parties whereas House of Commons seats were distributed to 2.5 Effective Parties. This considerable gap to a large extent reflects the way in which the FPTP virtuous circle still benefits Labour and the Conservatives as the two 'major' competing parties, even though the electorate has increasingly and repeatedly signalled its overall collective preference for a multiparty system.

It is well beyond the scope of this paper to analyse the extent to which UK *local authority* elections have historically produced a gap between ENP-votes and ENP-seats: this would involve a massive exercise in data collection and analysis that might

[3] The Effective Number of Parties is defined as $N = 1/\Sigma(P_i^2)$, where P_i is the proportion of seats (or votes) obtained by each party in the parliament. (See Laakso & Taagepera 1979.)

[4] There are other more technical ways of calculating disproportionality. A common method is the Gallaher (1991) Disproportionality Index which takes into account the differences between each party's vote share and its seat share. On this measure, disproportionality at Westminster stood at 15.0 in 2015, compared with a European average of 6.5 for the period 2011–15.

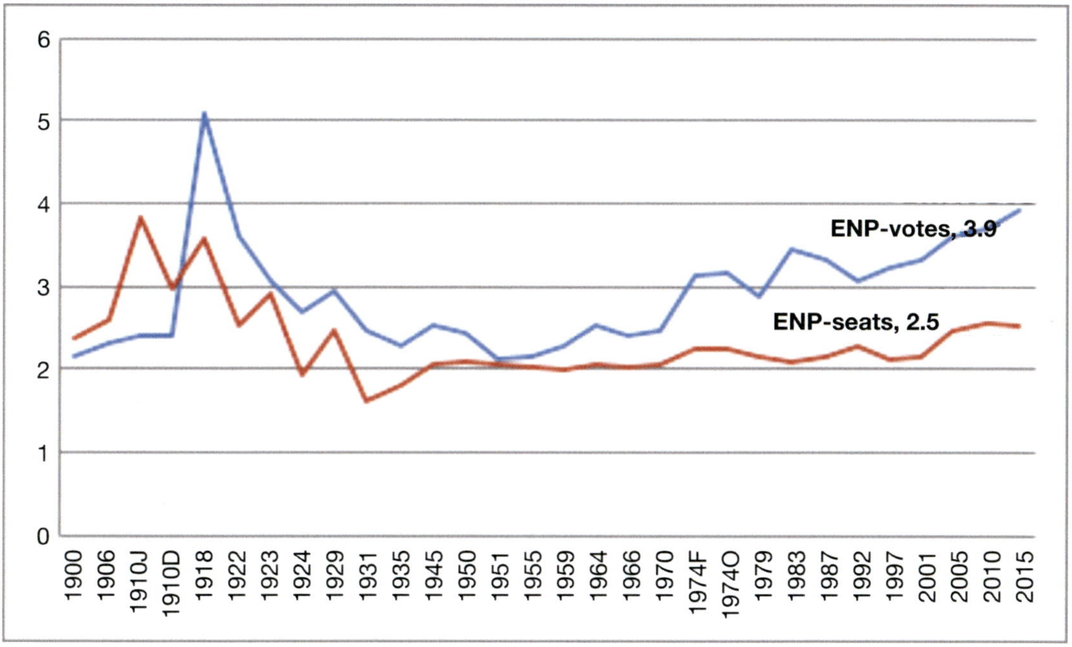

Figure 7. Effective Number of Parties in terms of votes and seats, UK 1900–2015.
Source: http://www.tcd.ie/Political_Science/staff/michael_gallagher/ElSystems/ and own calculations from sources cited in Figure 1.

well reveal nothing particularly interesting beyond an obvious parallel with what has been happening at Westminster since 1918. However, as far as the *devolved assemblies* are concerned, a similar set of calculations to those reported in Figure 7 can be undertaken for the relatively short period since 1998. Table 1 summarises the results of these calculations. The ENP-votes scores are all higher than in the Westminster parliament—as would be expected given that half the seats in the devolved assemblies are allocated by PR. However, as Table 1 shows, in all three contexts the ENP-*seats* scores are lower than their equivalent ENP-*votes* scores, implying that there is a degree of disproportionality even in the three devolved assemblies. In short, even in these assemblies the continuing FPTP component of the electoral rules constrains the representation of more peripheral parties, thereby reducing the degree of multipartism that would be expected purely on the basis of way people cast their votes.

Table 1. Effective Number of Parties (ENP) in terms of votes and seats and Gallaher Disproportionality Index measures; devolved assembly averages, 1998–2016.

	ENP-votes	ENP-seats	Gap votes–seats	Gallaher Index
Northern Ireland average, 1998–2016	5.11	4.54	0.57	3.61
Scotland average, 1999–2016	4.27	3.32	1.05	7.00
Wales average, 1999–2016	4.40	3.07	1.33	10.36

Source: Own calculations based on data, as in Figures 3–5.

The broad conclusions suggested by the foregoing discussion are straightforward. Notwithstanding Britain's tradition of First-Past-the-Post elections, the UK has been moving slowly towards a more fragmented, multiparty system since the 1950s. The process of fragmentation has been gradual and punctuated by brief periods of above-trend advance, but it has been inexorable. Voters have gradually been deserting the two major parties, even though the constraints of FPTP and its associated disproportionate translation of votes into seats have inhibited third-party (and fourth- and fifth-party) success. The explicit provision for regional list votes as a complement to FPTP in the devolved assemblies in Scotland, Wales and Northern Ireland has reduced (though not eliminated) disproportionality in these assemblies. Moreover, in Scotland and Wales, national assembly voting (as with European Parliament voting, which was based on PR regional lists from 1993) has almost certainly affected subsequent voting in Westminster elections. It has broken old habits and allowed some voters to support parties they previously considered marginal: Labour was almost a certainly a victim of this tendency in Scotland in the 2015 general election. Devolution, in short, has probably accelerated the movement towards multipartism in the Westminster parliament—even though FPTP still acts as a source of disproportionality by constraining the Effective Number of Parties in terms of *seats*.

WHAT EXPLAINS THE INCREASING FRAGMENTATION OF THE UK PARTY SYSTEM AND THE DECLINE OF SUPPORT FOR LABOUR AND THE CONSERVATIVES?

It is by no means a simple matter systematically to assess the factors that have undercut the 'virtuous circle' of the post-war two-party system. This is partly because the necessary data for evaluating the various possible explanations for vote (and, to a lesser extent, seat) fragmentation are unavailable and partly because of the statistical difficulty of estimating causal effects among variables that are potentially reciprocally related. With these constraints in mind, I offer an analysis that is speculative but 'consistent with the available evidence', rather than one that rigorously tests a more limited set of precise explanatory claims.

I begin with what I described earlier as the 'unmeasurable' factors. These are 'unmeasurable' in two senses—in terms of being able (a) accurately to measure how they have changed over the period since the post-war two-party system began to fragment in the 1950s and, consequently, (b) to assess their effects on the fragmentation process itself. There are arguably five main 'unmeasurables' that have contributed to party fragmentation.[5] The first is cultural—the *decline of deference*, the reduced preparedness of mass publics to defer to the wisdom, judgement and authority of elites. There has obviously always been a disposition among some sections of the public to challenge the status quo. It is nonetheless clear from World Values Surveys (WVS) conducted since 1980 that deference as a general characteristic is much less prevalent, both in the UK and elsewhere in the developed world, than it was in the immediate post-war years. The key evidence in this context relates to the levels of deference shown by different cohorts of WVS respondents: the younger the cohort, the lower the level of deference displayed. For example, those born after 1951 exhibit deference levels roughly half the levels shown by those born between 1921 and 1930 (Nevitte 2011). It is difficult to demonstrate that this general decline in deference has a direct impact on popular disaffection with the main parties of government, but it seems likely that it has played some sort of indirect role in increasing people's doubts about the wisdom of the actions of successive (Labour and Conservative) governments.

A second possible 'unmeasurable' factor underpinning party fragmentation relates to the *rise of 'alternative' identities*. Gilbert and Sullivan's Private Willis from *Iolanthe* is often quoted to exemplify the late-19th-century orthodoxy about the importance and ubiquity of *party* identity:

> How Nature always does contrive …
> That every boy and every gal
> That's born into the world alive
> Is either a little Liberal
> Or else a little Conservative!

By the late 1930s, of course, Labour had substituted for the Liberals in popular affections. However, as demonstrated below, party identifications have declined significantly since the early 1960s. They have been variously supplemented and replaced by a proliferation of new political and quasi-political identities—by Scottish and Welsh identities in those two countries, by ethnic and religious identities among

[5] Inevitably, I have omitted several factors that others might consider important here. For example, much has been made in the academic literature of the idea that the New Labour project alienated Labour's traditional working-class base and that this in turn weakened long-term working-class identification with Labour. There is certainly something in this idea. However, if it had simply been the New Labour policy platform that alienated Labour's working-class base under Tony Blair and Gordon Brown, one would have expected their departure and the abandonment of New Labour after 2010 to have restored Labour's working-class support. Voting patterns in the 2015 general election show clearly that it did not. (See Table 2 and Figure 10.) I can only plead that space constraints necessarily limit what can be presented here and leave it to the reader to add her/his own 'unmeasurables' to the list suggested.

the UK's growing ethnic minority population (Heath *et al.* 2013), and even for some by European identity (Isernia *et al.* 2012). The difficulty with trying to assess the changing importance of these 'new' identities is that there are no reliable baseline data extending back in time that might enable any changes in identity patterns to be measured and assessed. This means that although we know that these identities are important (especially national identities in Scotland and Wales) in determining party choices now, it is not possible assess how far they have driven out old party identities and therefore contributed to party fragmentation.[6]

A third 'unmeasurable' source of fragmentation is the *increased level of traditional media criticism* of politicians, which has in turn increased popular disillusion with professional politicians and established parties. It is easy to assert this proposition but far more difficult to demonstrate it. Nonetheless, we are all familiar with the more confrontational style of political interviewing on radio and television that has developed in the UK over the last three decades or so. And *The Daily Telegraph* and other newspapers have seemed to regard it almost as a duty in recent years to expose the peccadillos and errors of judgement made by politicians of all parties at every opportunity—a development that for many observers has contributed to the increasing lack of trust that voters have in politics and politicians (see for example, Whiteley *et al.* 2013). Although it is very difficult to establish empirically either the extent to which these changes have occurred and whether or not they have affected fragmentation, it would be unwise to conclude that they have had no effect.

A similar conclusion is suggested with regard to a fourth possible source of party fragmentation: the *rise and rise of social media conversations* and exchanges. Analysts are only starting to get a proper handle on how to measure and assess these exchanges, but it seems clear from anecdotal evidence that most of them involve participants listening and talking to people largely like themselves. The low transactions costs of social media interactions mean that it is relatively easy to form ever-smaller, more specialised political groupings in which the like-minded converse. This clearly makes it easier for 'groupthink' mechanisms to operate and for participants to reinforce each other in their views and to convince themselves that those views (since they are rarely contradicted) are widely shared. Again, it is difficult to assess either the extent of such social media conversations or to show that they connected to party fragmentation—

[6] Available British Social Attitudes time-series data on national identity in Scotland suggest that Scottish identity increased from around 58 per cent in 1979 to just over 70 per cent in 1992, since when it has remained more or less constant. (See http://www.bsa.natcen.ac.uk/latest-report/british-social-attitudes-30/devolution/trends-in-national-identity.aspx). Welsh identity in Wales fell from around 65 per cent in 2001 to 60 per cent in 2011. (See David Owen, 'Variations in National Identity, Diversity and Integration within the UK', https://www2.warwick.ac.uk/fac/soc/ier/people/dowen/20150715_d_owen.pptx).

but it seems likely that they have helped to reinforce the fragmentation process in the relatively recent past and that they will continue to be of relevance in the future.

The final 'unmeasurable' factor underpinning fragmentation concerns the *unintended consequences of elite decisions*. It is all but impossible to demonstrate the connections between specific decisions and such a generalised long-term process as party fragmentation. In my view, however, there are three identifiable decisions that have had—and will continue to have—important consequences for the unity and character of the Labour and Conservative parties, and which have therefore compounded the tendencies towards party fragmentation that were already underway. The first was the Blair government's decision to establish the Scottish Parliament from 1999. Blair's aim in devolving power was to preserve the union between Scotland and the rest of the UK by making modest concessions to Scottish demands for increased decision-making autonomy. At the same time, Blair introduced part-PR electoral arrangements that would minimise the chances of an SNP-led Scottish government (since all the other parties were pro-union), thereby making it difficult for the SNP to build further momentum for its core cause of independence. In the event, of course, Blair's plans rapidly went awry. In May 2007, the first SNP minority administration took office in Holyrood. It was so successful that it was elected with a majority in 2011. The knock-on consequence of the SNP's domestic success, even in the wake of an unsuccessful referendum in 2014, was that the party annihilated Labour in Scotland in the 2015 Westminster elections. To the delight of all lovers of irony, Labour's Scotland strategy had had the very opposite effect of what was intended—and party fragmentation at Westminster had been reinforced.

The second elite decision that increased the tendency towards party fragmentation at Westminster was Ed Miliband's reform of Labour leader-election rules in March 2014. John Smith had introduced One Member One Vote (OMOV) in September 1993, but the voting power of party activists had been curbed by the continuing existence of an electoral college in which MPs, MEPs and trade unions were also represented. Miliband's reforms introduced genuine OMOV and these operated for the first time in July 2015, following his resignation after the 2015 election defeat. The empowerment of the grass roots activists that this implied, combined with Labour MPs' decision to include Jeremy Corbyn as one of the balloted candidates for leader, produced an overwhelming victory for Corbyn as the representative of the party's radical left (a victory that was confirmed in a second ballot in October 2016). The unintended consequence of this concatenation of rule change and nomination naivety plunged Labour into a crisis over whether Labour should be an activist-driven campaigning party that articulates a radical voice for the dispossessed or a realistically aspirant party of government that, in office, could genuinely improve the lives of 'ordinary working people'. Corbyn's victory has given many Labour activists the voice and policies they have always wanted. But it has distanced the party from both the median voter and traditional Labour voters and left large numbers of Labour MPs wondering how on earth the party can ever recover electorally. As I will discuss in the final section, there is an opportunity here for a new centre-ground political force in the UK, if enough Labour MPs can convince themselves that the need for politicians to take practical action which improves ordinary people's lives is more important than notions of party loyalty and betrayal.

The third elite decision worth mentioning is David Cameron's decision, in the run-up to the 2015 general election, to promise an 'in/out' referendum on Britain's EU membership by 2017. Cameron clearly expected that he would be able to negotiate a deal (on improved membership terms for the UK) with the UK's EU partners that would be acceptable to the UK public, and that he would accordingly win any such referendum. His failure to understand the risks he was running or to campaign effectively for the deal he had secured resulted in his rapid political demise and his replacement by a Conservative government that seems bent on both a 'hard Brexit' and on moving the Conservatives firmly to the authoritarian right. The centre of gravity of the Conservative Party under Theresa May has shifted towards an anti-Europeanist, anti-immigrant, anti-human-rights stance that leaves the pro-EU social liberals, who formed the vanguard of the party under Cameron, very isolated. As with Labour's centrists, Tory centrists have an opportunity to defect from a party with which they no longer have very much in common. Again, this is an issue to which I return in the final section.

The factors outlined above offer an incomplete and largely anecdotal account of why party fragmentation has increased in Britain in recent decades. There are two further (measurable) factors, however, where more specific corroborating evidence can be provided. Yet even here, the corroboration is limited in the sense that these measurable factors all suffer from a potential 'endogeneity' problem (a problem, incidentally, that besets large swathes of social science research)—that is, they are all subject to the potential criticism that they are the *consequence* of declining support for the two main parties, rather than its *cause*. Given that the necessary data for resolving this sort of endogeneity problem are not available, I simply hypothesise that these two measurables do indeed underpin the fragmentation process and then examine the data to determine whether or not they are consistent with such a claim.

The decline of party identification

Party identification (or PID) is one of the most commonly used concepts in the explanation of voting patterns. It can be characterised in various ways, but in essence constitutes an individual's long-term predisposition to support one party rather than another—though such predispositions can change over time (Clarke *et al.* 2004). Analyses of PID typically differentiate among Very Strong, Fairly Strong and Not Very Strong Identifiers, all of whom are distinguished from No Party Identifiers. Identifying with a party is not a guarantee that an individual will support it, but Very Strong Identification with a party is a powerful indication that an individual will indeed vote for it at the next election. Equally, having No Party Identification generally signifies that an individual's vote is 'up for grabs' at any given election—that vote choices will be affected more by perceptions of leadership qualities, evaluations of policy platforms, and assessments of the likely managerial competencies of the rival leadership teams.

Figure 8 shows the aggregate changes in strength of party identification between 1964 (when PID was first systematically measured in the UK) and 2015. Fairly Strong Identifiers remain broadly constant at around 40 per cent of voters. Not Very Strong Identifiers—the least committed identifiers—increase from around 10 per cent to about 23 per cent. However, Very Strong Identifiers decline from 45 per cent of voters in 1964 to 15 per cent in 2015. And crucially, people with No Party Identification have increased from 5 per cent of the electorate to over 20 per cent. Figure 9 presents the data in a slightly different form, showing how PID strength has fallen for the two

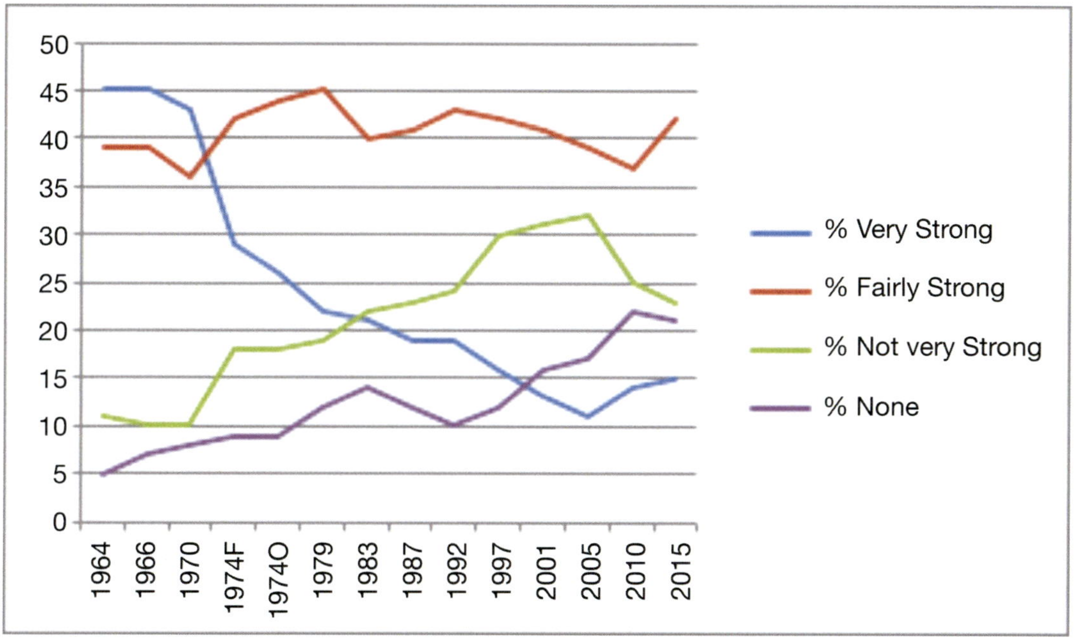

Figure 8. Percentage of Very Strong, Fairly Strong, Not Very Strong and No Party Identifiers, 1964–2015.
Source: British Election Study (BES) cross-section surveys, 1964–2015.

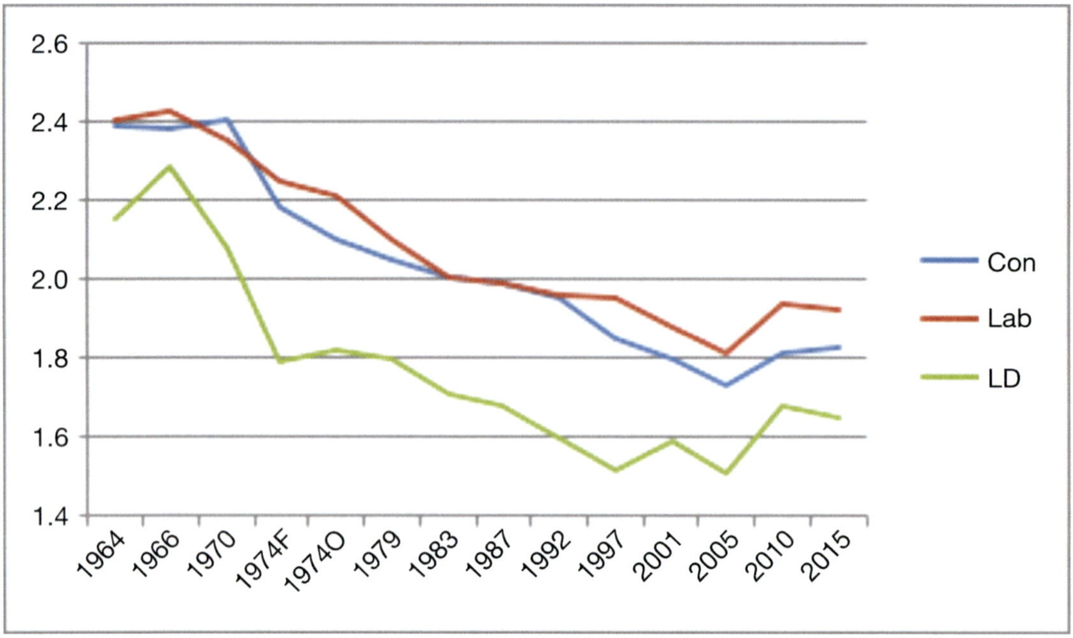

Figure 9. Strength of party identification with Conservative, Labour and Liberal Democrat parties, 1964–2015.

Source: BES cross-section surveys, 1964–2015. The index figures reported are calculated as averages of individual scores where Very Strong Identification with a party scores 3; Fairly Strong scores 2; Not Very Strong scores 1; and No Identification scores 0.

major parties and for the Liberal Democrats since 1964. For simplicity of presentation, the strength measures are presented in index form. The two figures tell the same story, however. Together, they show conclusively that voters have become progressively less committed to the main established political parties in the half century since 1964. It is hardly surprising in these circumstances that they have been prepared to vote for a wider range of newer, alternative parties—they have behaved more like discriminating consumers than committed partisans—thus contributing to the Westminster vote and seat fragmentation described in the previous section.

The decline of class-based voting

A second measurable factor that has contributed to party fragmentation in Westminster voting is the decline of social class as a source of voting choice. Traditionally, people from manual working-class families disproportionately supported Labour whilst non-manual middle-class voters disproportionately supported the Conservatives. Table 2 displays the relationship between vote and social class in 1964, and again in

Table 2. Class voting in the 1964 and 2015 general elections.

	Non-manual middle class	Manual working class
1964		
Conservative	62 (a)	28 (b)
Labour	22 (c)	64 (d)
Other	16	8
Class Consistency Index	76	
2015		
Conservative	43	33
Labour	31	33
Other	26	34
Class Consistency Index	12	

Source: BES cross-sections, 1964 and 2015. Column percentages reported. Class Consistency Index is measured as (a − b) + (d − c) [theoretical range 0–200].

2015.[7] The contrast between the two elections could not be clearer. In 1964, just under two thirds of middle-class voters supported the Conservatives and a similar proportion of working-class voters supported Labour: there was a very clear relationship between class and vote. By 2015, the class–vote nexus had weakened considerably. While the Conservatives garnered slightly more middle-class votes (43 per cent) than working-class ones (33 per cent), Labour's support was almost the same among the middle class (31 per cent) as it was among the manual working class (33 per cent). Class-based voting in fact declined progressively after 1964. Figure 10 reports a simple 'Class-Vote Consistency Index that can be calculated, for every general election since 1964, from tables analogous to those shown in Table 2. The data for 2016 relate to voting intentions rather than reported vote. As the figure shows, class has all but disappeared as a factor in vote choice.

The mechanism through which declining class-voting contributes to party fragmentation is simple. Parties with a clear class base, of the sort enjoyed by Labour and the Conservatives from the 1930s to the 1960s, find it relatively easy to garner votes from that class demographic. But a third-party challenger has to position itself to attract working-class votes from Labour and/or middle-class votes from the

[7] Although there are various ways of measuring class voting, the one used here is the most straightforward and allows for the longest over-time comparisons. Because this measure necessarily falls when the combined support for Labour and the Conservatives falls, it has been suggested that the rise of UKIP (which tends to garner more working-class than middle-class support) could mean that this simple measure under-estimates current class-based voting. Strictly, this is correct, though the effect is in fact very small. In the 2016 YouGov survey cited in Tables 5–8, UKIP derived 60 per cent of its support from working-class respondents and 40 per cent from the middle class. Given that UKIP voters constituted less than 11 per cent of the UK sample, the UKIP support pattern adds very little to the overall level of class voting in 2016 that is indicated in Figure 10.

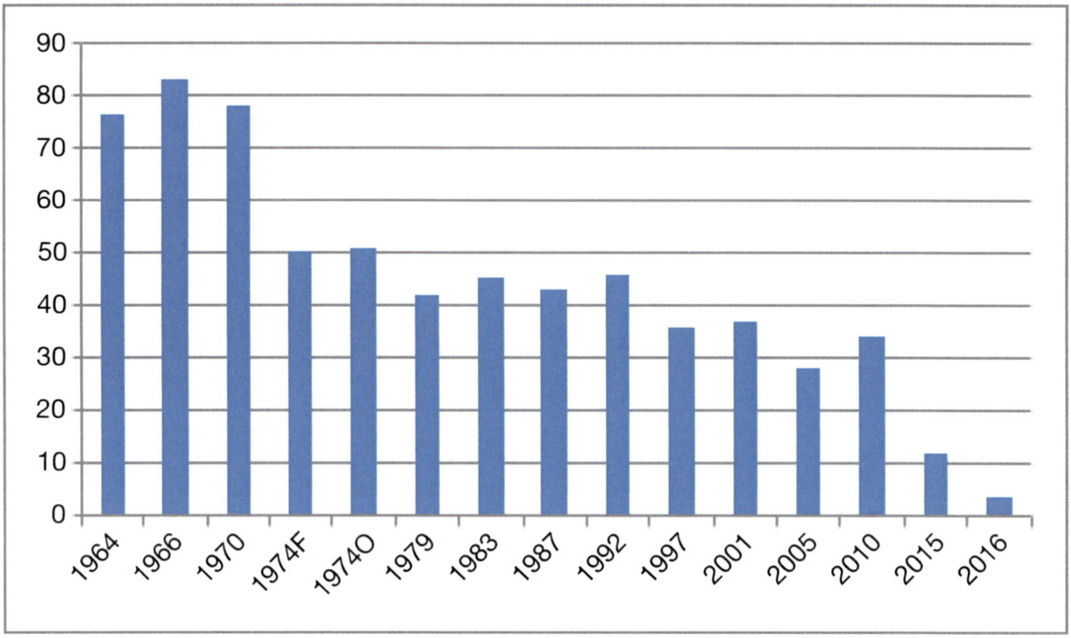

Figure 10. Class-Vote Consistency Index, 1964–2016.
Source: BES cross-sectional surveys 1964–2015; YouGov, 12-Nation Authoritarian Populism Survey October 2016. Index calculated as shown in Table 2. [Theoretical maximum score is 200; minimum is 0].

Conservatives. This is an extraordinarily difficult task to accomplish in constituencies of different types given that it is important to convey a consistent national-level campaigning message in order to present an image of policy and managerial competence. As class-based voting weakens, however, not only do the original class-based parties have to make new non-class appeals to attract support, but third parties too have an equal opportunity to make non-class appeals. In fact, as class-based voting declines, all parties increasingly have to engage in what Riker (1986) termed heresthetics—the conscious effort to focus political debates and divisions on 'new' issue dimensions or cleavages that are conducive to their own interests. The SNP, for example, has been outstandingly successful on restructuring political debate in Scotland around Scottish interests and which party is best placed to advance them. The decline of class as the basis of the vote has simply created more opportunities for newer parties to frame issues and mobilise support on a more level playing field than previously—though FPTP still represents a constraining influence by restricting the 'fair' translation of national vote share into Westminster seats (for all but the SNP).

The implication of the foregoing discussion is that the long-term declines of party identification and class-voting have both played roles in the growing fragmentation of Westminster voting. Tables 3 and 4 test this proposition. Table 3 shows the correlations, across the 14 elections 1964–2015, between (a) changes in vote fragmentation and (b) changes in party identification and class-voting. PID is measured as the percentage of the electorate with No Party Identification; class-voting is measured using the Class-Vote Consistency Index outlined above.[8] The table shows, as expected, that fragmentation is positively correlated with the proportion of the electorate with No Party Identification (r = 0.89: as the proportion of non-identifiers has increased, fragmentation has increased)) and negatively correlated with Class-Vote (r = −0.93: as class-voting has declined, fragmentation has risen).

Table 4 reports two simple multivariate models of vote fragmentation, 1964–2015. This table is included to establish that the declines in party identification and class-voting exert simultaneous, independent effects on party fragmentation. The left-hand segment of Table 4 presents an Ordinary Least Squares (OLS) model which suggests that both No Party Identification (b = 0.032) and Class-Vote (b = −0.014) exert statistically significant effects on fragmentation: fragmentation increases as the percentage of non-identifiers rises and as class-voting falls. However, inspection of the OLS model's residuals indicated that they are generated by a second-order autoregressive

Table 3. Correlations between (a) Effective Number of Parties-votes and (b) No Party Identification and Class-Vote.

	Fragmentation: Effective Number of Parties-votes
Per cent No Party Identification	+0.89
Class-Vote Consistency Index	−0.93

N = 14 (cases are general elections 1964–2015).
Source: Own calculations.

Table 4. Models of party fragmentation (Effective Number of Parties-votes), 1964–2015, OLS and autoregressive specifications

	OLS model			AR(2) model		
	Coeff.	St. Err.	Sig.	Coeff.	St. Err.	Sig.
Per cent No Party Identification	0.032	0.016	0.064	0.031	0.016	0.013
Class-Vote Consistency Index score	−0.014	0.004	0.004	−0.015	0.003	0.000
Constant	3.430	0.374	0.000	3.450	0.254	0.000
U_{t-1}				−0.509		0.054
U_{t-2}				−0.510		0.054
Corrected R^2	0.887			0.917		
Durbin–Watson	2.684			2.350		

Dependent variable is Effective Number of Parties-votes. Sample: General Election Events 1964–2015. N = 14.

[8] The raw data are presented in Annex 2.

process or AR(2). This violates the standard assumption of a random error term. The right-hand segment of Table 4 accordingly re-estimates the model as an AR(2). The results show that No Party Identification and Class-Vote continue to be statistically significant and correctly signed. With only 14 cases in this sort of time-series, it is risky to set too much store by statistical modelling of these relationships. However, the results are certainly consistent with the claim that the upward trend in fragmentation is significantly affected by the downward trends in PID and class-voting since 1964. This is not to say the 'unmeasurable' factors mentioned earlier are not also important—merely that their effects cannot readily be assessed empirically, even in the imperfect manner described in Tables 3 and 4.[9]

BRITAIN'S CURRENT POLITICAL TRIBES AND THE POTENTIAL FOR A PARTY-SYSTEM RE-ALIGNMENT

The referendum on the UK's membership of the European Union held in June 2016 highlighted the growing appeal of Authoritarian Populism (AP) among the British public. Indeed, since UKIP's emergence as an electoral force after the 2010 general election (and particularly after its performance in the May 2014 European Parliament elections), it has been clear that the politicisation and mobilisation of Authoritarian Populist sentiments have become an increasingly important feature of the UK political landscape. This is not to say that voting for extreme right-wing parties, or voting for UKIP, provides a simple measure of the extent of the electorate's AP thinking. Rather, AP is best viewed as a constellation of five sets of attitudes that relate to: the individual's position on the left–right ideological spectrum; cynicism about the importance and desirability of protecting human rights; concern about and opposition to immigration (an issue, at least until recently, consistently underplayed by successive governments); opposition to the EU; and strong support for a robust national defence and foreign policy (see Sanders *et al.* 2016). Adherence to this AP attitude set does not mean that the individuals involved will necessarily vote for Authoritarian Populist parties. However, their attitudinal dispositions mean that, given appropriate conditions and rhetoric, they are available for mobilisation by such parties in the future.

Table 5 reports the results of an exploratory factor analysis on five measures of AP attitudes. The results show clearly that a single dimension underlies the five measures. An alpha-scale test for uni-dimensionality among the same variable set

[9] Table A2 in Annex 2 takes the issue of causal direction a little further by regressing vote fragmentation on lagged values of PID and Class-Vote; and vice versa. The results are consistent with the conclusion that PID and Class-Vote are not endogenous to fragmentation.

Table 5. Exploratory factor analysis of five indicators of Authoritarian Populism, 2016.

Component variable	Range	Loading	Uniqueness
Left–Right Self-Placement	0–10	0.59	0.65
Britain Strong and Tough	0–1	0.54	0.71
Negative Immigration Emotions	0–4	0.67	0.54
Critical of Human Rights	1–5	0.73	0.47
Disapproval of European Union	1–5	0.73	0.47

Eigenvalue factor 1 = 2.15; eigenvalue factor 2 = 0.02. N = 1265. For precise variable definitions see Annex 4.
Source: YouGov 12-Nation Authoritarian Populism Survey, October 2016.

yields α = 0.75 (above the standard 0.7 cut-off), suggesting that the five measures do indeed form an Authoritarian Populist scale on which any given individual can be located. Analyses of the consequences of AP, not reported here, show that net of the effects of other key predictors, AP attitudes have powerful effects on Westminster voting intention, EU referendum vote and democracy satisfaction.

The same AP measures can also be analysed using cluster analysis, to establish whether there are groupings of individuals who constitute distinctive attitudinal types. It is not a simple task to decide how many clusters to estimate for any given set of variables and individuals. For the purposes of analysis here, 2-, 3-, 4- and 5-cluster solutions were estimated. The details are provided in Annex 3, which also provides a non-technical interpretation of the cluster analyses conducted here. The results in Annex 3 show that the 2-cluster solution fails to distinguish between two sorts of Authoritarian Populists—those in the centre of the political spectrum and those on the far right. Similarly, the 3-cluster solution fails to differentiate between centrist Authoritarian Populists and centre-right liberals. The 5-cluster solution, in contrast, identifies one cluster that contains only 12 (1 per cent) of the 1265 respondents sampled—a sure sign that this grouping is insufficiently important to merit serious consideration as a distinct 'type'.

As Table 6 indicates, however, the 4-cluster solution tells a compelling story about the UK's new political tribes, and their relative sizes, in an era of renewed authoritarian populism. Note that this story reveals a subtlety about contemporary British political attitudes that would not be evident if only left–right ideology were considered. The table reports the mean scores on each of the five AP measures for each of the four clusters. With minor exceptions, the mean scores on each AP component measure increase as we move down the table from *Liberal Internationalist Pro-EU Left* to *Authoritarian Populist Right*. (For example, the mean Critical of Human Rights score increases progressively from 2.08 to 3.83 as we move down the table.) The only major exception—and this is where the importance of considering more than just left–right ideology is borne out—relates to the mean left–right scale score for the *Liberal Pro-EU Centre-Right* (6.28)—which is significantly higher than the equivalent

Table 6. The UK electorate's four political tribes: four-cluster solution.

Cluster	Britain Strong and Tough	Disapproval of European Union	Critical of Human Rights	Negative Immigration Emotions	Left–Right Self-Placement	Per cent
Liberal Internationalist Pro-EU Left	0.10	1.79	2.08	0.31	3.07	37
Liberal Pro-EU Centre-Right	0.26	1.77	2.84	0.68	6.28	15
Authoritarian Populist Centre	0.44	4.36	3.65	1.72	5.02	29
Authoritarian Populist Right	0.53	4.46	3.83	1.71	7.79	19
Average (range)	0.30 (0–1)	2.96 (1–5)	2.94 (1–5)	1.00 (0–3)	4.96 (0–10)	

Source: YouGov 12-Nation Authoritarian Populism Survey, October 2016.

score for the *Authoritarian Populist Centre* (5.02). In short, there is a sizeable group (estimated at 15 per cent of the UK electorate) that is clearly to the right of the political spectrum but which equally clearly rejects AP attitudes and values. Together with the *Liberal Internationalist Pro-EU Left* (estimated at 37 per cent), these non-Authoritarian Populists represent just over half of the electorate, compared with the two groupings of Authoritarian Populists —the *Authoritarian Populist Centre* (29 per cent) and the *Authoritarian Populist Right* (19 per cent).

The key issue that follows from the identification of these four groupings or clusters ('tribes') is what consequences they might have for changing patterns of party support. Table 7 reports the relationship between Tribe and Vote based on column percentages. As the table shows, almost two thirds of *Liberal Internationalist Pro-EU Left* (tribe T1) (65 per cent) support Labour, though to a lesser extent they also support the Liberal Democrats and Others (in effect, Greens, SNP and PC). The *Liberal Pro-EU Centre-Right* (T2) strongly supports the Conservatives (67 per cent) and to a lesser extent the Liberal Democrats (17 per cent). The *Authoritarian Populist Centre* (T3) distributes its support across the Conservatives (42 per cent), Labour (21 per cent) and UKIP (25 per cent). The *Authoritarian Populist Right* (T4) is overwhelmingly Conservative (75 per cent), with most of the remainder supporting UKIP (21 per cent).

Table 8 reports the same data, but this time presenting row percentages. This enables us to analyse the spread of party support across the four tribes more easily. The results are instructive. The Conservatives have the most diversified support portfolio, deriving substantial support from T2, T3 and T4. This degree of dispersal is potentially a source of long-term electoral strength, though it is possible that Theresa May's authoritarian tendencies with regard to immigration may combine with a 'hard

Table 7. Vote intention by political tribe, 2016, column percentages.

	T1: *Liberal Internationalist Pro-EU Left* (37%)	T2: *Liberal Pro-EU Centre-Right* (15%)	T3: *Authoritarian Populist Centre* (29%)	T4: *Authoritarian Populist Right* (19%)
Conservative	7	67	42	75
Labour	65	17	21	0
Liberal Democrat	12	9	4	0
UKIP	1	0	25	21
Other	16	6	8	3

Source: YouGov 12-Nation Authoritarian Populism Survey, October 2016.

Table 8. Vote intention by political tribe, 2016, row percentages.

	T1: *Liberal Internationalist Pro-EU Left*	T2: *Liberal Pro-EU Centre-Right*	T3: *Authoritarian Populist Centre*	T4: *Authoritarian Populist Right*
Conservative	7	25	29	39
Labour	75	8	17	0
Liberal Democrat	63	20	16	1
UKIP	2	0	59	38
Other	62	10	21	7

Source: YouGov 12-Nation Authoritarian Populism Survey, October 2016.

Brexit' to alienate the remaining Conservative supporters in T2, the *Liberal Pro-EU Centre-Right*. Labour, in contrast, is largely dependent on T1 and risks losing its remaining supporters in T3 either to UKIP or to a newly authoritarian Conservative Party that strengthens its opposition to immigration and human rights and at the same promises more redistribution. UKIP, which is dependent entirely on AP support, is clearly vulnerable to the Conservatives now that its original raison d'être has gone and Euroscepticism dominates the Cabinet. Finally, the Liberal Democrats and Others are dependent primarily on the *Liberal Internationalist* T1 tribe for their support—and their efforts to increase their support levels there are likely to make life even more difficult for Jeremy Corbyn's increasingly sectarian Labour Party.

All of this suggests that the situation in the UK is ripe for a party realignment around the political centre. The Conservatives are clearly in a position to undercut UKIP and reinforce their support among T3 and T4 as the May government adopts a more aggressive foreign policy stance, stands firmly against immigration, and moves towards a hard Brexit. If there are no Tory defections from this increasingly Authoritarian Populist position, the Conservatives could become the dominant party of UK electoral politics. In these circumstances, however, the Conservative centre-left would have very little in common with anti-EU, anti-immigrant, anti-human-rights mainstream of the party. The Tory centre-left group in the Commons is almost certainly smaller than the 128 Conservative MPs who committed themselves formally to the Remain camp in the EU referendum. However, it is probably at least half that size, even after David Cameron's resignation as an MP. If the Tory centre-left could bring itself to put national interest above party loyalty (never a small matter!), it could defect to a new democratic centre party or even to the Liberal Democrats, with a realistic possibility of bringing the support of most of the T2 tribe with them.

Labour under Corbyn, for its part, is likely to see its support increasingly restricted to T1, the *Liberal Internationalist, Pro-EU Left*. Even though T1 (with a 37 per cent share) is numerically the largest single tribe, Labour has to compete for T1 support with other liberal parties, and it is seriously hampered in its electoral efforts by widespread negative voter perceptions of both its leadership and its managerial competence. Corbyn's overwhelming victory in the party's leadership vote in October 2016 means that Labour's centre-left has lost its battle for control of the party. Like the liberal Tories who are isolated in an increasingly Authoritarian Populist Conservative party, Labour's centre-left MPs have less and less in common with a leadership that fails to understand voters' concerns about immigration, and which sees Labour primarily as an activist-driven campaigning party that articulates a radical voice for the dispossessed rather than as a (necessarily compromising) party of government. In these circumstances, Labour's centre-left should seriously consider defection. The empowerment of Labour's grass-roots constituency activists under the post-2014 leadership rules and Corbyn's victory together mean that Labour stands no prospect of occupying the political centre ground of British politics. If Labour's centre-left (the majority of its current MPs) allow party loyalty to dominate their actions, they seriously risk condemning the British electorate to the electoral hegemony of an increasingly authoritarian Conservative government in the future. If, on the other hand, they recognise that the need to protect liberal, internationalist values is more important than personal ambition and misplaced loyalty to a party that has moved radically to the left, then defection to a new centre party could provide a plausible vehicle for protecting those values. A new centre party (or a reconstructed Liberal Democrat party) could realistically bid for dominance among T1 and T2 voters, giving it a serious chance of challenging the Conservatives in the next general election.

SUMMARY AND CONCLUSIONS

The UK party system has always been subject to change and occasionally, as with the replacement of the Liberals by Labour in the 1920s, to fundamental change. Since the 1950s, the electorate has increasingly signalled its collective preference, even at Westminster, for a more multiparty system. The Number of Effective Parties in terms of *votes* has increased from two in 1951 to almost four in 2015. To be sure, First-Past-the-Post has constrained the seat shares of alternative parties so that even by 2015 the Number of Effective Parties in terms of *seats* had risen to only 2.5.

With regard to the 'measurable' influences on this increasing fragmentation of voting preferences, the key drivers of change appear to have been the declines in class voting and party identification. Declining class voting increases the opportunities for alternative parties to open up new issues and cleavages while declining party identification makes more voters available for recruitment to alternative causes. In both cases, third parties can compete more effectively thereby increasing vote fragmentation. These 'measurables' have almost certainly been complemented by such 'unmeasurables' as the rise of alternative identities and increased media and social media criticism of politicians and conventional politics. These effects have been reinforced by certain decisions of party leaders that have added to the deeper centrifugal forces encouraging party fragmentation. In Labour's case, the decision to move to genuine One-Member-One-Vote in 2014, combined with a naïve approach to the Leader nomination by the Parliamentary Labour Party after the 2015 general election defeat, has enabled left-wing grassroots activists to take control of the party. This is a position they will not lightly relinquish, but it has seriously (some would argue, fatally) weakened Labour's electoral prospects by shifting the party's centre of political gravity too far away both from Labour's traditional support base and from the median voter. As far as the Conservatives are concerned, Cameron's overweening confidence and unpreparedness to listen to advice in committing to a referendum on Britain's EU membership and his subsequent failure properly to prepare public opinion before calling the referendum itself were hugely damaging to the project he was seeking to advance. They led to the termination of his pro-EU liberal leadership of the party and its replacement by a more hardline anti-EU and authoritarian May government.

Underpinning the rise of UKIP since 2010 and the Leave victory in June 2016 has been the growth of Authoritarian Populist sentiment among the UK electorate. Indeed, Authoritarian Populist attitudes (and their antitheses) now constitute an important defining dimension of UK public opinion and electoral politics. Cluster analysis of these AP attitudes suggests there are now four 'tribes' of UK voters: the *Liberal Internationalist Pro-EU Left*; the *Liberal, Pro-EU Centre-Right*; the *Authoritarian Populist Centre*; and the *Authoritarian Populist Right*. Under Corbyn, Labour's support base in the *Liberal Internationalist Pro-EU Left* is far too limited for it to prosper electorally—especially as it faces competition from other liberal parties such as the Liberal Democrats, the SNP and Plaid Cymru among that group of voters. At the same time, liberal pro-EU Conservatives have little in common with an Authoritarian Populist-dominated Conservative leadership that appears bent on hard Brexit and which draws most of its electoral support from the *Authoritarian Populist Centre* and

Authoritarian Populist Right. Indeed, on the key issues of Europe, human rights, immigration and the fiscally responsible mixed economy, the Conservative centre has much more in common with the vast majority of anti-Corbyn Labour MPs than it does with its own government and party activists. Conservatives do not have a history of splitting and Labour activists and MPs have a visceral fear (if not hatred) of it. However, the long-term loosening of party identifications and of class-based voting outlined above have created a new situation that is very different from previous occasions (such as 1931 or 1981) when serious splits in the major parties have been on the political agenda.

Fundamental policy differences within the two main parties are becoming increasingly evident. Combined with the new divisions in the electorate associated with the four tribes described above, Conservative and Labour centre liberals would have little to lose and much to gain by defecting from their respective parties. To avoid more party fragmentation and the vicious circle consequences of First-Past-the-Post, they could explore the possibility of working with the Liberal Democrats to form a new party of the liberal, democratic centre. Such a party grouping could expect to prosper in a general election, especially with Rump Labour fighting UKIP for working-class votes in the North and Midlands and the Conservatives and UKIP competing for Authoritarian Populist votes across the country. For some observers, the spectacle would be irresistible.

Acknowledgements
I am indebted to this journal's editors and an anonymous reviewer for their helpful comments on an earlier draft of this paper.

REFERENCES

Butler, David & Butler, Gareth (2011), *British Political Facts* (Basingstoke, Hants, Palgrave-Macmillan).

Clarke, Harold, Sanders, David, Stewart, Marianne & Whiteley, Paul (2004), *Political Choice in Britain* (Cambridge, Cambridge University Press). https://doi.org/10.1093/019924488X.001.0001

Duverger, Maurice (1954), *Political Parties: Their Organisation and Activity in the Modern State* (London, Methuen).

Gallagher, Michael (1991), 'Proportionality, Disproportionality and Electoral Systems', *Comparative Political Studies*, 10(1): 33–51. https://doi.org/10.1016/0261-3794(91)90004-c

Heath, Anthony, Fisher, Stephen, Rosenblatt, Gemma, Sanders, David & Sobolewska, Maria (2013), *The Political Integration of Ethnic Minorities in Britain* (Oxford, Oxford University Press). https://doi.org/10.1093/acprof:oso/9780199656639.001.0001

Isernia, Pierangelo, Fiket, Irena, Serricchio, Fabio & Westle, Bettina (2012), 'But Still it Does Not Move: Functional and Identity-based Determinants of European Identity', in David Sanders, Pedro Magalhaes & Gabor Toka (eds), *Citizens and the European Polity: Mass Attitudes Towards the European and National Polities* (Cambridge, Cambridge University Press), 110–139.

https://doi.org/10.1093/acprof:oso/9780199602339.003.0006
Laakso, Markku & Taagepera, Rein (1979), ' "Effective" Number of Parties: A Measure with Application to West Europe', *Comparative Political Studies*, 12(1): 3–27.
Nevitte, Neil (2011), 'The Decline of Deference Revisited: Evidence after 25 Years', paper presented at Mapping and Tracking Global Value Change: A Festschrift Conference for Ronald Inglehart, University of California, Irvine, 11 March
Riker, William (1986), *The Art of Political Manipulation* (New Haven, CT, Yale University Press).
Sanders, David, Scotto, Thomas & Reifler, Jason (2016), 'The Consequences of Authoritarian Populism in Britain', working paper, Department of Government, University of Essex.
Whiteley, Paul, Clarke, Harold, Sanders, David & Stewart, Marianne (2013), *Affluence, Austerity and Electoral Change in Britain* (Cambridge, Cambridge University Press).
https://doi.org/10.1017/CBO9781139162517

Note on the Author: David Sanders has taught politics at Essex University since 1975. He has recently completed a second term as Pro-Vice-Chancellor (Research) and is currently Regius Professor of Political Science in the Department of Government. He was co-editor of the *British Journal of Political Science* between 1990 and 2008 and was co-Director of the British Election Study from 1999 to 2012.
sanders@essex.ac.uk

To cite the article: David Sanders (2017), 'The UK's changing party system: The prospects for a party realignment in Westminster', *Journal of the British Academy*, 5: 91–124.
DOI https://doi.org/10.85871/jba/005.91

Journal of the British Academy (ISSN 2052–7217) is published by
The British Academy—the national academy for the humanities and social sciences.
10–11 Carlton House Terrace, London, SW1Y 5AH
www.britishacademy.ac.uk

ANNEX 1: THE TREND IN UK GOVERNMENT POPULARITY, 1947–2016

Government popularity measured as the percentage intending vote for the governing party, average of all published opinion polls. For the period of the 2010–15 coalition government, the figures are Conservative vote intention.

A simple trend function can be estimated as government popularity = 49.34 – 0.19 time. Both the constant and the coefficient are significant at $p < 0.000$; r^2 is −0.33. The

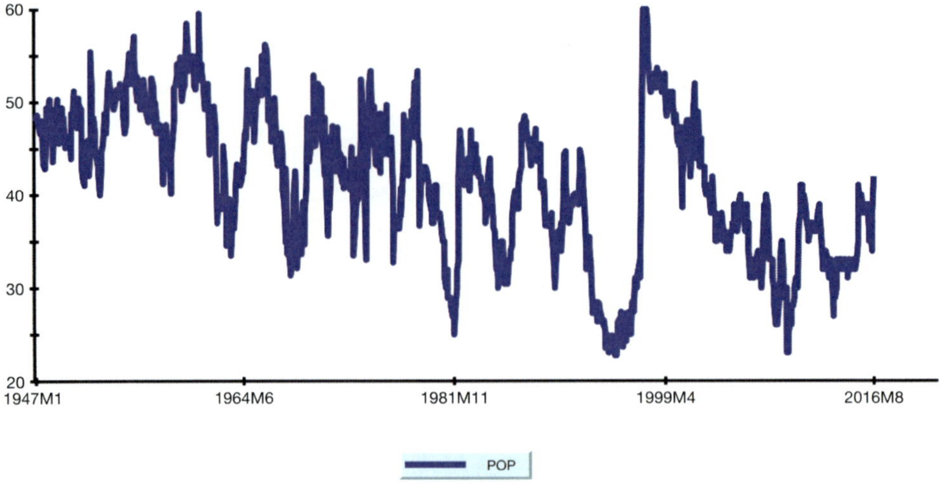

Figure A1. Monthly variations in government popularity, January 1947 – August 2016.

Table A1. Lagged endogenous variable model of UK government popularity, 1947–2016, with controls for key political events.

	Coefficient	St. Error	Significance
Government popularity t – 1	0.94	0.01	0.000
Time	0.001	0.0003	0.002
Change of government dummy	4.46	0.88	0.000
Suez Crisis (November 1956)	3.95	2.40	0.100
Devaluation Crisis (October 1967)	−4.84	2.40	0.044
Winter of Discontent (December 1978 – March 1979)	−2.70	1.02	0.008
Falklands War (May, June 1982)	6.72	1.54	0.000
Poll Tax (March 1990)	−4.80	2.40	0.046
ERM Crisis (October 1992)	−5.25	2/40	0.029
New Labour boost (May 1997)	7.01	2.82	0.013
Blair Honeymoon (May – October 1997)	3.75	0.94	0.000
Fuel Crisis (September 2000)	−6.55	2.40	0.007
Iraq War (May 2003)	−2.97	2.40	0.216
Financial Crisis (November 2007)	−5.87	2.40	0.015
Expenses Scandal (May 2009)	−7.37	2.40	0.002
Constant	2.84	0.55	0.000
U_{t-1}	−0.22	6.42	0.000
U_{t-2}	−0.05	1.33	0.184
Corrected R^2	0.91		
Durbin–Watson	2.00		

Dependent variable is government popularity, monthly average intending to vote for governing party as indicated by the average of all monthly polls. Estimation by Exact AR(2) Newton—Raphson Iterative Method after OLS diagnostics showed that the OLS residuals were generated by an AR(2) process. All independent variables other than lagged dependent variable are dummies (1 for the months specified; 0 otherwise). Sample: 1947M2–2016M8; N = 835.

more elaborate specification outlined in Table A1 includes controls for the major political events of the 1947–2016 period.

The results in the table show that the time-trend effect remains significant even when a lagged endogenous variable term and a battery of other effects and controls are included in the specification.

ANNEX 2: LAGGED MODELS OF PARTY FRAGMENTATION (EFFECTIVE NUMBER OF PARTIES-VOTES), PARTY IDENTIFICATION AND CLASS-VOTING, 1964–2015

When variables are potentially reciprocally related, Granger causality tests can be used to shed light on claims that any causal connection is from X to Y rather than from Y to X. The simplest way of effecting such tests is to see whether lagged values of X (e.g. X_{t-1}) predict Y_t and/or whether lagged values of Y predict X_t. We could conclude that X affected Y, for example, if X_{t-1} predicted Y_t but Y_{t-1} did not predict X_t. Table A2 undertakes these tasks. The coefficients of interest and their associated significance levels are highlighted in bold. As the table indicates, lagged ($t-1$) values of No Party Identification (No PID) and Class-Vote both significantly affect EPN-votes at time t, but lagged values of EPN-votes do not significantly affect either No Party Identification or Class-Vote. These results clearly support the idea that it is PID and ClassVote that affect party fragmentation rather than vice versa.

Table A2. Lagged endogenous variable models of EPN-votes, No Party Identification and Class-Vote, 1964–2015.

	EPN-votes$_t$			No PID$_t$			Class-Vote$_t$		
	Coeff.	St. Err.	Sig.	Coeff.	St. Err.	Sig.	Coeff.	St. Err.	Sig.
EPN-votes$_{t-1}$	−0.60	0.32	0.09	**−5.89**	**3.98**	**0.17**	**3.97**	**18.93**	**0.84**
No PID$_{t-1}$	**0.08**	**0.02**	**0.00**	0.91	0.25	0.01	−2.32	1.17	0.08
Class-Vote$_{t-1}$	**−0.02**	**0.01**	**0.03**	−0.16	0.08	0.08	0.49	0.38	0.23
Constant	4.29	1.18	0.00	28.39	14.57	0.08	35.77	69.24	0.62
Corrected R^2	0.86								
Durbin–Watson	2.02			2.00			2.08		
LM (C^2) 1	0.06		0.80	0.01		0.90	0.66		0.42

Sample: general election events 1964–2015. $N = 13$. Estimation by OLS. EPN-votes is the Effective Number of Parties in terms of votes cast. No Party Identification is the percentage of Non-Party-Identifiers in each BES cross-sectional survey. Class-Vote is the Class-Vote Consistency Index.

The raw data for these estimates are as follows:

Election	EPN-votes	No Party Identification	Class-Vote
1964	2.53	5	76
1966	2.42	7	83
1970	2.46	8	78
1974f	3.13	9	50
1974o	3.15	9	51
1979	2.87	12	42
1983	3.46	14	45
1987	3.33	12	43
1992	3.06	10	46
1997	3.22	12	36
2001	3.33	16	37
2005	3.59	17	28
2010	3.71	22	34
2015	3.91	21	12

ANNEX 3: CLUSTER ANALYSES OF UK RESPONDENTS, BASED ON THE FIVE AUTHORITARIAN POPULISM MEASURES

Cluster solution	Percentage in cluster	Left–Right Self-Placement	Britain Strong and Tough	Negative Immigration Emotions	Critical of Human Rights	Disapproval of European Union
2-clusters						
Cluster A1	66.5	3.86	0.24	0.88	2.71	2.84
Cluster A2	33.5	7.09	0.40	1.23	3.37	2.96
3-clusters						
Cluster B1	37.3	3.07	0.10	0.31	2.08	1.79
Cluster B2	29.2	5.02	0.44	1.72	3.65	4.36
Cluster B3	33.5	7.09	0.40	1.23	3.37	2.96
4-clusters						
Cluster C1	37.3	3.07	0.10	0 .31	2.08	1.79
Cluster C2	29.2	5.02	0.44	1.72	3.65	4.36
Cluster C3	14.9	6.28	0.26	0.67	2.84	1.77
Cluster C4	18.6	7.79	0.53	1.71	3.84	4.46
5-clusters						
Cluster D1	37.3	3.07	0.10	0.31	2.08	1.79
Cluster D2	28.2	5.10	0.44	1.67	3.61	4.34
Cluster D3	1.0	2.75	0.50	3.25	4.58	4.75
Cluster D4	14.9	6.28	0.26	0.67	2.84	1.77
Cluster D5	18.6	7.79	0.53	1.71	3.84	4.46

Cell entries, except where specified, are mean scores within the relevant cluster. Total = 1266; weighted by w8.

The key to interpreting this table is to begin by considering the 2-cluster solution. This indicates that in Cluster A1 (66.5% of the sample) the average Ideology (Left–Right Self-Placement) score is 3.86, indicating that on average these people are to the left of centre, whereas in Cluster A2 (33.5%), the average Ideology score is 7.09, indicating that these people are to the right of centre. Note that the differences in average scores across the four other component measures are all consistent with what we would expect of 'right-wing authoritarians': the A2 respondents on average all score more highly than their A1 counterparts on Britain Strong and Tough, Negative Immigration Emotions, Critical of Human Rights and Disapproval of European Union.

But these differences are averages, and averages can be misleading. The 3-cluster solution in effect splits the 66.5% A1 cluster into two separate clusters, B1 and B2, leaving B3 the same as A2 in the 2-cluster solution. This B1/B2 distinction is very instructive. It shows that A1 can be split into two very different groups: one on the left (B1, 37.3% of the sample), and one in the centre that, Ideology apart, looks very like the A2 = B3 cluster of 'right-wing authoritarians' referred to above. Indeed, the average scores for the four other component variables are higher for B2 respondents that they are for B3 — suggesting that the latter are, if anything, more Authoritarian Populist than the former.

The 4-cluster solution splits the A2 = B3 33.5% cluster into two new subgroups, C3 (14.9%) and C4 (18.6%). Again, the average scores for these two subgroups are very different. Even though both C3 and C4 are on the political right, the C3 cluster registers low average scores on the four remaining component variables, whereas the C4 cluster averages are much higher. Indeed, the C3 cluster represents what can be described as centre-right social liberals, whereas the C4 represents fully fledged right-wing Authoritarian Populists. The 5-cluster solution splits the C2 cluster into D2 and D3, but the number of cases involved is so small in D3 that this subgroup cannot sensibly be interpreted as a distinct 'political tribe'. Thus, I conclude that the 4-cluster solution is the most useful for understanding the UK's contemporary political tribes.

ANNEX 4: QUESTION WORDINGS FOR COMPONENT AUTHORITARIAN POPULISM MEASURES

Left–Right Self-Placement: Respondent's self-placement on 0–10 left–right scale.

Britain Strong and Tough: Question: From the list of foreign policy priorities, please select the one you think the United Kingdom should pursue in the 21st century (figures in parentheses indicate the percentage of respondents choosing each category): Helping the rest of the world by providing foreign aid and protecting human rights

(12%); Solving international problems by working with other nations and working through international organizations (44%); Protecting British interests by being strong and tough with other nations and maintaining a powerful military (33%); Avoiding involvement with other nations by simply minding our own business in international affairs (12%). The measure used is a dummy where 1 = chose the ‘strong and tough’ option, 0 = not.

Negative Immigration Emotions: Question: Please indicate which of the following emotions you feel towards immigrants: Angry, Happy, Disgusted, Hopeful, Uneasy, Confident, Afraid, and Proud. The measure is the sum of negative emotions (angry, disgusted, uneasy, afraid) specified by the respondent.

Critical of Human Rights: Statement: People who talk about protecting human rights are mainly interested in protecting the rights of criminals, not those of their victims. Strongly agree (19%); Agree (26%); Neither agree nor disagree (22%); Disagree (16%); Strongly disagree (11%).

Disapproval of European Union: Question: Overall do you strongly approve, approve, disapprove or strongly disapprove of the European Union? Strongly approve (13%); Approve (32%); Neither/Don’t Know (15%); Disapprove (22%); Strongly disapprove (19%).

Journal of the British Academy, **5**, 125–162. DOI https://doi.org/10.5871/jba/005.125
Posted 19 July 2017.

Globalisation and wage inequality

Keynes Lecture in Economics
read 28 September 2016

ELHANAN HELPMAN
Fellow of the Academy

Abstract: Globalisation has been blamed for rising inequality in rich and poor countries. Yet the views of many protagonists in this debate are not based on evidence. To help form an evidence-based opinion, I review in this paper the theoretical and empirical literature on the relationship between globalisation and wage inequality. While the initial analysis that started in the early 1990s focused on a particular mechanism that links trade to wages, subsequent research has considered several other channels, and the quantitative assessment of the size of these influences has been carried out in multiple studies. Building on this work, I conclude that trade played an appreciable role in increasing wage inequality, but that its cumulative effect has been modest, and that globalisation does not explain the preponderance of the rise in wage inequality within countries.

Keywords: globalisation, inequality, wages, trade.

BACKGROUND

While measures of globalisation—which assess the importance of international transactions in the world's economic activity—may include international trade in goods and services, international trade in financial and non-financial assets, and international migration, this article centres on the role of merchandise trade in the globalisation process. The role of international commerce in the evolution of the world's economy has a long history, dating back to biblical times more than three thousand years ago and extending to the Roman empire, the Dark Ages, the Middle Ages, and the post-Industrial Revolution era (see McCormick 2001, Findlay & O'Rourke 2007, Helpman 2011: chap. 1). Despite this long history, imports plus exports as a share of the value of output were very small until the beginning of the 19th century. Starting around 1820, when the value of world imports plus exports amounted to 2 per cent of the value of the world's output, the value of trade relative to income started to climb, and it kept climbing until the outbreak of World War I, exceeding 22 per cent in 1913. Judged by the evolution of the share of international trade in income, there have been two waves of globalisation since the beginning of the 19th century; the first started in the early part of the 19th century and ended with World War I, while the second started after World War II and continues until this very day. The ratio of trade to output declined between the wars.[1]

Likewise, the growth rate of income per capita in the world economy was negligible until the 19th century (see Maddison 2001). Starting from 1820 it accelerated and remained high until World War I. The growth rate was lower during the years between the two world wars, and then reached an unprecedented peak between World War II and the oil crisis of 1973, a period known as the Golden Age of economic growth. Moreover, even after the oil crisis the rate of growth of income per capita remained high by historical standards (see Helpman 2004: chap. 1). Evidently, trade and growth followed similar trajectories during these historical episodes.

Bourguignon and Morrisson (2002) constructed a data set from which they estimated the evolution of inequality of personal income in the world, beginning with the first wave of globalisation and ending in 1992. Using two common measures of inequality, the Gini coefficient and the Theil index, they showed that inequality increased dramatically during that time span. In their data the Gini coefficient was 0.5 in 1820 and close to 0.66 in 1992, while the Theil index was slightly above 0.52 in 1820 and exceeded 0.85 in 1992. Importantly, they decomposed the inequality of the world's distribution of personal income into a within- versus a between-country component, where the latter is calculated under the counterfactual supposition that the income level of every individual within a country equals the country's per capita income. The Theil index is particularly suitable for this type of decomposition because the within- and between-country Theil indexes add up nicely to equal the index of the world's distribution of income. According to updated data reported in van Zanden *et al.* (2014), which extend to the year 2000, overall inequality increased steadily until the middle of the 20th century and reached a peak in 1975. Importantly, however, the rise in inequality was primarily driven by the rise in inequality between countries; that is, over time, income per capita increased faster in rich countries than in poor countries, thereby widening the gap of income per capita between them.

[1] The rise in the trade–income ratio (imports plus exports relative to GDP) was temporarily interrupted after the oil crisis of 1973 and the recession of 2008; see http://data.worldbank.org/indicator/TG.VAL.TOTL.GD.ZS?end=2015&start=1960, accessed on 31 July 2016. According to these data, the trade–income ratio exceeded 50 per cent in 2008. I thank Alan Taylor for providing the data cited in the text. The drivers of globalisation have also changed over time; see Baldwin (2016).

Between the early 1980s and 2000 the Theil index of within-country inequality and the Theil index of between-country inequality changed little. Nevertheless, due to economic growth, extreme poverty declined dramatically in the world economy. Extreme poverty was originally defined as income of less than one dollar a day, and this threshold was updated to less than 1.25 dollars a day adjusted for purchasing power parity (PPP) in 2005. In 1981 close to two billion people, a bit more than half the population, lived in extreme poverty, while by 2008 this number had declined to less than 1.3 billion, or a little over 22 per cent (see Anand & Segal, 2015: Table 11.8). Noting that the world's population increased by about 50 per cent between 1981 and 2008, this reduction in poverty is impressive indeed.

These long-term trends in the world economy suggest that economic growth, globalisation in the form of expanding foreign trade, and income inequality are intertwined. Recent concerns about these issues are more narrowly focused, however, because inasmuch as the contribution of within-country inequality to total inequality of the world distribution of personal income was stable between 1981 and 2000, big changes occurred in individual countries afterwards. While inequality of income declined in a number of emerging economies, particularly in Latin America, it increased significantly in most OECD countries.[2] But earnings gaps between skilled and unskilled workers, which played a large role in rising income inequality from the late 1970s to the early 1990s, also increased in many less-developed countries that managed to significantly close the gap in their income per capita with the rich countries. The sources of this rise in inequality have been hotly debated and a great deal of research has attempted to unearth them.

THE RISE OF THE COLLEGE WAGE PREMIUM

In 1913 the top 1 per cent of US income earners received 18 per cent of US income. Their share declined to 8 per cent in the mid-1970s, after which it started to climb, reaching 13 per cent in 1990 and 18 per cent in 2008.[3] This U-shaped form of the share of top earners in a country's income is not unique to the United States, as shown by Atkinson *et al.* (2011). In other English-speaking countries, such as Canada and the United Kingdom, inequality evolved along similar lines. And, moreover, this pattern is

[2] Between the mid-1980s and 2013, income inequality declined slightly in Greece and Turkey, and changed very little in Belgium, the Netherlands and France. In all other OECD countries it increased substantially, and especially so in Finland, Sweden, New Zealand, the United States and Mexico (see OECD 2015: Figure 1.3).

[3] Source: The World Wealth and Income Database (WID), http://www.wid.world, accessed on 12 September 2015.

not restricted to top incomes; other measures of inequality, such as the Gini coefficient, show similar trends. For our purposes the more important observation is that inequality has been rising in many countries since the late 1970s, and this includes not only the English-speaking countries, the United States, United Kingdom, Canada, Ireland, Australia and New Zealand, but also the Nordic countries Sweden, Finland and Norway, as well as poorer countries such as India and China. An important source of this rise in inequality has been rising inequality of labour income, which attracted much attention in the early 1990s (see Katz & Autor 1999).

Katz and Murphy (1992) pointed out that despite the continuous rise in the number of college graduates relative to high school graduates in the US economy, the college wage premium rose sharply in the 1980s. This trend continued in later years. Autor (2014) showed that the relative supply of college graduates, measured by the share of their hours in the aggregate number of hours worked by the adult population, increased continuously from 1963 to 2012. At the same time, the college wage premium—which expresses in percentage terms how much more a college graduate earns than a high school graduate—followed a humped shape between 1963 and 1979 and sharply increased thereafter. According to these updated data, the college wage premium was 48 per cent in 1979 and had doubled to 96 per cent by 2012.[4] In 1987, the last year in the Katz and Murphy sample, the college wage premium was 63 per cent.[5]

From the vantage point of 1992, Katz and Murphy asked whether the rise in the college wage premium during the 1980s was driven by supply or demand factors, and they concluded that the dominant cause was an increase in the relative demand for skilled workers, and especially for those with a college degree. Following an analysis of alternative explanations, including the impact of foreign trade on wage inequality, they concluded: 'Although much of this shift in relative demand can be accounted for by observed shifts in the industrial and occupational composition of employment toward relatively skill-intensive sectors, the majority reflects shifts in relative labour demand occurring within detailed sectors. These within-sector shifts are likely to reflect skill-biased technological change' (Katz & Murphy 1992: 37). The conclusion that skill-biased technological change was the principal cause behind the widening gap in the wages of skilled and unskilled workers was subsequently echoed in additional studies. Other factors, such as the decline of unionisation, the decline of the minimum wage, and deregulation of labour and product markets, did not appear to

[4] I am grateful to David Autor for providing these data.

[5] Measured in constant 2012 dollars, the college wage premium increased from $17 400 in 1979 to about $35 000 in 2012; see Autor (2014).

play a large role in the rise of the college wage premium.[6] Attempts to disentangle the contribution of trade from the contribution of technology came out in favour of technology.

WHAT DOES BASIC THEORY TEACH US?

A celebrated result from the factor proportions trade theory, known as the Stolper–Samuelson theorem, was used to interpret the rising college wage premium. According to this theorem, in a country that trades low-skill-intensive and high-skill-intensive products on international markets an increase in the price of low-skill-intensive products raises the real wage of the country's workers with low skills and reduces the real wages of its workers with high skills.[7] And, alternatively, if the price of low-skill-intensive products falls, then the real wage of low-skilled workers declines while the real wage of high-skilled workers rises. In the former case the gap between the wages of low-skilled and high-skilled workers narrows while in the latter case it widens. These wage outcomes do not depend on the sources of price movements; they can result from a country's change in trade policy, such as magnified import protection or trade liberalisation, or from changes that occur in other countries that trade on international markets.

To interpret the rising college wage premium in light of this theorem, consider the following scenario. A group of less-developed countries expands its participation in foreign trade by joining the World Trade Organization or by reducing barriers to trade. Since compared to rich countries they specialise in low-skill-intensive products, their expanded role in world trade reduces the relative price of low-skill-intensive products. Under the circumstances the Stolper–Samuelson theorem predicts that the wages of low-skilled workers should decline in rich countries relative to the wages of high-skilled workers. Regarding high-skilled workers as college graduates then implies that the college wage premium should rise in the rich countries.

[6] See Bourguignon (2015: chap. 3) for a review of evidence concerning these factors in a variety of countries. In the United States, for example, the debate concerning the impact of the minimum wage on inequality led to a nuanced conclusion. Card & DiNardo (2002) argued that the decline of the real value of the minimum wage during the 1980s played a dominant role in the rise of wage inequality. On the other side, Autor *et al.* (2008) showed that the minimum wage had an impact on inequality at the lower end of the wage distribution, but not at the upper end where inequality increased most. In an updated recent analysis, Autor *et al.* (2016) found that the decline in the real minimum wage explains 30 to 40 per cent of the rise in wage inequality at the lower tail (the 50/10 percentile ratio) in the 1980s.

[7] In Stolper & Samuelson (1941), where the original theorem is stated, the assumptions restrict the economies to include two sectors and two factors of production. Jones & Scheinkman (1977) extended these results.

There is, however, a flip side to this argument. For less-developed countries to sell more low-skill-intensive products on world markets, the relative price of these goods has to *rise* in their home markets. The logic of the Stolper–Samuelson theorem then implies that the college wage premium should *decline* in these countries. In other words, the relative price of low-skill-intensive products and the skill premium should change in opposite directions in rich and poor countries.

Additional implications of this theory concern relative factor use. A higher college wage premium in rich countries induces manufacturers to economise on skilled workers. By the same logic a lower college wage premium in poor countries induces manufacturers to economise on low-skilled workers. For that reason, within sectors the ratio of high- to low-skilled employees should decline in rich countries and rise in poor countries. Evidently, once we subscribe to this mechanism we also buy into certain subsidiary implications. The empirical validity of these subsidiary implications provides a test of the extent to which the Stolper–Samuelson mechanism is suitable for explaining the rise in the college wage premium.[8]

EVIDENCE: THE FIRST PASS

The first attempts at empirically evaluating the role of foreign trade in raising the college wage premium relied heavily on the factor proportions trade theory. Katz and Murphy (1992) used factor content analysis to compute shifts in labour demand induced by US imports and exports. Factor content analysis consists of computing the services of various factors of production embodied in a country's exports and imports. By adding the net amounts of these services (from exports minus imports) to the country's factor endowment one obtains a notional country with the same characteristics as the original country except for its factor endowment. The autarky features of the notional country are then the same as the features of the original country that engages in foreign trade in terms of prices, factor rewards and consumption levels. It also implies that the output levels of the notional country's exportables equal the original country's output levels minus exports, and the output levels of the notional country's importables equal the original country's output levels plus imports. In the absence of trade, the country would be in autarky with the original factor endowment. Therefore the gap between the notional country's factor endowment and the original factor endowment, which equals the factor content of trade, represents the implicit *addition* of factor availability made possible by foreign trade. This modification of factor supplies affects factor rewards in contrast to autarky. An increase in supply

[8] Rodrik (2015) provides an excellent discussion of this type of use of models in economics.

depresses a factor's reward, while a reduction in supply raises its reward (see Krugman 2008). A similar analysis applies to changes in trade that result from changes in world prices by comparing the factor contents of trade before and after the price changes.

Katz and Murphy found that changes in US trade flows embodied flows of factor content that increased the demand for skilled relative to unskilled workers, thereby contributing to the rise in the wage gap between them. Yet, 'Although trade-induced changes in relative demand move in the correct direction to help explain rising education differentials in the 1980s, they are quite small relative to the increase in the relative supplies of more-educated workers over the same period' (65). They therefore concluded that foreign trade did not play a big role in the rise of the college wage premium. In a more detailed study of the factor content of trade flows with less-developed countries between 1980 and 1995, Borjas *et al.* (1997) concluded that trade accounted for 5 per cent of the rise in the US college wage premium. Immigrants, who consisted primarily of workers with less than a college degree, also raised the relative supply of low-skilled workers. They contributed another 5 per cent to the rise in the US college wage premium.

The Stolper–Samuelson mechanism was also employed by Krugman (1995) for evaluating the influence of trade with less-developed countries on wages. Although, he argued, in theory this mechanism can explain the empirical pattern, reasonable parametrisation of the theoretical model leads to the conclusion that it cannot explain the *magnitude* of the rise in the college wage premium.

A quantitative assessment of the impact of trade with less-developed countries on the US (or some other country's) college wage premium has to use an estimate of changes in the relative price of high-skill-intensive products, or prices of exports relative to imports (the terms of trade), and it has to use an estimate of the impact of such price changes on changes in the relative wage of skilled workers. It follows that the extent to which this mechanism explains the rise in the college wage premium depends on whether relative prices of high-skill-intensive products increased in the 1980s and how large that increase was, and on the size of the coefficient that translates relative price changes into changes in relative wages. In other words, the impact of trade on the college wage premium depends on how large this combined effect is in practice.

Lawrence and Slaughter (1993) estimated the relationship between sectoral skill intensity, measured as the employment of non-production relative to production workers, and price changes. They found no evidence that during the 1980s prices of high-skill-intensive products increased in the US more than prices of low-skill-intensive products. Leamer (1998) tracked sectoral prices relative to the overall producer price index during three decades: the 1960s, 1970s and 1980s. Textile and apparel were the low-skill-intensive sectors in his sample, and he found that their relative prices declined markedly, by 30 per cent, only in the 1970s. In the 1980s, when the college wage premium soared, the relative prices of low-skill-intensive products changed only slightly. One could of course argue that the price changes in the 1970s had the biggest impact on wages only in the 1980s, because the transmission of price shocks into wages was slow. But the credibility of this argument—which is not grounded in evidence—is questionable, even if one believes that the adjustment of wages to prices is not contemporaneous. Leamer (1998) also estimated 'mandated' factor price changes; that is, factor price changes mandated by the zero profit condition in competitive markets. Comparing the resulting estimates of mandated wage changes with wage data provides a test of the soundness of these estimates. It turns out, however, that these estimates are very sensitive to how much of the productivity growth is assumed to feed into prices, which limits the trustworthiness of the inferences drawn from this analysis (see Feenstra 2015: 87–91). Be this as it may, Leamer's main conclusion was that Stolper–Samuelson effects were strong in the 1970s but not in the 1980s. Apparently, other mechanisms are needed to account for the rise of the college wage premium in the 1980s.

Another challenge to the Stolper–Samuelson mechanism was presented by evidence from less-developed countries. A number of these countries implemented unilateral trade reforms in the 1980s and early 1990s, including Argentina, Brazil, Colombia, India and Mexico. Tariff reductions were far-reaching in these episodes, as they were in Chile's trade liberalisation in the 1970s (see Goldberg & Pavcnik 2007). According to the theory, these policies should have reduced the reward to skilled relative to unskilled workers, yet relative wages responded in the opposite direction. And similar to what happened in the rich countries, the use of skilled workers increased within sectors despite the rise in their relative cost (see Goldberg & Pavcnik 2007).

TRADE VS. TECHNOLOGY

As pointed out in in the previous section, Katz and Murphy (1992) concluded that the rise of the US college wage premium during the 1980s was most likely caused by skill-biased technological change, and the majority of the shift in relative labour demand occurred within rather than between sectors. What skill-biased technological change means in this context is that the efficiency of skilled labour increased faster than the efficiency of unskilled labour. If, alternatively, a decline in the relative price of low-skill-intensive products were the foremost cause of the rise in the college wage premium, we would have observed a reallocation of factors of production from low-skill- to high-skill-intensive sectors on the one hand and a reduction in the employment of high-skilled relative to low-skilled workers within all manufacturing industries on the other. Since the supply of college graduates increased markedly during that time period relative to the supply of workers with lower education levels, the allocation of college graduates to high-skill-intensive sectors should have been massive. No such shifts took place, however. According to the evidence in Berman *et al.* (1994), the relative employment of skilled workers *increased* in all US manufacturing industries, and these within-sector changes account for the majority of the rise in the aggregate employment of skilled relative to unskilled workers in manufacturing. The same type of employment shifts took place in other rich countries during the 1980s. While in the United States more than 70 per cent of the increase in the employment of skilled (non-production) workers occurred within manufacturing sectors, much larger shares (more than 90 per cent) were recorded in Australia, Belgium and the UK.

Skill-biased technological change can explain the above-described employment shifts together with the surge in the college wage premium, at least in theory. Furthermore, considerable evidence shows that advances in technology shifted factor demand toward highly skilled workers; sectors with faster increases in the demand for such workers were more innovative, more intensive in R&D, and more intensive in computer use.[9] On the other side, Machin and van Reenen (1998) found that in seven OECD countries the share of imports originating from less-developed countries played a minor role in explaining the rise in the employment of skilled workers within industries. This type of evidence was interpreted to imply that the role of foreign trade in the rise of the college wage premium was modest at best.

Leamer (2000) objected to this interpretation, arguing that for given world prices the data on shifts in wages and employment are not consistent with pure skill-augmenting technological change: that is, a productivity improvement of every skilled worker. If this were the case, wages of low-skilled workers would not change and wages of high-skilled workers would rise in proportion to the rate of technological improvement, so that wages *per effective* unit would not change. Under these circumstances the growth of effective units of skilled labour should not change factor proportions within industries, measured in effective units, but should shift resources from low-skill-intensive to high-skill-intensive sectors.

While theoretically correct, Leamer's argument relies on the assumption that world prices of goods do not change, which would be appropriate if the skill-biased technical change were a localised phenomenon in some small country. As pointed out by Krugman (2000), however, this assumption is quite inappropriate when the improvement in technology is widespread. In the latter case there is a direct effect on wages, captured by Leamer's analysis, and there is an indirect effect through changes in final product prices set in motion by the resulting supply shifts. Working out a

[9] See Berman *et al.* (1994) and Autor *et al.* (1998) for the US evidence and Machin & van Reenen (1998) for comparable evidence from the US, the UK, France, Germany, Denmark, Sweden and Japan.

complete model embodying these considerations, Krugman showed that the final outcomes are theoretically consistent with the patterns in the data.

Was skill-biased technical change ubiquitous? The evidence points to an affirmative answer. Berman and Machin (2000) showed that in the 1980s the within-industry contribution to increases in non-production workers' wage-bill shares was large in all twelve rich countries in their sample, with the exception of Sweden, and that changes in sectoral non-production workers' wage-bill shares were positively correlated across these countries. For nine of them, the upswings in their wage-bill shares were positively correlated with the US upswings, and only Austria and Belgium had a few negative correlations with other countries (see their Table 2). Berman and Machin also showed that during the same time period the within-industry contribution to the increase in non-production workers' wage-bill shares was large in all of the eighteen middle-income countries in their sample, with the exception of Korea, as well as in the poor countries in their sample, with the exception of Bangladesh. Furthermore, sectoral skill upgradings in the poor and middle-income countries were positively correlated with skill upgradings in the US sectors (see their Table 4), and sectoral skill upgradings in all these countries—rich, middle-income and poor—were positively correlated with US computer usage and OECD R&D intensity (see their Table 5). Evidently, changes in technology were widespread and exhibited similar patterns in countries at different levels of development.

Do similar patterns of wage changes in rich and poor countries necessarily contradict a foreign-trade-based explanation of the rising college wage premium? Undeniably, this evidence is at odds with the implications of the theoretical analysis above. Despite that, Feenstra and Hanson (1996, 1997) managed to develop a sensible modification of the theoretical model in order to qualitatively square the theory with this evidence. To this end they proposed to view the production process as a collection of many activities or intermediate inputs that differ in factor intensity. In these circumstances rich countries, with a high relative wage of unskilled workers, find it profitable to source low-skill-intensive intermediate inputs from poor countries. In other words, the rich countries specialise in high-skill-intensive production while poor countries specialise in low-skill-intensive production. When sourcing from foreign countries becomes cheaper, be it due to a decline in transport costs or improvements in technology, a rich country stops producing some of its least-skill-intensive intermediates and instead sources them from a poorer country. This change in the sourcing pattern can take place within firm boundaries by multinational corporations, as suggested by Feenstra and Hanson, or at arm's length, as suggested by Zhu and Trefler (2005). In both cases the reallocated activities are least-skill-intensive in the rich country and most-skill-intensive in the poor country. As a result, the demand for high-skilled labour rises in both countries relative to low-skilled labour, bidding up the relative wage of skilled workers in both. Evidently, this modified model has a built-in mechanism through which trade can raise the college wage premium in rich and poor countries alike. And, moreover, if all these activities and intermediate inputs are concentrated in the same industry, it also predicts a rise in the relative use of skilled workers within industries.

Feenstra and Hanson (1997) used data on US multinational corporations that operated assembly plants in Mexico during the 1980s to examine these implications. Those assembly plants, erected along the US border, imported intermediate inputs from the US and shipped back assembled products. This business strategy was profitable because the assembly could be done primarily by unskilled Mexican workers. Feenstra and Hanson found that US foreign direct investment in these plants, known as maquiladoras, was positively correlated with the rise of the share of skilled labour in Mexico's wage bill; in regions with larger foreign investment, the wage share of skilled labour increased more.

While this evidence confirms that offshoring of intermediate inputs affects relative wages in the destination country, it does not tell us how important this mechanism was in shaping US wages. The latter was addressed in Feenstra and Hanson (1999). Studying the 1970s and 1980s, they sought to evaluate the importance of offshoring versus technology in shaping US wages. Their estimates proved to be sensitive to the measure of sectoral use of high-tech equipment, which they employed as a proxy for a sector's technology level. Using the share of high-tech equipment in the capital stock as a measure of technology led them to conclude that about a quarter of the rise in the relative wage of non-production workers during the 1980s (1979–90) was due to offshoring and around 30 per cent was due to technology. But once more weight was given to more recent equipment, which presumably was more advanced, the contribution of offshoring halved and the contribution of technology more than tripled. In their review of the literature, Feenstra and Hanson (2003) re-estimated these relationships, giving the trade explanation as good a chance as possible, but the results did not change much.

My conclusion from the literature discussed so far is that while several mechanisms that link globalisation to the relative wages of skilled workers affected US wages during the 1980s, their impact on wage inequality was modest. Furthermore, although technological change has most likely played a bigger role, there is a paucity of quantitative evidence concerning its effects. In too many cases technological change is used as a default explanation when other alternatives are not compelling.[10]

[10] In fact, technological change plays a significant role in the Feenstra & Hanson (1996, 1997, 1999) story line concerning the role of foreign trade, because it is used to motivate the rise in offshoring.

BROADENING THE CANVAS

A vibrant literature has recently re-examined the relationship between foreign trade and wages, motivated by new theoretical developments on the one hand and new facts on the other. Three expansions of the standard model are at the core of this enterprise: firm heterogeneity within industries, worker heterogeneity beyond the classification into two groups of low-skilled and high-skilled individuals, and labour market frictions such as unemployment, wage bargaining and costly mobility. Each of these features adds a distinct facet to the theory, helping to address issues that were beyond the reach of previous scholarly work.

Firm heterogeneity

Firm heterogeneity was introduced into trade theory in response to the discovery during the 1990s of new patterns in previously unavailable data sets. In these data firms exhibited substantial heterogeneity within industries in terms of productivity and size, and only a fraction of firms exported. Furthermore, exporters differed systematically from non-exporters, with exporters being larger and more productive.[11] Melitz (2003) provided the canonical model that is consistent with these patterns, and various elaborations of his approach were applied to the study of trade and wages.[12]

Melitz assumed that labour is homogeneous and entrepreneurs pay an upfront 'entry' cost to acquire a manufacturing technology. The entry cost may consist of R&D or the cost of forming a business enterprise. Importantly, however, the productivity of the manufacturing technology becomes known only after the entry cost is sunk, and only the *distribution* of productivity is known when the entry decision is made. A company's business strategy is formed after entry, when the productivity of its technology becomes known. At that stage staying in business entails bearing a fixed operating cost in every period. For this reason only firms with a high enough productivity level are profitable, while low-productivity firms are not. The latter cut their losses by closing shop. Companies that stay in business may also export, except that exporting entails a fixed cost of establishing a beachhead in every destination country. For this reason only firms with high enough productivity levels can profitably export. In sum, not all entrants into an industry stay, and among those who do the

[11] Bernard and Jensen (1995, 1999) discovered these patterns in US data, while subsequent studies confirmed them in many other countries, including Canada, Colombia, France, Mexico, Morocco, Spain and Taiwan (see Helpman 2011: chap. 5).

[12] An alternative, less-influential model, was developed by Bernard *et al.* (2003). See, however, the discussion of Burstein & Vogel (2016) below for an interesting application.

more-productive enterprises export while the less productive serve only the domestic market. This structure replicates the main patterns in the data.[13]

In Melitz (2003) all workers are paid the same wage, independently of whether they are employed by high- or low-productivity firms, by exporters or by non-exporters. For this reason international trade impacts the wage level but not wage inequality. Nevertheless, as we shall see below, by adding more features firm heterogeneity can generate a non-degenerate wage distribution that responds to foreign trade.

Assortative matching

Matching has a long tradition in economics, be it for the assignment of firms to locations, of individuals to houses, or workers to firms. Becker (1973) applied it to marriages, deriving a condition under which there is positive assortative matching (PAM). For illustrative purposes, suppose that there are a fixed number of 'men' and a fixed number of 'women' and the number of men equals the number of women. Moreover, men can be ranked by a single characteristic from low to high and so can women. A marriage consists of pairing a man and a woman, and every pair produces a value based on the characteristic of the man and the characteristic of the woman, and this value is higher the higher the characteristic of either the man or the woman.

What types of matches maximise aggregate value? Becker showed that if the value of a match exhibits complementarity, then positive assortative matching maximises the aggregate value of marriages; that is, the man with the largest value of the masculine characteristic is matched with the woman with the largest feminine characteristic, the man with the second largest masculine characteristic is matched with the woman with the second largest feminine characteristic, and so on, until the man with the lowest masculine characteristic is matched with the woman with the lowest feminine characteristic. Complementarity of the values of matches means that when the masculine characteristic is replaced with a larger one, the increase in the value of a match is larger as the feminine characteristic is larger. In other words, the marginal gain from a masculine characteristic is increasing in the attractiveness of the woman in the match. And, symmetrically, the marginal gain from a feminine characteristic is increasing in the attractiveness of the man in the match. This property is also known as supermodularity. Becker then showed that in a 'competitive' marriage market the resulting marriages satisfy PAM.

The same logic can be applied to matching workers with managers or firms. All we need is to identify a worker characteristic, say ability, and a characteristic of managers, say managerial ability, or a characteristic of firms, say technological sophistication, in

[13] See Melitz & Redding (2014) for a review of the original contribution and its many extensions.

order to study the matching of workers to managers or firms. An important difference between these types of matches and those in the above-described marriage market is that while one man is typically matched with one woman in a marriage, many workers are matched with a single manager or a single firm. These models use a stronger notion of complementarity in order to obtain clear portrayals of inequality; they assume that the *natural logarithm* of the value of a match exhibits complementarity. This property is also known as log supermodularity. This implies that a marginal increase in the characteristic of one party raises the marginal value of the other party's characteristic *proportionately more* than the value of the match.[14]

This last feature has the following implication. Suppose, for concreteness, that workers with ability levels between *a* and *b*, measured in appropriate units (e.g., years of schooling), are matched with firms whose technological sophistication lies between *c* and *d*, also measured in appropriate units. Then workers with higher ability are matched with more-sophisticated firms. In particular, workers with ability *a* are matched with firms whose technological sophistication is *c* while workers with ability *b* are matched with firms whose technological sophistication is *d*. In this event more-able workers are paid higher wages, and the rate at which wages rise with ability depends on how strong the complementarity between worker ability and firm sophistication is in the productivity function. The rate of wage increase in turn determines wage inequality in this ability range.

Now suppose that due to a change in the economic environment (e.g., a change in relative product prices), the workers with abilities *a* to *b* match with more-sophisticated firms, so that every worker is now employed by a more-sophisticated firm. Under the circumstances the relative wage gap between any pair of workers with different ability levels is now larger than it was before. For this reason wage inequality is now higher than it was before.

This illustrates an important property of economies of this type: shifts in matching can aggravate or mute wage inequality. For this reason, globalisation can impact inequality through its influence on the assortative matching of workers with firms. Ideas of this type have been applied to models with heterogeneous workers in order to study the impact of trade on wages. They make it possible to examine the impact of trade on wage inequality at different parts of the distribution, comparing, for example, inequality at the top-end with inequality at the bottom-end of the distribution (see below).

[14] For this condition to be necessary and sufficient for the inequality results derived in these studies, characteristics and quantities of the two parties have to interact in specific ways; see Eeckhout & Kircher (2016).

Labour market frictions

There is little doubt that labour markets are subjected to a variety of frictions that prevent instantaneous adjustment of employment and wages. Some of these frictions are designed by governments, such as minimum wages or firing costs; other are ingrained in a functioning economy, such as the cost of finding a job or the cost of switching jobs. The latter may arise in turn from costs of moving to a different location, to a different industry, or to a different occupation. Additionally, in many countries labour unions play a major role in wage determination, be it within firms, within industries, or at the country level.

Many studies examined the influence of labour market frictions—which vary substantially across countries—on foreign trade and wages, shedding light on wage inequality (see Helpman 2011: chap. 5 for a review). A key implication of such frictions is that unemployment emerges as a natural outcome, providing business firms have leverage over labour compensation. Details of the mechanism differ, depending on the form of the labour market frictions, but the qualitative outcomes are often comparable.

Search and matching in labour markets, of the type developed by Mortensen and Pissarides (1994) and Diamond (1982a, b) for the study of macroeconomic determinants of unemployment, is a prime ingredient in recent studies of trade and wages. In this framework firms post vacancies and unemployed workers search for jobs. Workers are matched with vacancies, but only some workers succeed in finding a job and only some vacancies are successfully filled. The degree of success of the matching process depends on characteristics of the labour market; in more-efficient markets more matches are realised and some markets favour workers more. Matched firms and workers engage in wage bargaining. Failure to reach an agreement is costly to the workers and the firms, because it raises the number of unfilled vacancies for firms and the number of unemployed for workers. As a result, every party has an incentive to reach an agreement. Understandably, wage bargaining takes place in the shadow of these costs, which consequently impact the wage agreement. International trade modifies the choices available to firms and the employment opportunities available to workers. Through changes in these options trade modifies wages and employment.

Skills play a noteworthy role in shaping individual earnings, notwithstanding the fact that luck matters too. Yet skills are difficult to measure, and they depend on a host of individual characteristics, such as ability, talent, schooling and experience. Since the work of Mincer (1974), however, three observable worker characteristics—education, experience and gender—have been used for explaining differences in wages across individuals. As successful as this approach has been, it explains only a fraction of the variation in wages. The residual fraction—which cannot be explained by observable worker characteristics—is referred to as the 'residual inequality' (see Katz & Murphy 1992). Residual inequality increased over time and the sources of this increase are still debated. The next two sections discuss the impact of trade on wages through observable worker characteristics, while the following section discusses the impact of trade on residual inequality.

OBSERVABLE ATTRIBUTES

Needless to say, it is necessary to think about workers as being heterogeneous in order to study how trade impacts the wages of different types of workers. Whereas most of the discussion has so far focused on two types of workers, skilled and unskilled, the matching mechanism introduced in the previous section can encompass richer patterns of worker heterogeneity in order to study wage inequality across the entire spectrum of wages. Besides, matching can take a variety of forms. Workers can be matched with capital equipment, with managers, with firms, or with sectors, and the consequences of trade for wages depend on these particulars. In this section I discuss workers who have observable attributes and firms that have technologies that cannot be modified. In particular, firms cannot invest in R&D in order to enhance their productivity. The possibility of technology upgrading is explored in the next section.

Costinot and Vogel (2010) developed a variant of the factor proportions trade model that features multiple sectors and multiple types of workers, in which markets are competitive and workers are matched with sectors.[15] One interpretation of their model is that sectors produce intermediate inputs that are traded internationally, and every country uses these intermediate inputs to assemble its own final consumer goods. Another interpretation is that workers are matched with tasks (i.e., a sector is re-labelled to be a task), and the tasks are combined to produce a final product. In the latter case a country relies on tasks performed in other countries for producing its own consumer goods. This interpretation might be appropriate, for example, for trade in business services. Be this as it may, workers differ in a single dimension, call it ability (they call it skill), and the productivity of a worker with a given ability varies across sectors. Critically, the productivity of a worker with a specific ability level depends only on her sector of employment and it does not depend on how many or what type of other workers are employed in this industry. In addition, sectors can be ordered by a single characteristic, say technological sophistication, so that the natural logarithm of output per worker, which depends on the worker's ability and the sector's sophistication,

[15] Ohnsorge & Trefler (2007) is a predecessor that studies trade and wages with an assignment model in which workers sort across sectors.

exhibits complementarity; i.e., the productivity function is log supermodular. In these circumstances there is positive assortative matching: higher-ability workers are matched with more-sophisticated sectors in every country.

In this type of world, international trade has an unambiguous effect on wage inequality when the countries differ in factor endowments in a way that exhibits a clear ranking of relative ability abundance.[16] This means the following: Suppose that the world consists of two countries and for any two ability levels one country has relatively more workers with the higher ability (this is known as the monotone likelihood ratio property). In this case we can state unambiguously that this country is high-ability abundant compared to the other country. The opening of trade between a high-ability abundant country and a low-ability abundant country improves matches for all workers in the former and worsens them for all workers in the latter. That is, in the skill-abundant country trade leads to a reallocation of labour across sectors so that every worker is employed in a more-sophisticated industry, and the opposite happens in the other country. As explained in the previous section, when workers are matched with more-sophisticated sectors (or firms) the gap in wages between every higher-ability and every lower-ability worker rises, leading to more wage inequality. It follows that trade raises wage inequality in the high-ability abundant country and lowers wage inequality in the low-ability abundant country. These results are similar in spirit to the implications of the simple two-sector factor proportions trade model with low-skilled and high-skilled workers. Except that here linearity of the technology prevents the mixing of different types of workers in a single sector.

Trade alters matching in more complex situations as well. Of particular interest is trade between countries that differ in the *diversity* of factor endowments (what Costinot and Vogel call North–North trade).[17] For concreteness, suppose that there is an ability level such that one country is high-ability abundant above this skill level and low-ability abundant below this skill level, compared to the other country. Then it is reasonable to think about the former country as having a more diverse factor endowment. To be sure, this is a particular way in which endowments differ across countries, but it proves to be instructive for the purpose at hand. In these circumstances trade worsens the matches of low-ability workers and improves the matches of high-ability workers in the country with a more diverse factor endowment, and the opposite occurs

[16] Generally speaking, with many ability levels it is possible for one country to have relatively more higher-ability workers at the lower end of the ability distribution but relatively fewer higher-ability workers at the upper end of the ability distribution, as well as more complicated patterns of relative abundance of abilities.

[17] Grossman & Maggi (2000) provided the first theoretical analysis of the impact of diversity on trade flows; Bombardini *et al.* (2012) provided empirical evidence. See Grossman (2013) for a review of this literature.

in the country with the less diverse factor endowment. As a consequence, wage inequality declines at the lower end of the wage distribution and rises at the upper end of the wage distribution in the more diverse country, and the opposite happens in the less diverse country. This illustrates that globalisation does not have to raise or reduce inequality in a country along the entire wage spectrum; it can impact inequality differently at different ability intervals.

The last point comes out even stronger in Grossman *et al.* (2017), who study a two-sector economy that employs two factors of production: workers and managers. Factor intensity differs across sectors, so that one sector is worker intensive and the other is manager intensive. Unlike the standard model, however, both workers and managers are heterogeneous, with varying ability levels. As a result, there are two types of matches: matches of inputs with sectors and matches between inputs within sectors. In other words, certain types of workers and managers are employed in the worker-intensive sector and the other workers and managers are employed in the manager-intensive sector. At the same time, within every sector workers match with managers. To distinguish the matching of inputs with sectors from the matching of inputs within sectors, the term *sorting* is used for the former and the term *matching* is used for the latter.

The total factor productivity of a firm that employs a manager with workers who share a common ability level is higher the higher the ability of either the manager or the workers; the productivity function is log supermodular and it depends only on the attributes of the workers and the manager, notwithstanding the fact that there is diminishing marginal productivity in the number of workers per manager.[18] Furthermore, while individual firms have no incentive to mix the abilities of managers or workers, every sector employs workers and managers with multiple abilities.

What types of workers and managers are employed in each sector depends on technological features and product prices. Through product prices international trade affects the sorting of inputs to sectors and thereby the matching pattern between workers and managers within every sector. The matching pattern determines in turn the inequality of workers' wages and managers' earnings. While log supermodularity of productivity ensures PAM within sectors, sorting across sectors does not necessarily satisfy PAM. In other words, in every sector firms with better managers employ better workers, but if, say, a group of the best managers sort into the exporting sector it is nevertheless possible for a group of the least-able workers to sort into this sector too. Sufficient conditions for one or the other sorting pattern depend on cross-sectoral comparisons of factor intensities and features of the productivity functions. In this

[18] A firm's production function is separable in quantities and abilities of inputs in a way that makes total factor productivity dependent only on abilities, and it exhibits constant returns to scale in quantities.

environment elements from the factor proportions theory interact with matching and sorting in determining the impact of globalisation on inequality.[19]

To illustrate the richness of this framework consider an economy in which the best workers and the best managers are employed in one industry and the least-able workers and managers are employed in the other. Also suppose that factor intensities do not differ much between the sectors. How will inequality change when globalisation changes product prices? Suppose that it raises the price of the product produced by the industry with the least-able factors of production. Then inequality of earnings across sectors declines, as would be predicted by the factor-specific trade model (see Helpman 2011: section 3.3).[20] There is indeed an element of factor specificity in this framework that emanates from the sorting pattern, because the least-able factors of production are somewhat specific to their sector of employment as are the most-able factors of production. This semi-specificity is responsible for the narrowing of the inequality of earnings between the sectors. On the other side there is re-matching of workers and managers in every industry. More workers and managers are attracted to the low-ability sector in response to the price hike. But this means that the range of abilities expands together with employment in the low-ability sector and contracts in the high-ability sector, because the former sector attracts the least-able workers and managers from the latter sector and these employees are more able than the low-ability sector's original employees. As a result, matching improves for one factor of production, either workers or managers, in both sectors, and matching deteriorates in both sectors for the other factor of production (see their Proposition 6). Consequently, within-sector compensation inequality rises in both sectors for the input whose matching has improved and declines in both sectors for the input whose matching has deteriorated. In short, globalisation leads to a negative correlation between the within-sector inequality of wages and managerial earnings, and it narrows the earning disparities between sectors.[21]

Matching between workers and managers is also analysed in Antràs *et al.* (2006). In their framework there is a managerial hierarchy. Every manager has a team of workers. The ability of a worker determines the range of production problems he can

[19] Grossman *et al.* (2017) report in their online appendix that the average compensations of managers and workers were positively correlated across twelve Brazilian manufacturing sectors in 1994. One might conclude that at least in this case an equilibrium with PAM across sectors is more relevant for an analysis of the impact of globalisation on inequality than one with the opposite sorting pattern.

[20] The original sector-specific model was developed by Jones (1971).

[21] Grossman *et al.* (2017) report in the online appendix that the change in the inequality indexes of worker wages and management earnings between 1986 and 1994, a time interval that covers a major trade liberalisation episode, were weakly negatively correlated across twelve Brazilian manufacturing sectors, in line with this prediction.

handle. If he encounters a problem that is outside this range, he forwards it to his manager and she solves the problem if it happens to be in the range that she can handle. Solving a problem requires a fixed amount of time on the part of the manager. Every person can handle problems whose upper bound is determined by her ability, and therefore more-able individuals can solve all the problems that less-able individuals can solve, and more. A problem without a solution prevents the worker from contributing to output. This structure produces a complementarity between the ability of the worker and the ability of the manager.

Individuals are heterogeneous in ability and ability is continuously distributed. There is a single sector that produces homogeneous output by teams of workers and managers. The economy is competitive, yielding positive assortative matching between workers and managers. That is, better workers are matched with better managers. And since higher-ability individuals have a comparative advantage in management, the highest-ability individuals sort into management and the rest become production workers. The resulting matches generate a wage distribution among production workers and a distribution of earnings among managers.

Starting with two closed economies, say North and South, Antràs *et al.* examine the impact of globalisation on wage and earnings inequality. In autarky workers match with managers who reside in their own country, whereas in a globalised world, workers in one country can match with managers in another country. As a result, globalisation leads to a rematching of workers and managers around the globe, a form of offshoring, which changes the distribution of income.

When the ability distributions are uniform between zero and an upper bound, and one country has a larger upper bound, it is natural to refer to the latter as North and to the former as South. When other things are the same in these countries, globalisation can lead all individuals in South to be employed by northern managers. And because these workers have the lowest abilities, they work for the lowest-ability managers in North. Alternatively, depending on parameter values, some southern individuals can be managers in a globalised world. In this event the least-able individuals in South are employed by southern managers, while the most able individuals are employed by the best northern managers. However, in all cases southern workers improve their matches.

Focusing on the absolute difference in wages of the highest- and lowest-ability workers as a measure of inequality, Antràs *et al.* show that globalisation raises wage inequality within the group of southern workers. It also raises wage inequality within the group of northern workers if management consumes little time and the skill gap between North and South is large. Otherwise globalisation reduces wage inequality among northern workers. Moreover, globalisation reduces earnings inequality among southern managers but has ambiguous effects on earnings inequality among northern managers.

The role of matching between firms and workers in shaping wage inequality in a Melitz-style economy was analysed by Sampson (2014). Recall that the original model was developed to explain differences between exporting and non-exporting firms within industries, using variation in productivity across firms as an essential ingredient. But labour was treated as a homogeneous input and therefore all workers were paid equally. By including workers with diverse abilities, Sampson's economy generates a wage distribution and this distribution differs between globalised and non-globalised economies. Unlike the competitive environments discussed above, here only labour markets are competitive, while firms engage in monopolistic competition in product markets. A firm's total factor productivity depends on its technology and its workers' ability level, and the productivity function exhibits log supermodularity. As a result there is positive assortative matching between firms and workers; better firms—with more-productive technologies—match with more-able workers. The matching pattern shapes wage inequality. Inequality of wages within an ability interval is higher when the workers are matched with more-sophisticated (higher-productivity) firms.

To understand the impact of trade on inequality in this economy, it is necessary to account for the fact that trade changes the distribution of productivity of active firms. While at entry every firm draws its technology from the same pool, independently of the degree of globalisation, the productivity level of the least-productive active firms *does* depend on the degree of trade openness. The fraction of exporting firms depends on the fixed cost of exporting and when this cost is low all firms export. Consequently, the productivity distribution of incumbent firms varies with the fixed cost of exporting.

In a world of *symmetric* countries with a low fixed export cost, all firms export and trade leads to an increase in the productivity level of the least-productive firms that remain active in the industry, bringing about a rightward shift in the productivity distribution of incumbents. This shift leads in turn to a rematching of workers and firms that improves the matches of all workers. As a result, wage inequality rises. Although the case in which all firms export is not the most realistic, it helps isolate a mechanism through which globalisation raises wage inequality: the rightward shift in the distribution of active technologies. The conclusion is that '... at sufficiently high levels of trade integration [that inspire all firms to export] wage inequality is always greater over all workers than in autarky' (Sampson, 2014: 176). When the fixed export cost is not low enough to induce all firms to export, the results are more nuanced.

Analytical frameworks that embrace rich heterogeneity among workers are needed for understanding recent developments that exhibit ample patterns of change in earnings inequality. To illustrate, in the United States the ratio of the fifth to the first decile of the earnings distribution increased from 2.137 in 2000 to 2.146 in 2007, while the ratio of the ninth to the fifth decile increased from 2.240 to 2.397, pointing to a rise in inequality above and below middle-income levels.[22] Similar rises of inequality between 2000 and 2007 were reported for Ireland, Japan and Korea. In contrast, in France both ratios declined: the ratio of the fifth to the first decile declined from 1.561 to 1.521, and the ratio of the ninth to the fifth decile declined from 2.112 to 2.093. Moreover, in Canada and the UK the ratio of the fifth to the first decile declined while the ratio of the ninth to the fifth decile increased, and in Germany and Sweden the former ratio increased while the latter declined. Evidence of this type confirms the need for analytical frameworks capable of shedding light on inequality in different segments of the distribution.

Sorting and matching have also been used to study the impact of globalisation on growth and inequality, the main idea being that both growth and inequality respond to trade exposure and therefore both are endogenous in the long run. This view, developed in Grossman and Helpman (2017), contrasts with the alternative views that either inequality influences growth or that growth influences inequality (see Helpman 2004: chap. 6). This is not to deny that during the transition to a long-run growth trajectory current inequality can temporarily affect future growth or that current growth can temporarily affect future inequality; the argument is instead that eventually growth and inequality are jointly determined by fundamental characteristics of the world economy. These characteristics include innovation technologies, specialised resources used by these technologies, the ability to convert research and development experience into usable knowledge, and the like.

Grossman and Helpman (2017) showed that trade accelerates growth and raises inequality when countries benefit from research and development done by their trade partners or there are international capital flows. Otherwise, trade accelerates growth but reduces inequality. The quantitative significance of these findings is yet unknown.[23]

A detailed quantitative study of wage determinants in the US economy, which incorporates workers with multiple attributes that sort into multiple occupations, is provided in Burstein *et al.* (2016). In their analytical framework workers differ by education and gender, and labour productivity varies across occupations as a function of worker type and the type of equipment combined with the worker's labour input. Computer usage provides an explicit channel through which technology impacts wage inequality, because the spread of personal computers was uneven across occupations as well as across workers with different characteristics within occupations; it was biased toward more-educated workers and toward women. A rapidly falling price of

[22] These and the following data are from OECD.StatExtracts accessed on 28 February 2014.

[23] There is also a literature on trade and induced technical change that I do not discuss in this paper. See Acemoglu (2003) and Acemoglu *et al.* (2015).

computers, a reflection of technological change, encouraged growth in the adoption of computers in the workplace, which affected in turn the composition of labour demand and the structure of wages. On the supply side a rising relative supply of more-educated workers also affected the composition of employment and wages.

Between 1984 and 2003 the log of the skill premium, defined as the average wage of workers with a college degree relative to those without a college degree, increased by 15.1 log points (see Burstein *et al.* 2016: Table 3).[24] This skill premium would have declined by 11.4 log points due to changes in labour supply had there been no changes in labour demand. Yet shifts in labour demand increased the skill premium by 26.5 log points. About 60 per cent of this demand effect was due to computer usage, and 18.5 per cent was due to shifts in demand for different occupations. Labor productivity accounts for the remaining sources of demand shifts, where labour productivity is estimated as a residual. The large impact of computers on the skill premium emanated from two sources: the comparative advantage of educated workers in computer use, and the comparative advantage of educated workers in computer-intensive occupations.

In order to assess the impact of globalisation on the skill premium, it is necessary to assess how trade impacted labour demand via computer usage and occupational employment. Burstein *et al.* found that if the American economy had had no access to international markets for equipment (including computers), then between 1984 and 2003 the rise in the skill premium would have been lower by 2.1 percentage points, and if the US economy could not have traded occupation services the skill premium would have been lower by 1.3 percentage points (see their Tables 7 and 8). Each of these estimates represents only a fraction, 13 per cent and 27 per cent respectively, of the contribution of computers and occupations to the rise in the skill premium. In other words, international trade had a modest impact on wage inequality.

OBSERVABLE ATTRIBUTES AND TECHNOLOGY CHOICE

The previous section described the impact of globalisation on wage inequality in the presence of the matching of heterogeneous workers with heterogeneous firms. The nature of these matches determined the slope of the wage function, and foreign trade impacted these matches through changes in the sorting of workers into different

[24] This is a bit lower than the college wage premium in Autor's (2014) data, where the college wage premium is defined as wages of workers with a college degree relative to workers with a high school degree. In Author's data the college wage premium was 58 per cent in 1984 and 86 per cent in 2003, which yields log(1.86) – log(1.58) = 0.164. I thank Jonathan Vogel for clarifying this point.

activities and the distribution of technologies in those activities. Nonetheless, firms could not invest in order to improve their technologies. Although firms acquired manufacturing technologies, the cost of a technology was uniquely determined by market conditions. The outcome of the investment could be uncertain, yet there was no way to invest more in order to draw a technology from a more attractive distribution. In this section I discuss wage inequality that arises when workers are heterogeneous and firms can choose among technologies of varying quality.

Yeaple (2005) provided an early analysis. In his model workers vary by ability. There is a traditional sector supplying a homogeneous good in which there is no technology choice and labour productivity rises with ability. In contrast, two technologies are available in the advanced sector that supplies varieties of a differentiated product and labour productivity rises with worker ability for each technology. One of these technologies surpasses the other in terms of productivity, but the better technology requires higher fixed costs of operation. A firm that enters the industry in order to produce a brand of the differentiated product can choose one technology or the other. Finally, higher-ability workers have a comparative advantage in the advanced sector and within this sector they have a comparative advantage operating the better technology. This leads the least-able workers to sort into the traditional sector, the most-able workers to sort into the advanced sector in order to operate the better technology, and workers with mid-range abilities to sort into the advanced sector in order to operate the inferior technology.[25] Under the circumstances wage inequality at the upper end of the distribution is determined by the labour productivity of the better technology, wage inequality at the lower end of the distribution is determined by the labour productivity of the traditional-sector technology, and in the middle range wage inequality is determined by the labour productivity of the inferior technology in the differentiated product sector. Inequality across these groups depends in turn on the comparative advantage of workers across the three technologies.

When two symmetric countries trade with each other and there are fixed and variable trade costs, there is no trade in traditional goods. With low enough fixed export costs there is trade in differentiated products, however, and if both technologies are employed, then all firms that invest in the better technology export. Although there are circumstances in which all firms—independently of their technology—export, the interesting case arises when not all of them do. Whenever only a fraction of the firms exports, those who adopted the poorer technology serve only the domestic market. That is, with selection into exporting there is a stark contrast between

[25] Depending on the distribution of skills and the available technologies both technologies are used in the advanced sector or only one of them. The discussion in the main text proceeds under the assumption that both technologies are used.

exporters and non-exporters: the former employ a better technology and hire more-able workers.

A reduction in variable trade costs prompts more firms to adopt the better technology in the differentiated product sector, the most-able workers among those operating the worse technology switch employment to firms operating the better technology, and the least-able workers among those who operate the inferior technology switch employment to the traditional sector. Relative wage changes conform to changes in employment: they rise for high-ability workers operating the advanced technology, decline for middle-ability workers operating the inferior technology, and do not change for workers manufacturing traditional goods.[26] The result is wage and employment polarisation. Since labour market polarisation has been documented in the United States and sixteen European countries (see Goos *et al.* 2009, Autor 2014), this analysis identifies a mechanism through which globalisation might have contributed to this outcome, although there is no good evidence to support the claim that globalisation played a big role in causing polarisation.[27]

Similarly to Yeaple (2005), Bustos (2011a) also assumed that firms in the differentiated product industry can adopt one of two technologies: a high-fixed-cost technology, measured in units of final output, that is efficient at large volumes of output, and a low-fixed-cost technology that is efficient at low volumes of output. Unlike Yeaple, however, she had no homogeneous sector. In addition, she assumed that there are only two types of workers, high-ability skilled workers and low-ability unskilled workers; that both types of workers are essential in production; and that the technologies differ in factor intensities: the large-scale-efficient technology uses more-skilled relative to unskilled workers.

These features were combined with firm heterogeneity. Every entrant to the industry acquires a random firm-specific productivity level that affects proportionately its variable production costs. Higher-productivity firms gain the same variable cost advantage in both technologies. As a result, higher-productivity firms have a comparative advantage in the use of the large-scale-efficient technology. Naturally, whether a firm chooses to use this technology depends on how productive the firm is and how large the skill premium is. An exceedingly high wage of skilled workers relative to the unskilled can make the variable cost of production with the large-scale-efficient technology so high as to offset the advantage this technology has over the small-scale-efficient technology at high output levels. When the skill premium is not that high, both technologies are used by incumbents and high-productivity firms adopt the large-scale-efficient technology.

[26] This means that wages rise also for workers who switch from the inferior to the superior technology and decline for workers who switch from the inferior technology to the traditional sector.
[27] This type of polarisation is sometimes described as the 'hollowing out of the middle class'.

Fixed export costs lead to selection of the most-productive firms into exporting. And with suitable parameter restrictions some firms exit the industry after entry, the least-productive incumbents serve only the domestic market and adopt the small-scale-efficient technology, while the remaining incumbents export. Among the exporters lower-productivity firms adopt the small-scale-efficient technology while the higher-productivity firms adopt the large-scale-efficient technology.

Bustos used this framework to study the impact of MERCOSUR—the free trade area established in 1991 between Argentina, Brazil, Paraguay, Uruguay and Venezuela—on Argentinean firms.[28] In her model a reduction in variable trade costs leads to exit from the industry of some of the least-productive firms and it induces exporters who use the small-scale-efficient technology to switch to the large-scale-efficient technology. It also leads some of the non-exporters (at the upper scale of the non-exporters' productivity distribution) to start exporting, with the most successful among them adopting the large-scale-efficient technology. Evidently, these within-industry reallocations raise the relative demand for skilled workers, both because a larger fraction of firms adopt the large-scale-efficient technology and because market shares are reallocated from firms that use the low-skill-intensive technology to firms that use the high-skill-intensive technology. As a result, the skill premium rises.

Brazilian tariff cuts were used to assess the response of the share of skilled workers in the employment of Argentinian firms (Brazil was Argentina's largest trade partner). These tariff cuts varied across sectors and provided a source of variation that differentially affected firms in different industries. Among firms above the median size 76 per cent exported, while only 38 per cent of firms exported among those below the median size. The estimates suggest that the average reduction of the tariffs, which amounted to 23 per cent, brought about an 8 per cent reduction in the share of skilled workers in firms below the median and an increase of 6 per cent in the share of skilled workers in firms above the median. These figures represent a significant shift in labour composition across firms. The skill composition was affected both among production and non-production workers, with the strongest effect on the share of skilled workers among non-production workers taking place within firms at the top quartile of the size distribution.

The positive correlation between firm size or productivity and the relative use of skilled workers is not unique to Argentina. It was documented for the United States by Bernard *et al.* (2007), for Mexico by Verhoogen (2008), and for Chile by Harrigan and Reshef (2015). In combination with selection into exporting this feature generates

[28] Bustos (2011b) studied the impact of MERCOSUR on the technology upgrading of Argentinean firms. She found that most of the upgrading occurred within firms that switched from nonexporting to exporting status in response to the free trade agreement.

an increase in the relative demand for skilled workers within sectors in response to trade liberalisation. Under the circumstances globalisation can raise the relative employment of skilled workers within industries even when it raises the skill premium. For this reason globalisation can lead to a pervasive rise in the skill premium, and therefore in wage inequality, in both developed and developing countries. While the Stolper–Samuelson mechanism magnifies the rise in the skill premium in rich countries and moderates it in poor countries, wage inequality may rise in all of them. The question is whether this theoretical possibility generates quantitatively substantial results, however. Burstein and Vogel (2016) provide an answer.

They constructed a quantitative model of international trade with 60 countries and a region that encompasses the remaining parts of the world's economy, a large number of traded sectors, and service sectors that do not engage in foreign trade. Within sectors firms are heterogeneous and higher-productivity firms employ relatively more-skilled workers (worker heterogeneity is limited to skilled and unskilled workers). There is oligopolistic competition with limit pricing, as in Bernard *et al.* (2003), that results in variable markups. The model is calibrated to data in 2005–7. Holding constant endowments and technologies, they use the model to carry out counterfactual experiments. In one experiment trade costs are increased so as to drive all countries to autarky. The differences between autarky and the 2005–7 outcomes provide estimates of the impact of globalisation.

Importantly, in this counterfactual both skilled and unskilled workers gain from trade; that is, moving from autarky to trade raises the real wages of both types of labour everywhere. Moreover, in all countries, with the exception of Russia, trade raises the wages of skilled workers proportionately more than the wages of unskilled workers. As a result, the skill premium rises in almost all countries (see their Figure 2). This means that the Stolper–Samuelson effects are overwhelmed by the within-industry reallocations, including selection into exporting. Nonetheless, the rise of the skill premium varies across countries, being larger in more open economies and in net exporters of skill-intensive products. The rise in the skill premium is largest in Lithuania, amounting to 12 per cent, compared to an average of 5.1 per cent. It rises by 2 per cent in the United States and by 0.5 per cent in Brazil.

A comparison of 1975–7 with 2005–7 counterfactuals also features a pervasive rise in the skill premium, with the Philippines experiencing the largest rise, and this largest increase is a little more than half the rise in Lithuania's skill premium from autarky to 2005–7. This quantitative analysis suggests that the contribution to the rise of wage inequality of within-sectoral heterogeneity, selection into exporting, and factor proportions, is significant, yet modest.

RESIDUAL INEQUALITY

Residual inequality refers to the component of earnings that is not explained by workers' observed characteristics. After estimating a wage equation by regressing log wages on worker characteristics such as education, experience and gender, the inequality of log wages can be decomposed into inequality due to observed characteristics and inequality due to unobserved characteristics. The latter component represents residual inequality. While different measures of dispersion can be used, such as the 90/10 percentile wage ratio, the standard deviation of log wages, or the Theil index of the distribution of wages, the decomposition into an observed and an unobserved part is essential for identifying residual inequality.

Katz and Murphy (1992) pointed out the contribution of residual inequality to the rise in the college wage premium in the 1980s in the United States. But the contribution of residual inequality to the rise in wage dispersion was challenged by labour economists, and particularly by Lemieux (2006), who attributed this rise to an 'episodic' event and to compositional changes. In response, Autor *et al.* (2008) conducted a detailed analysis of the data, concluding that the rise in inequality was not episodic, and especially so in the upper-tail of the wage distribution (the 90/50 percentile ratio), where inequality increased nearly consistently from 1980 to 2005. Moreover, while changes in the composition of the labour force exerted upward pressure on residual wage inequality from the late 1980s to 2005, it was concentrated in the lower part of the wage distribution and '... changes in earning dispersion within narrowly defined demographic groups, remain a key force in the evolution of both upper- and lower-tail U.S. residual wage inequality' (301). They found that between 1973 and 2005 the 90/10 percentile ratio of wages of males increased by 34.6 log points, of which 12.8 log points were attributed to residual inequality and about two thirds of the latter resulted from the rise of the 90/50 percentile ratio.

Rising residual wage inequality played a major role in rising wage dispersion in other countries too. In Sweden, for example, residual wage inequality accounted for 70 per cent of wage dispersion in 2001 (measured as the standard deviation of log wages) and it contributed 87 per cent to the rise in wage inequality between 2001 and 2007 (see Akerman *et al.* 2013: Table 3). Likewise, residual wage inequality accounted for 59 per cent of wage dispersion in 1994 in Brazil, where it also accounted for 49 per cent of the rise in wage inequality between 1986 and 1995 (see Helpman *et al.* 2017). Evidently, the importance of residual wage inequality is not confined to rich countries alone.

A number of studies addressed the potential impact of globalisation on residual wage inequality, emphasising alternative mechanisms of wage determination, such as labour market frictions in the form of fair wages (Egger & Kreickemeier 2009,

Amiti & Davis 2012), efficiency wages (Davis & Harrigan 2011), and search and matching (Davidson *et al.* 2008; Helpman *et al.* 2010, 2017). Combined with firm heterogeneity, each one of these mechanisms generates a wage distribution among workers with similar characteristics, because these models predict that within the same industry firms with higher productivity pay a higher wage to the same type of workers. The positive correlation between firm size and wages, known as the wage-size premium, has been known for a long time (see Oi & Idson 1999). By combining international trade with a wage-size premium mechanism, recent studies have shown that due to selection into exporting, exporting firms—which are larger and more productive than non-exporters—pay significantly higher wages. The relationship between exporting and wages then implies that trade impacts wage gaps between workers employed by firms with different characteristics, as a result of which trade impacts residual wage inequality.

To illustrate, first consider the model of fair wages employed by Amiti and Davis (2012). There, wages are assumed to be an increasing function of profits, and since profits consist of a fraction of revenue minus fixed costs, wages are increasing in a firm's revenue. But revenue depends on a firm's business strategy: it can serve only the domestic market or also export, and it can choose to purchase only domestic intermediate inputs or also imported intermediates. Since both exporting and importing entail fixed costs, firms select into exporting and importing, with the most-productive firms engaging in both. In other words, the most-productive firms pay the highest wages, they export their final output, and they import intermediate inputs. On the other side there are firms that do not import intermediate inputs and do not export their output; these are the least-productive firms that serve only the domestic market. As in Melitz (2003), there is a productivity threshold above which firms stay in the industry. Under these circumstances trade weeds out the least-productive firms and shifts market shares toward producers that engage in foreign trade.

Studying a trade liberalisation episode in Indonesia during the 1990s, Amiti and Davis (2012) showed that tariff cuts had different effects on wages paid by firms that were internationally oriented than on firms that were domestically oriented. In addition, cuts in tariffs on final goods had different effects from cuts in tariffs on intermediate inputs. Since only 5 per cent of the firms imported inputs and exported a fraction of their output, 10 per cent exported output but did not import inputs, and 14 per cent imported inputs but did not export, the data provided rich variation for examining the differential effects of the tariff cuts on wages. In these data, exporters paid 27.5 per cent higher wages than domestic firms, importers of intermediate inputs paid 46.8 per cent higher wages, and firms that both imported intermediates and exported final output paid 66.4 per cent higher wages (see their Table 1A). These wage premia declined to 7.6 per cent, 14.6 per cent and 25.4 per cent, respectively, after controlling for firm employment and industry fixed effects. And moreover, exporters were larger and more productive than domestic firms, importers were larger and more productive than exporters, and firms that imported and exported were the largest and most productive, suggesting selection into trade in line with the theory. Also in line with the theory, they found that reductions in output tariffs increased wages paid by exporters and decreased wages paid by non-exporters. In contrast, cuts in tariffs on intermediate inputs increased wages paid by large importers and reduced wages paid by non-importing firms. Since their data allowed them to estimate these effects only on average wages paid by the Indonesian firms, some of the wage responses might have been related to the rematching of different types of workers with firms, thereby reflecting changes in worker composition. While they argued that these compositional effects were small, it remains a concern for evaluating the quantitative outcomes. In any case, Amiti and Davis have not provided a summary estimate for the impact of this trade liberalisation episode on overall wage inequality.

Helpman *et al.* (2010) developed a theory of trade and wages that builds on search and matching in the labour market. In this theory firms post vacancies and unemployed workers search for jobs. A fraction of the workers are matched with a fraction of the vacancies, and the productivity of a worker in a specific job is a random draw from a known distribution. Firms can screen workers in order to improve the mix of their workforce, but this process is costly and imperfect. As a result, a firm can improve the average productivity of its workers but it cannot assess the productivity of each one of them. Because firms differ in total factor productivity, more-productive firms have a stronger incentive to engage in screening and they therefore end up with higher labour productivity due both to their core productivity and to the better fit of their workers to the jobs in their firms. Selection into exporting provides firms that have large core productivity levels with the strongest incentives to screen, which skews the final labour productivity distribution in comparison to the distribution of core productivity.

This skewness plays an important role in the determination of wage inequality within sectors populated by heterogeneous firms, because following matching and screening every firm bargains with its workers over wages, and this multilateral wage negotiation leads to higher wages being paid by more-productive firms. The more-productive firms are bigger and the most productive among them select into exporting. As a result, exporters pay higher wages than non-exporters, in line with the evidence. An important implication of this theory is that ex-ante identical workers are paid different wages, with those who have been matched and retained by more-productive firms earning more. In addition, trade liberalisation has non-monotonic effects on wage inequality within sectors. Starting from autarky, sectoral wage inequality rises initially in response to reductions in trade impediments. In the process, the fraction of exporting firms rises. But inequality peaks when the fraction of exporters is less than one. Further reductions of trade impediments reduce wage inequality until—when all firms export—inequality reaches the level of a closed economy. While real wages are higher than closed-economy wages when all firms export, wage *inequality* is the same in both cases. It follows that when only a fraction of the firms export, wages are always more unequal than they are in autarky.

This model yields simple equations that describe the variation across firms in an industry of wages, employment, and selection into exporting. Helpman *et al.* (2017) extended this theoretical model to allow firms to differ also in the fixed cost of exporting and in the ability to screen workers. They then showed how the resulting equations for the cross-sectional variations within industries can be used to estimate employment and wage premia for exporters, and how these estimates can in turn be used to characterise wage inequality. However, their estimation methods require rich data sets, because they require data on individual workers and individual firms, and information on which workers are employed by every firm in the sample. Fortunately, data sets of this type are now available for a number of countries, and they illustrated their methodology with Brazilian data.

Brazil liberalised its economy over a number of years, culminating with a major trade liberalisation in 1991 with the formation of the MERCOSUR free trade area. Helpman *et al.* (2017) used administrative data for manufacturing industries, which cover the formal sector, to estimate the model for every year starting in 1986 and ending in 1998. These data cover about 6 million workers and over 90 thousand firms. From the workers' data they estimated Mincer wage equations, including an occupation-specific component for every firm. The distribution of these firm-specific and occupation-specific components was then taken to represent residual wage inequality. While the variation of wages across firms accounted for 55 per cent of wage inequality in 1994, the variation across firms of the estimated firm-specific components accounted for 39 per cent of wage inequality (where inequality was measured by the standard deviation of log wages). In comparison, observable worker characteristics contributed only 13 per cent to wage inequality. Using the maximum likelihood estimates of the model, they calculated that the standard deviation of log wages predicted by the model was 0.46 in comparison to 0.42 in the data, that the predicted Gini coefficient was 0.25 in comparison to 0.22 in the data, and that the predicted 90/10 percentile ratio was 3.24 in comparison to 2.95 in the data. Since only between 5 per cent and 9 per cent of the firms exported, the overall fit for non-exporters was better than for exporters.

Using the 1994 estimates, Helpman *et al.* simulated the impact of trade impediments on inequality. First, they found that reductions in trade impediments first raise inequality until it peaks, followed by declines in inequality in response to further declines in trade frictions, as predicted by the theoretical model. Second, they found that declines in variable trade costs lead to a higher peak of inequality than declines in fixed export costs. When disregarding the multiple destinations of different exporters, the former peak was 10.7 per cent above autarky while the latter was 7.6 per cent above autarky. Allowing for multiple destinations raised the former peak to 23.3 per cent above autarky and the latter to 19.0 per cent (see their Figures 1 and 3). Evidently, multiple export destinations, which feature in the data, amplify the effects of trade on residual wage inequality.

CONCLUSIONS

A major conclusion from my review of the literature is that the prevalent view that globalisation is primarily responsible for the large increase in the inequality of labour compensation has no basis in the evidence. Yes, globalisation impacted the wages of different types of workers to different degrees, and yes, it contributed to an increase in the wages of skilled relative to unskilled workers through multiple channels. Yet, in sum, all these effects explain only a fraction of the rise in wage inequality in rich and poor countries alike.

This conclusion does not deny the fact that foreign trade, foreign investment, and offshoring have adversely affected certain workers. Trefler (2004) found, for example, that the US–Canada free trade agreement of 1989 increased temporarily (for about three years) the level of unemployment in Canada; and Autor *et al.* (2013) found that imports from China had large differential employment effects across US commuting zones, where employment declined more in zones whose industries were more exposed to import competition from China. But these consequences, as painful as they were for the affected workers, do not imply necessarily that globalisation is responsible for the large wage differentials observed in the data.[29]

[29] Autor *et al.* (2013) also report wage effects, but their estimates of the impact of Chinese imports on wage differentials across commuting zones are perplexing. Despite the fact that imports from China consisted predominantly of manufactured products, they found no difference in wage impacts across these zones in the manufacturing sector for college graduates or for non-college graduates (see their Table 7). At the same time, they found somewhat larger declines in the wages of non-college workers than of college graduates in non-manufacturing sectors in zones more affected by Chinese imports, which is puzzling. In a more recent study, Chetverikov *et al.* (2016) found differences across commuting zones in wages of workers in different quantiles of the wage distribution, with more adverse effects on low-wage workers in the zones more affected by import competition from China. Yet the largest differential wage decline at the bottom of the wage distribution amounted to only 2.6 per cent over a decade for zones with the average rise in exposure to imports from China. Using individual-level data, Autor *et al.* (2014) also found differential impacts across commuting zones on workers with different earnings levels, where higher earners were affected less negatively than lower earners. The point remains, however, that the size of these effects is just not large enough to explain the observed rise in inequality.

While the finding that globalisation has had only moderate effects on wage inequality may disappoint some observers, the development of research tools in this area has been nothing but gratifying. To begin with, major methodological advances have been made. While studies of trade and wages focused initially on effects arising through the neoclassical channel, subsequent work introduced a host of additional considerations, such as selection into exporting, variation across firms in productivity and factor intensity, technology upgrading, matching, and residual inequality. In addition, new data sets became available to study the relationship between trade and wages, and these data sets were employed to examine trade liberalisation episodes in individual countries as well as to explore quantitatively the interactions between multiple countries. All in all more than twenty years of research have greatly enhanced our understanding of this important issue and they have produced a host of quantitative estimates. And while this cumulative knowledge may not be the last word on the subject, it would be a shame to conduct the debate on the impact of globalisation on inequality without utilising this body of work.

Acknowledgements
I thank Gene Grossman, Oleg Itskhoki, Gianmarco Ottaviano, Stephen Redding and Thomas Sampson for comments.

REFERENCES

Acemoglu, Daron (2003), 'Patterns of Skill Premia', *Review of Economic Studies*, 70: 199–230. https://doi.org/10.1111/1467-937X.00242

Acemoglu, Daron, Gancia, Gino, & Zilibotti, Fabrizio (2015), 'Offshoring and Directed Technical Change', *American Economic Journal: Macroeconomics*, 7: 84–122. https://doi.org/10.1257/mac.20130302

Akerman, Anders, Helpman, Elhanan, Itskhoki, Oleg, Muendler, Marc-Andreas & Redding, Stephen (2013), 'Sources of Wage Inequality', *American Economic Review (Papers and Proceedings)*, 103: 214–19. https://doi.org/10.1257/aer.103.3.214

Amiti, Mary &. Davis, Donald R. (2012), 'Trade, Firms, and Wages: Theory and Evidence', *Review of Economic Studies*, 79: 1–36. https://doi.org/10.1093/restud/rdr016

Anand, Sudhir & Segal, Paul (2015), 'The Global Distribution of Income', Chapter 11 in Anthony B. Atkinson & François Bourguignon (eds), *Handbook of Income Distribution, vol. 2A* (Amsterdam, North–Holland). https://doi.org/10.1016/b978-0-444-59428-0.00012-6

Antràs, Pol, Garicano, Luis & Rossi-Hansberg, Esteban (2006), 'Offshoring in a Knowledge Economy', *Quarterly Journal of Economics*, 121: 31–77. https://doi.org/10.1093/qje/121.1.31

Atkinson, Anthony B., Piketty, Thomas & Saez, Emmanuel (2011), 'Top Incomes in the Long Run of History', *Journal of Economic Literature*, 49(1): 3–71https://doi.org/10.1257/jel.49.1.3.

Autor, David H. (2014), 'Skills, Education, and the Rise of Earnings Inequality Among the "Other 99 Percent" ', *Science*, 344(6186): 843–51. https://doi.org/10.1126/science.1251868

Autor, David H., Katz, Lawrence F. & Krueger, Alan (1998), 'Computing Inequality: Have Computers Changed the Labor Market? *Quarterly Journal of Economics*, 113(4): 1169–214. https://doi.org/10.1162/003355398555874

Autor, David H., Katz, Lawrence F. & Kearney, Melissa S. (2008), 'Trends in U.S. Wage Inequality: Re-assessing the Revisionists', *Review of Economics and Statistics*, 90: 300–23 https://doi.org/10.1162/rest.90.2.300.

Autor, David H., Dorn, David & Hanson, Gordon H. (2013), 'The China Syndrome: Local Labor Market Effects of Import Competition in the United States', *American Economic Review*, 103(6): 2121–68. https://doi.org/10.1257/aer.103.6.2121

Autor, David H., Dorn, David, Hanson, Gordon H. & Song, Jae (2014), 'Trade Adjustment: Worker Level Evidence', *Quarterly Journal of Economics*, 129(4): 1799–860. https://doi.org/10.1093/qje/qju026

Autor, David H., Manning, Alan & Smith, Christopher L. (2016), 'The Contribution of the Minimum Wage to US Wage Inequality over Three Decades: A Reassessment', *American Economic Journal: Applied Economics*, 8: 58–99. https://doi.org/10.1257/app.20140073

Baldwin, Richard (2016), *The Great Convergence: Information Technology and the New Globalization* (Cambridge, MA, The Belknap Press of Harvard University Press).

Becker, Gary (1973), 'A Theory of Marriage I', *Journal of Political Economy*, 81: 813–46. https://doi.org/10.1086/260084

Berman, Eli & Machin, Stephen (2000), 'Skill-biased Technology Transfer around the World', *Oxford Review of Economic Policy*, 16: 12–22. https://doi.org/10.1093/oxrep/16.3.12

Berman, Eli, Bound, John & Griliches, Zvi (1994), 'Changes in the Demand for Skilled Labor in U.S. Manufacturing Industries: Evidence from the Annual Survey of Manufacturing', *Quarterly Journal of Economics*, 109: 367–98. https://doi.org/10.2307/2118467

Bernard, Andrew B. & Jensen, J. Bradford (1995), 'Exporters, Jobs, and Wages in U.S. Manufacturing, 1976–1987', *Brookings Papers on Economic Activity: Microeconomics*, 67–112. https://doi.org/10.2307/2534772

Bernard, Andrew B. & Jensen, J. Bradford (1999), 'Exceptional Exporter Performance: Cause, Effect, or Both?' *Journal of International Economics*, 47: 1–25. https://doi.org/10.1016/S0022-1996(98)00027-0

Bernard, Andrew B., Eaton, Jonathan, Jensen, J. Bradford & Kortum, Samuel (2003), 'Plants and Productivity in International Trade', *American Economic Review*, 93: 1268–90. https://doi.org/10.1257/000282803769206296

Bernard, Andrew B., Jensen, J. Bradford, Redding, Stephen J. & Schott, Peter K. (2007), 'Firms in International Trade', *Journal of Economic Perspectives*, 21: 105–30. https://doi.org/10.1257/jep.21.3.105

Bombardini, Matilde, Gallipoli, Giovanni & Pupato, Germán (2012), 'Skill Dispersion and Trade Flows', *American Economic Review*, 102: 2327–48.

Borjas, George J., Freeman, Richard B. & Katz, Lawrence F. (1997), 'How Much do Immigration and Trade Affect Labor Market Outcome?" *Brookings Papers on Economic Activity*, 1: 1–90.

Bourguignon, François (2015), *The Globalization of Inequality* (Princeton, NJ, Princeton University Press).

Bourguignon, François & Morrisson, Christian (2002), 'Inequality Among World Citizens: 1820–1992', *American Economic Review*, 92: 727–44. https://doi.org/10.1257/00028280260344443

Burstein, Ariel & Vogel, Jonathan (2016), 'International Trade, Technology, and the Skill Premium', *Journal of Political Economy* (forthcoming).

Burstein, Ariel, Morales, Eduardo & Vogel, Jonathan (2016), 'Changes in Between-group Inequality: Computers, Occupations, and International Trade', mimeo, 13 September.

Bustos, Paula. (2011a), 'The Impact of Trade Liberalization on Skill Upgrading: Evidence from Argentina', Barcelona BGSE working paper: 559.

Bustos, Paula (2011b), 'Trade Liberalization, Exports, and Technology Upgrading: Evidence on the Impact of MERCOSUR on Argentinean Firms', *American Economic Review*, 101: 304–40. https://doi.org/10.1257/aer.101.1.304

Card, David & DiNardo, John E. (2002), 'Skill-biased Technological Change and Rising Wage Inequality: Some Problems and Puzzles', *Journal of Labor Economics*, 20: 733–83. https://doi.org/10.1086/342055

Chetverikov, Denis, Larsen, Bradley & Parmer, Christopher (2016), 'IV Quantile Regression for Group-level Treatments, with an Application to the Distributional Effects of Trade', *Econometrica*, 84 (2): 809–33. https://doi.org/10.3982/ECTA12121

Costinot, Arnaud & Vogel, Jonathan (2010), 'Matching and Inequality in the World Economy', *Journal of Political Economy*, 118: 747–85. https://doi.org/10.1086/655858

Davidson, Carl, Matusz, Steven J. & Shevchenko, Andrei (2008), 'Globalization and Firm Level Adjustment with Imperfect Labor Markets', *Journal of International Economics*, 75: 295–309. https://doi.org/10.1016/j.jinteco.2008.02.004

Davis, Donald R. & Harrigan, James (2011), 'Good Jobs, Bad Jobs, and Trade Liberalization', *Journal of International Economics*, 84: 26–36. https://doi.org/10.1016/j.jinteco.2011.03.005

Diamond, Peter A. (1982a), 'Demand Management in Search Equilibrium', *Journal of Political Economy*, 90: 881–94https://doi.org/10.1086/261099.

Diamond, Peter A. (1982b), 'Wage Determination and Efficiency in Search Equilibrium', *Review of Economic Studies*, 49: 217–27. https://doi.org/10.2307/2297271

Eeckhout, Jan & Kircher, Philipp (2016), 'Assortative Matching with Large Firms', mimeo.

Egger, Hartmut & Kreickemeier, Udo (2009), 'Firm Heterogeneity and the Labor Market Effects of Trade Liberalization', *International Economic Review*, 50: 187–216. https://doi.org/10.1111/j.1468-2354.2008.00527.x

Feenstra, Robert C. (2015), *Advanced International Trade: Theory and Evidence* (Princeton, NJ, Princeton University Press).

Feenstra, Robert C. & Hanson, Gordon H. (1996), 'Foreign Investment, Outsourcing and Relative Wages', in Robert C. Feenstra, Gene M. Grossman & Douglas A. Irwin (eds), *The Political Economy of Trade Policy: Papers in Honor of Jagdish Bhagwati* (Cambridge, MA, The MIT Press) chapter 6.

Feenstra, Robert C. & Hanson, Gordon H. (1997), 'Foreign Direct Investment and Relative Wages: Evidence from Mexico's Maquiladoras', *Journal of International Economics*, 42: 371–93. https://doi.org/10.1016/S0022-1996(96)01475-4

Feenstra, Robert C. & Hanson, Gordon H. (1999), 'Productivity Measurement and the Impact of Trade and Technology on Wages: Estimates for the U.S., 1972–1990', *Quarterly Journal of Economics*, 114: 907–40. https://doi.org/10.1162/003355399556179

Feenstra, Robert C. & Hanson, Gordon H. (2003), 'Global Production Sharing and Rising Inequality: A Survey of Trade and Wages', in Kwan Choi & James Harrigan (eds), *Handbook of International Trade* (New York, Basil Blackwell) 617–868. https://doi.org/10.1002/9780470756461.ch6

Findlay, Ronald & O'Rourke, Kevin H. (2007), *Power and Plenty: Trade, War, and the World Economy in the Second Millennium* (Princeton, NJ, Princeton University Press).

Goldberg, Pinelopi K. & Pavcnik, Nina (2007), 'Distributional Effects of Globalization in Developing Countries', *Journal of Economic Literature*, 45: 39–82. https://doi.org/10.1257/jel.45.1.39

Goos, Maarten, Manning, Alan & Salomons, Anna (2009), 'Job Polarization in Europe', *American Economic Review*, 99: 58–63. https://doi.org/10.1257/aer.99.2.58

Grossman, Gene M. (2013), 'Heterogeneous Workers and International Trade', *Review of World Economics*, 149: 211–45. https://doi.org/10.1007/s10290-013-0152-7

Grossman, Gene M. & Helpman, Elhanan (2017), 'Growth, Trade, and Inequality', http://scholar.harvard.edu/files/helpman/files/growth_trade_and_inequality_032117gg.pdf.
Grossman, Gene M. & Maggi, Giovanni (2000), 'Diversity and Trade', *American Economic Review* 90 (5): 1255–75. https://doi.org/10.1257/aer.90.5.1255
Grossman, Gene M., Helpman, Elhanan & Kircher, Philipp (2017), 'Matching, Sorting, and the Distributional Effects of International Trade', *Journal of Political Economy* 125(1): 224–64. https://doi.org/10.1086/689608
Harrigan, James & Reshef, Ariel (2015), 'Skill-biased Heterogeneous Firms, Trade Liberalization and the Skill Premium', *Canadian Journal of Economics*, 48: 1024–66. https://doi.org/10.1111/caje.12167
Helpman, Elhanan (2004), *The Mystery of Economic Growth* (Cambridge, MA, Harvard University Press).
Helpman, Elhanan. (2011), *Understanding Global Trade* (Cambridge, MA, Harvard University Press). https://doi.org/10.4159/harvard.9780674061019
Helpman, Elhanan, Itskhoki, Oleg, Muendler, Marc-Andreas & Redding, Stephen J. (2010), 'Inequality and Unemployment in a Global Economy,' *Econometrica*, 78: 1239–83. https://doi.org/10.3982/ECTA8640
Helpman, Elhanan, Itskhoki, Oleg & Redding, Stephen J. (2017), 'Trade and Inequality: From Theory to Estimation', *Review of Economic Studies* 84, 357–405.
Jones, Ronald W. (1971), 'A Three-factor Model in Theory, Trade and History', in Jagdish N. Bhagwati, Ronald W. Jones, Robert A. Mundell & Jaroslav Vanek (eds), *Trade, Balance of Payments and Growth: Papers in International Economics in Honor of Charles P. Kindleberger* (Amsterdam, North-Holland) 3–21.
Jones, Ronald W. & Scheinkman, Jose A. (1977), 'The Relevance of the Two-sector Production Model in Trade Theory', *Journal of Political Economy*, 85: 909–35. https://doi.org/10.1086/260615
Katz, Lawrence F. & Autor, David H. (1999), 'Changes in the Wage Structure and Earnings inequality', in Orly Ashenfelter & David Card (eds), *Handbook of Labor Economics, Volume 3* (Amsterdam, North-Holland) 1463–555. https://doi.org/10.1016/s1573-4463(99)03007-2
Katz, Lawrence F. & Murphy, Kevin M. (1992), 'Changes in Relative Wages, 1963–1987: Supply and Demand Factors', *Quarterly Journal of Economics*, 107: 35–78. https://doi.org/10.2307/2118323
Krugman, Paul R. (1995), 'Growing World Trade: Causes and Consequences', *Brookings Papers on Economic Activity*, 1: 327–62. https://doi.org/10.2307/2534577
Krugman, Paul R. (2000), 'Technology, Trade and Factor Prices', *Journal of International Economics*, 50: 51–72. https://doi.org/10.1016/S0022-1996(99)00016-1
Krugman, Paul R. (2008), 'Trade and Wages, Reconsidered', *Brookings Papers on Economic Activity*, 2: 103–38. https://doi.org/10.1353/eca.0.0006
Lawrence, Robert & Slaughter, Matthew J. (1993), 'International Trade and American Wages in the 1980s: Giant Sucking Sound or Small Hiccup?' *Brookings Papers on Economic Activity*, 1: 161–211. https://doi.org/10.2307/2534739
Leamer, Edward E. (1998), 'In Search of Stolper–Samuelson Linkages between International Trade and Lower Wages', in Susan M. Collins (ed), *Imports, Exports, and the American Worker* (Washington, DC, Brookings Institution Press) 141–202.
Leamer, Edward E. (2000), 'What's the Use of Factor Content?' *Journal of International Economics*, 50: 17–50. https://doi.org/10.1016/S0022-1996(99)00004-5
Lemieux, Thomas. (2006), 'Increased Residual Wage Inequality: Composition Effect, Noisy Data, or Rising Demand for Skill', *American Economic Review*, 96: 461–98. https://doi.org/10.1257/aer.96.3.461

Machin, Stephen & van Reenen, John (1998), 'Technology and Changes in Skill Structure: Evidence from Seven OECD Countries', *Quarterly Journal of Economics*, 113: 1215–44. https://doi.org/10.1162/003355398555883

McCormick, Michael (2001), *Origins of the European Economy: Communications and Commerce, AD 300–900* (New York, Cambridge University Press).

Maddison, Angus (2001), *The World Economy: A Millennial Perspective* (Paris, OECD). https://doi.org/10.1787/9789264189980-en

Melitz, Marc J (2003), 'The Impact of Trade on Intra-industry Reallocations and Aggregate Industry Productivity', *Econometrica*, 71: 1695–725. https://doi.org/10.1111/1468-0262.00467

Melitz, Marc J. & Redding, Stephen (2014), 'Heterogeneous Firms and Trade', in Gita Gopinath, Elhanan Helpman & Kenneth Rogoff (eds), *Handbook of International Economics, Volume 4* (Amsterdam, North Holland) 1–54. https://doi.org/10.1016/b978-0-444-54314-1.00001-x

Mincer, Jacob A (1974), *Schooling, Experience, and Earnings* (New York, The National Bureau of Economic Research).

Mortensen, Dale T. & Pissarides, Christopher A. (1994), 'Job Creation and Job Destruction in the Theory of Unemployment', *Review of Economic Studies*, 61: 397–415. https://doi.org/10.2307/2297896

OECD (2015), *In It Together: Why Less Inequality Benefits All* (Paris, OECD Publishing).

Ohnsorge, Franziska & Trefler, Daniel (2007), 'Sorting it Out: International Trade with Heterogeneous Workers', *Journal of Political Economy*, 115: 868–92. https://doi.org/10.1086/523657

Oi, Walter Y. & Idson, T. L. (1999), 'Firm Size and Wages', in Orly Ashenfelter & David Card (eds.), *Handbook of Labor Economics, Volume 3* (Amsterdam, Elsevier) 2165–214. https://doi.org/10.1016/S1573-4463(99)30019-5

Rodrik, Dani (2015), *Economics Rules: The Rights and Wrongs of the Dismal Science* (New York, W. W. Norton & Company).

Sampson, Thomas (2014), 'Selection into Trade and Wage Inequality', *American Economic Journal: Microeconomics*, 6 (3): 157–202. https://doi.org/10.1257/mic.6.3.157

Stolper, Wolfgang W. & Samuelson, Paul A. (1941), 'Protection and Real Wages', *Review of Economic Studies*, IX: 58–73. https://doi.org/10.2307/2967638

Trefler, Daniel. (2004), 'The Long and Short of the Canada–U.S. Free Trade Agreement', *American Economic Review*, 94: 870–95. https://doi.org/10.1257/0002828042002633

van Zanden, Luiten, Jan, Baten, Joerg, Foldvari, Peter & van Leeuwen, Bas (2014), 'The Changing Shape of Global Inequality 1820–200: Exploring a New Dataset', *The Review of Income and Wealth*, 60(2): 279–97. https://doi.org/10.1111/roiw.12014

Verhoogen, Eric. (2008), 'Trade, Quality Upgrading, and Wage Inequality in the Mexican Manufacturing Sector: Theory and Evidence from an Exchange Rate Shock', *Quarterly Journal of Economics*, 123: 489–530. https://doi.org/10.1162/qjec.2008.123.2.489

Yeaple, Stephen R. (2005), 'A Simple Model of Firm Heterogeneity, International Trade, and Wages', *Journal of International Economics*, 65: 1–20. https://doi.org/10.1016/j.jinteco.2004.01.001

Zhu, Susan Chun & Trefler, Daniel (2005), 'Trade and Inequality in Developing Countries: A General Equilibrium Analysis', *Journal of International Economics*, 65: 21–48. https://doi.org/10.1016/j.jinteco.2003.11.005

Note on the author: Elhanan Helpman is the Galen L. Stone Professor of International Trade at Harvard University and a Distinguished Fellow of the Canadian Institute for Advanced Research. He holds a BA degree in Economics and Statistics from Tel Aviv University, an MA degree in Economics from the same institution, and a PhD degree in Economics from Harvard University. He also is Professor Emeritus at Tel Aviv

University, where he served as the Archie Sherman Professor of International Economic Relations. Helpman's contributions include studies of the balance of payments, exchange rate regimes, stabilisation programmes, foreign debt and political economy. He is a cofounder of the 'new trade theory' and the 'new growth theory'. He is a Foreign Honorary Member of the American Academy of Arts and Sciences, a Corresponding Fellow of the British Academy, a member of the European Academy of Sciences and Arts and a Distinguished Fellow of the American Economic Association. He was President of the Israeli Economic Association and President of the Econometric Society. He received the Mahalanobis Memorial Medal, the Bernhard Harms Prize, the Rothschild Prize, the EMET Prize, the Nemmers Prize, the Onassis Prize, the BBVA Frontiers of Knowledge Award, the Jean-Jacques Laffont Prize, and the Israel Prize.
ehelpman@harvard.edu

To cite the article: Elhanan Helpman (2017), 'Globalisation and wage inequality', *Journal of the British Academy*, 5: 125–162.
DOI https://doi.org/10.85871/jba/005.125

Journal of the British Academy (ISSN 2052–7217) is published by
The British Academy—the national academy for the humanities and social sciences.
10–11 Carlton House Terrace, London, SW1Y 5AH
www.britishacademy.ac.uk

Journal of the British Academy, **5**, 163–176. DOI https://doi.org/10.5871/jba/005.163
Posted 19 July 2017.

The stress test: Can stress ever be beneficial?

Joint British Academy–British Psychological Society Lecture read 22 September 2016

IAN H ROBERTSON
Trinity College Dublin

Abstract: The human brain needs an optimal amount of challenge in order to perform optimally. This is because challenge activates the neurotransmitter noradrenaline (NA) which, at optimal levels, facilitates good brain performance; in contrast, when levels of NA are either too low (sleepy, jaded, bored, mood low) or too high (stressed, anxiety, pressure), the brain underperforms because of the key neuromodulatory effect of noradrenaline. Moderate amounts of stress can actually increase performance and attention to such a 'sweet spot' and hence to higher levels of cognitive performance with resulting improved confidence. Stress arises when people perceive the demands made upon them to exceed their ability to cope with these demands. But this in turn depends upon appraisal of the stress and in particular whether the stressors are seen as challenges to be overcome or threats to be avoided. A 'challenge' mindset makes it easier for individuals to use adversity to attain this optimal zone of performance and build resilience. Furthermore, moderately stressful events in a person's life have a number of potentially beneficial effects including emotional resilience, better chronic pain tolerance and even enhanced cognitive function.

Keywords: stress, anxiety, mood, attention, adversity, resilience, cognitive function, chronic pain.

Attitudes to stress have changed considerably over the last hundred years in the developed world. Anecdotal accounts of parenting and schooling from the first part of the 20th century are replete with tales of harsh treatments that aimed to 'toughen' children and adolescents, with corresponding attitudes to adults. The inevitable psychological casualties of such regimes, along with the growth of psychological and sociological research, eventually helped trigger a more person-centred approach to psychological vulnerabilities that came to prevail, in the Western world at least, during the late 20th and early 21st centuries.

Remarkably, however, this change has coincided with a very significant increase in diagnosed psychological problems linked to perceived stress. Stress can be defined as the perception that the demands made upon one exceed one's resources to cope with these. The resulting emotion is anxiety. Almost one in five UK citizens are estimated to suffer a significant anxiety disorder in any one year (Fineberg *et al.* 2013), with a similar estimated prevalence in the USA (Kessler *et al.* 2005). Chronic anxiety lowers mood and there has been a remarkable escalation in the prescription of SSRI (selective serotonin re-uptake inhibitors) drugs across the developed world for the treatment of both anxiety and mood disorders.

For example, the population of England in 2013 was 53 million and during that year the number of prescriptions for antidepressants was 53 million (most of which would be repeat prescriptions and not just new ones). Just two years later, in 2015, this figure had risen to 61 million (http://content.digital.nhs.uk), which represents a doubling in a decade.

This remarkable level of mass-medication of populations represents a considerable challenge in understanding stress—increasing treatment should surely reduce the disorder, whereas in contrast we are seeing a progressive rise. According to the World Health Organization, depression is now the single leading cause of disability worldwide (http://www.who.int/mediacentre/factsheets/fs369/en/).

How are these two social phenomena—the abandonment of the 'grin and bear it' approach to psychological distress on the one hand, and the massive expansion of diagnosis and treatment on the other—related, if at all?

One possibility is that the actual level of psychological distress has not increased, but rather it is being diagnosed more readily. This argument does not hold up, however, because self-reported mood has actually been declining over the last 70 years in the USA, at least. The average score on a standard measure of depressed mood (MMPI depression scale) among students has risen steadily over that period—by around 20 per cent on average (Twenge *et al.* 2010).

Young Westerners, then, report themselves to be significantly less happy now than they did 70 years ago, and hence under more stress. There are a number of socio-cultural–economic reasons for this which are neither fully understood nor within the scope of the present paper to explore.

In this paper, I set out the evidence that one key psychological factor may play a part in this epidemic of distress—namely a failure to understand and embrace the positive effects that moderate levels of stress can have on mind, body and emotions.

This seemingly counter-intuitive approach to moderate stress understandably runs against the grain of a mental health movement that seeks to minimise stress and anxiety, if for no other reasons than of awakening unpleasant resonances of the 'grin and bear it' approach to psychological distress that pertained in the first half of the 20th century.

Yet the evidence, as will be seen in the course of this paper, is quite strong that properly embraced, moderate adversity and its associated stress can have quite significant beneficial effects which, if appreciated and used, could help individuals harness moderate stress rather than seek to avoid it and have it medicalised.

A related question is whether the medicalisation of stress represented by antidepressant prescribing figures causes as many problems as it solves? Is stress always something to be treated—or can it sometimes have beneficial effects? This paper will examine the extent to which attitudes to, and tolerance of, adversity, can influence psychological well-being. I will also ask whether, under certain circumstances, stress can have positive effects that a possible over-reliance on prescription medications may mask. Answering these questions, however, requires me to address some questions about the human brain and behaviour that ostensibly have little to do with stress.

WHY DO CIVIL ENGINEERS BUILD BENDS IN ROADS WHERE THERE IS NO GEOLOGICAL NEED TO DO SO?

Civil engineers avoid building long, straight roads because experience has taught them that unless curves are built into them, drivers tend to lose concentration and drive off them (The Highways Agency 2016). This is because *sustained attention* is one of the hardest tasks for the human brain to achieve and is the major cause of accidents not just on roads, but also on railways across the world when train drivers travel through red lights due to lapsed attention (Edkins & Pollock 1997).

Attention refers to the capacity to control, moment to moment, the contents of awareness. There are three broad categories of attention (Robertson *et al.* 1996), the most common being selective attention, which refers to the ability to choose to attend to one strand of information from the external (e.g. one person's voice against a background of many) or internal (e.g. memory of a particular conversation) environment. Selective attention can be deployed across sensory modalities: for example, allowing you to focus your mind on the clarinet against the complex sounds of an orchestra.

The second category of attention is attentional switching, where focus is shifted from one stream of information (e.g. the melody of the clarinet) to another (e.g. the words sung by the accompanying vocal soloist).

Sustained attention is the third category of attention and refers to the ability to keep one's mind on routine tasks and over-ride the brain's tendency preferentially to process novelty and change over predictable repetition.

Sustained attention is hence required in situations that have no intrinsic attention-grabbing properties such as change, novelty, emotional tone, threat or challenge. Video-games, for example, require little sustained attention because their designers are expert at externally controlling our attention through these variables. In contrast, reading a book or listening to a lecture demand that we can keep our mind on the task in hand by internally- rather than externally-driven processes.

My colleagues and I in Dublin and Cambridge found that we could measure sustained attention using a simple computerised test called the SART (Sustained Attention to Response Task) which simply required people to press a button to every number between 1 and 9 which appeared at a rate of just slower than one per second, *except* the number 3 (Robertson *et al.* 1997). This apparently very easy task resulted in a surprising number of errors with people uttering 'Oops', or worse, when they found themselves 'tricked' into pressing the 3 when they had not intended to.

This SART turned out to be an excellent laboratory measure of the type of sustained attention needed to keep your mind on a dull, repetitive situation like driving a train on a long straight track. It is also, it turns out, a pretty good measure of people's propensity to make absent-minded slips in everyday life, as colleagues in Canada showed after reviewing the SART literature (Smilek *et al.* 2010).

We therefore considered the SART to create the laboratory equivalent of the long straight road that makes it so difficult for drivers to concentrate. What is the equivalent of the road with bends it, however? Tom Manly and I tested the hypothesis that if you increased the proportion of no-go targets in the test, it would be experienced as more difficult, compared to the very low frequency version, because it would involve more frequent switches between press and no-press modes. This is in fact what happened—paradoxically as the test became more 'difficult' (i.e. more like the road with bends in it), the proportion of absent-minded false presses decreased (Manly *et al.* 1999).

What is more, while the low-frequency (straight-road) SART distinguished clearly between people who were more or less prone to everyday absent-mindedness, the high-frequency (bendy road) task did not, as Figure 1 shows.

Attention Deficit Hyperactivity Disorder (ADHD) is a common childhood complaint that persists in altered form into adulthood in approximately 50 per cent of cases (Bellgrove *et al.* 2005). A key symptom of this problem is a difficulty in keeping attention focussed on the task in hand, resulting in great distractibility and behavioural difficulties in children, not least in the school classroom. Our research suggests that the sustained attention system is particularly impaired in ADHD, while the selective attention system is relatively spared (Manly *et al.* 2001).

Noradrenaline (NA) is one of the brain's key neurotransmitters or 'chemical messengers'. It is produced deep in the mid-brain in a tiny structure called the locus coeruleus, and is triggered whenever we are engaged, excited, frightened, alerted, curious, challenged or generally aroused (Sara 2009). NA is a 'neuromodulator', because in the right quantities, it helps different parts of the brain synchronise sweetly with each other to produce fluent performance in mental or physical tasks.

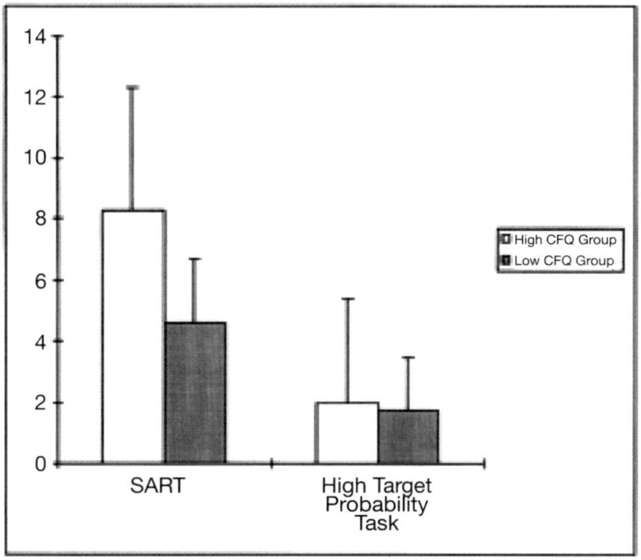

Figure 1. Fewer absent-minded errors as a task becomes more challenging (Manly *et al.* 1999).

We discovered that both in children with Attention Deficit Hyperactivity Disorder, and in healthy young adults, a highly specific link existed between the availability of noradrenaline in the brain and the ability to sustain attention—in particular the propensity to make SART errors (Bellgrove *et al.* 2006, Greene *et al.* 2009).

The prefrontal cortex of the brain, which occupies that region above the eyes and from the ears forward, has long been linked to high-level 'executive' control over our behaviour, where planning, flexibility, judgement and inhibition of irrelevant activity are emphasised. Attention is a crucial part of such complex behaviour, and sustained attention is particulary important in that it involves over-riding more primitive impulses to respond to immediately attractive stimuli in favour of colourless longer-term goals (such as not crashing a train, for example).

We also found that a particular region of the brain—the right prefrontal cortex, was implicated in the ability to sustain attention. We showed this in two separate functional Magnetic Resonance Imaging (fMRI) studies in Cambridge and Toronto where we compared which brain regions were active—in each it turned out to be the right dorsolateral prefrontal cortex—when people were trying to keep their mind on the SART test, compared to when they were not (O'Connor *et al.* 2011, Manly *et al.* 2003).

Then, using a quite different methodology, colleagues in Belgium gave the SART to people who had the misfortune to suffer a stroke, and examined damage to which part of the brain best predicted having difficulty doing the SART accurately. These researchers confirmed the fMRI findings by showing a very specific linkage of SART errors to right prefrontal cortex lesions (Molenberghs *et al.* 2009). A subsequent meta-analysis of scores of different studies of sustained attention tasks confirmed the involvement of the right dorsolateral prefrontal cortex in sustaining attention to routine, boring tasks (Singh-Curry & Husain 2009).

But had these two disparate correlates of the SART—right prefrontal cortex on the one hand, and the neurotransmitter noradrenaline on the other—anything to do with each other? A review of the literature showed that indeed they had—studies which used drugs to increase activity specifically in the noradrenaline system consistently found that the brain region that increased its activity in response was the right dorsolateral prefrontal cortex (Bush *et al.* 2012, Grefkes *et al.* 2010, Chamberlain *et al.* 2007).

One major challenge of following through on this link between sustained attention and noradrenaline is that it has not been possible directly to observe NA activity in the waking human brain. We were able to overcome this hurdle in Dublin where Peter Murphy, Redmond O'Connell, Josh Balsters and I showed that the eye's pupil was an accurate indicator of NA activity in the human brain.

We are familiar with people's pupils dilating in pleasure or attraction, which reflects the brain's increasing NA activity as part of an emotional response. But the pupil also dilates whenever we pay attention to something through being curious, surprised, engaged or challenged. This is quite different from the pupil response to changes in light—for example, the pupil dilating when it becomes dark. This latter pupil response is controlled by the neurotransmitter acetylcholine, while the pupil's 'attention response' is controlled by noradrenaline.

We showed that this was the case by looking at the pupil's response to targets that participants had been trained to pay attention to, while simultaneously measuring the brain's activity using fMRI, in the part of the brain known to produce NA, the locus coeruleus. For the first time, our group demonstrated that whenever the pupil got bigger in response to a target, the locus coeruleus increased its activity.

But one other finding confirmed an early finding in psychology, the Yerkes–Dodson curve (Yerkes & Dodson 1908). This inverted-U-shaped curve demonstrates an important principle of many human functions, including those of many neurotransmitters, namely that peak performance (say in accuracy of response, or speed of thinking, or reliability of memory) is achieved where there are intermediate levels of 'arousal'. For example, if alertness levels are low because it is very early in the morning, a person may be sluggish in their ability to do mental arithmetic. Similarly, if alertness levels are too high because of high anxiety, arithmetic performance may be similarly impaired. In the median zone, at the peak of the inverted U, there is a 'sweet spot' of performance.

Animal research has shown that NA and some other neurotransmitters—dopamine, for example—share this inverted-U-shaped function, and this fact in relation to NA was thought to underpin the Yerkes–Dodson curve.

We were able to show for the first time that the human pupil response showed this Yerkes–Dodson-type curve (Murphy *et al.* 2014). Just before every target, the pupil diameter was measured, and then the quality of attention (measured by the variability of the speed of response, a very sensitive measure of attentional focus) for responses at different pupil diameters measured. We found that small and large pre-target pupil diameters were associated with poor attention, in contrast to medium diameters which were associated with very good sustained attention (Murphy *et al.* 2011), as seen in Figure 2, where lower scores represent better attentional focus.

So, in addressing the question as to why civil engineers build unnecessary bends in long roads, the answer is that it is to engineer a level of arousal closer to the 'sweet spot' represented by moderate levels of noradrenergic activity in the locus coeruleus. Like many of the brain's neurotransmitters, this inverted-U-shape function dictates that both too low (under-stimulation, low challenge) and high (over-stimulation, very high challenge/stress) levels impair attention.

Driving down an unremittingly straight road places too great a demand on the brain's capacity for sustaining attention and loss of focus and alertness result, with potentially dangerous outcomes. Civil engineers have learned by trial and error that

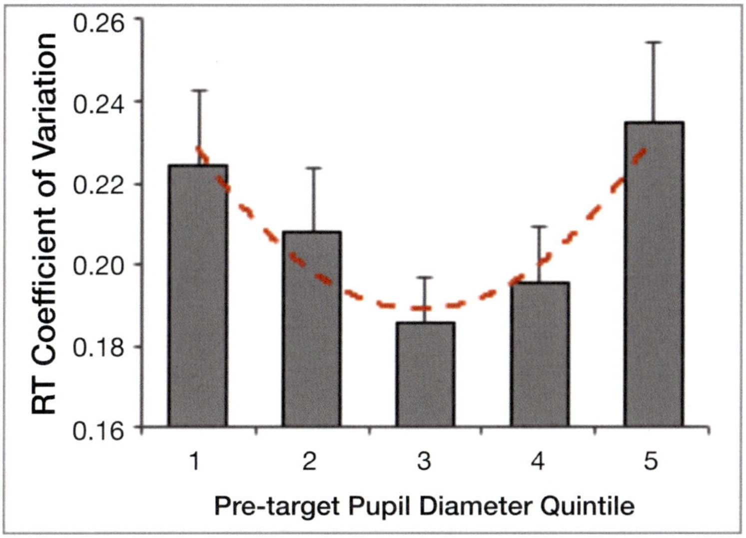

Figure 2. Optimal focus with moderate levels of pupil dilation/noradrenergic function.

they have to build 'challenge' into their roads in order to trigger the driver's brain to produce sufficient NA to maintain reasonable driving performance.

We were able to put this principle into practice with people suffering from traumatic brain injury (TBI) in whom disruption of frontal lobe activity commonly leads to a number of difficulties, including difficulty in sustaining attention (Robertson *et al.* 1997). We were able temporarily to improve their cognitive and emotional functioning. We did this using a simulated hotel receptionist job situation where they had to perform a number of different tasks and remember not to neglect any one task through giving equal time to each. On average TBI individuals missed out one complete task—a really poor job performance—compared to control, non-impaired individuals.

We then tried to increase their alertness levels by ringing a buzzer randomly and occasionally during the task—the equivalent of putting a bend in the long straight road. This simple intervention led to them—temporarily, of course—showing normal performance on the receptionist task, probably because their brain was temporarily nearer its optimal level of NA activity due to the arousing stimulus (Manly *et al.* 2002).

We put this principle into more long-term use in adults with ADHD, many of whom, we had discovered, were chronically short of NA in their brains and hence had major problems with attention. With Redmond O'Connell in Dublin we showed that you could train them to give temporary boosts to their arousal by feeding back to them using a device called a Skin Conductance Response (SCR) device, which measures the skin's sweatiness. This measure is a very good marker of the brain's state of arousal and by allowing people to see what their arousal levels are on the screen of a computer, they can learn to control it up or down, which is the principle of 'biofeedback'.

We trained these adults with ADHD to generate spikes of arousal at important times when they would otherwise be liable to make an absent-minded or impulsive slip (O'Connell *et al.* 2008) and subsequently we developed a self-administered training programme that produced extended improvement in ADHD symptoms, cognitive function and depression in blind follow-up three months later (Salomone *et al.* 2015).

These findings led to a second, related, question regarding the relationship between stress and arousal.

WHY IS HIGHER CORTISOL ASSOCIATED WITH *BETTER* PERFORMANCE IN LOW-MATHS-ANXIETY STUDENTS AND WITH *WORSE* PERFORMANCE IN HIGH-MATHS-ANXIETY STUDENTS?

Cortisol is the human stress hormone, part of the body's 'fight or flight' response, and a useful short-term energiser of human performance in conditions where urgent action is required. Short-term, cortisol boosts mental and physical performance, but when it is elevated over prolonged periods, it can cause damage to the body and brain.

In any stressful situation—for example, performing in front of a critical audience —it is normal to see cortisol levels go up in healthy people. And this is true in one study where people had to perform mental arithmetic in front of a critical audience—a stressful situation that caused all participants to generate big increases in cortisol (Mattarella-Micke *et al.* 2011).

All participants were equally arithmetically capable, but half were, even before the experiment, anxious about their ability, while the other half were not.

As might be expected, among the maths-anxious students, the more their cortisol levels surged, the worse they performed. But what was very strange was that the reverse was true for the maths non-anxious students—the more their cortisol levels rose, the *better* they performed. This is likely because the anxious students were already high in arousal because of this, and the extra arousal created by performing difficult problems in front of an audience pushed them over beyond their 'sweet spot' of functioning, and hence to poorer performance.

The low-maths-anxiety students on the other hand, were probably at lower levels of arousal and the challenge of performance pushed them *up* towards their 'sweet spot'. Stress for them, therefore, fuelled better performance because of this.

In a much darker domain, stress appeared to bolster cognitive performance in a much more enduring, counter-intuitive way. My colleagues in Dublin working on the Irish Longitudinal Study on Ageing (TILDA) found that roughly one in fifteen of the fifty- to ninety-year-olds reported that they had been sexually abused as children. This wasn't the surprise—such figures are fairly typical of research studies worldwide. As is usually the case, in adulthood these abuse victims were more depressed and also less physically healthy than their contemporaries. This fairly typical finding is explained by the prolonged stress-linked damage to the body caused by being subjected to early abuse. So the picture here fitted with what we already knew, except in one respect: despite their other problems, they were cognitively better on a number of cognitive tests including their ability to remember lists of words, their speed of thinking, and their ability to control their attention ('executive function') than non-abused people in the study of the same age, social and educational background (Feeney *et al.* 2013) Because of the size of the study—nearly 7,000 people—we could rule out other physical, social and mental factors that might have caused the differences.

Stress also has other unexpected effects amidst human suffering. One Dutch study measured cognitive abilities in more than a thousand people in their early seventies, and then again three years later (Comijs *et al.* 2011). The seventies is a difficult decade for many, with new pressures on people, such as a spouse succumbing to serious ill-ness. Conflicts with families can also spring up during the major changes that are so common at this time of life. The Amsterdam group were no exception—over three quarters of them reported having experienced at least one very significant 'life event' during the three years. And those whose partners had suffered a serious illness showed *better* cognitive function than those who had not. Furthermore, people who had run into severe conflict with other people—family, friends, neighbours, etc—were *also* cognitively sharper three years later.

This is very likely because stress raises noradrenaline levels in older people, some of whose relatively undemanding lifestyles might have resulted in low levels of noradrenergic stimulation. The challenge and stress of looking after a seriously ill partner, or the demands of coping with family conflict, may have raised these levels to nearer the optimum 'sweet spot' that is beneficial to cognitive functioning.

These and other findings led me to propose a theory to explain how 'cognitive reserve' functions to reduce risk of dementia. Cognitive reserve is the term coined for a combination of education, intelligence level and mental stimulation that together strongly predict vulnerability to Alzheimer's Disease (Stern *et al.* 1996). Education level is one of the strongest predictors of reduced risk of dementia, yet there has been no adequate theory of how a social variable like education might influence a biological variable such as Alzheimer's Disease. My noradrenergic theory of cognitive reserve was the first attempt at such a theory.

All forms of mental challenge, including moderate stress, increase noradrenaline (NA) levels in the brain. Providing NA stays near its 'sweet spot', then it not only improves cognitive functioning but also helps the brain form new connections and new brain cells (Robertson 2013), a view that has subsequently been supported in studies in other laboratories (Wilson *et al.* 2013, Clewett *et al.* 2016).

But it is not only in old age that stress can be beneficial. Young adults who have experienced moderate levels of adversity in their lives have lower levels of emotional vulnerability than is the case for those who have had no or little adversity (Seery *et al.* 2010a). Those who have experienced moderate stressors in their life are also much less likely to be disabled and off work if they suffer chronic back pain, compared to those who have suffered little or no adversity (Seery *et al.* 2010b).

Could this help explain the rising levels of distress across generations? Have more recent generations been protected against adversity in the relatively prosperous and stable Western world that has existed since World War 2? Has the switch to a more 'psychological' approach to stress, contrasting with the 'grin and bear it' attitudes of previous generations, led to a relative over-protection of younger people? If we accept the results by Seery and colleagues about the role of moderate adversity in emotionally toughening younger people against various adult emotional and physical ailments, then this must be seen as a tenable hypothesis.

*****

Stress, in moderate levels, can have positive emotional, cognitive and physical consequences, but this depends on appropriate cognitive appraisal and a resulting optimal level of arousal. Some adversity appears to be essential in life so that individuals can learn habits of managing stress, but also so that they can experience the optimisation of noradrenaline levels in the brain that properly appraised 'challenge' can cause.

The inverted-U-shaped function of stress—too much *or* too little can be bad for you—is related to the inverted-U-shaped function of key brain neurotransmitters such as noradrenaline. Given that NA is a key component of the 'fight or flight' stress response, this is not particularly surprising.

The question arises whether in our anxiety as a culture to avoid the harsh 'grin and bear it' attitudes of our forebears, we have lurched too far into a realm where any stress is seen as bad and to be avoided. Has this resulted in Western cultures in over-protection of youngsters from what otherwise might be psychologically strengthening experiences of mild adversity, albeit with some inevitable attendant greater risk?

Linked to this approach to distress are the psychological implications of administering medication to millions of people for their psychological distress. What message does this convey to them about the causes of their emotional difficulties? Does it imply that their emotions are caused by biological factors outside of their control? And if so, does that then sabotage their abilities to benefit from moderate levels of stress and the psychological and physiological learnings—'inoculation'—that can arise from them?

Stress can be beneficial to both emotional and cognitive functioning. By realising this fact, and understanding how it happens, we can hope that people may learn to cope better and benefit from the lessons that moderately severe stressors can teach us.

This summary cannot go into the full detail of the fascinating science surrounding the positives of stress and the reader is referred to my book on the subject (Robertson 2016) for a fuller account.

Acknowledgments
I would like to thank my wonderful colleagues in Cambridge, London, Dublin and Toronto with whom I have worked over the last 35 years. I would also like to thank the British Psychological Society for inviting me to give the annual Joint British Academy – British Psychological Society Lecture which the current paper documents. My grateful thanks to the British Academy for their support, expertise and hospitality.

REFERENCES

Bellgrove, M. A., Gill, M., Hawi, Z., Kirley, A. & Robertson, I. H. (2005), 'Dissecting the Attention Deficit Hyperactivity Disorder (ADHD) Phenotype: Sustained Attention and Spatial Attention Asymmetries in Relation to Dopamine Transporter (DAT1) Transporter', *Neuropsychologia*, 43: 1847–57.https://doi.org/10.1016/j.neuropsychologia.2005.03.011

Bellgrove, M. A., Hawi, Z., Gill, M. & Robertson, I. H. (2006), 'The Cognitive Genetics of Attention Deficit Hyperactivity Disorder (ADHD): Sustained attention as a Candidate Phenotype', *Cortex*, 42: 838–45. https://doi.org/10.1016/S0010-9452(08)70426-X

Bush, G., Holmes, J., Shin, L. M., Surman, C., Makris, N., Mick, E., Seidman, L. J. & Biederman, J. (2012), 'Atomoxetine Increases Fronto-Parietal Functional MRI Activation in Attention-Deficit/ Hyperactivity Disorder: A Pilot Study', *Psychiatry Research*, 211: 88–91. https://doi.org/10.1016/j.pscychresns.2012.09.004

Chamberlain, S. R., Campo, N. D., Dowson, J., Müller, U., Clark, L., Robbins, T. W. & Sahakian, B. J. (2007), 'Atomoxetine Improved Response Inhibition in Adults With Attention Deficit/ Hyperactivity Disorder', *Biological Psychiatry*, 62: 977–84. https://doi.org/10.1016/j.biopsych.2007.03.003

Clewett, D. V., Lee, T.-H., Greening, S., Ponzio, A., Margalit, E. & Mather, M. (2016), 'Neuromelanin Marks The Spot: Identifying a Locus Coeruleus Biomarker of Cognitive Reserve in Healthy Aging', *Neurobiology of Aging*, 37: 117–26. https://doi.org/10.1016/j.neurobiolaging.2015.09.019

Comijs, H. C., van den Kommer, T. N., Minnaar, R. W. M., Penninx, B. W. J. H. & Deeg, D. J. H. (2011), 'Accumulated and Differential Effects of Life Events on Cognitive Decline in Older Persons: Depending on Depression, Baseline Cognition, or ApoE ε4 Status', *The Journals of Gerontology Series B: Psychological Sciences and Social Sciences*, 66B: 111–20. https://doi.org/10.1093/geronb/gbr019

Edkins, G. & Pollock, C. (1997), 'The Influence of Sustained Attention on Railway Accidents', *Accident Analysis and Prevention*, 29: 533–9. https://doi.org/10.1016/S0001-4575(97)00033-X

Feeney, J., Kamiya, Y., Robertson, I. H. & Kenny, R. A. (2013), 'Cognitive Function is Preserved in Older Adults with a Reported History of Childhood Sexual Abuse', *Journal of Traumatic Stress*, 26: 735–43. https://doi.org/10.1002/jts.21861

Fineberg, N. A., Haddad, P. M., Carpenter, L., Gannon, B., Sharpe, R., Young, A. H., Joyce, E., Rowe, J., Wellsted, D. & Nutt, D. J. (2013), 'The Size, Burden and Cost of Disorders of the Brain in the UK', *Journal of Psychopharmacology*, 27: 761–70. https://doi.org/10.1177/0269881113495118

Greene, C., Bellgrove, M. A., Gill, M. & Robertson, I. H. (2009), 'Noradrenergic Genotype Predicts Lapses in Sustained Attention', *Neuropsychologia*, 47: 591–4. https://doi.org/10.1016/j.neuropsychologia.2008.10.003

Grefkes, C., Wang, L. E., Eickhoff, S. B. & Fink, G. R. (2010), 'Noradrenergic Modulation of Cortical Networks Engaged in Visuomotor Processing', *Cerebral Cortex*, 20: 783–97. https://doi.org/10.1093/cercor/bhp144

Kessler, R. C., Chiu, W. T., Demler, O. & Walters, E. E. (2005), 'Prevalence, Severity, and Comorbidity of 12-Month DSM-IV Disorders in the National Comorbidity Survey Replication', *Archives of General Psychiatry*, 62: 617–27. https://doi.org/10.1001/archpsyc.62.6.617

Manly, T., Robertson, I. H., Galloway, M. & Hawkins, K. (1999), 'The Absent Mind: Further Investigations of Sustained Attention to Response', *Neuropsychologia*, 37: 661–70. https://doi.org/10.1016/S0028-3932(98)00127-4

Manly, T., Anderson, V., Nimmo-Smith, I., Turner, A., Watson, P. & Robertson, I. H. (2001), 'The Differential Assessment of Children's Attention: The Test of Everyday Attention for Children (TEA-Ch), Normative Sample and ADHD Performance', *Journal of Child Psychology and Psychiatry*, 42: 1–10. https://doi.org/10.1111/1469-7610.00806

Manly, T., Hawkins, K., Evans, J., Woldt, K. & Robertson, I. H. (2002), 'Rehabilitation of Executive Function: Facilitation of Effective Goal Management on Complex Tasks Using Periodic Auditory Alerts', *Neuropsychologia*, 40: 271–81. https://doi.org/10.1016/S0028-3932(01)00094-X

Manly, T., Owen, A. M., Datta, A., Lewis, G., Scott, S., Rorden, C., Pickard, J. & Robertson, I. H. (2003), 'Enhancing the Sensitivity of a Sustained Attention Task to Frontal Damage. Convergent Clinical and Functional Imaging Evidence', *Neurocase*, 9: 340–9. https://doi.org/10.1076/neur.9.4.340.15553

Mattarella-Micke, A., Mateo, J., Kozak, M. N., Foster, K. & Beilock, S. L. (2011), 'Choke or Thrive? The Relation Between Salivary Cortisol and Math Performance Depends on Individual Differences in Working Memory and Math-anxiety', *Emotion*, 11: 1000–5. https://doi.org/10.1037/a0023224

Molenberghs, P., Gillebert, C. R., Schoofs, H., Dupont, P., Peeters, R. & Vandenberghe, R. (2009), 'Lesion Neuroanatomy of the Sustained Attention to Response Task', *Neuropsychologia*, 47: 2866–75. https://doi.org/10.1016/j.neuropsychologia.2009.06.012

Murphy, P. R., Robertson, I. H., Balsters, J. H. & O'Connell, R. G. (2011), 'Pupillometry and P3 Index the Locus Coeruleus–Noradrenergic Arousal Function in Humans', *Psychophysiology*, 48: 1532–43. https://doi.org/10.1111/j.1469-8986.2011.01226.x

Murphy, P. R., O'Connell, R. G., O'Sullivan, M., Robertson, I. H. & Balsters, J. H. (2014), 'Pupil Diameter Covaries with BOLD Activity in Human Locus Coeruleus', *Human Brain Mapping*, 35: 4140–54. https://doi.org/10.1002/hbm.22466

O'Connell, R. G., Bellgrove, M. A., Dockree, P. M., Lau, A., Fitzgerald, M. & Robertson, I. H. (2008), 'Self-Alert Training: Volitional Modulation of Autonomic Arousal Improves Sustained Attention', *Neuropsychologia*, 46: 1379–90. https://doi.org/10.1016/j.neuropsychologia.2007.12.018

O'Connor, C., Robertson, I. H. & Levine, B. (2011), 'The Prosthetics of Vigilant Attention: Random Cuing Cuts Processing Demands', *Neuropsychology*, 25: 535–43. https://doi.org/10.1037/a0022767

Robertson, I. H. (2013), 'A Noradrenergic Theory of Cognitive Reserve: Implications for Alzheimer's Disease', *Neurobiology of Aging*, 34: 298–308. https://doi.org/10.1016/j.neurobiolaging.2012.05.019

Robertson, I. (2016) *The Stress Test: How Pressure Can Make You Stronger and Sharper* (London, Bloomsbury).

Robertson, I. H., Ward, T., Ridgeway, V. & Nimmo-Smith, I. (1996), 'The Structure of Normal Human Attention: The Test of Everyday Attention', *Journal of the International Neuropsychological Society*, 2: 525–34. https://doi.org/10.1017/S1355617700001697

Robertson, I. H., Manly, T., Andrade, J., Baddeley, B. T. & Yiend, J. (1997), ' "Oops!": Performance Correlates of Everyday Attentional Failures in Traumatic Brain Injured and Normal Subjects', *Neuropsychologia*, 35: 747–58. https://doi.org/10.1016/S0028-3932(97)00015-8

Salomone, S., Fleming, G. R., Shanahan, J. M., Castorina, M., Bramham, J., O'Connell, R. G. & Robertson, I. (2015), 'The Effects of a Self-Alert Training (SAT) Program in Adults with ADHD', *Frontiers in Human Neuroscience*, 9. https://doi.org/10.3389/fnhum.2015.00045

Sara, S. J. (2009), 'The Locus Coeruleus and Noradrenergic Modulation of Cognition', *Nature Reviews Neuroscience*, 10: 211–23. https://doi.org/10.1038/nrn2573

Seery, M. D., Holman, E. A. & Silver, R. C. (2010a), 'Whatever Does Not Kill Us: Cumulative Lifetime Adversity, Vulnerability, and Resilience', *Journal of Personality and Social Psychology*, 99, 1025–41. https://doi.org/10.1037/a0021344

Seery, M. D., Leo, R. J., Holman, E. A. & Cohen Silver, R. (2010b), 'Lifetime Exposure to Adversity Predicts Functional Impairment and Healthcare Utilization Among Individuals with Chronic Back Pain', *Pain*, 150: 507–15. https://doi.org/10.1016/j.pain.2010.06.007

Singh-Curry, V. & Husain, M. (2009), 'The Functional Role of the Inferior Parietal Lobe in the Dorsal and Ventral Stream Dichotomy', *Neuropsychologia*, 47: 1434–48. https://doi.org/10.1016/j.neuropsychologia.2008.11.033

Smilek, D., Carriere, J. S. A. & Cheyne, J. A. (2010), 'Failures of Sustained Attention in Life, Lab, and Brain: Ecological Validity of the SART', *Neuropsychologia*, 48: 2564–70. https://doi.org/10.1016/j.neuropsychologia.2010.05.002

Stern, R. A., Silva, S. G., Chaisson, N. & Evans, D. L. (1996), 'Influence of Cognitive Reserve on Neuropsychological Functioning in Asymptomatic Human Immunodeficiency Virus-1 Infection', *Archives of Neurology*, 53: 148–53. https://doi.org/10.1001/archneur.1996.00550020052015

The Highways Agency (2016) *Design Manual for Roads and Bridges. Road Geometry* (London, HM Stationery Office).

Twenge, J. M., Gentile, B., Dewall, C. N., Ma, D., Lacefield, K. & Schurtz, D. R. (2010), 'Birth Cohort Increases in Psychopathology Among Young Americans, 1938–2007: A Cross-temporal Meta-analysis of the MMPI', *Clinical Psychology Review*, 30: 145–54. https://doi.org/10.1016/j.cpr.2009.10.005

Wilson, R. S., Nag, S., Boyle, P. A., Hizel, L. P., Yu, L., Buchman, A. S., Schneider, J. A. & Bennett, D. A. (2013), 'Neural Reserve, Neuronal Density in the Locus Ceruleus, and Cognitive Decline', *Neurology*, 80: 1202–8. https://doi.org/10.1212/WNL.0b013e3182897103

Yerkes, R. M. & Dodson, J. D. (1908), 'The Relation of Strength of Stimulus to Rapidity of Habit-formation' *Journal of Comparative and Neurological Psychology*, 18: 459–82. https://doi.org/10.1002/cne.920180503

Note on the author: Ian Robertson (www.ianrobertson.org) is Emeritus Professor of Psychology at Trinity College Dublin, Visiting Professor at University College Dublin and at the University of Texas at Dallas (Center for BrainHealth). His book *The Stress Test: How Pressure Can Make You Stronger and Sharper*, published by Bloomsbury, is an account for the lay reader of 35 years of research which are summarised in the book and more briefly in this paper.
iroberts@tcd.ie

To cite the article: Ian H. Robertson (2017), 'The stress test: Can stress ever be beneficial?', *Journal of the British Academy*, 5: 163–176.
DOI https://doi.org/10.85871/jba/005.163

Journal of the British Academy (ISSN 2052–7217) is published by
The British Academy—the national academy for the humanities and social sciences.
10–11 Carlton House Terrace, London, SW1Y 5AH
www.britishacademy.ac.uk

Journal of the British Academy, **5**, 177–199. DOI https://doi.org/10.5871/jba/005.177
Posted 25 July 2017.

The duty to be generous (karam): Alternatives to rights-based asylum in the Middle East

Lecture on Africa, Asia and the Middle East
read 14 March 2017

DAWN CHATTY
Fellow of the Academy

Abstract: The international standard of providing protection to a category of people who have crossed state borders and fit the legal definition of 'refugee' is a rights-based construction fashionable in public discourse at present. Middle Eastern constructions of duty-based obligations to the guest, stranger, and person-in-need are, however, less well understood. This article explores the disconnect between international rights-based protection approaches to refuge and duty-based asylum (*karam*) commonly accepted in Middle Eastern societies. Returning to an exploration of Marcel Mauss' *Essay on the Gift*, it asks whether we are abrogating our moral responsibilities when we permit a 'rights-based approach' to asylum to prevail. In other words, when we mainstream 'rights' do we repress our human urge to provide refuge to those in need? Should we perhaps be looking for a more holistic engagement with humanitarian assistance and delivery that brings together a duty-based responsibility with a 'rights-based' approach?

Keywords: refuge, asylum, sanctuary, rights-based protection, duty-based asylum, *karam*, humanitarian assistance, *The Gift*

More than 60 per cent of the world's refugees currently huddle along the eastern (and southern) rim of the Mediterranean Sea. These—more than 10 million people—include Palestinians, Iraqis, and now Syrians who have fled violent conflict in their countries over the past century. Providing assistance to these enormous numbers of people has not been easy. Refuge, asylum, and sanctuary in the Middle East have become highly contested notions with many international human rights concepts competing with local and regional understandings. The international legal standard of providing protection to a category of people who have crossed international borders and fit the legal definition of 'refugee' is a rights-based hegemonic construction in public discourse at present. Local and regional Middle Eastern constructions of duty-based obligations to the guest, stranger, and person-in-need are, however, less well understood or appreciated in the West.

The international legal definition of refugees are those: who are outside of their country of nationality or habitual residence; who have a well-founded fear of being persecuted because of race, religion, nationality, membership of a particular social group, or political opinion; and who are unable or unwilling to avail themselves of the protection of that country, or to return there for fear of persecution (Article 1A (2) of the 1951 Convention). Those who meet this definition are deemed worthy of our sympathy and have rights enshrined in the United Nations 1951 Convention on the Status of Refugees and its 1967 Protocol.[1] None of the countries of the Middle East adhere to the 1951 United Nations Convention on the Status of Refugees; and Turkey, which is a signatory of the 1951 Convention and its 1967 Protocol, maintains a geographic reservation which restricts the definition of a 'refugee' to within the European arena. Thus, it is not surprising that these Middle Eastern countries hosting the majority of the world's refugees are often taken to task by Western commentators for not abiding by the United Nations rights-based conventions; while countries who have adopted rights-based legislation host relatively few refugees in comparison.

An alternative notion which this paper explores is the 'duty' approach to providing refuge and asylum, the social and sometimes religious duty to provide hospitality/generosity to the stranger that is widespread in the Middle East and exists in a 'folk' rendering in many societies. This is best expressed through the institution of *karam* (generosity/hospitality). Using as case studies the Syrian response to the Iraqi refugee crisis which commenced in 2003 and the Turkish, Lebanese, and Jordanian response to the Syrian refugee crisis which commenced in 2011, this paper explores the disconnect between international rights-based approaches to refuge and the duty-based ones commonly accepted in Middle Eastern civil societies, public culture, and national ideologies. It concludes by asking the question 'Do we abrogate our moral responsibilities when we permit "a rights-based approach" to asylum to prevail?' In other words, when we mainstream 'rights' and expect agencies and international organisations to operate under such a mandate do we repress our universal urge to provide refuge to those in need? Should we perhaps be looking for a more holistic or comprehensive engagement with humanitarian assistance and delivery that brings together both duty and moral responsibility with a 'rights-based' approach?

[1] The full text of the 1951 Convention and the 1967 Protocol can be found at http://www.unhcr.org/protect/PROTECTION/3b66c2aa10.pdf

BACKGROUND

In October 1945, at the end of World War II, a United Nations Charter was signed in San Francisco to save future generations from 'the scourge of war'. Yet within a very short period of time, the world community felt that the United Nations Charter did not sufficiently define the fundamental rights to which it referred. A drafting Committee, the Commission on Human Rights, chaired by Eleanor Roosevelt, was formed to prepare what was initially conceived as an International Bill of Rights. The Committee met over two years and finally on 10 December 1948 the Universal Declaration of Human Rights was adopted by the UN General Assembly by a vote of 48 in favour, none against, and eight abstentions. In that Declaration, Article 13 provided the rights of citizens to leave their country and Article 14 declared that everyone has the right to seek and to enjoy in other countries asylum from persecution.[2]

By December 1949 the United Nations High Commission for Refugees (UNHCR) was created by the United Nations General Assembly, thus ending the 'Nanson' Era of the 1920s and 1930s which provided refugees—mainly Russians and later Armenians and Assyrians—with travel documents, thus assisting them to cross borders in the search for work.[3] With the 1951 Refugee Convention, refugees became differentiated from economic migrants, and their desire for sustainable livelihoods while encamped was overlooked (Long 2013). Until the end of the Cold War the population of concern for the United Nations Agency for Refugees (UNHCR) numbered in single-figure millions. However, by the 1990s the number of people of concern to the Agency had climbed precipitously and hovered around the 35 million figure for about a decade (it is currently at over 60 million). The template for providing protection was based on the encampment model developed, some would argue, from practices initiated during the 2nd Boer War (1900–2) to remove people from areas of conflict and to control their access to food, shelter, and communications with the outside world, thus creating a passive and pliable population for ease of management. Over the course of the following 100 years, camps for the displaced by war were increasingly organised according to this military template.

[2] This provision declared that everyone has the right to seek and to enjoy in other countries asylum from persecution. Despite endorsing Article 14, most Western states have since made the process of reaching 'other countries' irregular if not illegal. The growth of the smuggling industry across the Mediterranean is one case in point. See http://www.ohchr.org/EN/UDHR/Documents/UDHR_Translations/eng.pdf

[3] Fridtjof Nanson was appointed the first High Commissioner for Refugees by the League of Nanson in the wake of the massive displacement of peoples after World War I. In1922 he began issuing passports to some of the 800,000 Russians stripped of their citizenship by Lenin the year before. In the 1930s these passports were extended to Armenian, Assyrian, and Turkish refugees.

Such 'camp' approaches to the provision of 'refugee' rights (health, shelter, food, and water) were increasingly at the expense of almost all other rights, including education of children, social security, and sustainable livelihoods (Harrell-Bond 1986, Jamal 2000, Crisp 2003, Crisp & Slaughter 2009). In the context of the middle-income countries of the Middle East, this 'one size fits all' template for protecting refugees has faced serious challenges in its failure to address the wider social concerns of the displaced. These include the specific socio-historical context of the dispossessed (e.g. Syrians traumatised by 45 years living under a controlling police state, fear of engaging with officials), the behaviour of youth (e.g. the rise of male youth gangs, particularly in camps, and the apparent 'selling and buying' of young refugee women), and a desperate search for sustainable livelihoods (e.g. the selling of camp rations, working illegally). It would seem that the paradigm of the refugee camps as a global humanitarian mechanism needs to be reconsidered in the face of the massive Syrian and, and before it, the Iraqi social disarticulation.

Until 2009, the UNCHR promoted camps globally as the most effective and efficient way in which to provide the 'right to life' to those who were displaced generally by armed conflict. The displaced who avoided entering refugee camps were regarded as 'irregular' (UNHCR 1997). However, with the Iraqi refugee crisis following the invasion of that country in 2003, UNHCR took a long hard look at its policies. It recognised that most Iraqis fleeing into Syria and Jordan had purposively bypassed the camps set up for them and sought refuge and sanctuary, instead, in the major cities. This left the UN agencies and other international aid providers scrambling to make contact and search for alternative ways of providing the basic right to life services enshrined in UN statutes and covenants. A high-level field mission in 2008 resulted in a new set of directives recognising the rights of the displaced to self-settle in urban centres (UNHCR 2009). Applied to the specific Iraqi refugee population in Syria and Jordan, it became a 'gold standard' for UNHCR operations. But lessons learned from the Iraqi crisis (which are discussed in detail below), reaching out and working with the self-settled refugees, have proven extraordinarily difficult to operationalise in the complex Syrian humanitarian crisis. Country-specific innovative measures to assist the self-settled are being tested piecemeal by various agencies (Senior Humanitarian Aid practitioner, personal communications, 2014). Little, if any, attention has been directed to gaining a holistic understanding of the customs, social traditions, public culture, and behaviour of the refugees and their hosts in the Middle East.

The Iraqi case

Iraqi forced migrations did not start in the past decade but rather nearly a century before, at the end of World War I. The Paris Peace Conference of 1919 saw the dismantling of the Ottoman Empire and the widespread displacement of groups impacted by the creation of 'mandated' neocolonial states in the region. Over the course of ensuing decades, wave after wave of Iraqis fled their country, following or creating linkages in bordering states that had once been part of the Ottoman Empire. In the years following the 2003 invasion, Iraqis did not flee when expected and then when they did set out into exile, they refused to enter the internationally organised holding camps, choosing to settle on their own in urban centres. Even as one of their host countries, Syria, imploded into spasms of violence and bloodshed, the international community raced to create new holding centres outside the borders with the country. Yet only a few thousand Iraqis moved out of Syria and fewer returned to Iraq. International assumptions regarding refugee behaviour in this part of the world appeared to be unravelling, and a fresh understanding of mobility and the duty to provide refuge, asylum, and hospitality was required.

In March 2003 the US, supported by the UK launched its first set of air strikes on Baghdad. 'Operation Iraqi Freedom' was officially underway. In the six-month build-up to this military venture there had been estimates that a Western military engagement would cause the displacement of more than one million people within Iraq and across its borders. The UNHCR and numerous NGOs made preparations to receive this wave of humanity in Jordan, Syria, and Iran. In Syria, the UNHCR negotiated the upgrading or building of three campsites in eastern Syria and at the border crossing. In Jordan, the UNHCR worked closely with the Hashemite Charitable Society to set up a refugee holding site near its eastern border with Iraq. In addition, the UNHCR stockpiled relief items at the southern port of Aqaba for immediate dispatch should that prove necessary. In Iran, the government's Bureau for Aliens and Foreign Immigrants (BAFIA) prepared ten campsites with the help of the UNHCR.

Despite the dire predictions, few Iraqis fled Iraq in 2003 (Chatty 2003). No Iraqi refugees crossed the border into Iran. In Syria just over 200 Iraqis crossed the border and took refuge at El Hol camp. In Jordan, more than 1,200 refugees arrived at the border crossing between Iraq and Jordan and found themselves trapped, unable to cross over into Jordan and unwilling to go back into Iraq. These were mainly third-country nationals trapped in a 'no-man's land': Iranian Kurds, Iranian Arabs, and Palestinians. Two months after 'Operation Iraqi Freedom' had begun, some 550 Palestinians and a few hundred other Arab refugees were allowed entry into the Jordanian refugee camp at Ruwaishid.

We now know that between 2006 and 2010 more than one million and possibly two million Iraqis fled the sectarian explosion and general insecurity which descended on Iraq in the years after the Anglo-American invasion (Sommer-Houdeville 2017). These forced migrants largely sought refuge but not 'refugee status' in the neighbouring countries of Syria, Jordan, Egypt, Lebanon, and Turkey. They were mostly middle-class professionals who found their way to the large cities where they could become invisible. Indisputably, Syria hosted the largest number of displaced Iraqis as temporary guests. By 2012, with Syria imploding in armed uprisings and rebellion, many in the humanitarian aid regime expected Iraqis to return to Iraq or to attempt a crossing into Lebanon or Jordan. But again expectations were proven unfounded. Only several hundred Iraqis returned to Iraq. Most hunkered down in the Syrian-government-controlled urban and suburbs neighbourhoods that had accepted them and had provided them with refuge and hospitality.

Why had estimates of displacement and humanitarian aid needs been so far from the mark? How was the original forecast of one million refugees in 2003 calculated and why was this figure so readily accepted by the humanitarian aid agencies? We now know that in the first few years after 2003 most Iraqis did not cross international borders. Instead most were internally displaced within the country's borders. In 2003 some 300,000 Iraqis were displaced, mainly Arabs who had recently been forced to settle in Kurdish villages surrounding the northern Iraqi town of Kirkuk by Saddam Hussein's regime.

Ten years on and still the international humanitarian aid regime is not getting it right. Expectations of Iraqis returning to Iraq did not come about either in 2003 or in the years since. An expected surge of return from Syria after 2011 resulted in the Iraqi government setting up reception/detention camps on the Iraq/Syria border which were never filled. An International Organization for Migration (IOM) report identified that between 2010 and 2013 a total of 76,000 Iraqis had returned to the country (IOM 2015). Iraqi, Syrian, and other Arab exiles continue to confound international *humanitarian* aid organisations actors when policy and programming are developed for them within the framework of international rights-based humanitarianism.

The fundamental errors in judgement which have made the Iraqi case so controversial are two-fold: historical and cultural. Anglo-American strategists drawing up a post-invasion plan assumed that the Iraqi people would welcome the invasion and behave as most Europeans would: flee from areas of armed conflict and return when security had been reimposed. This judgement was based on flawed intelligence as well as on an assumption that Iraqis would regard 'Operation Iraqi Freedom' as a liberation campaign by the Anglo-American powers. What was not recognised by these powers was the extent to which Iraqis regarded the Anglo-American campaign as a neocolonial assault on their homeland. Most Iraqis preferred to stand their ground and, sheltering among familiar neighbours and kin, safeguarded their holdings, while affirming their Iraqi-ness. The Anglo-American assumption that Iraqis might flee and later return to recover their property and possessions—as guaranteed by international law—was not one that many Iraqis, or any Middle Easterner, for that matter, would make. The historical lessons of Palestine and Palestinian refugees have been deeply engrained in the Middle Eastern social psyche. Witnessing the traumatic catastrophe of the Palestinian Arabs in 1948 when 750,000 fled their homes in the anticipation of returning as soon as fighting in their neighbourhoods or villages and towns stopped, and the decades of protracted displacement and temporariness that followed, in part due to Israeli rejection of their right to return as well as Arab states' unwillingness to permanently resettle them, have contributed significantly to Iraqi migration decision-making. If you flee war in your homeland, you may not be allowed to return when fighting ends.

The Iraqi cultural response to dispossession and displacement—one that is beginning to be recognised as more pervasive and widespread globally—has proved to be very much at odds with international expectations of the behaviour of the 'model' refugee who seeks out and succumbs to the ministrations of humanitarian aid as manifested in prefabricated and rigidly administered holding camps. Sites of 'bare life', where all agency and self-sufficiency are stripped away and the refugee enters a liminal status between citizen and outcast, is a fair description of contemporary internationally sanctioned and operated refugee camps (Agamben 1998).

The Syrian case

The current displacement from Syria inevitably follows the pathways of Iraqi and Palestinian refugees before them (Marfleet and Chatty 2009). Those movements and occasionally return migrations have changed social identities and notions of belonging and reshaped both host societies as well communities of origin (Chatelard 2010, Chatty & Lewando-Hundt 2005, Van Hear 1998). Regarded as temporary guests rather than 'refugees' by their hosting authorities, some have become part of 'near-diasporic' communities while others have integrated or created new identities and ties of belonging to a reshaped host society (Cohen 1997, Vertovic 2001). In Lebanon the impact of flows of displaced people both internally and from across its borders is seen as a threat to an already weak and brittle public sector. Turkey, on the other hand, perhaps with important international relations goals, has set up a system of temporary protection and refugee assistance of a standard far superior to any achieved in the region by the international humanitarian aid regime.

UN estimates are that over 85 per cent of the Syrian refugee flow across international borders is self-settling in cities, towns, and villages where they have social networks.

In other words, only 10–15 per cent of the Syrian refugee flow is into camps. This includes 25 non-UN camps in Turkey, three UN camps in Jordan and none in Lebanon (ECHO 2015). Overall, there has been a general rejection of 'encampment' by most Syrians in Jordan and in Lebanon; while in Turkey the response is more complex (Kirisci 2013).

By August 2016, about 15 per cent of the approximately 2,800,000 Syrian refugees in the country actively sought out the 'non-standard' camps managed by AFAD, the Turkish Disaster Relief Coordination Institution under the Office of the Prime Minister. These camps have been described as 'five-star' by international experts (International Crisis Group 2013); some have cynically suggested that such a model cannot be sustained as it is too expensive in the long term. These Turkish camps do much more than give food and clothes; most camps have classrooms, hospitals, areas for recreation, sports, and religious worship, laundry and television rooms, meeting tents, and even hair salons. They do not conform to the 'camp' template designed by the UNHCR; rather they take on the appearance of small towns. More than any other feature, they are open access and provide their residents with opportunities to come and go.

In contrast, in Jordan, an estimated 600,000 Syrians flooded into the country over a short period of time. This led to fears in some quarters that these refugees would destabilise the country if they continued to disperse and self-settle throughout the country. The Jordanian government then abandoned its laissez faire policy and determined that all newly arriving Syrians would be placed in UN-sponsored camps. Thus, new arrivals after the summer of 2012 have been rounded up by the Jordanian army as they crossed the border and handed over to the IOM for processing and entry into the UNHCR border camps at Zaatari and at Azraq.

In Lebanon, an estimated 1,100,000 Syrians have crossed the border and are self-settled in thousands of small units throughout the Bekaa Valley and along the coastal cities of the country, making standard humanitarian relief mechanisms hard to deliver. The international aid regime has persisted in recommending the establishment of formal official refugee camps in the country. But these requests have been consistently rejected by the government (White *et al.* 2013).

From all three of these countries there is much to be learned not only about dignity in exile and refugee protection, but also about the nature of local and regional notions of hospitality, sanctuary, and refuge, identity and belonging as well as how social capital and networks emerge in the hosting community. Although under-researched, historical examples in the Middle East do show that successful 'near-diasporic' resettlement or return are clearly associated with the manner of reception and accommodation of exiles and forced migrants in host communities (Chatty 2010, Loizos 1999, Shields 2016).

OTTOMAN LEGACIES, ARAB CUSTOMS, AND PUBLIC CULTURE

The Ottoman legacy of mobility and migration

The end of World War I saw the collapse of the Ottoman Empire and its dismemberment along lines proposed in several secret wartime agreements undertaken by the French, British, and Russian governments. The Sykes–Picot Agreement as well as the Balfour Declaration set out the neocolonial borders of the southern region of the Ottoman Empire. However, even prior to this final collapse, the Ottoman state had been pushed to accommodate the dispossession and forced migration of millions of its subjects within the Empire. This was a response to failed attempts to repulse competing claims to borderlands largely from Tsarist Russia which forced the creation of an independent Bulgaria, Serbia, and Romania out of the European Ottoman Empire. And in the process, as detailed by Justin McCarthy, the Russians dispossessed and ejected the native populations of Circassia and Abkhazia in the Caucasus, forcing the Ottomans to take in more than 800,000 Caucasian peoples. A further 900,000 Turks were also forced by the Russians into the Ottoman Empire which then had to find food and shelter for them when the existing population was already poor (McCarthy 2001).

By 1857 the Sublime Porte in Constantinople (Istanbul) set out a code of conduct to deal with this mass influx of refugees and migrants. This was the Refugee Code to welcome refugees and migrants into the Empire. Three years later, a Refugee Commission was established (1860) to facilitate refugee settlement in, first, the Ottoman Europe (the Balkans) and then later, near the end of the 19th and early 20th century, in the southern provinces of the Empire—Anatolia and Greater Syria (Chatty 2010: 97). The Commission oversaw the management of international aid—mainly missionary—coming into the Ottoman Empire. But, more importantly, it set a precedent for how to receive and best integrate refugees, exiles and migrants alike. It co-ordinated in-country aid and the feeding, clothing, and sheltering of several millions of refugees as they progressed through and near cities to eventual sites where they were encouraged to settle. There were no internment or holding camps. Rather than trying to provide basic emergency aid in a fixed location, the Ottoman state encouraged local communities to assist this flow of humanity and to provide hospitality to their largely Muslim 'brothers' and 'sisters'. In addition, the state set out incentives for self-settlement. Forced migrants who turned into settlers were provided with up to 17 acres of land to start farming. They were provided with seeds, draft animals, and money to buy farm equipment. They were expected to build their own houses—often in the style of their original homeland—or to get local people to build for them. They were prohibited from selling their new land holdings for fifteen years in an effort to make sure that local investors and entrepreneurs did not take advantage of these new settlers and in order to give these newcomers time to adapt and acclimatise (Chatty 2010: 98). Until 1878 forced migrants were largely settled in rural areas. Only later did the Ottomans commence the construction of new migrant districts in the neighbourhoods of towns and cities—the Muhajirin district of Damascus, for example, was first established to house the forced migrant settlers from Crete in the late 1890s.

The Paris Peace Conference at the close of World War I resulted in the British gaining the League of Nations mandate administrations over the Kingdom of Iraq (former Ottoman regions of Basra, Baghdad, and Mosul) and the French being granted the mandate authority over Greater Syria (modern Syria and Lebanon) in 1920. These mandates were not locally popular and uprisings, rebellion, and armed conflict greatly marred their authority. The Arab Revolt of Syria (1925–7) drew in large elements of the country's population. When the British gave up their mandate of Iraq in 1932 after a decade of battling local insurgencies, they left behind their Assyrian supporters who had worked with them as gendarmeries. Thus the first massive wave of Assyrians fled Iraq for Syria, Lebanon, Turkey, and the West.

In French-mandated Syria, refugees continued to flow into the country from Iraq, from Turkey, from Palestine, as well as from the Balkan states of Albanian, Bulgaria, and the Caucuses. These newcomers were granted citizenship. Although there was some disquiet in a few intellectual corners at the idea of Armenians, Assyrians, and Kurds becoming citizens in a country which was largely Arabic speaking, this disgruntled attitude gave way to muted appreciation of many of these minority social groups who took part in the country-wide demonstrations against the continued French neo-colonial grip over the state throughout the 1920s and 1930s (White 2004, 2011). The modern nation state of Syria was rapidly becoming a country of minorities sharing notions of local cosmopolitanism and conviviality (Chatty 2010, 2013, Rabo 2008).

The Ottoman *millet*

What was remarkable about the Ottoman Empire was the way that its organising ethos was not based on ideas of ethnic superiority of one community over another but rather on religion. Belonging was tied to social places rather than physical spaces. In other words, the Ottoman subjects recognised the superiority of Islam in the Empire, but were also cognisant of its tolerance of the *Ahl-il-Kitab*—its Jewish and Christian communities. This acceptance was based on religious tenets as well as economic and political realism. European mercantile interests in the Christian and Jewish communities in the Middle East as well as Ottoman principles of self-governance for these ethno-religious groups resulted in the establishment of protected communities, *millets* whose religious and social affairs were organised from within the structured and specific mechanisms of the church or synagogue.[4] It was the legacy of these '*millets*' that shaped the way in which the great forced migrations of the 19th and 20th centuries were absorbed into the fabric of the societies and cultures of the Middle East.

The term *millet* (which comes from the Arabic *milla*, a religious community or denomination) originally meant both a religion and a religious community. The Ottomans regulated and institutionalised the *millet* system in the 19th century. Thus, Muslims, for example, might be ethnically and linguistically Turks, Arabs, Kurds, Albanians, Bosnians, Circassians, and others. Jews, especially in the northern provinces were mainly Sephardic, the descendants of those who had been given refuge after being expelled from Spain and Portugal in the 16th century; but there were also many *Mizrahi*, or Oriental Jews. The Christians were mainly Orthodox and comprised Greeks, Serbs, Bulgarians in the Balkans, and Arabs in Palestine and Syria (McCarthy 2001). In some areas, ethnic groups were fairly homogenous. In others they were widely dispersed. Constantinople in the late 1800s was a mix of ethno-religious minorities. But records only identified religious or *millet* affiliation. At the end of the 1900s Constantinople was 56 per cent Muslim, 22 per cent Greek Orthodox, 15 per cent Armenian, and 4 per cent Jewish. While Muslims were a large majority in the Asiatic provinces, and a significant one in the European areas of the Empire, most regions had significant Christian and Jewish minorities. Few non-Albanians, for example, lived in Albania. But there were Muslim, Catholic, and Orthodox Albanians. Ethnically, most of west and central Anatolia was Turkish; the southeast was Kurdish; while the Levant and Arabia were mainly Arab. Yet these regions also had significant religious 'majorities' and 'minorities': Muslim, Christian, and Jewish adherents. In many other areas there was a thorough mix of ethnic groups and religious affiliations. Sometimes it was villages of one ethnic group or religious affiliation adjacent to another ethnic group or religious affiliation. In some cases, single villages and small towns had a number of ethnic and religious groups. Thus it was impossible to manage these widely dispersed peoples on the basis of territoriality. And at the same time, ethnic and culturally similar linguistic groups were establishing wide-ranging networks of ethno–co-religionists throughout the Empire. As Argenti elaborates, a sense of shared existence between neighbours of different cultural and religious backgrounds characterised the 'peace that reigned over Anatolia' and the southern provinces for so much of the Ottoman Empire (2017: 10).

[4] The term *millet* was used by the Ottoman administration to identify and designate Ottoman non-Muslims. It dates back to the reign of Sultan Mahmud II (1808–39). Before the 19th century the term meant Muslims within the Empire and Christians outside it (Quataert 2000: 173).

The late 19th and early 20th centuries left a profoundly negative mark on the history of human settlement and political engineering. The Ottoman Empire, which had developed a largely successful multicultural and religious pluralism, was gradually dismantled by pressures from within as much as from outside. This demise came quickly, although it was prefixed by a nearly century-long reweaving of the peoples of the Balkans, eviction of the Muslim peoples in the Caucasus, and the remixing of the largely Muslim peoples in Anatolia with the departure of the Orthodox Greeks and Armenian Christians. The numerous forced migrations that accompanied this era are too complex and also too contested to be dealt with adequately here in this paper. However, it may be enough to say that this upheaval saw an entire Empire on the move. Furthermore the deterritorialised aspects of belonging tied to the Ottoman ethno-religious *millets* laid the foundations for later elaborations of migrations, mainly circular and back-and-forth between relations, co-religionists, colleagues, customers, and creditors in the modern Arab successor states of the Empire.

The Empire's century-long struggle against collapse saw the rise of numerous nationalisms followed by short-term movement and large-scale migration within its borders. Several million people were uprooted between about 1875 and 1925 from the Balkans, or more specifically Bulgaria, Macedonia, Thrace, and western Anatolia. These forced migrants found their way to Anatolia and further south to Syria, Lebanon, Jordan, and Egypt. Armenians in the heartland of Armenia also moved into the Syrian provinces, and to Egypt where they found long-settled co-religionist communities. Kurds, Palestinians, and Circassians and Chechnyans were also spread throughout the southern provinces of the Empire in a combination of forced and voluntary migrations throughout the 19th and 20th centuries. The unmixing of peoples initially followed religious rather than linguistic lines. The Muslims moved south and east, and the Christians moved north and west. Thus, it was not only ethnic Turks who retreated towards Ottoman core areas, but also other Muslims, notably Bulgarians and Bosnians, as well as Circassians and Crimean Tatars who had fled earlier from Russia to the Ottoman Balkans. These movements, some for trade and others the result of nationalist struggle and war, created a carpet of locally cosmopolitan and migratory communities in the Middle East in the aftermath of the collapse and carving up of the Ottoman Empire at the end of World War I.

The Ottoman Empire was remarkable for having 'uncoupled the essentialised relationship linking ethno-religiously defined peoples to places' (Argenti 2017: 9). These dispossessed Ottoman peoples took with them the memory of a multi-ethnic and multi-religious empire as well as the singular remembered and partially imagined homelands where culturally distinct peoples would nevertheless form an interdependent social whole. Over the next few decades, two further peoples were to become dispossessed and forced from their homelands or have their lands politically transformed underfoot: the Palestinians and the Kurds. Their dispossession has added to the region's cultural experience of movement and forced migration and plays an important contemporary role in the networking and migration decision-making of the current wave of dispossessed and displaced Iraqis and Syrians.

Legacy of the *millets*, notions of solidarity, and hospitality

In 2004 Human Rights Watch observed the situation around Kirkuk where some Iraqi populations were fleeing and others were returning. They reported that:

> Much of the Arab population brought to the rural areas in the north during the Arabisation campaign [of Saddam Hussein] fled during the war. … Human Rights Watch is not aware of a single massacre committed against Arab settlers by returning Kurds or other minorities. This is an experience vastly different from that of the Balkans, where bloodshed was routine during the various 'ethnic' cleansing campaigns that characterized those conflicts (Human Rights Watch 2004).

During the past five years of the armed conflict in Syria, there has been little 'ethnic cleansing of minorities' of the sort seen in the Balkans, though some might argue that Homs has been ethnically cleansed of its majority Sunni population by the Asad regime along with other specifically targeted sites. In general, relations between displaced, host communities, and returning groups were not what the humanitarian aid regime was expecting based on its experience in other continents and contexts. One explanation for this resistance to conducting 'ethnic' cleansing may lie in the historical antecedents of ethnic tolerance in the immediate region, a legacy of the *millet* system. But it may also be explained by reviewing the nature of group solidarity and concepts of generosity and hospitality in the Arab world.

The Arab expression 'I against my brother; I and my brother against my cousin; I, my brother and my cousin against the world' perfectly describes the layered outlook on alliances and enmity among families, lineages, and tribes throughout the Arab world. Though largely regarded as a form of organisation exclusive to the Arab Bedouin tribes, it is the segmentary nature of alliance and network building on the basis of real or fictive kinship which extends to urban folk as well. Generally, the members of a recognised social unit support each other generously, take in its members when moving from place to place, and often make migratory moves together—both forced and voluntary. Expulsion of an individual in the modern political context of Iraq and its neighbours often means moving the entire extended family. Thus, individuals had a large group to rely on and the whole group had each other to rebuild lives shattered by politics or conflict.

The unit was often represented by a leader, generally the strongest and most charismatic male of the extended family group or lineage. This leadership was also vested in a moral authority which could be augmented or lost by behaviour which either respected or disregarded family norms and custom, particularly with regard to generosity and hospitality (Chatty 1977). One could argue that the Asad regime relied on developing much the same authority built on 'acts' of public generosity to the nation, such as commissioning statutes of President Asad outside of football stadiums, libraries, opera houses, and other monumental projects. The citizens then reacted to this 'politics of public dissemination' by acting as if they revered their leader (for more detail see Wedeen 1999). *Karam*, the Arabic term which can be translated as hospitality or generosity, is ultimately also about security, protection, and respect. The family or lineage's reputation is in many ways hostage to correct behaviour with a guest/stranger, as inappropriate behaviour might lead to disrespect, danger, and insecurity (Shryock 2004). With identity and security based on family, lineage, and ethno-religious *millet*s, movement did not represent a decoupling, or deracination, but rather a wide horizontal network of support and solidarity. Relatives, close and distant, were spread over a wide region far beyond the confines of the modern nation state and could be called on for support, shelter, and security when needed. In the case of Iraqi refugees entering Syria, the Asad regime adopted the role of the 'paterfamilias' of the nation, extending 'hospitality' to the Iraqi refugees as a moral duty rather than as a rights-based act derived from international law.[5] Another term commonly used in the Middle East with respect to providing hospitality to the stranger is *thawaab* (merit, or duty, or correct behaviour). Its religious overtones refer to collecting merit by good behaviour for the Day of Judgement. Variants of the term exist in Turkish, and also in Persian.

Notions of hospitality and generosity and the ways in which such acts augment individual and family honour are fundamental to an understanding of many societies and cultures (some of these notions are rooted in Ancient Greek philosophy, as illustrated in the treatment of the stranger and exile in *The Iliad* and later *The Odyssey*). They are also developed in Kantian Ethics where the duty 'to do good' is primordial. Perhaps the universality of this 'moral economy' is best articulated in Marcel Mauss' *Essay on the Gift*, a seminal study of gifting (providing hospitality) based on ethnographic and historical records of the time. Mauss' short but magisterial work explored alternatives to the modern capitalist economy in the wake of the most brutal and destructive war—World War I—that had yet been experienced by mankind (Mauss 2016 [1925]). His detailed ethnography reveals that the practice of gifting has not disappeared in industrial society (though we may not recognise it). And that, as with *karam,* gifting creates a relationship and requires a return. Excessive gifting or inappropriate return can result in hostility and insecurity. The practice of gifting,

[5] I do not wish to make the association that the state opened its borders as an act of national generosity. Instead, I would suggest that the regime was cynically using the language of individual acts of generosity for its own security purposes and perhaps also to benefit from international humanitarian assistance.

according to Mauss, is often found among the 'masses' (host communities) who have evolved a better sense of the 'general interest' of society and express it in mutuality and solidarity. The *Essay*, thus, is an implicit and explicit assessment of how generosity/ hospitality and the duties and obligations are kept alive in many societies and might also be kept alive in Europe. It is Mauss' conviction that deep attentiveness to human exchange—material, intellectual, moral, and spiritual—might give life to post-war recuperation from the tragedies and travesties of war for which 'we must weep' (Mauss 2016 [1925]:11).

Hospitality redefined in Western rights-based practices

The notions of generosity and hospitality, of mutuality and solidarity are particularly redolent in the Middle East. In many Western countries, however, 'hospitality' has become a dominant notion in legislated asylum and immigration practices built upon international legal obligations. It is used in official discourse and in social analysis and is found in such fundamental terms as host country, reception centres, and asylum hotels (Rozakou 2012: 562). However, tension and perhaps even a transformation in the moral economy of Europe—the traditional view of social norms and obligations—has resulted in growing tensions between the discourse and practices of compassion and legally framed repression as highlighted in the deportation dramas at Sangatte in 2002 (Fassin 2005) and the 'Jungle' at Calais in 2016. How is it, Michael Herzfeld asks, that 'in contemporary societies justly famed for their hospitality and warmth, we often encounter the pettiest form of bureaucratic indifference to human needs and suffering' (1992: 142)? Is this a response to the 'mainstreaming' of the 'rights' of refugees and asylum seekers in the West which results in a growing depoliticisation and disinterest in active moral response or responsibility? In another context, it has emerged very clearly in recent scholarship that mainstreaming of 'gender' in international and non-government agencies has resulted in a lack of interest or sense of responsibility for 'gendering' in internal policy and external programming (Pialek 2008).

It may be that in the face of such mainstreaming of 'rights' of refugees in Europe a form of mutuality and solidarity as identified by Mauss is gradually emerging to resist the political reframing of 'social duty' into 'rights-based law'. In France and now also in the United Kingdom, Germany, and Sweden a call for civil action paralleling (or resisting) state positioning is developing in public culture.[6] The seeming

[6] For example, in the UK, voluntary groups such as Rural Refugee Network are active in supporting Syrians once they arrive in the country and helping to place them with local families; in Germany a refugee charity, Willkommen, was set up in the Hamburg train station to orient refugees as they arrived; and in Sweden a movement called VI STÅR INTE UT ('We can't stand it anymore') is growing among professional people and others who are protesting against the inhuman treatment of refugees.

growing indifference in state regulations in Europe and the UK to moral obligations to refugees and asylum seekers in the face of extraordinary suffering appears to be changing. Fassin, in his explorations of moral anthropology asks why in societies which have become hostile to asylum seekers and immigrants does there remain 'a sense of common humanity collectively expressed through attention paid to human needs and suffering' (2005: 366). The recent French moves to regulate and control hospitality and criminalise those who offer succour to the illegal immigrant or refugee are seen by some as an attempt to impose official rights-based law (bureaucratic indifference) on everyday life.

Yet public discourse in France has resulted in a plea among some intellectuals to redefine hospitality and refocus attention on human need and suffering. This group refers to the French 'myth of hospitality' and calls for remission of these rights-based laws. It argues for the need to have both an ideal, national policy based on rights of categories of people but also to recognise and permit the private engagement of individuals based on a sense of moral duty and obligation (Fassin 2005). This movement calls to mind Derrida's 'Law of Hospitality' which refers to absolute and unconditional hospitality in contrast to the French efforts to legislate a 'pact of hospitality' (Derrida and Dufourmantelle 2000). The latter, clearly derived from Mauss' seminal essay, is conceptualised as a contract that specifies rights-based rules and duties of the guest and the host. These then are spelled out in asylum and immigration laws of the state as well as in practices of humanitarian actors in receptions, centres, refugee camps, and holding centres. The former relates to the idealised norms and obligations of compassion for humanity which drive a local community-based effort to provide sanctuary to these needy 'guests'.

A similar discourse has existed in the United Kingdom, where the accommodation of asylum seekers in immigration centres, or 'asylum hotels' has been in public debate for most of the past decade. Britain has a mythology of hospitality 'to those fleeing from political and religious persecution' (Cohen 1994: 72). The accommodation of strangers, particularly 'neighbours' from the Continent, has long been part of normal social conventions of hospitality and one might say a customary legal right: Belgians in the 1940s, Hungarians in the 1960s, and Bosnians in the 1990s. But hospitality to the more distant stranger is another matter. After several years of inertia, challenges to the country's rights-based determinations regarding who among refugees and asylum seekers may benefit from the state is emerging. Local civil society (as well as local councils) efforts to set into motion forms of support and sponsorship for refugees from Syria as well as other acts of moral clarity are on the rise (see, for example, the work of the British Rural Refugee Network based in Hampshire http://www.ruralrefugeenetwork.org).

Yet, the impulse to be hospitable has come to be separated all over Europe from the granting of asylum. The latter is an act which the host state or nation can engage in within the framework of political laws and the limited protections set out in international law. The former is an individual social act associated with generosity and 'gift-giving' and is more in the realm of moral justice. Accommodating strangers in the UK is no longer an act of individual generosity, but rather a political act of hospitality which can easily elide into hostility. The current detention of asylum seekers fleeing political persecution is the phenomenon which this calls to mind. The collapsing of hospitality to the stranger which is often accompanied by growing hostility emerges from the conditionality set by the state structure. As Derrida argues, a distinction has emerged in the West between the ethics of hospitality (as cultural norm) and the politics or law of hospitality which reigns conditionally. No nation state in Europe would unconditionally open its doors to strangers. Absolute hospitality would undermine the very condition of the nation or state (Derrida and Dufourmantelle 2000). If this argument were to be followed to its logical conclusion, then the nation's hospitality would be based on the assumption that the national space could be conceived of in terms of hosts and guests, the nation as a house in which hospitality could be offered and received. In the liberal democratic states and constitutional monarchies of Europe this would simply not be possible without undermining the sovereignty of the nation. In the authoritarian and constitutional monarchies of the Middle East, however, this is exactly what is developing; hospitality to the stranger is both a national as well as an individual act.

Contrary to the dominant discourse on refuge and hospitality in the West where asylum seekers are placed in a liminal space in state-run detention centres and camps (Agamben 1998) and denied full social existence as a member of a nation state, I am arguing here that the notions of hospitality and generosity are so important in Middle Eastern cultures as to make it nearly impossible for the state to adopt international refugee law which seems to carry with it the 'pettiest form of bureaucratic indifference to human needs and suffering' which Herzfeld identified (1992). National or domestic asylum laws are not part of the legislation of most countries of the Middle East largely because hospitality to the stranger is deeply rooted in notions of individual, family, and group reputation. Public culture around the generosity of the father figure ruler (monarch or dictator, it doesn't matter) is significant. The state is seen as the family which is hospitable to the stranger. Providing hospitality/asylum increases one's reputation for generosity. The setting up of 'halfway' houses or state facilities, as well as international humanitarian holding camps, becomes unnecessary if not repugnant.[7]

[7] The Palestinian refugee case is particularly complicated as it was not at its core an issue of refuge or asylum. Rather it was fundamentally a rejection of the unilateral ending of the British Mandate and the revocation of all citizenship rights of Muslim and Christian British Mandate citizens, but not Jewish British Mandate citizens.

In the Middle East the idealised understanding of the state is that it, the state, is the 'host family', and that the actual acts of hospitality are a matter for the local community and the private individual to enact as a private act or via the church or mosque or other charitable organisation. In Jordan, Lebanon, and Turkey, local 'coexistence' initiatives have emerged that are bringing together refugees from Syria with local hosting communities. These local and regional associations set up both by resident Syrians and by nationals now dwarf the measures put into place by the international humanitarian aid regime (Syria Regional Refugee Response 2016). In Jordan, for example, Generations for Peace works to smooth out relations between refugee youth and local youth. In Lebanon, a Syrian-founded and organised NGO, Sawa4Syria undertakes to help Syrians empower themselves and 'take control of their present and their future'. While in Turkey, despite tight government control and restrictions on the activities of IGOs and NGOs, civil society local initiatives are emerging to provide various forms of hospitality for Syrians, such as Ala Syria, which work towards developing skills among the youth for their eventual return to Syria. Studies of refugee reception in exile have not yet considered the impact which generous accommodation and access to skills training and education facilitate may have on local integration and, in some cases, successful reintegration to places of origin (Chatty *et al.* 2014, Sirriyeh 2016).

The refugee camp as a reception centre is not part of Middle Eastern positionings with regard to the stranger. The forced migrant is welcomed or tolerated as a guest, generally temporarily but sometimes of long duration. The ideal of an 'Arab nation' persists in the rhetoric and the practices of some Arab states. Syria, for example, practised a near unconditional hospitality which saw it permit all Arabs into the country without visas.[8] Other Arab states have less rigid visa requirements for entry of Arabs compared to entry of other 'foreign nationals'. Only pressure from the international community and, in particular, the UN Agency for Refugees in the period after the mass influx of Iraqis into the country saw the imposition of a temporality to its hosting—Iraqis could get a three-month entry visas at the border on application. These restrictions were later relaxed and one-month visas at the border were reinstated, with renewal in country common.

Middle Eastern notions of hospitality assume that the national space can be conceived of in terms of the host and guest. The nation becomes a house or home in which hospitality can be offered and received. A relationship of power, as first articulated by Mauss, is implicit in Derrida's neologism of *hostipitalité*; *hostis* connects the figure of the stranger and host while *potis* calls up the semantics of power and sovereignty. In this sense the host is thus someone or something which has the power to give

[8] Bahrain, in earlier decades, received Omani exiles unconditionally and educated an entire generation before their return to the Sultanate of Oman in the 1970s.

to the stranger [generosity] but remains in control (Derrida 2000, Mauss 2016 [1925]). This provides a clear philosophical fit with the Arab notion of *karam* [generosity/hospitality] and the network of solidarity and support which it can engender. The widely used popular expression '*bayti, baytak*' (my home is your home) or even '*watani, watanak*' (my country is your country) perfectly exemplifies the notion of the host who has the power to provide generosity to the stranger/guest and who retains that power. The act of hosting does not diminish that power. On the contrary it enhances the *karam* and thus the reputation of the host. In addition, the act of hosting creates greater security by enlarging the network (*wasta*) of the host and at the same time manages hostility. One day the host may become a stranger somewhere and seek hospitality/refuge, thus setting into motion a reciprocal cycle of hospitality and refuge among members of different *millet*s which are the antecedents to the modern Arab nation states in the Middle East.

CONCLUSION

Iraqi and Syrian exiles and refugees have regularly confounded the international system of humanitarianism. Iraqis did not flee their country when expected to nor did they return in the numbers expected after 2011. They have eschewed the holding centres and containment camps set up for them on barren border lands and sought refuge, sanctuary, and hospitality from their Arab hosts in populous localities and urban centres. The Iraqi rejection of camps caught the international community off guard and has since resulted in a rethink at UNHCR and other refugee agencies. Only a few years ago, refugees who evaded camps were 'criminalised' for such acts. However in 2009, largely as a result of the Iraqi crisis, UNHCR issued new guidelines to address the bureaucratic requirements for effectively dealing with the urban, self-settled refugee. Displaced Syrians have also largely avoided the holding centres and camps set up for them in the region and instead sought out self-settlement and opportunities for local accommodation and integration. But the Syrian numbers are gigantic compared to those from Iraq. Whereas the one million or more Iraqis found hospitality regionally, Syrian numbers overwhelmed the hosting communities. With 10 per cent of the population of Jordan made up of refugees from Syria, and 30 per cent of the population of Lebanon made up of displaced Syrians, it is no wonder that the 'house' has become full and some of those seeking asylum have had to look further afield to the northern shores of the Mediterranean. This one might say is what happens when a duty-based approach faces the pressure of extreme numbers; some will need to move on.

Iraqi and Syrian exiles and their hosts have largely rejected the contemporary international notion of the separation of the stranger/asylum seeker from the rest of society. These acts have a resonance and clarity with the historical context of the late Ottoman Era and its system of *millet* communities spread far and wide over its Arab provinces. With the collapse of the Ottoman Empire and the neocolonial imposition of British and French Mandates in the interwar years, migration, forced and voluntary, characterised the region creating widespread and large-scale networks of families, lineages, and tribes throughout. The considerations of social capital, networks, and alliances then became significant when Iraqis came to deciding the time, the place, and the route to flee their devastated country. In addition, notions of hospitality and refuge operated at the individual and community level—not by government decree. Escape and exile—though by their very nature dangerous and insecure—were more easily converted into security and asylum in the public consciousness. The granting of hospitality was seen not only as a public good but also as an act which enhanced the host's reputation. Thus asylum as an aspect of hospitality became a requirement for the individual citizen as well as the social collective. These social and ethical norms underpin the success of self-settlement and local community hosting in the Middle East.

The international humanitarian aid regime's prioritising of protection to a category of people who fit the legal definition of 'refugee' is a rigid, rights-based construction that leaves many gaps in its implementation. Those who do not wish to be categorised as legal refugees or who fail to meet the formal criteria fail to access international support. Local and regional Middle Eastern constructions of duty-based obligations to the guest, stranger, and person-in-need can, with strategic support, offer a wider range of people sanctuary and asylum sanctuary. A holistic approach which taps into the social and ethical norms of hospitality in local contexts can only improve and extend the delivery of rights-based asylum as provided by international humanitarian organisations. This we see is happening in Europe and elsewhere. In the Middle East, most states have not adopted the international standard for refugee protection. However the social reality is that *karam*, as a social obligation, effectively operates to provide the asylum seeker with sanctuary and refuge in an environment where international protection does not exist.

REFERENCES

Agamben, Giorgio (1998) *Homo Sacer: Sovereign Power and Bare Life* trans. D. Herrer-Roazen (Stanford, CA, Stanford University Press).

Argenti, Nicolas (2017), 'Post-Ottoman Topologies: The Presence of the Past in the Era of the Nation State', *Social Analysis.* https://doi.org/10.3167/sa.2017.610101

Chatelard, Geraldine (2010), 'What Visibility Conceals: Re-embedding Refugee Migration from Iraq', in eds Dawn Chatty, Bill Finlayson *Dispossession and Forced Migration in the Middle East and North Africa* (London, British Academy).

Chatty, Dawn (1977), 'Land, Leaders and Limousines: Emir and Sheikh', *Ethnography* 16(4): 385–97. https://doi.org/10.2307/3773263
Chatty, Dawn (2003), ' "Operation Iraqi Freedom" and its Phantom 1 Million Iraqi Refugees', *Forced Migration Review*, 18: 51.
Chatty, Dawn (2010) *Dispossession and Displacement in the Modern Middle East* (Cambridge, Cambridge University Press). https://doi.org/10.1017/cbo9780511844812
Chatty, Dawn (2013), 'Guests and Hosts', *Cairo Review*, 9: 76–85.
Chatty, Dawn & Lewando-Hundt, Gillian (eds) (2005) *Children of Palestine: Experiencing Forced Migration in the Middle East* (Oxford, Berghahn Books).
Chatty, Dawn *et al.* (2014), 'Ensuring Quality Education for Young Refugees from Syria (12–25 Years): A Mapping Exercise', Forced Migration Policy Note, Refugee Studies Centre, Oxford Department of International Development, University of Oxford.
Cohen, Robin (1994) *Frontiers of Identity: The British and the Others* (London and New York, Longman).
Cohen, Robin (1997) *Global Diasporas: An Introduction* (London, Routledge). https://doi.org/10.4324/9780203228920
Crisp, J. (2003), 'No Solutions in Sight: The Problems of Protracted Refugee Situations in Africa', Evaluation and Policy Unit Working Paper no. 75, United Nations High Commission for Refugees, Geneva.
Crisp, J. & Slaughter, A., (2009), 'A Surrogate State? The Role of the UNHCR in Protracted Refugee Situations', New Issues in Refugee Research Paper no 168, United Nations High Commission for Refugees, Geneva.
Derrida, Jacques (2000), 'Hostipitality', *Agnelaki*, 5(3): 3–18.https://doi.org/10.1080/09697250020034706
Derrida, Jacques & Dufourmantelle, Anne (2000) *Of Hospitality: Anne Dufourmantelle Invites Jacques Derrida to Respond* trans R. Bowlby (Stanford, CA, Stanford University Press).
ECHO (2015), 'Refugee Crisis in Europe', European Civil Protection and Humanitarian Aid Operations.
Fassin, Didier (2005), 'Compassion and Repression: The Moral Economy of Immigration Policies in France', *Cultural Anthropology*, 20(3): 362–87. https://doi.org/10.1525/can.2005.20.3.362
Harrell-Bond, B. (1986) *Imposing Aid: Emergency Assistance to Refugees* (Oxford, Oxford University Press).
Herzfeld, Michael (1992) *The Social Production of Indifference: Exploring the Symbolic Roots of Western Bureaucracy* (Chicago, IL, University of Chicago Press).
Human Rights Watch (2004), 'Reversing Ethnic Cleansing in Northern Iraq', *Human Rights Watch* 16(4E).
International Crisis Group (2013), 'Blurring the Borders: Syrian Spillover Risks for Turkey', Report 225, International Crisis Group, https://www.crisisgroup.org/middle-east-north-africa/eastern-mediterranean/syria/blurring-borders-syrian-spillover-risks-turkey
IOM (2015)', Iraqi Returnees from Syria following the 2011 Syrian Crisis', International Organization of Migration.
Kirisci, Kemal (2013) *Syrian Humanitarian Crisis: The Fundamental Difficulties Facing Turkey* (Washington, DC, Brookings Institution).
Jamal, A. (2000), 'Refugee Livelihoods in Kakuma, Kenya', Evaluation and Policy Unity Working Paper no. 5, United Nations High Commission for Refugees, Geneva.
Loizos, Peter (1999), 'Ottoman Half-lives: Long Term Perspectives on Particular Forced Migrations', *Journal of Refugee Studies*, 12(3): 237–63.https://doi.org/10.1093/jrs/12.3.237
Long, K. (2013), 'When Refugees Stopped being Migrants: Movement, Labour and Humanitarian Protection', *Migration Studies*,1(1):4–26. https://doi.org/10.1093/migration/mns001
Marfleet, Philip & Chatty, Dawn (2009), 'Iraq's Refugees—Beyond "Tolerance" ', RSC Forced Migration Policy Brief no. 4. Refugee Studies Centre, University of Oxford.
Mauss, Marcel (2016 [1925]) *The Gift Expanded Edition* trans. Jane Guyer (Chicago, IL., Hau Books).

McCarthy, Justin (2001) *The Ottoman Peoples and the End of Empire* (London, Arnold).
Pialek, Nicholas (2008), 'Is this Really the End of the Road for Gender Mainstreaming? Getting to Grips with Gender and Institutional Change', in *Can NGOs Make a Difference? The Challenge of Development Alternatives* Eds A. Bebbington, S. Hickey & D. Mitlin (London, Zed Books) 279–97.
Quataert, Donald (2000) *The Ottoman Empire, 1700–1922* (Cambridge, Cambridge University Press).
Rabo, Annika (2008), 'Narrating Ethnic and Religious Heterogeneity in Contemporary Aleppo',. in *9th Mediterranean Research Meeting*, Robert Schuman Centre,European University Institute, Montecatini.
Rozakou, Katerina (2012), 'The Biopolitics of Hospitality in Greece: Humanitarinasm and the Managment of Refugees', *American Ethnologist*, 39(3): 562–77. https://doi.org/10.1111/j.1548-1425.2012.01381.x
Shields, Sarah (2016), 'The Greek–Turkish Population Exchange: Internationally Administered Ethnic Cleansing', *Middle East Research and Information Project* (267). http://www.merip.org/mer/mer267/greek-turkish-population-exchange
Shryock, Andrew (2004), 'The New Jordanian Hospitality: House, Host and Guest in the Culture of Public Display', *Comparative Studies in Society and History*, 46(1): 35–62. https://doi.org/10.1017/S0010417504000039
Sirriyeh, Ala (2016) *Inhabiting Borders, Routes Home: Youth, Gender, Asylum* (London, Routledge).
Sommer-Houdeville (2017), 'Remaking Iraq: Neoliberalism and a System of Violence after the US Invsion, 2003–2011', Stockholm Studies in Sociology 66, University of Stockholm.
Syria Regional Refugee Response (2016) 'List of Partners'. http://data.unhcr.org/syrianrefugees/partnerlist.php
UNHCR (1997), 'Policy on Refugees in Urban Areas', December, United Nations High Commission for Refugees, Geneva.
UNHCR (2009,) 'Surviving in the City: A Review of UNHCR's Operation for Iraqi Refugees in Urban Areas of Jordan, Libya and Syria', Policy Development and Evaluation Service, United Nations High Commission for Refugees, Geneva.
Van Hear, Nicholas (1998) *New Diasporas: The Mass Exodus, Dispersal, and Regrouping of Migrant Communities* (Seattle, WA, University of Washington Press).
Vertovic, Steven (2001), 'Transnationaloism and Identity', *Journal of Ethnic and Migration Studies* 27(4): 573–82. https://doi.org/10.1080/13691830120090386
Wedeen, Lisa (1999) *Ambiguities of Domination: Politics, Rhetoric and Symbols in Contemporary Syria* (Chicago, IL, University of Chicago Press).
White, Ben, Haysom, Simone & Davey, Eleanor (2013), 'Refugees, Host States, and Displacement in the MIddle East: An Enduring Challenge', *HPN: Humanitarian Exchange Magazine*, (59): 20–1.
White, Benjamin (2004) French Minorities Policy in Mandate Syria: Discourse, Domination, and Orwell's Elephant', in *British Society for Middle Eastern Studies Annual Conference*, London.
White, Benjamin Thomas (2011) *The Emergence of Minorities in the Middle East: The Politics of Community in French Mandate Syria* (Edinburgh, University of Edinburgh Press). https://doi.org/10.3366/edinburgh/9780748641871.001.0001

Note on the author: Dawn Chatty is Emeritus Professor in Anthropology and Forced Migration, former Director of the Refugee Studies Centre in the Department of International Development, and Emeritus Fellow at St Cross College, University of Oxford, UK. She is also a Fellow of the British Academy. Her research interests include: Syria and its displaced peoples, coping strategies and resilience of refugee

youth, nomadic pastoralism and conservation, gender and development, health, illness and culture. Her recent books include: *From Camel to Truck* (2nd edition, White Horse Press, 2013), *Dispossession and Displacement in the Modern Middle East* (Cambridge University Press, 2010), *Dispossession and Forced Migration in the Middle East and North Africa* (ed. with Bill Finlayson, Oxford University Press, 2010), *Deterritorialized Youth: Sahrawi and Afghan Refugees at the Margins of the Middle East* (ed., Berghahn Books, 2010), *Nomadic Societies in the Middle East and North Africa: Facing the 21st Century* (Leiden, Brill, 2006), *Children of Palestine: Experiencing Forced Migration in the Middle East* (ed. with Gillian Lewando-Hundt, Berghahn Books, 2005), and *Conservation and Mobile Peoples: Displacement, Forced Settlement and Sustainable Development* (ed. with Marcus Colchester, Berghahn Press, 2002).
dawn.chatty@qeh.ox.ac.uk

To cite the article: Dawn Chatty (2017), 'The duty to be generous (karam): Alternatives to rights-based asylum in the Middle East', *Journal of the British Academy*, 5: 177–199.
DOI https://doi.org/10.85871/jba/005.177

Journal of the British Academy (ISSN 2052–7217) is published by
The British Academy—the national academy for the humanities and social sciences.
10–11 Carlton House Terrace, London, SW1Y 5AH
www.britishacademy.ac.uk

Journal of the British Academy, **5**, 201–250. DOI https://doi.org/10.5871/jba/005.201
Posted 9 October 2017.

Some turns in a 'journey to the West': Cosmological proliferation in an anthropology of Eurasia

Radcliffe-Brown Lecture in Social Anthropology
read 29 March 2017

WANG MINGMING
Peking University

Abstract: In Eurasia, cosmological traditions have been at the same time different and related as well as 'similar'. Furthermore, the hierarchy of the so-called great and little traditions seen as making up the landscape of Eurasian cosmologies is reversible over time, with the little traditions—whose 'life-giving myths' and 'animism' have made the social anthropologies of the South (e.g., Australia, South America, and Melanesia) and the North (e.g., the frontiers of the Arctic Circle and Siberia) relevant to those of the East and West—the more resilient.

Keywords: cosmology, social anthropology, history, great and little traditions, inter-civilisational interactions, Eurasia.

In the autumn of 1935, the ancestor whom we are honouring here journeyed to the East. During his stay at the University of Yenching, an Occidental educational institution with its Oriental-style campus situated in the northwestern outskirts of the city of Beijing (Beiping at the time), Alfred Radcliffe-Brown delivered a series of lectures to some of the pioneers of Chinese social sciences. These lectures, combined in a certain 'Chinese way' by Wu Wenzao (1990), the leader of the 'Chinese School of Sociology', with Robert Park's human ecology and Bronislaw Malinowski's (1948) ethnographic science, played a major role in the opening up of the 'Chinese phase in social anthropology' (Freedman 1963). Radcliffe-Brown was meanwhile reading extensively from Marcel Granet's sociology of Chinese cosmology, which convinced him that the concept of *yin–yang* was the Eastern counterpart of the ancient Greek idea of the 'union of contraries', fundamental to his own 'science of society'.[1]

[1] At Yenching, Radcliffe-Brown came to know that in the social worlds of the Chinese, archaic practices such as ancestral worship and cosmological ideas such as *yin* and *yang* had continued to be effective.

Eighty years after his 'China trip', I received, with deep gratitude, the invitation to pay the present tribute to the mentor of mentors. I can be said to be much more fortunate than most of my predecessors in the East. When those in China whom Radcliffe-Brown taught were bearing all the hardships induced by the party-state-mobilised campaigns against 'bourgeois mentalities', I was just a child. In the period during which these pioneers were allowed back to their universities and academies, I was stabilising my career as a professional anthropologist. And then, they left our world one by one ...

But coming to this remote 'holy place' is inevitably both privilege and ordeal. The debts our mentors owed to their mentors and those I have owed to my mentors, as well as what we together have owed to such intellectual exchanges as those occurring in the 1930s and in the post-Cultural-Revolution periods, have piled up to make a mountain, compared to the weight of which my return, however ambitiously designed, is a small offering. I decided to offer what I now deliver, an exploration of the historical and relational qualities of 'Old World' cosmologies.

In an age in which archaic cosmologies, or, so to speak, age-old 'wisdoms of the world' are evoked either as radical critiques of hegemonic myths or summarily relativised as the legends of cultures or 'ontologies', the complexity of differences, similarities, and relations in and between traditions, to which our forerunners had begun to attach importance, need to remain at the centre of our anthropological concern. I will expound this point with constructive criticism of the self–other dichotomy, core to the ethnographic theories of witchcraft, 'primitive religion', 'savage mind', and 'civilisation', and to such scholarly new fashions as 'ontological anthropology'.

In Western anthropology, due to the subject's peculiar archaism, and perhaps anarchism, Eurasian traditions have most often been placed at the margins of ethnographic worlds. Leaving aside the benefits or otherwise of the ethnographic politics of such center–periphery relations, I wish to carry forward Radcliffe-Brown's accomplishments in comparative method, in which he always insisted on basing comparison on an inter-continental association of socio-logics and worldviews.[2]

Through some regional visitations inspired by a selection of relevant writings, in a so-called 'journey to the West', I move 'here and there', from the West to the South, from the South to the West and the East, from the North to the South, and back to the North and its intermediaries, thereby tracing the interaction of cosmological

With great curiosity, he began to develop a project to 'modernise' Granet's history of *Chinese Civilization* which he had begun to read during his Chicago years (Wu 1936). He involved several Chinese scholars in his project, seeking to gain from them an understanding of the ancient Chinese kinship system (Pan 1936) and its continued practice in contemporary lineage organisations (Lin 1936). Unfortunately, the implementation of the project was prevented by the Japanese attack in 1937 (Radcliffe-Brown 1977a, Stocking 1995: 353).

[2] Notwithstanding his emphasis on the 'primitive,' Radcliffe-Brown included ancient Chinese, Greek, and Roman cosmologies as relevant models (Radcliffe-Brown 1977a, 1977b).

traditions within and beyond the boundaries between worlds. My observations and thoughts from different places lead to an argument. In crossing the borders of some 'ethnographic regions' (Fardon 1990), I establish a link between two things: a resistance to typological contrasts, and, by synthesising Chinese and Western perspectives, images of what I have elsewhere defined as 'intermediaries' (Wang 2008), 'reciprocal alterity' (Wang 2014a), and 'supra-societal systems' (Wang 2015), concepts which should become clearer as my argument proceeds. I shall argue that, insofar as the traditions we study consist in certain cosmologies, then, be they Western or Eastern, Northern or Southern, they are internally varied and externally related.

The argument I make is more historical than 'sociological' and may strike some as removed from what Radcliffe-Brown envisaged for social anthropology. Nonetheless, I have taken it as close to the lesson he taught our forebears in the East and which is available only as a Chinese-language publication, namely that past–present and inside–outside relations are ethnographically complex (Wang 2016).[3] The lecture follows several directional turns (and perhaps returns) within which a framework of exposition unfolds.

MAGIC IN THE WEST

In my 'journey', I flew over the yellow and grey *landmass*, legendarily the enormous test Xuanzang, the Tang monk, was put to in his pilgrimage to the holy place in the West (India). But flying by aircraft instead of travelling on foot, I arrived smoothly at my destination, the greenest margin of Eurasia, from where I begin my narrative.

In the East, the case of England, in particular that of modern England, has been familiarised in varied ways. In Chinese late imperial times, England was known as the homeland of 'maritime barbarians (*yangyi*)' who, by means of giving free play to the 'hard power' of trade and war, brought major cosmic chaos to the Central Kingdom. But in due course, the negative side of the 'maritime barbarian' became forgotten. England was reconceptualised in our Occidentalist discourse in terms of 'soft power', the birthplace of such 'stranger-sages' as Darwin and Huxley, and was seen by both reformers and revolutionaries as the source of advanced institutions and social thought which would rescue their *tianxia* (all-under-Heaven) (Wang 2012) from History. For several decades of the post-imperial age, Frederich Engels' *The*

[3] In 'Some Suggestions for the Sociological Investigation of Rural Life in China' (Bulang [Radcliffe-Brown] 1936), a lecture delivered at Yenching (unavailable in English), Radcliffe-Brown focused on two aspects beyond 'synchronic or monochronic study': (1) the relation between ethnographic localities and other localities and between these localities and the greater areas of which they are parts, and (2) the changes in relations along the 'vertical' (historical) line.

Condition of the Working Class in England (1887) altered our image of the West again. England became synonymous with the world of the miserable. But in the late 1930s a positive image returned, as Max Weber's *The Protestant Ethic and the Spirit of Capitalism* (1930) redefined 'soft power' and inspired the minds of reformers.

In critiquing the 'post-colonialist' negligence of non-Western perspectives of alterity, I recently compiled a genealogy of Chinese Occidentalism (Wang 2014a) and set it against Edward Said's *Orientalism* (1978). We can continue adding images of modern England to this genealogy. But here I limit my attention to the fact that I go against the view of most of my colleagues in the East who view England in terms of simple linear history, whether good or bad. I argue instead that England is in fact made up of a history of plural cosmological traditions jostling ambivalently with each other.

Let me illustrate the point by referring to the magisterial study of the seeming 'decline' of magic by the English historian Keith Thomas (1973). In drawing our attention to the 'mental climate of early modern England', Thomas shows how new socio-logics and worldviews were promoted to replace old ones and how the promotion of the new cosmologies was complicated by the return of the mentalities and practices of magic. In so doing, Thomas demonstrates the replay of episodes in the dramatic interaction of magic and the modern.

According to Thomas, among the English, 'religion' was traditionally understood as 'a ritual method of living, not a set of dogmas', much as social anthropologists since Robertson Smith, Durkheim, and Radcliffe-Brown have viewed 'primitive religion' (Evans-Pritchard 1962, 1965). In late medieval times, the commoners paid hardly any attention to the difference between practising magic and performing ritual in the Church, and they well deployed the 'confusion' to press the Church into accepting the reality of what was happening. Consequently, not only were Church practices 'degraded', but magical practices were redesignated as religious ones. During the Protestant Reformation, however, this old religiosity was abandoned and a new one inserted into English society, which elevated the importance of the individual's faith in God and in scientific naturalism (Thomas 1973: 88). Thus, compared to the medieval Church, this reformed Anglican Church, much more rational and more hostile to magic, sought to forge a new direct link between the individual and God.

As Protestantism grew, the various late medieval, performatively efficacious procedures designed to serve the social and spiritual needs of the population were simplified, and the needs themselves redefined as what the individual should separately shoulder. Protestantism 'presented itself as a deliberate attempt to take the magical elements out of religion, to eliminate the idea that the rituals of the Church had about them a mechanical efficacy, and to abandon the effort to endow physical objects with supernatural qualities by the formula of consecration and exorcism' (Thomas 1973: 87). In a word, in paving the way for rationality and science,

Protestantism encouraged the individual to take a critical approach, and substituted the old legends of miracles with the norm of 'natural explanation'. The resultant split or rupture in the older Church created a gap which magic filled and so enjoyed a revival. So, while the campaigners for Protestantism and science were busily 'inventing' modernity from the very soil of the English country, various kinds of magic were flourishing, presenting the campaigners with a heavy burden.

The revival of magic was also observed in urban settings. Amazingly, as Thomas insists, in the 17th century 'It was in London that the sects, with their prophesies and healing miracles, were most successful; and it was there that the busiest astrologers had their practices.' And because the metropolis harboured every kind of popular magician, it 'was not exempt from witchcraft accusations' (796–7).

No history is a one-way street. The 'natives' of England in the 17th century persistently remained unconcerned by the 'distinction between magic and medicine.' Because of the persistence of magic, the expansion of naturalist cosmology in the form of an opposition between moral culture and material nature (Leach 1982: 36), proved to be nothing like a smooth process. 'Magic occupied the vacuum left by science' (Thomas 1973: 794–800), and its role in modern society continued to be 'more extensive than we yet appreciate' (799).

I see *Religion and the Decline of Magic* as making a good case for the anthropology of civilisations as envisaged by Robert Redfield half a century ago in several non-Western contexts—Mexico, India, and China. For medieval, modern, and 'late capitalist' England could largely be described in Redfield's terms as a long-term process in which old and new 'great traditions'—i.e., 'primary' and 'secondary' civilisations—came subsequently to reform the persons and things belonging to the 'little tradition' (Redfield 1973: 40–59, Wilcox 2004: 109–36). However, as I have also come to realise, to be applied in the English context, Redfield's theory of civilisation needs a couple of reformulations.

In its original definitions, 'primary' refers to the older civilisations internal to the societal wholes of the peasantries, while 'secondary' refers to the civilising process of modernisation intruding from outside—from the Christianities and the industrial power of the West—into such wholes as 'individualising forces'. In England, the sequence or order of the internal and the external seems reversed. With the 'primary' acting from the Romans outside and sometimes 'resisted' from within and the 'secondary' springing from within and exported abroad, England has indeed represented a different way of civilisation. In addition, the contestation of traditions in modern periods seems to end in what the historically optimistic Redfield had not expected: as Thomas points out, by removing the earlier ritualisation of religion, Protestant rationality left a gap that magic returned to fill in the lives of ordinary people, thus nurturing the needs of commoners who still equated ritual with magic.

In this regard, despite Macfarlane's caution,[4] I cannot help but associate the fortunes of English magic with what anthropologist Marshall Sahlins suggests about the new fortunes of Third World cultures. With the observation that 'culture is not disappearing', Sahlins (2000) argues that the cultural struggles of non-Western peoples have succeeded in undoing 'the received Western opposition of tradition versus change, custom versus rationality' (514).

Concentrating on the 'structures of conjuncture' between the West and the rest at the margins of the modern world-system, Sahlins hardly goes into the equivalent events occurring in the West. However, in effect, in these events the teleological structure extended to history has likewise been faced with a problem. The problem, in particular that defined by Thomas as the unanticipated persistence and revival of magic, has resonance with what Louis Dumont observes when attempting to explore different ways of modernity in modern France and Germany. As Dumont tells us, 'There are the new universal, modes of being that modern technics and perhaps modern ideas impose or carry with them, and there are older modes of being, proper to a population or a region, that manage to survive, more or less lively, more or less weakened or maimed by the former and their association with them' (1994: 4). In other words, the forces complicating the civilising process of the modern have not been from without but from within, but the outcome—sometimes explained in sociology as the resurgence of 'Axial Age' traditions in the multitude of modernities (Eisenstadt 2003)—has been similar to the persistence of the old in the 'other worlds'.[5]

To be succinct, by associating Thomas's case of England with the dramas of the interaction of traditions in non-Western contexts, we can arrive at the conclusion that the continuity of 'witch beliefs' is a more pervasive phenomenon than we have imagined.[6]

[4] In *The Origin of English Individualism* (1978), Alan Macfarlane warns us against the danger of drawing parallels between England's transition and those in the currently developing Third World. According to him, England's transition took centuries longer than we have imagined. Even within Western Europe, it represents a special example—'special' because individualism had already been prevalent in the peasantry a few centuries before industrialisation. Drawing parallels between the untypical example and the hoped-for transitions can result in more intense trauma and difficulties in the Third World (202).

[5] The persistence of 'culture' seems also close to that of 'folk belief' in China where the contexts in which each of the 'civilising processes' of the Neo-Confucian, missionary, revolutionary, and reformist projects have one after another given new life to 'superstition' (Wang 2004, 2009).

[6] In Continental Europe, historical circumstances and cultural patterns there are undoubtedly not the same (Macfarlane 1978: 2–3); nevertheless, similar phenomena to 'superstitious persistence' must have been existent, otherwise we cannot properly explain classical anthropologists' broad inclusion of all the Continental 'cultural survivals', such as Arnold van Gennep's ethnographic accounts of the 'folkloric' in France, and the local foundation of the ethnos of Velkskunde and Völkerkunde in Germany (Stocking 1987: 46–77, 186–237).

OTHER IN THE SELF, SELF IN THE OTHER

'Magic' in early modern England is not the same as 'primitive religion', or, to be more fashionable, 'Amerindian perspectival ontology' in Amazonia (Viveiros de Castro 1998), divination in Cuba (Holbraad 2012), or shamanic 'body–soul dialectics' in Siberia (Willerslev 2007). However, in the so-called 'superstition' of persistent magical practices, there is a cosmology close to what is often perceived as 'animism'. It echoes what is designated in China as *mixin* ('confused belief'), an old concept employed by Chinese authorities to refer to the mental state of 'popular religion' (Feuchtwang 1989, Wang 2011). This is a kind of 'universalism', which, as Thomas notes, ignores the 'naturalistic' or 'rationalistic' distinction between humans and non-humans (be they divinities, tangible things, or intangible Powers).

The case Thomas makes for English magic, together with such recent ethnographies of contemporary Western witch-hunting allegations as Jean La Fontaine's *Speak of the Devil* (1998), reveal not only the blindness of Occidentalism to other phenomena than those of intruding remote Occidental Powers, and the misfortunes they brought to the 'Mandate of Heaven', but also challenges our discipline's 'location of cultures'. The anthropology of witchcraft, founded by E. E. Evans-Pritchard (1937) in an African context, presented 'superstition' as a hybrid of spirituality and physicality and made it look as if it had existed only in other parts of the world than the West.

But the 'mythical realities' of magic turned out to be far more universal than what was ethnographically represented as remote 'local knowledge'. Witchcraft and witchcraft beliefs are not absent or extinct in the West; on the contrary, their continued lifeforms, sometimes described as distant 'cosmologies of capitalism' surviving the 'civilisation' of colonial modernity (Sahlins 1988), have in fact been quite evident in the civilising West, not only in its early state but also in its 'high time'.

As La Fontaine points out, witchcraft and witchcraft beliefs have continued to exist in the age in which the most sophisticated technologies and scientific knowledge as well as the most powerful bureaucracy in human history have dominated Western social life. Some witchcraft accusations, based on certain myths of satanic abuse, continued to form a major part of English public life (La Fontaine 1998: 177–92). By the end of the last century, the naturalist approach to beliefs in supernatural phenomena had been deeply embedded in the civilisation of England. It supported a sceptical attitude (held mostly by independent intellectuals) towards the allegations of satanic abuse; nevertheless, 'the surface change hid a continuity that indicates the tenacity of the campaign and the importance, to both sides, of issues that underlie both the old and the new forms of witch-hunting' (163).

Admittedly, even if it could be said to refer to expressions of certain 'witchcraft beliefs', contemporary folklore of satanic abuse is different from witchcraft itself; but for the allegations to be justified, it indeed requires the actual existence of its 'target phenomena'. So, as La Fontaine reckons, if there has indeed been a continuity of witch-hunting, then, at least to those who organised the campaigns, there must have been a continuity of witchcraft. This, to those who took the sceptical approach based on a belief in the triumph of reason, could not be the case. However, if we relate witchcraft to a broader category—e.g., non-operational 'superstitious activities'— we are able to find numerous such 'cultural survivals'. [7]

Presently, historical circumstances have altered; but the altering of condition and cosmology has not led to a 'breakthrough' in the structure of relationship of traditions. What is more, the campaigners opposing 'superstition' have turned out to be equally 'superstitious'. For they have treated science as if it was ethico-ideological guidance, 'trusted' in technology as if it would perform miracles, and made their political claims sound as if they were as effective as the 'confusions of beliefs'.

Perhaps the predicaments of modernity and tradition explain why the ethnographer of science, Bruno Latour has given one of his books the title *We Have Never Been Modern* (1993), which would have been more inspiring had he extended his scope of the anthropology of the moderns to the sphere of magic. On this, perhaps we can append a theoretical implication. To our appreciation of the implication of modernity being among traditions, or even being one tradition among several others, historians like Thomas and anthropologists like La Fontaine have made major contributions. By bringing to light the fact that different cosmologies—even those as mutually contradictory as modern and traditional—share the fate of being co-present in history, the historian and the anthropologist of Western magic and witchcraft have given us a new sense of 'existence'.

'... he who cannot find wonder, mystery, awe, the sense of a new world and an undiscovered realm in the place by the Grays Inn Road will never find those secrets elsewhere, not in the heart of Africa.'[8] What Arthur Machen famously said about London may be exaggerated; but it conveys something relevant to the issue we have just raised. The Chinese proverb 'seeking far and neglecting what lies close at hand (*shejin qiuyuan*)' seems to apply well to some aspects of anthropology.

Needless to say, the pursuit of 'the view from afar' (Lévi-Strauss 1985) has its recognised merits, and we often remain unwilling to embrace the enterprise of repatriated anthropology (Marcus & Fischer 1986: 111–36). However, reading about English magic, one wonders if it is unproblematic to sacrifice the 'unnecessary' traditions

[7] As Thomas also argues, in today's England, 'astrologers and fortune-tellers continue to be patronised by those for whom psychiarists and psycho-analysts have not provided a satisfactory substitute'. On the other hand, 'contemporary doctors and surgeons engage in many ritual practices of a non-operational kind' (Thomas 1973: 799).

[8] Cited from Ackroyd (2001: 503).

within anthropology's own birthplace (the West) as the price for the recursion of the subject's civilisational self-identification. And does not the anthropological distancing of the other, intended as emancipating our discipline's understanding of life, society, and world from the singularising process of 'civilisation', end, unfortunately, in the 'expulsion' of human understanding of being in the universe, core to what we mean by 'cosmology'?

COSMOLOGIES OF THE WEST AND THE REST

To specify the issue, let me dwell on our French colleague Philip Descola's *Beyond Nature and Culture* (2013), a project which, for the very reason we have just indicated, has regrettably failed in its attempt to subvert the burgeoning hegemony of the distancing dichotomy in anthropology.

In this book, Descola provides an extensive comparative perspective. Perhaps because he has been reoriented towards an animistic mode of knowledge, the author has freed himself from earlier comparative frameworks. What are given up are certain disciplinary derivatives of naturalism, which, as Claude Lévi-Strauss (1977) indicated some decades ago, are deeply troubled by the classical issue of whether the affinity between cultures 'is to be explained by a common origin or by an accidental resemblance between the structural principles which govern the social organisation and religious beliefs in both areas' (133). Unlike most of the preceding comparisons, which sought either to explain away the troubling relationship between 'singularity and multitude' or to place singularity (Western) outside multitude (the rest), Descola simply situates the 'one' among all others, making the modern European catalogue of persons and things a member of a larger catalogue of types.

The 'ontologies' Descola fetches from the distant and compares with the near (naturalism) are mainly two—animism and totemism—and these can be characterised in the anthropologist's own words as follows:

> Naturalism and animism are all-inclusive hierarchical schemas that are the polar opposites of each other. In the one, the universality of physicality extends its system to cover the contingencies of interiority; in the other, the generalization of interiority becomes a means of attenuating the effect of differences of physicality. Totemism, in contrast, appears as a symmetrical schema characterized by a double continuity of both interiority and physicalities, the logical complement to which can only be another symmetrical schema. (Descola 2013: 9)

With such distinctions in hand, Descola proceeds to map the geographic distribution of the ontologies in his chapter on the non-autonomous essence of the wild and the domesticated, where he dwells most heavily on the remote realms of animism and totemism, the nomadic spaces, the Amazonian gardens and forests, the rice paddy, the hunters' resorts, and so on. He then contrasts these realms with the modern dwellings of naturalistic existence, whose 'structural faults', as he reveals, have become apparent since the Enlightenment. Between the two worlds, Descola adds a long frontier, made up of medieval European, ancient Chinese and Mexican, and contemporary African constructs of 'analogism'.

The frontier ontology is defined as 'a mode of identification that divides up the whole collection of existing beings into a multiplicity of essences, forms, and substances separated by small distinctions and sometimes arranged on a gradual scale so that it becomes possible to recompose the system of initial contrasts into a dense network of analogies that link together the intrinsic properties of the entities that are distinguished in it.' As Descola continues, the mode 'is a hermeneutic dream of plenitude that arises out of a sense of dissatisfaction' (201–2).

Eventually Descola creates a certain trichotomic division of the world, close to that envisaged long ago by Marcel Mauss (1990). For Mauss, the three-fold worlds are the circles of the primitive, the historically archaic, and the modern, while for Descola, they are those of the 'primitive' (animistic or totemic), the analogist, and the naturalist. The worlds, constituted with the same concentric structure of the 'three rings' (Wang 2015: 136–66), are compared from a viewpoint opposing them to ethnocentrism.

Seemingly, this kind of worldscape is similar to the Japanese ethnologist Umesao Tadao's map of Eurasian civilisations.[9] Both are opposed to the old dualisms such as that of East and West, both are adapted to the concentric conception of Eurasia. Nonetheless, a major difference exists between the two. While Umesao presented the core areas of Eurasia (India, China, and Arabic worlds) as encircled by British, French, German, and Japanese 'advanced modern civilisations' from East and West, Descola, engaging all available ethnographies of 'primitive ontologies' from his own South and some others' North (Ingold 1986, Pedersen 2001), depicts it in terms of the

[9] By the late 19th century at the latest, Japanese intellectuals had invented their own Orientalism and Occidentalism. Siding with Western Europe, they tended to see China and India, despite both being situated to the West of Japan, as 'Oriental,' and to regard Japan and Western Europe as both 'Occidental'. So, in the Japanese perspective, Orientalism refers to Japanese narratives about China and India, while Occidentalism denotes the Western and modern civilisation. In the post-war decades, Umesao Tadao (2003) reworked the old dichotomy into a new concentric model of Eurasia. He substituted the 'nonsensical' diametric model of East and West with his concentric model of two zones. According to this new perspective of the world, Japan and Western Europe (Great Britain, France, and Germany) form a unity of advanced civilisations (Zone One), encircling Zone Two (China, India, Arabic worlds, and Russia), the core areas of Eurasia. While advanced capitalism and bourgeoisie control of power are the characteristic systems of Zone One countries, the opposite scenarios—undevelopment and revolutions—are seen in Zone Two (38–61).

dichotomy between the lands of totalitarian analogism and aggressive naturalism and those of animism and totemism surrounding them. Compared with Omesao's ethnocentric and modernist perspective, Descola's approach is thus considerably more alter-centric and archaic. Whatever it ends in, it allows the author to derive a comparative anthropology from subverting the accepted hierarchy of centre–periphery relations.

As an endeavour in making modern naturalism 'more accommodating to nonmodern cosmologies and better adapted to the circulation of facts and values' (xvii), *Beyond Nature and Culture* tells us a great deal about different ways of being in the universe. It brings into play not only the different 'ontologies' of the 'low' natives, and the 'high' shamans, but also those of the priests, poets, artists, scientists, and even Confucians. By means of centring the remote and marginalising the near, and identifying the middle, he successfully relativises Western modern socio-logics and worldviews.

I see good reason to believe that Descola 'offers a radical change in the current anthropological trajectory' (Sahlins 2013: xii). However, this has not prevented me from feeling somewhat disconcerted by the implicit contrasts lurking behind the trichotomy.

In Descola's overall depiction, the naturalistic 'mode' on this side of the planet is now chiefly organised by the thinking subjects in Europe who all the time since the emergence of modernity feel a need to choose between being human or otherwise, and demand a naturalistic schema in which they can locate their own lives; and by contrast, the 'natives' on the other side who appear much more 'cosmopolitan'—living, as they do, in enchanted social morphologies on the blurred boundaries between interiority and physicality, enjoying conceptual mobilities along the animistic, totemistic, analogical journeys, while remaining in their own traditions of cosmological anthenticity. This picture of contrasted cultures has struck me as what may be labelled 'typological self-identification'.

Descola's mental travel departs from the wonders of the 'unthinking' side of the Earth, where the wisdoms of the world are found in the local ontological realities. Neither does Descola end his travel simply in the West (he arrives at a conclusion concerning all humans), nor does he characterise the non-naturalist cosmologies as all alien to Europe (he seems to say that the ancients in the West were not that different from others). Nonetheless, in imposing a certain scepticism upon the possibility of creating functional hybrids out of components of what he perceives as 'irreconcilable properties' (Descola 2013: 392), he has drawn out a circle of boundaries around naturalism and attributes it to the modern (Western). In so doing, he has made the 'anthropology of nature', supposedly complementary to the 'anthropology of culture', dependent upon the principles with which Evans-Pritchard enhanced the efficacy of the anthropology of witchcraft.

FROM INNER NEW GUINEA TO ANCIENT GREECE TO CHINA: 'UNITIES OF DIVERSITY'

Any anthropology which feeds itself on such a contrast between self and other inevitably misses the fact that any society, culture, or civilisation is a 'unity of diversity' (Fei 1988). Even in the most distant realms which some would identify as the worlds of animism and totemism, cosmologies can be far more varied and divided than we have imagined. For instance, in the region of the Mountain Ok in inner New Guinea, among the small population of 15,000 individuals, the variation the anthropologist Frederick Barth (1987) found in the local cosmological systems is as enormous as that found in 'complex societies'. More or less similar to Descola's Achuar, the Mountain Ok people, whose languages are closely cognate, physical types indistinguishable, and house and dress strikingly similar, are a group who live in a 'simple economy', with their subsistence based on horticulture and extensive hunting and collecting of forest and streambed products as well as raising domestic pigs. However, among them, 'religious practices and beliefs vary dramatically as between groups and communities' (2–3). Internal cultural contrasts can easily be detected in the cults of ancestors, symbolism in initiation, ideas of conception, and uses of fire. Even the major modes in which religious and cosmological ideas are expressed differ dramatically between Mountain Ok communities.

As Barth notes, in locating personally remembered events, while Baktaman consolidate their vision in terms of the change 'from a better past when the ancestors were alive and taro and welfare were better, to a present time (since e.1950) when steel axes have replaced stone axes (both obtained externally through ceremonial trade) and the blessing of ancestor has failed', Telefolmin have developed from the same set of concerns and experiences certain more embracing and abstract concepts. What is more, on their part, the Bimin-Kushusmin 'have created a different and cyclical vision. Baktaman envision the beginning of human life from a kind of covenant with the original ancestor—the tree-foraging, ground-burrowing "white" marsupial who bestowed taro and instituted clan organisation' (49). Thus, as Barth argues, if there is an Ok cosmology, then it is distributed as sub-traditions between numerous places (villages and temples), and these sub-traditions are subject to constant oscillations between public performances and personal 'magical' rituals.[10]

In comparing his 'Neolithic' Ok example with those found in the 'complex societies' where the development of literacy has produced a novel durability of verbal statements, Barth tends to see the non-literate Ok people as keeping more multivocal and multivalent sacred symbols (75–6). We have no answer to the question of whether

[10] This is perhaps similar to the pendulum of the ideal types of hierarchy and egalitarianism in Highland Burma (Leach 1954)

civilisations with literacy are in fact less multivalent than the 'primitive societies'; but we are certain that they are no less multivocal. As I shall show, as with Barth's Mountain Ok cosmology, a civilisation fed on literacy can be understood as the precipitate of a cultural history of changeability, producing parallelism, convergence, and divergence.

We first move to the North, to look at the cosmological examples of the 'Axial Age' provided by Greece and China. Descola avoids simply following the ancient Greek definition of naturalism (172–3). However, in most places, he models the West in such a way that his narratives remind us of what the French mythologist Jean-Pierre Vernant (2006: 157–260) said decades ago about classical Greek cosmology.

As Vernant postulates, prior to the coming of age of philosophical cosmologies, the early model of what may be called 'geometric naturalism' had evolved quietly in the life of Greek society. This kind of 'geometry' was political, in that the *meson*, or middle, defines the shared and public domain (the *xunon*), as opposed to what is private and individual. This geometrical form of centre–periphery relations originated in the Greeks' domestication of a religious worldscape primarily charted by the 'Easterners'; but it was a radically different cosmology from those patterned in the kingdoms of the Oriental.

On the basis of this observation, Vernant makes the following contrast between East and West:

> In the Eastern Kingdoms, political space took the form of a pyramid, dominated by a king, with a hierarchy of powers, prerogatives, and functions stretching from top to bottom. In the city-state, in contrast, political space is symmetrically organized around a central point, as a geometrical schema of reversible relationships governed by equilibrium and reciprocity among equals. (Vernant 2006: 214)

In presenting the geometry of ancient Greece, Vernant emphasises that this is a culture of political space with a perspective on the universe. Matured in Anaximander's philosophy, archaic Western cosmology defined the earth as immobile and situated geometrically at the centre of the universe so that all the surrounding stars could be seen as equally moving around it. By contrast, in the so-called 'Eastern kingdoms', astronomy was 'arithmetic' rather than 'geometric'. There, accurate knowledge of certain celestial phenomena was well developed, but no geometric model was advanced to represent the movement of the stars in the sky (198–9).

The contrast Vernant sets up intrigues us as being similar to that between naturalism and analogism established by Descola, especially when he relates analogism to Louis Dumont's Indian hierarchy (Dumont 1980) and Marcel Granet's Chinese relationalism (Granet 1930, 1932). The two theorised comparisons of archaic cosmologies together define the deeply historical geo-cosmic models behind Occidental democracy and 'Oriental despotism'. However, this contrast makes little sense of each of the areas of East and West.

I do not mean that ancient Greek and Chinese 'wisdoms of the world' were the same. As I can appreciate, certain important differences existed between the two 'ends' of Eurasia, and these can be exemplified with different 'myths of creation', in particular those of Kronos and Pangu.

Drawing on Edmund Leach (1981: 124–31), Anthony Aveni (1995) argues that the myth of Kronos, the religious pendulum bridging the calendars of 'work and days' and the almanac, is based on the myth narrated as 'a lengthy genealogical catalogue of alternating good and evil deities who represent different parts and powers of a highly animate, personified universe' (58). In it, creation or the origin of the order of time is traced back to the separation of Father-Heaven and Mother-Earth: 'For the Greeks, Kronos created the pattern when, out of the homogenous symmetry of chaos, he polarised the universe. He made time when he parted the earth and the sky, when he separated the male principle that fell into the sea to become its own opposite, the female principle in the form of Aphrodite' (63).

In the Chinese 'genesis' myths—if they can be called such—Pangu (literally 'Plate Ancient'), a hairy giant with horns on his head and clad in furs, is the closest to Kronos. Legends suggest that in the beginning there was only chaos or 'con-fused (I have added an '-' to 'confused', to avoid the word being confused with 'confusion') complexity' (*hundun*). Over about 18,000 years, this coalesced into a cosmic egg. From the egg, Pangu emerged and began to order the world. Like Kronos, he sought to separate sky from earth and *yin* from *yang* with a swing of his giant axe. But unlike Kronos, Pangu did not go back and forth in-between sky and earth: to keep sky and earth apart, he simply stood between them and pushed up the sky. This task took 18,000 years; with each day the sky grew ten feet (three metres) higher, the earth ten feet wider, and Pangu ten feet taller. The myth continues that after the 18,000 years had elapsed, Pangu himself became the original source of all things in the world (Yuan 1991: 73–5).

A certain contrast can be drawn from the different myths. In the ancient Greek myth, by means of separation, Kronos 'performed out' the mobile element of time. In early China, in a comparable myth, the 'division of labour' between the male and female principles, perceived as 'natural' in being what originally existed, were only reproduced by Pangu. It seems arguable that the myths of Kronos and Pangu represent two different types of cosmology: one classificatory and, perhaps, 'analytical'; the other 'holistic'.

However, this does not mean that there is no 'reciprocal translatability' (Lévi-Strauss 1970) or 'transformation of each other' (Goody 1996) between the two: while the classificatory Kronos is insignificant without the reference of its opposite, chaos, or the 'con-fused complexity', the 'holistic' Pangu was reliant, in its own making, on the 'pre-existent senses' of the distinctions between celestial and earthly levels and persons and objects. More importantly, internal variation seems to be characteristic of the philosophical cosmologies in West and East,

Let us return to the issue of ancient Greek 'naturalism'. According to philosopher Rémi Brague, this is not the whole story of ancient Greek cosmology. The Greek 'Axial Age' saw Socrates's 'sociologism' and Plato's cosmologism, as well as such other schools as Atomism, the Scriptures, and Gnosticism (Brague 2003). Thus, apart from the Greece invented by Socrates and restored by Plato, there were three other Greeces. These four models were also 'anthropologies' because they all related the world to human knowledge and judgement.

As Brague explains,

> Out of the Greek concept of the world as kosmos there arose an anthropological dimension. This might appear paradoxical if, as I have assumed, the concept of 'world' only becomes possible at the moment when man has been excluded from its contents. In fact, the Greek idea of world contains an implicit appeal to the idea of subject, which it obliquely draws into it. Man is completely excluded from any active role in the construction of the world. But it is exactly because man does no 'making' to the world, because his presence adds nothing to any part of the world and his absence takes nothing from it, that he is able to appear as the subject to which the world shows itself in its totality. (Brague 2003: 24–5)

In each of the four models, there are thus the intrinsic ontological value of the world and the interest a knowledge of it has for humans. It is by way of these two means of access that the four models offer different perspectives, including the following:

> In the Timaeus Plato responds in a very positive way to the two questions about the value and the interest of the world: the world is what is best, and knowledge of it is supremely interesting, since such knowledge and it alone, enables us to reach the fullness of our own humanity. For Epicurus, the world such as it is is not bad, but it has no more value than any other arrangement of atoms; a knowledge of it, in theory, is not indispensible, but it is useful in fact, since it enables one to be assured. For those who claim to be of Abraham, the world is good, and even 'very good,' because it is the work of a good God; a knowledge of it is also useful, since it leads to a knowledge of the Creator. For Gnostics the world, the work of a clumsy or perverted demiurge, is bad. (70)

Brague also tells us that at a later stage, some of those diverse 'concepts of things/persons' got marginalised by the Abrahamic vision of the world; but the Abrahamic vision itself was not a way of being post-traditional—it restored the archaic cosmology of sacrifice and managed by so doing to stay on a higher plane. The Abrahamic vision, as Henri Hubert and Marcel Mauss (1981) tell us, in fact stayed 'down' in the tracks of the exchange ethics of classical sociologism.

Were one to take 'sociologism' and exchange ethics as naturalistic 'socio-centric modes', one would reduce all these into different manifestations of naturalism and analogism: for instance, Atomism into the original statement of naturalism and cosmologism into socially related cosmic patterns. In whatever ways these can be related to the typology entertained in Descola's *Beyond Nature and Culture*, the overall impression we just gained from reading the cosmologies of Antiquity reveals the plurality of thoughts, a closer examination of which would show that the Greek 'Axial Age' was not a 'society' with a correspondent cosmological tradition, be it analogism, naturalism, or something else, but a world in which a variety of traditions coexisted and interacted over space through time to make the *polis*. The shapes of the civilisation, being not devoid of relations with other shapes, were not that different from those that anthropologists observe in such 'living Neolithic societies' as that of the Mountain Ok. Not only in the Western part of Eurasia but also in the Eastern can such a culture history of internally varying traditions be reconstructed.

In an interview (Kohn 2009), regarding the overall patterns of the four modes, Descola gives the following synopsis:

> 1) animism, in which differently embodied kinds of humans and non-humans share a similar interiority, this is exemplified by Amazonian multinaturalism; 2) naturalism, where humans and nonhumans share a physicality but only humans have an interiority, a mode best exemplified by modern western science; 3) totemism, where certain groupings of humans and non-humans are united because they share interior as well as physical attributes, a mode found in Aboriginal Australia; and, 4) analogism, in which humans and non-humans are understood to be made up of fragmented essences, essences whose relationships can be mapped onto similarly linked essences possessed by other entities, this is a mode exemplified, as you note, by the ancient Inca State. (Kohn 2009: 141)

The four modes Descola has alloted to their own rooms of existence have impressed me as mostly available—though in a most cases in combined forms or in fragments—in ancient China.

Influenced by Edward Burnett Tylor, who spent seven lengthy chapters on animism in his masterpiece *Primitive Culture* (1871), a number of early-20th-century Chinese scholars extended the concept of 'survival' to their own culture, and they discovered a great number of expansive systems of animistic customs and beliefs among the peasants and ethnic minorities (e.g., the Heze in the Northeastern frontiers, see Ling 1931) as well as in the classical records (Jiang 1928). But as a neatly defined type, animism seems not to find a precise counterpart in written Chinese philosophies. However, once combined with naturalism, it becomes 'Chinese', as in the ontology shared by first-generation Daoist philosophers.

For instance, Zhuangzi (Chuang-tzu), who rejected almost all forms of classification, said that 'the sages ... see things in the light of Heaven [Chinese notion of Nature]. [For them], the "this" is also "that". The "that" is also "this" ' (Chuang-Tzu 1989 [edn]: 44). Like the animists, Zhuangzi did not differentiate humans ('this' or 'that') from non-humans ('that' or 'this') or non-humans from humans, and he even often described his own physical transformation into a flying bird and a dreaming butterfly; but he did not see the sameness between humans and non-humans in the light of 'culture' which he would attribute to Confucian socio-logics—he saw it instead in the light of Heaven, the ultimate level of existence which, as more or less the 'natural law' of nothingness but not being, was definable neither in terms of materiality nor in terms of spirituality.

Zhuangzi's 'depersonification' and 'declassification' of the world, as philosophical thinking, were undoubtedly not the same as either animistic, perspectival cultural universalism or natural relativism (Viveiros de Castro 2012). Articulated as a response to the situation associated with the over-pervasiveness of deity cults, although it seemed to include an ontology of metamorphosis, Daoist philosophy seemed far from the universalism of 'interiority'. A more appropriate understanding of it requires a situational approach: the cosmology emerged out of its confrontation with another philosophy, also concerned with the pervasiveness of deity cults in the 'little traditions'—Confucianism—which was in turn derived from certain sociologistic reactions to the cosmologism of Daoism.

Confucius nurtured his ideal of 'being social' neither in the non-human world nor in human society, but in the intermediary between nature and civilisation, and he derived his socio-logics from the correspondence between 'geo-cosmic patterns' and 'human (social) order' (Fung 2011: 56–89, 398–419). Although he did not explicitly trace human ancestry to non-humans as most totemists did (Viveiros de Castro 2012: 73–104, Ingold 2000: 132–52), he did strongly emphasise the political efficacy of kinship, which, to him, not only made proper relations for the living but also related them as living persons/things with ancestors as subject/objects.

It is true that in ancient Chinese cosmologies, the *xing* (nature) of an existing being is 'not produced by a dynamic opposition between mind and matter' (Descola 2013: 207). However, the terms '*xing*' does not simply mean what expresses 'the distinctions that are established between the states of elements and the proportions of their respective mixtures' (Ibid.). As I will explain, even if we insist on 'discovering' certain 'analogistic' remnants in Chinese cosmologies, we should be warned against treating parts as wholes.

At the beginning of the 20th century, Wang Guowei (1908), the mentor of almost all modern Chinese historians, argued that, in classical times, apart from the two different philosophies just mentioned, a third philosophical tradition emerged in the classical poetic excursions, in which the thinker and poet Qu Yuan transgressed the boundary between the two schools by means of analogising the Confucian socio-centric worldview to the ideal of 'other things' in the wilds. Unlike Confucius, who 'by respect for the Spirits keeps them at a distance' (Confucius 1998 [edn]:73),[11] as Wang (1908) argues, Qu Yuan's mind was all the time among the Spirits. We should not consider Qu Yuan's poems to be the same as what is expressed in 'the savage mind'; but the kind of spiritual excursions he made in his poetic creativities also mapped the relationship of the fragmented essences of humans and non-humans onto similarly linked essences possessed by other entities, and it has been said to be pervasive throughout the history of Chinese literature and 'wild' or vernacular historiography (*yeshi*). Because Qu Yuan moved between Daoism and Confucianism, he made in his own mind (and heart, I must add) a good synthesis. His poems proved to have 'ten thousand things (*wanwu*)'—plants, animals, landscapes, celestial beings, ancestral spirits, etc—talking just like living humans[12]—to inspire and lift him up beyond chaotic human worlds onto the higher plane of wisdom. These entities also proved to have many of the sociological anxieties which Confucius had; but they were more animistic, because they made a large sum of non-humans contrastively relevant to humans.

SYNOPSIS OF A GEOHISTORY OF SOME VARIED AND RELATED MODELS

In integrating culture and nature into a social system (Descola 1994), one accomplishes a critique of sociologism and environmentalism, whose common error has been its naturalistic dualism. However, one contines to be faced with the difficulties of freeing the social from the restrictions of the idea of self-contained cultures. The ontologies under speculation are still discrete ways of 'identification' and 'relations', of persons identifying themselves with things, and things identifying themselves with persons (Descola, 2013: 112), and 'the external links between beings and things that are detectable in typical behavior patterns and may be partially translatable into concrete social norms' (113). Still, they are altered expressions of the composite mode of dividual

[11] This explains why modern Confucianists like Qian Mu (2004) do not believe that China has anything to do with animism, which they, in most cases, identify with the West, where, as they perceive it, the Spirits are everywhere.

[12] Therefore, Qu Yuan can be said to be greatly different from the Western philosopher Ludwig Wittgenstein, who as Eduardo Viveiros de Castro (2012) notes, does not believe in the possibility of human–animal communication, and he is more similar to the Amerindians, for whom, as Viveiros de Castro describes, 'lions, or rather jaguars, not only can talk, but we are perfectly able to understand what they say—they "speak of" exactly the same things as we do' (112).

and individual persons and groups who are related with each other only to the extent that 'each party is irreducibly differentiated from the other' (Strathern 1988: 13–14). These altered expressions surely make a syntax of the combinations of physicalities and interiorities, but, having been characterised as usual as the manifestations of the differences determined by cultures, they remain removed from the so-called 'ontological realities', which, as I believe, often gain their identities across the boundaries of cultures.

What Sahlins brilliantly argues about the dialectic of inter-cultural identification and relation can be repeated here as a critique of the topological view of ontologies:

> Divinities or enemies, ancestors or affines, the Others are in various ways in the necessary conditions of a society's existence. Sources of power and cultural good things, though they may also be dangerous, these beings from the beyond represent a predicament of dependency in which all peoples find themselves. All must construct their own existence in relation to external conditions, natural or social, which they did not create or control, yet cannot avoid. They are constrained in some ways, if never the only possible way, by the passage of the seasons, the annual rainfall, the customs and actions of their neighbors. In such respects, no culture is sui generis. And a more or less self-conscious fabrication of culture in response to imperious outside 'pressures' is a normal process—dialectic or schismogenic, perhaps, but not pathogenic. (Sahlins 2000: 489)

Because no society exists alone, 'The dialectic of similarity and difference, of convergence of contents and divergence of schemes, is a normal mode of cultural production' (Sahlins 1999: 411).

As Sahlins proposes, to 'fetch' the facts of the related cultures, we can simply revisit the ethnographies which have well indicated that 'cultures were never as bounded, self-contained and self-sustaining as postmodernism pretends that modernism pretends'. However, being more concerned with the dialectic of similarity and difference of the related 'Old World' traditions, I have chosen to add to the ethnographic enterprise a synoptic geo-history of the political cosmologies in the Eastern part of Eurasia.

Chinese geo-cosmic perspectives have been studied as advanced in the 'age of chronology', beginning in the 8th century BCE within the geographic confines of the 'agrarian civilisation' of the 'Central Plains'. In most of the available interpretations, the civilisation has been understood as different from the 'frontiers' where most of the nomads and hunter-gatherers were. It thus has been represented with hardly any reference to the ontologies of the 'peripheral peoples.' Instead of the identification and relations between hunters and prey, humans and 'beasts', herdsmen and animals, the cosmologies in the 'agrarian' world have been construed with reference to plants, soil, water, birds, butterflies, wind, and sky, and the 'ecologies of relationship' they yielded have been seen as neither the primitive way of sharing and trust, nor the pastoralist ontology of power—dominance and subordination (Ingold 2000: 61–76). That is to say, they have been characterised as something 'similar to that of the farmer who does no more than encourage the growth of his plants and in no way intervenes in the process of germination and growth' (Gernet & Vernant 1990: 84).

However, 'adaptation', a concept often appearing in the characterisation of 'agrarian civilisation' rendered by Western sinologists and by modern Chinese intellectuals alike,[13] represents only the tip of the iceberg of the universe of the varied cosmological ideas in the East, even if we only speak about China's 'Central Plains'.

Liang Qichao (1902), in mapping the histories of classical Chinese ideas in geographic terms, and writing as early as 1902, demonstrated that the 'hundred schools of thought' were all deeply rooted in the varied local worlds of the culturally differentiated regions. The higher level regional division was that between North and South, roughly corresponding to the division between the two major civilisations advanced along the Yellow River and the Yangtse River. In different eco-geographic situations, the two great civilisations advanced different agricultural and political systems, and founded different discursive traditions. In the North, agriculture was conducted in harsher environments, where for their limited livelihood, the humans competed among themselves. In the contexts of tension, stronger political powers were developed, and thinkers, be they Confucians or Legalists, had their minds oriented toward pragmatics, action, hierarchy, and state power. In the South, in contrast, agriculture, conducted on more fertile land and in friendlier environments, more easily yielded great harvests, and there thus saw, on the one hand, less serious social tensions, and on the other hand, more non-humanistic ontologies. There in the South, thinkers, with their eyes more open to the universe, were more inclined to develop metaphysics, inaction, equality, and anarchy. As Liang concludes, in the North, thinkers made efforts to make the rulers and the commoners follow the way of Heaven which they ought to fear, whereas in the South, they sought to remain in the state of inaction under Heaven (143–58).

[13] A certain Eastern negation of the naturalist dichotomy has become dominant in past decades. In two mutually related works, the late Fei Xiao-tong provides such a negation. In one work, 'Re-examining the Cultural Constructs of the Interrelationship Between Humans and Nature' (Fei 2004), Fei puts the ancient Chinese perspective of Heaven–human (nature–culture) unity side by side with the worldview of the world's 'ethnic peoples' and treats them as an alternative to the Western dichotomous cosmology, which, as Fei argues, has been behind all industrial powers and the man-made disasters they have brought to the world; in another work, 'On Extending the Frontiers of Traditional Sociology' (Fei 2009), argues that Western social sciences, constructed upon the destructive cosmological basis of dichotomism, cannot continue to be beneficial; alternatively, a new sociology conceptualised in the Eastern philosophical terms of Heaven–human unity must be invented. Leaving aside the issue of Fei's past devotion to rural industrialisation, we still find in his critiques, which can definitely impress many of us as finely in line with recent cosmological reconsiderations in Western anthropology, a sense of ethnocentrism.

In addition to the Northern (Confucian and Legalist) and Southern (Daoist) schools, there were other schools: for instance, the one invented by Mozi. Born in the archaic kingdom of Song situated between North and South, Mozi combined the two major schools into a third. He embraced the Confucian orientation toward pragmaticism and action, but he also adopted Daoist metaphysics and inaction (148).

In each of the higher level schools, there were sub-schools, which became more divided in the periods in which communication (including debates) between different cosmological traditions became frequent. Convergence often yielded not only combination but also differentiation. Being virtually a 'great tradition', each of the sub-traditions tended to uproot itself in order to join the more 'universal' dialogues with the other greater schools. However, what made its self-identity tangible was paradoxically its link to local culture. For instance, Yellow River Valley in the North had two major sub-regions: the West (upper basin of Yellow River) and the East (lower basin of Yellow River), the latter open to the sea, the former situated within the confined agricultural areas restricted by the mountains. Confucianism was prevalent in both the sub-regions. Nonetheless, in the Western sub-region, it was much more concerned with the worldly affairs of humans, whereas in the Eastern sub-region, faced with pressures from the popular great tradition of the necromancers' cosmology, it had to allow more space for speculation about 'celestial issues' (150–1).

A kind of 'geographic determinism' hidden in Liang's narrative worries many of us; but this depiction of the regional dynamics of cosmological formation has impressed me as well illustrating the temporal and spatial variations of cosmology in the long centuries of the pre-imperial period (the so-called 'Axial Age'). The variations stemming from the constant inter-regional division and interaction in fact had emerged in an earlier period than Liang's age of 'the hundred schools'.

Long before the 'hundred schools' gave voice, in late Neolithic times, in conceptualising the oneness, similarity, or distinction between humans and non-humans, and in advancing their wisdoms of the world, the peoples occupying different regions had come to differentiate the beings residing in the cultivated and the wild, the house and the mountains, and the worlds below and beyond. They seemed not to be satisfied with such binaries, and they multiplied them with a concentric geo-cosmic model of quarters surrounding the centre or, conversely, the centre orienting to the quarters. The model, later known as that of 'five quarters/directions (*wufang*)' or, alternatively, that of 'pentology', could be said to be a composite one, a model mediating the reciprocating binaries (inside and outside, self and other) and the hierarchical triads (upper, middle, and lower levels, e.g., Heaven, humans, and Earth) and making the combination of horizontality (binaries) and verticality (triads) possible.[14]

[14] A recent astro-archaeological reinterpretation of numerous findings has indicated that the model had been applied in late Neolithic times in various spatial patterns of the sacrificial platforms situated

In late Neolithic times, there had not been the 'Central Kingdom', and the Eastern part of Eurasia formed a multitude of the 'regional chieftains (*fangguo*)', and so, as the Chinese archaeologist Su Bingqi (1999) points out, was just like the 'sky sown with stars (*mantian xingdou*)'.

Following Liang's three-fold division of cultural areas, the historian and mythologist Xu Xusheng (1932) long ago mapped these 'chieftains' into three major groups (Xu 1932). According to Xu, these groups, who jointly made the history of civilisation through their contestations, comprised Chinese (the Western group), 'barbarians'—the 'Eastern barbarians' (known as Yi) and the 'Southern barbarians' (known as Man)—each inhabiting West, East, and South.

The archaic geo-cosmic model of 'pentology' seems to have been shared by all the 'chieftains', but it also seems to have been variously conceptualised in different 'cultural areas'. While in the Eastern basin of the Yellow River, the archaic kingdoms had their worlds more vertically oriented, placing more emphasis on the link between the low (humans) and the high (gods and Heaven), in the West the kingdoms put more emphasis on the middle realms (mountains and rivers) in which they sought to become connected with the ancestors, the non-humans, and Heaven. For instance, in the Shang dynasty (approximately 1600 to 1046 BCE), whose founders brought with them the tradition of one of the archaic kingdoms in the East and the Northeast, the model combined a certain 'ancestral landscape' (Keightley 2000) in a system of Di, in which the categories of supreme heavenly deities and ritual practices worked together to erect the verticality of the kingly. In the Zhou dynasty (1046–256 BCE), whose founders were the descendants of several of the archaic chieftains in the West previously attached to Shang as fiefs, the Shang model was reconstituted with political ontologies derived from the ancestors in the West, and was much more horizontal (binary, feudal, reciprocal, and 'outward-going') (Wang 2014a: 49–86). In addition, there was a third version in the South, a less politico-religious one, in which the Miao group or the 'Southern barbarians', having been excluded from the contest of dynastic alternations in the North, found their own opportunities to expand into the South.

Compared with the earlier models of political space, classical cosmologies were more theorised; but they continued to be transformations of the earlier models. Specifically, Zhuangzi's world was centred in the outside, the further outward being the higher; Confucius's world was centred in the middle, in which sagacity or civilisation between culture and nature was the higher; and Qu Yuan's world was centred in the outside as 'the most inner inside', contrastive to the ordinary and thus lower self.

outside human settlements in the uncultivated fields between mountains and low rivers in different areas and in numerous jade ritual objects unearthed near these platforms (Feng 2007: 124–75).

As Liang also brilliantly reveals, between the 2nd century BCE and the 3rd century AD, the classical schools of thought took turns to shape and reshape the imperium. In the first empire (Qin, BCE 221–7), Legalism overshadowed Confucianism; in Western Han (BCE 202–8 AD), Legalism lost its dominant position, and Confucianism regained its hegemony. In Eastern Han (25–225 AD), Confucianism cleared away almost all other schools of thought and, with direct support from the emperor, succeeded in turning all the intellectual debates into those concerning the annotations of the scriptures. However, soon after the Eastern Han perished during the period of 'disintegration' of the Three Kingdoms (220–80) and the Six Dynasties (222–589), the Southern school, Daoism, returned to the ideological stage; now, having become 'neo-Daoism', it created a long phase of 'political nihilism'.

The agrarian core of the East Asian continent, complex enough with all its sub-regions and sub-traditions within its confines, existed among other regions. Whereas the Western basin of the Yellow River was often under siege from the 'barbarians' known as the Rong and the Di in the Northwest and North, the Eastern part on the one hand tied itself to the basin of the Huai River in the South and on the other hand drew its civilisation from the constant exchanges of goods and ideas with the peoples living in the linguistic and cultural region comprising the vast land from Siberia to Northeast China. The South of the agrarian world was likewise surrounded by other 'quarters'. While the peoples speaking Sino-Tibetan and Mon-Khmer languages occupied all the high plateaux and mountains to the Southwest, those speaking Malayo-Polynesian languages occupied the islands, coast, and hills in the Southeast, forming two other outer 'quarters'. In these surrounding zones to the North and South, there were the nomadic livestock-raisers of the steppe, the mountain peoples, and those with mixed cultures of gathering, hunting, livestock-raising, agriculture, and fishing, who developed different ontologies out of different environments of relationship.

Many sino-centric historiographies have endorsed the cultural achievements of the sage kings, the archaic dynasties, and the classical thinkers in and around the 'Central Plains' as the only civilising forces. However, such achievements were actually accomplished in a much wider geo-historical context in which the 'barbarians' in the outer realms, with their own expansive systems of hard and soft power, also occupied a major position.

In order to enable their authority to be broadly received, the emperors ruling their world (all-under-Heaven) during the periods of unification usually adopted inclusive cultural politics towards other cultures. For instance, Wudi, the greatest Han emperor of (reigning between BCE 156 and 187), whose combined form of authority reminds me of the charismatic leaderships in the modern villages Stephan Feuchtwang and I (2001) have jointly studied, not only made good efforts to blend the Northern schools of Confucianism and Legalism into his 'ceremonial laws' and bureaucracy and to draw from the Southern Liang kingdom Sima Xiangru's kind of poetic vision for all-under-Heaven (Wang 2010: 236–339) but also tried his best to cherish the non-Han cosmologies.

Living his life as an emperor over two thousand years ago, Wudi could not be an actor in the modern drama of 'superdiversity' which, following Steven Vertovec (2007), anthropologist David Parkin (2016) has recently described in terms of a multi-scalar and overlapping interpenetration of cultural lifestyles, religions, and languages that, since the 1990s, new migrants have brought to the world's metropoles.[15] Nonetheless, Wudi was also a person with different identities which he expressed at different space–times. He, likewise, operated as a node in a strand of related activities, which in turn was related to other nodes along a hierarchical chain of networking, setting up a good example of what may be defined anthropologically as 'scale'.

A paragraph from Granet's book suggests a lot about that:

> He sought less to create a religion of the imperial person, than to become the high priest of syncretistic worship, abounding in splendid ceremonies. He called to him the scholars and magicians of the North-east as well as the sorcerers of the country of Yue, while he had brought into his palace the golden idol which the king of Hiu-ch'u worshipped, and into his study the celestial Horse taken from the Prince of Ferghana. He consulted the fates by means of chicken-bones after the methods of the Barbarians of the South-east, and in the Chinese manner by using shells of tortoises. He sacrificed on flat hillocks as well as on high terraces. He spent great sums on alchemy, spiritualism and traditionalist literature. He had hymns composed, classic in form and inspiration, and patronized the poems in which Ssuma Siang-ju imitated, it is said, the poetry peculiar to the country of Ch'u. (Granet 1930: 123)

The celestial Horse which Wudi loved came from the direction from which the nomadic powers intruded on the agricultural world. This pointed to the outer zones beyond the Great Wall, the long belt comprising the regions of the Northeast, North (the Mongolian grasslands), Northwest, and Tibetan plateau (Lattimore 1967). The peoples living in these zones were undoubtedly varied; but in common they derived their military, political, and civilisational competence from both their local cultures and their interactions with the 'agrarian' world. When the opportunity was ripe, they raised their local traditions to higher levels of greater scale, and at such levels, they invented their own arts of domination with cultural borrowings from the sinic world. Arriving from the perilous frontiers, they pressed a major part of the Chinese

[15] According to Parkin, instead of making the societies in the global cities individualised, 'superdiversity' has produced more dividual persons and newly mixed speech communities which 'can no longer be ranged alongside each other as relatively self-contained and clearly distinct from each other' (Parkin 2016).

population into the South, created their own kingdoms in the North during the periods of 'split and war',[16] and, eventually, in the so-called 'late imperial' times, established such great empires as Yuan (1271–1368) and Qing (1644–1912), in both of which some of the Han ways of the world were mobilised, together with such those of Tibetan Buddhism, as parts of the 'barbarian' whole of civilisational plurality.

While the North was faced with heavy pressures from the horse-riding barbarians, the South, from where Wudi of Han learnt the skills of sorcery and chicken-bone divination, became more and more important. The provinces along the tributary rivers of the Yangtse were settled in the 6th century. Consolidation of this new expansive region was completed under the South Song dynasty (1127–1279) whose capital itself was located in the city of Hangzhou in the Southeast. Further South, in Guangdong and Fujian, by the middle of the Tang dynasty, colonialisation and cultural advance were achieved. From the Yuan to Qing dynasties, the Southwestern areas, including Yunnan and Guizhou, were brought under imperial administrative and cultural control.

Compared with the countries beyond the Great Wall, the Southern countries were further from the imperial capital. In Charles Patrick FitzGerald's comparison (1972), while the 'Northern barbarian' countries 'were close to the capital (almost always in the North), and their hostile power could strike at the heart of the empire, resulting in two total conquests and two which were confined to North China', the Southern frontier was 'less dramatic': 'No power arose in the South capable of challenging the rulers of China, nor even of arresting for long the slow, steady spread of her Southward drive' (xix). However, it was in the South that Chinese civilisation came into direct contact with cultural influences emanating from another great centre: India. In the Southeast, before the Chinese system of local administration was charted, Hinduism and Buddhism had their own sacred architectures erected. In the Southwest, the native chieftains (*tusi*) had long developed close ties with the Hinduised kingdoms in Southeast Asia. Along with the increase in Chinese elements, the places in the South became more and more like the meeting points of different civilisations. Such places are exemplified by the towns of Dali in the Southwest (Liang 2010) and Quanzhou (Wang 2009) in the Southeast. To them, in conjunction with the 'little traditions' symbolised for the Han emperor by the magics of sorcery and chicken-bone divination,

[16] While others have adopted the trichotomy of Antiquity, Medieval, and Modern to frame Chinese history, I have followed historian Chi Ch'ao-ting (1963) in characterising the two millennia of imperial times in terms of two long cycles of unity and 'split', namely from the first period of unity and peace between the 3rd century BCE and the 3rd century AD to the phase of 'split' and war between the fall of Han in 221 to the late 6th century, and that between the second period of unity and peace of Sui and Tang (581–907) and the second phase of 'split' and war between the early 10th century and the early 13th century, which was followed by several long centuries of unification and peace.

came Confucianism and Daoism from the North, Hinduism and Buddhism from Southeast Asia, and such other religions as Islam, Manichaeism, and Catholicism.

The interactions between civilisations were not restricted to the Southern margins of the Han world. The co-presence of different civilisations had been more than apparent in the Northern imperial capital of Xi'an (Xiang 1933). As early as the Han dynasty, Buddhism had been introduced into the Chinese world from the West and the South, and by the time of the South and North Dynasties (420–589), it had created a 'Buddhist phase in Chinese history' (Liang 1902: 199–214). In the post-Tang periods of disintegration (the 10th to the 13th centuries), particularly during the Song Dynasty (960–1279), Confucianism revived. However, depending now not only on older versions of Confucianism but also on Buddhism, it was rejuvenated in both the 'Central Plains' and in the South as Neo-Confucianism. Not long after the invention of Neo-Confucian tradition, the 'history of the heart (*xinshi*)' emerged in such writings as those by the sorrowful Zheng Sixiao of South Song (Chen 2001) as a Southern Chinese intellectual response to the 'Northern barbarian' intrusions. According to Wu Han (1956), this kind of response, combined with sinified Manichaeism, was what was behind the Han popular anti-barbarian movements in late Yuan, which resulted in the establishment of the Neo-Confucian Ming.

The gaze we cast on ancient China confirms that cosmological traditions, be they 'great' or 'little', were diverse and interactive. Even if the notion of 'agrarian civilisation' is useful for our appreciation of the overall pattern of 'Chinese cosmology', it contains very little about the schools of cosmological thought as developed in the creative alternations of regional 'sub-traditions' in history and in the inter-cultural relations with the 'external' worlds to each of which the civilisation sometimes opened itself up and from which it sometimes closed itself off.

Such creative alternations and relations can be patterned in structural and historical terms. To a great extent, what we have drawn from Liang's geo-history of the great traditions of cosmology and from the later counterparts of centre–periphery relations suggests an idea of the structure of relationships. Such 'geo-histories', as we may name them, are undoubtedly 'etic perspectives;' but they are also in full relationship with the 'emics', for instance, with the transformative model of centre and quarters, whose 'ideal types' conditioned the alternations ('historical processes') and made the imperium a system of recognised and re-enacted relations defined by Granet (1930) in terms of the 'religion of the imperial person'.

'SAVAGE WITHIN'

We have passed by the West and the East as well as the South; in each of the 'quarters' we have observed the varied nature of cosmology, and have followed with interest the phenomena of the interaction of traditions. Obviously, between the examples provided so far, there have been discrepancies. The modern dramas of the interaction of traditions occurred between two contesting cosmologies situated 'vertically' in the higher and the lower planes (the emergent Protestant tradition as against persistent 'superstition', and the rational as against the 'magical'); comparatively speaking, those taking place in both ancient Greece and classical, early and 'middle-age' China involved a number of 'horizontally distributed' traditions.

The discrepancy may have stemmed from the greatly different scales of the 'societies' compared, or from the greatly different periods to which the chosen societies belonged (early modern absolutist states or modern nation states and the ancient civilisations and empires). But whatever explains it, it holds true that the one-to-one model developed by Redfield is far from being sufficient.[17]

Stanley Tambiah (1970) has argued that Redfield looks insufficiently into the varied and cumulatively changing qualities of the great traditions, apart from paying too little attention to the referential and legitimating function of texts and knowledge among the commoners (3–4). Suspending the issue of whether Redfield's model itself is a social science extension of the notion of the folklore of the singular culture nation(-state), we would just add that great and little traditions vary not only historically but also 'synchronically'.

If we follow Wu Wenzao (1990: 254–62) in thinking that China should be compared with Europe as a whole but with not one of its nations, we will find great similarities between the two civilisational ensembles.[18] Each of the ensembles involves several major 'sub-traditions', each of which was associated with the others in developing its

[17] In making us aware of the importance of great traditions in 'peasant societies', Redfield not only opens our eyes to history and humanistic studies but also makes it possible for us to involve ourselves in comparative studies of civilisations. In addition, in distinguishing great and little traditions, Redfield, quoting his colleague McKim Marriott (1956), points to the direction of interactions of traditions. He emphasises that between the higher learning and the lower in both traditional and modern societies are constant interflows of cultural elements, including 'universalisation' (great traditions taking up and heightening some elements of folk beliefs and practices) and 'parochialisation' (little traditions' reformation of great tradition as local cult).

[18] As Mauss (2006) points out, the 'nations' advanced their own political and legal regimes which functioned to mark themselves off from each other; however, such regimes, in their own making, also depended heavily upon inter-national and inter-civilisational borrowing of 'myths, tales, money, commerce, fine arts, techniques, tools, languages, words, scientific knowledge, literary forms and ideals' (38). Consequently, the 'nations' all had, within them, all the available elements of the civilisations, and associated with the civilisational ensembles.

own characteristics, and each of which was differentiated from the others in borrowing cultural elements from them. The mutual borrowings and self-identities of the great traditions of modern individualism in France and Germany (Dumont 1994) as well as in England (Macfarlane 1978) are more or less comparable to the older interactions of cosmologies in the 'Central Plains' of China. In addition, if we compare European nations with the core regions of the Eastern end of Eurasia, then we can also say that like the latter the former are surrounded by certain intermediate and outer 'quarters' which in turn form certain interactional relationships with the 'core.' Meanwhile, the variations of cosmology are not unique to the Old World. On the contrary, similar situations are also found in the 'remote places'.

In anthropology, the dualist division of the world has been achieved through making the primitive radically more authentic or original than the civilized;[19] in philosophy, it has reached a high key through attributing the 'logos' of the word 'cosmology' to Antiquity and its continuation into the 'middle age', and through defining primitive worldviews as, at their best, cosmography (descriptive accounts of the world) and cosmogony (the story of the emergence of things) (Brague 2003: 2–4). By means of relating modernity to magic and comparing Eurasian interactions of traditions to their counterparts in 'Neolithic' parts of the world, we have attempted to 'mingle' self and other. Our point is not new. It is a renewed expression of what Franz Boas said long ago about the primitive and the advanced: like all the 'advanced civilisations', the 'primitive cultures' have long histories behind them, and in the situation of the tribal, humans also live in accordance with their 'conventional prescriptions and rules' (Boas, 1974: 68), so much so that those factors, including the divergent traditions, attributed to the 'civilised' have also existed in the 'primitive.' It is also a re-decipherment of the relation between great and little traditions.

We have scrutinised the spread of the indomitable vitality of the 'primitive' into the great traditions when relating ancient Chinese cosmological models to the political ontological legacies of the contesting regional kingdoms established on the bases of late Neolithic local cultures, and we have offered a synoptic geo-history to illuminate the divergence and mutual dependence as well as the constant inversions, in the overall pattern of 'civilisation', between centre and quarters, Chinese and 'barbarians',

[19] Like the 'ethnographic regions' in which they are situated, the philosophical concepts in Eurasia and the modes drawn from the 'savage mind' are different: whereas the ancient Eurasian cosmologies are inscribed as philosophies, the modes of the 'savage mind' are philosophical only after they have been deciphered by the anthropologists; whereas the Eurasian cosmologies are overtly political, the 'native modes' are not really so unless they are related to the anthropologists who write ethnographies of them (this implication of ethnography has been recognised as Roy Wagner's discovery (Wagner 1981). These differences have benefitted the anthropology of the tribal, and given a 'peripheral status' to the anthropology of the civilised.

and 'agrarian' and 'tribal', which, in later periods, were associated with the 'world religions'.

In spite of all our references to 'classical scholarship', our reconsiderations have been projected to question the belief that the prehistoric worldviews were not subjects of humanistic studies, and to warn ourselves against erasing the traces of the 'primitive' in the places where the discipline of anthropology was instituted.[20]

TO THE SOUTH: THE LIMITS OF CIVILISATIONS

To understand our difficulty in achieving a shared 'common fate', I now pursue a couple more directional turns, between the South, the central place for ethnographic life-worlds beyond Eurasia, and the North, home to literacy, world religions, great traditions of philosophy, and anthropology itself.

Regarding the direction of the South, Zhuangzi's story entitled 'The happy excursion (*xiaoyao you*)' can be said to be potentially relevant to our future discussions: the thinker roamed the landmass of Eurasia to discover in its end (the 'Great Lake') between Heaven and Earth the ontology of being happy.[21] However, because here we are not concerned with the Daoist philosophy of the 'equality of things (*qiwu*)', we leave this aside, and limit our attention to such works as Hegel's *The Philosophy of World History* (1956 [edn]) and Lévi-Strauss's *Tristes Tropiques* (1997).

These two Western masterpieces can be said to form a pair of landmarks. They were written by the two great thinkers living in two different epochs of the history of the interaction between 'Europe and the people without history' (Wolf 1982), and they are comparable because they both celebrate the 'great divide' between worlds. Between them, one (Hegel's) speaks of a world civilisation and treats it as the global progress of spiritual liberation. It has the consequent realisation of 'freedom' informed by a variety of cultures arranged as a sequence of steps toward history's own future, and it locates the New World (the South) at the lowest level. In a discussion of the geographic background of civilising freedom, the book engages with a depiction of the 'non-historical character' of the South, which, as Hegel (1956: 96–120) foresees, has its future externally determined by the spiritually free European settlers, especially the Protestants in North America. Along the way, America is divided into two parts, North and South, whose contest, as Hegel famously foretells, would end in the South becoming the burden of History.

[20] To me, the 'prehistoric' is more universal and global than has been imagined, and our historical and ethnographic 'parochialisation' of it has proven to be problematic.

[21] This is that 'the perfect man has no self; the spiritual man has no achievement; and the true sage has no name' (Chuang-Tzu 1989: 30).

The other book, Lévi-Strauss's *Tristes Tropiques,* also draws heavily on the contrastive shapings of the two worlds. However, unlike Hegel's, it expresses not only the author's disappointment at the civilising North, but also sadness about the progress of History. He takes the New World for inspiration or mental liberation, and makes the South the 'primary mode' which, as a cosmographic order, is both better, in terms of its closeness to the original, and more desirable, in terms of its scientific value, than the 'secondary modes'.

A strong sense of 'sentimental pessimism' has hindered Lévi-Strauss from giving a necessary tribute to the civilisation in which he writes cultures into myths (it is this civilisation that has enabled him to express himself so well); but it has not prevented him from inventing another anthropology of civilisations. Unlike Hegel who treats non-Western Eurasian civilisations as necessary steps toward the singular Civilisation, Lévi-Strauss supposes all civilisations to be secondary to 'culture', the mental intermediary between nature and society (Lévi-Strauss's 'culture' is almost the same as Confucius's sagehood) from which the natives in the South have continued to draw out their worlds. Lévi-Strauss says:

> It [Anthropology] shows that the basis is not to be discovered in our civilization: of all known societies ours is no doubt the one more remote from it. At the same time, by bringing out the characteristics common to the majority of human societies, it helps us to postulate a type, of which no society is a faithful realization, but which indicates the direction the investigation ought to follow. (Lévi-Strauss 1997: 477)

Before the first printing of *Tristes Tropiques*, Lévi-Strauss had travelled quite extensively in some ancient parts of Eurasia. In the same book, *Tristes Tropiques*, he speaks about his impressions. Let us jump from the pages on over-populated India and the bad future of São Paulo, over the long chapters on the Indian tribal worlds, to the last chapters, where we discover an anthropological critique of all civilisations.

We should quote at length Lévi-Strauss's own narrative:

> Mankind has made three major religious attempts to free itself from persecution by the dead, the malevolence of the Beyond and the anguish of magic. Over intervals of approximately five hundred years, it originated in turn Buddhism, Christianity and Islam; it is a striking fact that each stage, far from constituting an advance on the previous one, should be seen rather as a regression. For Buddhism, there is no Beyond: its whole teaching can be summarized as a radical criticism of life, such as humanity would never again be capable of leading the sage to deny all meaning to beings and things: it is a discipline which abolishes the universe, and abolishes itself as a religion. Christianity, yielding again to fear, restored the other world, with its hopes, its threats and its last judgment. It only remained for Islam to bind this world to the other world: temporal and spiritual were brought together. The social order acquired the prestige of the supernatural order, and politics became theology. In the last resort, the spirits

> and phantoms, which superstition had always failed to bring to life, were replaced by masters who were only too real, and who were furthermore allowed to monopolize an after-life which added its burden to the already crushing weight of life here below. (Lévi-Strauss 1997: 499)

The issue of life and death, to Lévi-Strauss, was the issue of mankind's social bondage. Buddhism differentiated itself from primitive cults, but it retained the pre-Buddhist sense of placid femininity—a kind of 'third sex'—which frees human beings from 'the battle of the sexes'. Buddhism promised a return to the unifying kindness of the maternal breast, It kept a hope for the mutual belonging of human beings. However, 'the historical solutions offered by Buddhist morality face us with two chilling alternatives: anyone who gives an affirmative reply to the question shuts himself up in a monastery; anyone who replies in the negative can achieve easy satisfaction in the practice of egotistical virtue' (503). By contrast, Islam developed, according to a masculine orientation, a closed entity and a tendency to exclusion. In Buddhist civilisation, the infinite universal inclusion of alterity is thus central, while in Islam, the exclusion of the Other is the most characteristic (498). Christianity almost had a chance to synthesise the two into a good civilisation—into a posteriori reconciliation between the two extremes—but 'as a transition from one to the other the middle term of a series which, because of its internal logic, and geographical and historical factors, was destined thereafter to develop in the direction of Islam' (499).

Neither does Lévi-Strauss believe in what Radcliffe-Brown (1977a) saw as shared by the primitives and the Eurasians, nor does he believe in what (Catholicism) gave Evans-Pritchard and Mary Douglas hope (Douglas 1981). He meditates anthropologically on the ruins of history, and reaches a conclusion regarding the disappointing treatments of alterity in different civilisations: Buddhist universal kindness, Christian passion for dialogues, and Islamic fraternity. In the chapter leading to the closing of his narrative, he argues that none of the world religions managed to rescue, from history, the opportunity of inter-civilisational fusion—for him, the ideal way of 'being together' as humanity.

By the end, the lonely anthropologist-hero leaves himself roaming in several worlds, as he sighs, 'each truer than the one it encloses, and itself false in relation to the one which encompasses it' (504), and asserts the value of his hyper-science of the concrete, 'Kantism without a transcendental subject'. When he wrote his magisterial monograph on the elementary structure of kinship, he had been inspired by Granet's sinological sociology in advancing his own theory of alliance and exchange. However, because he has become so sad about history, he turns Granet's mapping of civilisation in the 'Extreme East' into a contrastive reference to the structure of 'the savage mind' or, in effect, 'Neolithicity' (Rowlands 2014), as one might say, which is not so much the 'original affluent sociey' as Sahlins (2003) describes it, but as culture's original way of just being 'semi-detached' from nature.

Both Hegel and Lévi-Strauss dwell upon the 'great divide' of historic fortune existing between the divided worlds of North and South. To them, and to many other philosophers and anthropologists consciously or unconsciously following in their footsteps, the 'other' side still remained in the 'primal stage', while on this side, civilisations, having being through the 'metal ages', continued to advance in the direction of expansive innovation. In the comparisons, the fact that post-Stone-Age civilisations were also 'invented' out of some prior Neolithic legacies is not denied; but for different purposes, the prehistoric foundations of the Old World are, in one way or another, described either as background to Eurasia's acquisition of civilisation or as a history of the degeneration or even loss of the primal. In the paradoxical attitudes to history, a certain historical truth is bypassed: not only did kings derive their 'ornaments' from distant alterities in the margins (Helms 1993, Wengrow 2010),[22] but there were also thinkers doing similar things. Thus civilisations, even the classical great traditions, were indispensable to the 'primal.'[23]

CIVILISATIONS AND THEIR RELATIONS IN THE NORTH

Evidently the parts of Eurasia that have concerned anthropologists were known in the history of religions as Indo-European and Semite. Since the 18th century, these, together with peoples of the vast regions of East and North Asia defined earlier as 'Turanian' (the 'non-Aryan' hunters, nomads, and farmers in the Eastern area of Eurasia), were seen as making up three major 'dialectical' or 'civilisational' entities formed in the deep past in which the unity of humanity had just begun to split up (Müller 1855, 2010).[24] In Western academia, these eventually provided three major regional foundations for a number of mythological and sociological theorisations—to

[22] Archaeological evidence has shown that prior to the 'urban revolution' (Childe 1950), in the late neolithic age, several geo-cosmological modes had been advanced in the peripheral areas removed from the metallised Central Plains, where jade had continued and transcended stone as being the medium between Heaven and Earth (Yang 2005), and it was from these modes that a sequence of early dynastic models of natural/social virtue were derived.

[23] Confucius always talked about his ideas as if they had been from Zhou, whose ideal kingly virtue had in turn stemmed from the sovereigns of what we now call the late Stone Age; Laozi and Zhuangzi talked about their concepts as if they had been from the age in which there had been no politics; Qu Yuan often hunted in the deep and high mountains for his ideal 'Lady' as if the mountains without humans had been truer than the social world of humans.

[24] Max Müller postulates that when time approached the age of the nations (the Bronze Age), these regions then became further divided and their languages got further refined, and in the process, 'nations' emerged.

mention just a few, the Indo-European model of 'trifunctions' (Dumézil 1970), Semite totemism and sacrifice (Smith 1893, Hubert & Mauss 1981), Chinese relationalism (Granet 1930), and grassland 'nomadology' (Deleuze & Guattari 1986). Undoubtedly, each of the divided civilisations has its core area of origination and existence, and each, as a characteristic collectivity of persons, things, and divinities, is distinct from the others, so much so that it can be illustrated as an example for comparison.[25] However, as we can see in the case of the East, through time, and in the intermediary spaces between societies, the constant interactions between cosmologies on a horizontal plane have created situations in which each has engaged the others in its own making.

Thus, the Great Wall, the extensive line of garrisons set up as the frontier line between the Han and the 'barbarians', did not prevent the Han from getting involved in the 'conjuncture' with 'barbarians' (Rong and Di) from the outside, specifically from the West and North. In the Northeast, Mongolia, Xinjiang, and the Tibetan Plateau many of these 'barbarians' from the transition of the 8th century had adopted Buddhism, Manichaeism, Islam, and even Christianity. It was by blending their 'peripheral traditions' and the 'world religions' that the 'barbarians' continued their interactions with the 'sinic world', which likewise combined its own traditions with others. From the 1st century AD people living in the 'Central Plains' had to depend upon India to gain a Buddhist understanding of the human condition (death, or the future of life)[26]. As the Dutch sinological ethnologist J. J. M. de Groot (1884) pointed out, the Han had their doors open in the direction of India. Between the 9th and the 13th centuries, maritime trade from the Southeast Coast brought with it incoming

[25] In his *Clan, Caste, and Club* (1963), Francis Hsu compares Chinese, Hindu, and American (Western) civilisations and argues that these are three different approaches to the world, characterised respectively by situation-centredness or mutual dependence (Chinese), individual-centredness (American), and supernatural-centredness or unilateral dependence (Hindu). Although Hsu claims his comparison to be a continuation of his early work on contrasting Chinese and American, it seems obvious that his trichotomy is based on a schema he inherited from Chinese culturological ancestors living in late imperial and early Republican times who saw Eurasia as composed of Eastern, Western, and Hindu worlds.

[26] Mark Elvin (1985: 170) has noted the difference between Indian and Chinese understandings of the human condition; as he says, the Indians believed in the continuous cycle of rebirths among living beings into lives of suffering, the wheel of samsara. The Chinese believed, 'by and large, in a unique personal existence, no doubt fortified by the concept of a structure of kinship ascendants and descendants, stretching indefinitely back into the past and indefinitely forward into the future, in which the individual occupied his unique place. ... The Chinese, for whom birth and life are positive goods, felt no such need of such ideas of cyclical rebirth. They were, until the coming of Buddhism, innocent of soteriology.' As de Groot (1884) points out, however, it is the difference that made Indian ontology complementary to Chinese.

Moslems, who became entrusted by the Han and then the Mongols as superintendents of trade affairs.[27]

Lévi-Strauss (1977), endeavouring to balance similarity and difference, presents a concept of transformations (in my understanding, alternations of relationship structures corresponding to alternations of space–time), which he applies not only to the study of myths but also to the cross-regional transformations of the synthetic structure of varied reciprocal, 'ethnocentric', and hierarchical models of socio-spatial organisation along the America–Pacific continuum.

This understanding of regional variations of complex structure and their cosmological outcomes is from the study of the 'mythology' of the South; but it is relevant to the anthropology of the North.[28] As in the South, in the North, in each of the societies, on the one hand, there exist social phenomena which are limited to it; on the other hand, there are hyper-social or civilisational phenomena 'which are common to several societies, more or less related to each other' (61). Phrased in Lévi-Strauss's own terms, none of the social systems is 'simple', each being 'sometimes open to external influences and quick to absorb them; sometimes withdrawn into itself, as if to give itself the time to assimilate these foreign contributions and put its own stamp on them' (Lévi-Strauss 2013: 122). All are complex, being combinations of different modes, each yielding its own composite structure, which gives it a distinctive imprint and allows the extent of its distinctiveness to decrease or increase in accordance with the circumstances of inter-societal and inter-civilisation interactions.[29]

'Societies live by borrowing from each other, but they define themselves rather by refusal of borrowing than by its acceptance' (Mauss 2006: 44). Considering the fact that civilisations are often associated with a certain level of good or bad non-combinational 'self-awareness of culture', one must refrain from supposing that the actual unities or pluralities in Eurasia can be described in terms of 'con-fusions' or, in terms of Chinese Pangu myth—'confused complexities' (*hundun*); nonetheless, it is paradoxically true that such 'con-fusions' are precisely what Lévi-Strauss is getting at in spite of his linguistic logo-centrism—we should not forget that in radicalising

[27] History continued to be that of such interaction when East came into contact with Europe, including the 'delayed return' of European Enlightenment for the 'gifts' of the old Chinese inventions of printing, gunpowder, etc. René Étiemble (1988) pushed China into interaction with the 'maritime barbarians' from further West, which in turn resulted in additions of Occidental and Oriental cosmologies.

[28] Let us note that Lévi-Strauss's *mythologique* of transformations is close to what Mauss says about civilisations: different from societies which are 'unfit to travel'. Civilisations 'are naturally able to do so', 'almost by themselves they overflow the (often difficult to determine) boundaries of a given society', and they are thus 'hyper-social' (Mauss 2006: 60).

[29] The 'elementary form of social life' can be said to be constituted with the phenomena of the social 'whose relative importance varies according to time and space' and those of the hyper-social 'whose size cannot be fixed a priori' (Mauss 2006: 60–1).

against Eurasian civilisations he in fact deploys his concept of 'alliance', actually a theory of 'mixing' as the prime value!

Needless to say, any focused inquiries into the complexities of inter-civilisational relations in Eurasia would lead us to see more than the idea of structure. As Lévi-Strauss (1970) himself reveals, this is defined in an abstract sense, a 'form of mental gymnastics, in which the exercise of thought is carried to its objective limits' (11) and so becomes visible. In front of us is an extensive landscape of transformations achieved historically on both the horizontal and vertical planes.

Regarding the 'horizontal plane', pre-modern India and China seem to form a related pair of examples. If pre-modern Indian society could be characterised in terms of 'caste', then it could be seen as a more rigid hierarchy, a transcending whole encompassing agents and social categories along the vertical line of priests, warriors, and producers (Dumont 1980); and if pre-modern Chinese hierarchy could be conceptualised as '*chaxugeju*' (the order of stratified closeness), then it could be said that the Chinese way had a propensity to involve a different order of relations, a certain hierarchical system of concentric networks reciprocally related (Fei 1992). Cosmographically, India and China shared the model of quarters surrounding the centre. However, the model seems to have been established on varied bases. The Indian variation (Mandala) has impressed us as vertical in principle, with the linkage between below and above located right in the centre; whereas the Chinese variation, the pentology of *tianxia* (all-under-Heaven), notwithstanding its similarity to the 'galactic polity' of Mandala (Tambiah 1985), is less so, in most cases, with the linkage (made of the five sacred mountains) situated outside the centre, in the intermediary circle transiting to the outside, reaching beyond but not above. Compared to India, China thus could be said to be more 'diametric'.

Nonetheless, as we have seen in the above, the Chinese 'order of stratified closeness' did not remain the same; on the contrary, it varied through time in the transformations of the structure of relationships between the regions. On the Hindu side, as Tambiah's depiction (1970) of change in the structural relationship between the 'triads'—kings, monks, and commoners—in the Southeast Asian context shows, similar transformations were observable.

The dynamics in the transformations of relationship structure often involved cosmologies from the 'exterior'. For instance, it was precisely from India that the Chinese living in ancient times, having been through all the Confucian illusion and disillusion of their own particularistic concentricity, borrowed the ontology of what Lévi-Strauss has called 'universal kindness' (Wang 2014a: 117–52).[30]

[30] Thus, not surprisingly, Chinese turned Avalokitesvara, the handsome-looking young male bodhisattva of compassion into the comforting mother Goddess of Mercy (Overmyer 1972).

Redfield (1973) argues that, in studying the civilisations of the 'Old World', anthropologists have 'taken on some part of the responsibility for the study of a composite structure comprised of little and great traditions which have interacted in the past and which are still interacting today' (50). This idea of a 'composite structure' roughly reflects what we have said about ancient India and China. Nonetheless, evidently what occurred in the interface between the two civilisations transcended the boundaries Redfield draws between civilisations. In the interface, or where the interactions of great and little traditions within each of the core culture regions of the civilisations took place, there also occurred 'inversions of self and alterity' which made composite structures horizontally expansive.

The achievements of these so-called 'inversions' can be understood as the formation of expansive regional systems linking the world of the Kula Ring (Damon 1990) with India and China to make an extensive ensemble contrastable with the Western end of the Euro-Asia landmass (Damon 2016), or those linking South and Southeast Asian civilisations with the 'Neolithic' in Africa through the circulation of objects and ideas along the land and sea routes to create a 'civilisation' removed from the Bronze-Age centres of the Bronze-Age 'urban revolution' (Rowlands 2014).[31] Such formations were quietly made by means of hidden mobility over the past few millennia and they have resulted in turning the civilisations of the North (Eurasia) and the South (the Pacific world) into part of each other. Often, such 'horizontal transformations' that made the great cross-regional formations were realised through alternations along the 'vertical line' of the more or less class-divided great and little traditions in history.

In many of the examples I have encountered in my field journeys, I note that, while great traditions in the civilisations existed as supra-societal patterns of relationships linking communities, groups, and 'nations' into higher level 'communities', they, being restrictive as well as universalising, also tended to form parochial boundaries. Consequently, the geographic coverage of such great traditions often turns out to be more confined than what they 'encompass'. By contrast, notwithstanding their 'communal', 'particularistic', and 'parochial' characteristics, 'little traditions' have also been far more inclusive.

A few notes on the inversion of the 'ranks' of the great and the little in the areas within and beyond the Great Wall can validate the point. In Eurasia, little traditions

[31] As Lévi-Strauss (1977: 245–68) shows, another linkage existed between the societies distributed in America and Asia: in prehistoric times, a long land bridge connected Asia and America, and along the edge of the Eastern part of Eurasia, a boulevard-like passageway allowed humans and their creativities to circulate freely from Southeast Asia to North America, via the long coasts in the East. Other connections in other direction could also be located in the intermediaries Westward, between Africa, South Asia, and Island Southeast Asia.

whose histories can be traced back to the Neolithic age[32] still exist everywhere, beneath each of the civilisations. In an urban setting in Southeast China (Wang 2009), 'folk religions' have existed as 'little traditions' inside and outside the world religions, including Confucianism, official imperial cults, Daoism, Buddhism, Islam, Manichaeism, Christianity, socialism, and the 'market economy'. Throughout the late imperial dynasties and modern regimes, these 'little traditions' have allowed into themselves the 'great traditions', some of which (for instance, the Ming official Neo-Confucian ceremonials) have been imposed on them from top-down, and some of which (for instance, Buddhism) they have 'borrowed' from other parts of the world. As a result, these 'traditions' have 'interiorised' elements from 'exterior' and 'upper levels', and made them (often described in terms of 'great traditions') 'diffused' in the life-worlds of the neighbourhoods of the city. In a rural setting, linking local cults horizontally over larger areas to the great pilgrimage centres in the four quarters, 'folk religion', by means of making an alternation along the vertical line of the hierarchical order of the civilised and the 'vernacular', invents its own world-scape in the annually re-enacted model of the age-old 'pentology' of quarters around the centre, in accordance with which the human world is represented as a greater unity than is defined in the 'great traditions' (Wang 2016). This kind of 'inversion' is true of the situations not only in the Southeast but also in the 'frontiers' of the Southwest and Northeast.

In a recent collection of a dozen case studies which my former students analysed in Southwest China (Wang & Shu 2015), several modes of 'cultural combination' are examined. Situated in the China–Southeast Asia–India Continuum (Wolf 1982: 44–50), the Southwest can be called a 'corridor' or a system of 'corridors.' It is a passageway where varied 'great traditions' from North, South, East, and West encounter each other,[33] and, in Mauss's words, it is a line of 'frontiers' whereby civilisations overflow, 'either by spreading from specific centres by their own powers of expansion, or as a result of the relationships established between societies' (Mauss 2006: 37). However, the passageway or the line of frontiers is not a zone empty of people; on the contrary, the region also has an extensive variety of home places of tens of 'peripheral peoples'. The civilisations to which the groups are attached can be said to include all known 'great traditions', especially 'Axial Age' civilisations from all over Eurasia. However, these are religions with strong local characteristics, and core to such characteristics are the 'prehistoric folk religions' such as Miao witchcraft, Yi

[32] Thus Granet argues that the early imperial Chinese sacrificial systems were, in their 'improvisations', dependent upon 'the social pact which the aboriginal communities celebrated at their seasonal gatherings' before the Age of Chronology (Granet 1932: 9).

[33] For centuries, the region has undergone the impacts of a variety of civilisations, not only the more recent ones such as Qing, Christian, and Chinese Communist 'great traditions' (Harrell 1995), but also the preceding ones such as various Buddhisms and Islam.

and Naxi magic writing, Bai mountain worship,[34] Tibetan bon, and the like. In the Southwest, local rituals have thus proven to be 'synthetic texts' in which varied historicities, life-giving myths, calendrical systems, identities, and sanctive powers converge; local native chiefs are 'persons of varied personalities', whose lives are examples of varied traditions; and the towns are 'ports of trade' through which the interflows of goods, people, images, and symbols are exchanged.

In Xinjiang, in the famous cross-roads of civilisations from East and West, as a remarkable ethnological survey (Apar *et al.* 2010) has demonstrated, Qam (a local term for Shamanism according to the authors) has continued to be practised by all the Uygur Moslem groups. The survey covers a large variety of topics, including Yygur shamanic concepts of spirits, cosmic entities, human and non-human beings, and ghosts, and magical applications of shamanic techniques and rituals, and divination. One chapter also provides a rich set of data on the interpretations by Uygur religious (Islamic) specialists on shamanism. In the more formal interviews, these specialists tend to express a shared hostility toward Qam, arguing that animistic beliefs and magical practices, being bound up with vernacular notions of spirits and demons as well as satanic powers, are heretic. However, interestingly, in less formal conversations, they express other viewpoints, and some of them even quote from the Koran loose sentences to justify the vernacular ideas of demonic power and magical efficacy (72–80).

In Urumqi, I conversed with the authors of the survey and realised that the ethnologists shared a very interesting sense of history. For them, the shamanic practices they observe among the Uygur and other ethnic groups had existed in 'prehistorical times' in the periods prior to the spread of the world religions in Xinjiang and they are 'sincerely shared' by the divided '*minzu* (nationalities)'. Liu Xuetang (2009), one of the three authors of the survey, has also published an archaeology book, in which he has considered 'primitive religion' in Xinjiang in terms of the link between the vast areas of inner Asia, central Europe, and Siberia.

In the pre-modern Tibetan world, as in that of the neighbouring world of the Han, the landscape of religious cosmology seemed to comprise mystic, sociologic,

[34] In rural Dali in Yunnan, among the Bai, the inner orders of the villages are often organised according to the Confucian model of the lineage. It thus seems that, ever since the Ming, Dali has been totally civilised by Confucianism. However, in fact, such Confucian 'inner orders' have been encompassed by a greater ritual geography. This is a system of local cults (*benzhu*) which integrates local communities to the native Bai deity cults housed in the temples in the great mountains (Liang 2005). Had we adopted Redfield's distinctions, we would have seen Confucianism in ethnic Southwest China as a great tradition, and the Bai local cults and pilgrimages as the opposite. True that the latter consist in a variety of 'folk cults'. However, seen from the cultural region of Dali, they in fact form a much greater geographic unity. In this unity, the 'secondary' Confucian civilisation in the villages is included as a mere part of the 'primary' Bai civilisation.

and synthetic modes. In Tibetological anthropologist Geoffrey Samuel's terms, Tibetan Buddhism consisted of at least two orientations: 'Shamanic Buddhism' and 'Clerical Buddhism'. These were fundamentally different attitudes toward the world and human experience: the former evoked an alternative mode of reality for the social through Tantric ritual, and worked toward the transcendence of 'enlightenment', while the latter emphasised the acquisition of merit through virtuous activities, including scholarship, philosophical analysis, and monastic discipline (Samuel 1993). Samuel also says that most of the actors in Tibetan religious history did not see the two orientations as mutually exclusive. Although major figures in the Tibetan 'great tradition' seemed to be oriented toward either shamanic or clerical aspects, they generally operated in both modes, and in so doing shaped their cosmologies into such different syntheses as Gelugpa and Rimed.

The synthetic modes or 'composite structure' of Buddhism could be said to form the 'great tradition' of Tibet, whose higher learning rested in the transmission and elaboration of an omnipresent system of monasteries. The system of monasteries was not only where the doctrines of the schools of thought of Tibetan Buddhism were transmitted but also provided the links and lines of communication through which the great tradition reproduced itself as a culture region (Spengen 2000: 62–3).

However, beside the Buddhist modes, there was another extensive cultural system in Tibet. This was another shamanic complex—'folk religion' (Samuel 1993: 19–22). The pervasiveness of 'folk religion' achieved its own manifestation in the fact that even the Lamas were sometimes 'like the Siberian shamans or the "diviners" or "prophets" of sub-Saharan Africa', getting themselves engaged in realigning humans with their society and with the universe (21). Rolf Alfred Stein alternatively calls this 'folk religion' the 'religion of men'. Different from the 'religion of gods' (Buddhism), the 'religion of men' kept its own vitality through legends told by old men of the clan, which 'were always uttered in a poetic style characterised by the use of metaphors, cliches and proverbial sayings' (Stein 1972: 192).

Formed in shamanism and in the vernacular, this shamanic complex, the 'ancient matrix' the Tibetans shared with other peoples living in the surroundings, made the Tibetan civilisational 'self' a composite site of 'ethnocentrism' and 'alter-centrism'. Stein argues that the dual cultural identity the Tibetans have shared has stemmed from the Tibetan acceptance of Buddhism. As he puts it:

> As was the fashion in China, the Tibetans imagined themselves as the centre of a square made by other lands, at 'the navel of the earth,' as they say. At the same time, unlike China, they maintained a surprising humility that sprang from the dominance of Buddhist beliefs. They always regard themselves as savages living in the north of the world. ... They speak of the 'little known country of barbarous Tibet,' they describe themselves (like the 'wild' Horpas) as 'red-faced flesh-eating demons' and

> many a time call themselves stupid, rough and dull, all this of course in relation to the civilizing influence of Buddhism. (Stein 1972: 40)

If these words have expressed Tibetan perspectives on civilisational self-identity, then they can be interpreted in other terms: by saying that 'we are barbarians', the Tibetans were just truthful to their own history—as Stein also suggests, it is the 'ancient matrix' that made Tibet a culture region and related it broadly to the neighbouring peoples. Many Tibetan songs and legends were related to Ge-sar of Phrom, a local version of 'Caesar of Rome' (39); and the Tibetan primal 'barbarian condition' was often confused with that of the nomads ('Turks' and 'Tartars') supposedly reigning in the North (41). It was precisely in the vast space in which shamanism or 'religion of men' continually reconstituted itself, that the most radical inversion of the hierarchical pattern of 'great and little traditions' took place. The Mongols, like the Tibetans, were originally shamanists, but as soon as they inaugurated their empire in the early 13th century, they not only put Buddhists at its service, but also advanced a highly tolerant attitude towards other religions and philosophies, from Buddhism to Christianity, from Manichaeism to Islam, from Confucianism to Daoism. Eventually, the empire turned most of the Eurasian great traditions into components of its original plurality nurtured in the fertile lands of the 'religion of men'.

CONCLUSION

For a long time, Eurasia, with its affiliated islands, has been diametrically divided and concentrically patterned. In the diametrical schema, Eurasia has been seen as comprising two parts, West and East, or Europe and Asia; in the concentric imaginaries, alternatively, the two parts have been jointly located in the 'circle' of the middle, contrasted with the fringes to the South and to the further North. The societies and civilisations in the Eurasian landmass, especially those with written records, have been compared, by the deployment of the concentric model, with the 'savages', the 'non-literate' in the outer rings imagined as living in more or less 'backward' life-worlds with their discrete cosmologies. They have also been compared, by the extension of the diametrical schema, with the 'more civilised' among their own kinds, celebrated as those who keep in their treasure houses the secrets of scientific and democratic as well as politico-economic efficacies, or, contrarily, remembered as those who, by way of depriving their own 'authenticity', bring infelicity to history.

In the 'journey to the West', I followed the conventional directions, but I proceeded in the manner of boundary-crossing to pursue reorientations. I departed from the destination of the 'journey', the modern West, where I browsed a history of magic and an ethnography of witch-hunting allegations. The persistence of what may be defined as 'little traditions' in the core of the West, associated with the internal divisions and external challenges of individualism, and with the fortunes of the interplay between 'global modernity' and 'peripheral cultures', itself became revealing: it brought to light the paradox of othering in the Occidentalist and anthropological discourses.

Turning my attention to a part of the ethnographic world, I encountered the method of 'contrasting cultures', which has regained its dominance in certain comparisons of cosmologies. As we critiqued, even when meant to emancipate our understandings of life, society, and world from the singularising 'civilisation', it has misled us into regarding other cosmologies as remaining 'outside us' and in a state of non-change, and 'this' or 'our' cosmology as being exceptionally capable of 'making history'.

In 'considering others in our own places (*tuiji jiren*)', following the visit to the West, I allowed my mind to travel between the South, the West, and the East. The internal diversity of 'traditions' within societies, seen in the dramas of the interaction of traditions in the modern West, is also found in the South, in the 'living Neolithic societies', and in the regional cultures and philosophies of the West and East of the 'Axial Age'. I examined an ethnography of the sub-traditions of inner New Guinea, a history of four cosmological models in ancient Greece, and a perspective on the 'three kingdoms' of Chinese political thought. With a synthesis of these I sought to illustrate the 'unities of diversity' in the South and the North. In so doing, I moved between opposite directions, reconsidering the distinctions between the 'savage' and the 'civilised', which are often reasserted to maintain the disciplinary boundaries between ethnography and philosophy.

To explore the dialectics of 'inside and outside', 'isolation and communication', I continued my 'journey' inspired by a geo-history of cosmological thoughts in the East. Such thoughts arose in the East in close relationship to each other and with preceding traditions founded upon the local cultures of different regions in and around the 'Central Plains'. Regaining their vitality by being blended with other thoughts coming in from the non-Chinese worlds, from the places beyond the Great Walls and beyond the Yangtse, they continued throughout the two millennia of empire to have an impact on the life of society.

Cosmologies are not only models of 'human relations', broadly defined as intermediaries between humans and others (other humans, things, and divinities) (Wang 2014b),[35] but also models of relations between models. To inquire into the multi-modal models of cosmology anthropologically, it is important to revisit the sites

[35] Surely, these can be considered in terms of the 'unconstrained creations of the human imagination' transcending the 'constrained real life experience of those who invent them' (Leach 1982: 213).

of relations between South and North, East and West and to pay more attention to the interactive and synthetic qualities of cosmological configuration in different 'ethnographic regions'.

But revisiting Hegel's optimistic history of the world and Lévi-Strauss's 'sad' reflections on Eurasian 'world religions' and the numerous ethnographic repetitions of them, we have come to realise that we have yet to accustom ourselves to making an association between the 'principles' of cosmology in the North (Eurasian civilisations) and the South ('primitive cultures') (Radcliffe-Brown 1977a).

In the South, in the world beyond the seas, 'when either a singular person or a collective group comes into relation with another, that relation is sustained to the extent that each party is irreducibly differentiated from the other' (Strathern 1988: 14). Such related transformations of the meaning of relationship between 'socio-ego' and alterity in the broad sense of the term have been studied in such a way as to create more complex personalities than we have lived with in the North. Nonetheless, as I must point out, these 'ontologies' are not contrary to those found in the North. In the North, in Eurasia, notwithstanding their distance from the 'original state' of mind where 'myth operate in men's minds without their being aware of the fact' (Lévi-Strauss 1970: 12), the 'conscious models' such as those found in the Western and Eastern ends of Eurasia are likewise invented out of their configurations of self–other relations, and out of their differentiated blendings of so-called ontological 'interiority' and 'physicality'. As Radcliffe-Brown (1977a, 1977b) pointed out long ago, in the great philosophical and religious traditions that we have habitually excluded from our ethnographic scope,[36] we can in fact find similar 'principles' of socio-logics and worldviews to those shared by the 'primitives'.

Besides, certain deep histories of the linkage between Eurasian 'civilisations' and the so-called 'animistic ontologies' found in the fringes or in places far away can be excavated not only along the Pacific Rim (Damon 2016) and along the networks linking Eurasia to the 'primitive worlds' of Africa (Rowlands 2014), but also along the intermediaries between civilisations at the core of Eurasia. I further journeyed to the Southeast, Southwest and Northwest of China, and the Tibetan Plateau, where I secured several examples of the interaction of traditions.

[36] Thus, the argument that we should take seriously what the natives say, i.e., pigs are persons, persons are pigs, and bodies are concepts, reminds me of another sense of 'con-fusion' in the north. In the year 1195 in the South Song Dynasty, the great Neo-Confucian thinker Cheng Hao had a similar idea. When asked how to understand the self with reference to the other, Cheng Hao said: 'there is a level beyond things outside humans and humans themselves; this is heaven-reason, or what explains both things and humans. If we understand heaven-reason, then we also understand things and humans.' And Cheng Hao added that, 'plants are me' (Wang 2005: 169–70).

In these 'intermediaries' or 'corridors' (Wang 2008), in the 'contact zones' between the civilisational ensembles—be they Indo-European, Semite, or Turanian linguistic 'hyper-social systems' (Mauss 2006: 57–74), be they 'world religions', the trafficking or exchange of myths, tales, arts, words, literary forms, ideals, money, commerce, techniques, and technologies has been highly constant and constitutes a landscape of related traditions dramatically different from what Redfield (1973) and his associates conceptualised in terms of what may be seen as the 'vertical' transmission of traditions.

In the past two or three thousand years, situated on the 'frontiers' of the civilisations, the intermediaries on the one hand have been the extensive geographic belts along which the 'hyper-social systems' of the 'great traditions', expanding along the line of what I have defined as 'horizontal' from their primary spheres of existence towards the 'exterior', have met one another and created such cultural combinations as Chinese, Tibetan, or Southeast Asian Buddhism. On the other hand have been the habitats of the 'peripheral peoples' in which, through joining the cross-regional networks of mobility of persons, things, and divinities and through 'assimilating' the bypassing 'civilisations', the vernacular traditions have 'survived' the expansion of the 'great traditions', or have even transformed their 'parochialities'—for instance, their pervasive shamanic 'interiority' and techniques—into the 'universal' substrata of the regional 'hyper-social systems'.

The examples from the intermediaries are special but not exceptional. As we observed at the beginning, in the West—for instance, in England—while anthropologists are inculcating in themselves the habit of 'contrasting to know', the flexible nexus of traditions continues to evoke the old life-giving myths of 'animistic cosmology', to re-enliven itself in the core spheres of influence of the modern 'great tradition' of individualistic and naturalistic reason. Although the co-presence of 'great and little traditions' in each of the nations of the modern West can be depicted as a struggle within a new social hierarchy conceptualised as a new quest for enlightenment, evidently the 'great tradition' itself is more internally varied and externally related than it is usually represented: Isn't what we accept as scholarly and scientific in fact dependent upon the debates or contests of divergent views in a similar way to that in which, as I insisted, the making of the 'Axial Age' philosophies in the West and the East were dependent upon the contests of the 'four Greeces' and the 'three Chinas'? Shouldn't we describe the 'whole' of the new social hierarchy of 'great and little traditions' in terms of what has been constituted in the 'social environment' of a larger ensemble which, by living together as 'all-under-Heaven' for millennia, has constantly interacted with other ensembles? Hasn't Western anthropology, in all its efforts—often made through intellectual contests—to achieve the 'views from afar', bought into the 'society of naturalism' in which it has been a part the cosmological contents and forms from the distant, and, has it not re-enlivened the complexity of the archaic in the modern?

The past is the prologue. Past experience, remembered, can inspire our understanding of the present and the future; and I imagine that so long as we continue to exist on Earth under Heaven, in the future, we will continue to live among the others, and the others will continue to live among us, in the situations in which we and other humans, other things, and other divinities, converge and interact to make history, and that, as in the past, our different cosmologies as different approaches to 'living in the universe' will remain related—peacefully or otherwise—with their counterparts, here or there, at different levels of existence, observable in another 'journey to the West'.

Acknowledgements

I am deeply grateful to the British Academy for the opportunity to give the lecture. While preparing the text, I gained a lot of encouragement and advice from Professor David Parkin, to whom, I have felt enormously indebted. In the two separate places (London and Aberdeen) in which a much shortened version of the lecture was delivered, Professors Richard Fardon and Tim Ingold raised the same intriguing issue as to whether history should be seen as 'external' to cosmology which I will carry on considering. Sincere thanks are due to them. In the past decade, while older friends such as Professor Stephan Feuchtwang have continued to come together in the activities I organise, contributing inspiring papers to them, newer friends like Professors Frederick Damon and Michael Rowlands, who share my interest in the long-term history of trans-regional cosmologies, have brought a great number of new ideas from which I have benefitted a great deal. I thank them for inspiration.

REFERENCES

Ackroyd, P. (2001), *London: The Biography* (London, Vintage Books).

Apar, A., Ormel, D. & Liu, M. (2010), *Weiwuerzu Saman Wenhua Yicun Diaocha (A Survey of the Cultural Survivals of Shamanism among the Uighers)* (Beijing, Minzu Chubanshe).

Aveni, A. (1995), *Empire of Time: Calendars, Clocks, and Cultures* (New York, Rodansha International).

Barth, F. (1987), *Cosmological in the Making: A Generative Approach to Cultural Variation in Inner New Guinea* (Cambridge, Cambridge University Press). https://doi.org/10.1017/CBO9780511607707

Boas, F. (1974), 'The Aims of Ethnology', in G. W. Stocking Jr. (ed.), *A Franz Boas Reader: The Shaping of American Anthropology, 1883–1911* (Chicago, University of Chicago Press), 67–70.

Brague, R. (2003), *The Wisdom of the World: The Human Experience of the Universe in Western Thought* (Chicago, University of Chicago Press).

Chen, F. (2001), *Jingzhong Qishu Kao (A Study of the Mysterious Book from the Old Well)* (Shanghai, Shanghai Wenyi Chubanshe).

Chi, C. (1963), *Key Economic Areas in Chinese History: As Revealed in the Development of Public Works for Water-control* (New York, Paragon Books).

Childe, G. (1950), 'The Urban Revolution', *Town Planning Review*, 21: 3–17. https://doi.org/10.3828/tpr.21.1.k853061t614q42qh

Chuang-Tzu (1989 edn) *A Taoist Classic: Zhuang-Tzu,* trans. with introd. Y. Fung Yu-Lan (Beijing, Foriegn Languages Press).

Confucius (1996 edn), *The Analects*, trans. Arthur Waley (Hertfordshire, Wordsworth Editions).

Damon, F. (1990), *From Muyu to the Trobriands: Transformations along the Northern Side of the Kula* (Tuscan, University of Arizona Press).

Damon, F. (2016), 'Deep Historical Ecology: The Kula Ring as a Representative Moral System from the Indo-Pacific', *World Archaeology*, https://doi.org/10.1080/00438243.2016.1220326

de Groot, J. (1884), *Buddhist Masses for the Dead at Amoy* (Leiden, E. J. Brill).

Delueze, G. & Guattari, F. (1986), *Nomadology: The War Machine* (New York, Semiotext(e)).

Descola, P. (1994), *In the Society of Nature: A Native Ecology in Amazonia*, trans. N. Scott (Cambridge, Cambridge University Press).

Descola, P. (2013), *Beyond Nature and Culture*, trans. J. Lloyd (Chicago, University of Chicago Press).

Douglas, M. (1981), *Edward Evans-Pritchard* (Kingsport, Penguin Books).

Dumézil, G. (1970), *Archaic Roman Religion,* 2 vols (Chicago, University of Chicago Press).

Dumont, L. (1980), *Homo Hierarchicus: The Caste System and its Implications* (Chicago, University of Chicago Press).

Dumont, L. (1994), *German Ideology: From France to Germany and Back* (Chicago, University of Chicago Press).

Eisenstadt, S. (2003), *Comparative Civilizations and Multiple Modernities* (Leiden, Brill).

Elvin, M. (1985), 'Between the Earth and Heaven: Conceptions of the Self in China', in M. Carrithers, S. Collins & S. Lukes. (eds.), *The Category of the Person: Anthropology, Philosophy, History* (Cambridge, Cambridge University Press), 156–89.

Engels, F. (1887) *The Condition of the Working Class in England in 1844* trans. F.K. Wischnewetzky (New York, J. W. Lovell, English publication).

Étiemble, R. (1988), *L'Europe Chinoise*, 2. vols (Paris, Gallimard).

Evans-Pritchard, E. (1937), *Witchcraft, Oracles and Magic among the Azande* (Oxford, Clarendon Press).

Evans-Pritchard, E. (1962), 'Religion and the Anthropologists', in his *Social Anthropology and Other Essays* (New York, The Free Press of Glencoe), 158–71.

Evans-Pritchard, E. (1965), *Theories of Primitive Religion* (Oxford, Oxford University Press).

Fardon, R. (1990), 'Localizing Strategies: the Regionalization of Ethnographic Accounts', in R. Fardon (ed.), *Localizing Strategies: Regional Traditions of Ethnographic Writing* (Edinburgh, Scottish Academic Press & Washington, Smithsonian Institution Press), 1–36.

Fei, X. (1992), *From the Soil, the Foundation of Chinese Society*, trans. with introd. G. Hamilton & Z. Wang (Berkeley, University of California Press).

Fei, X. (ed.) (1999), *Zhonghua Minzu Duoyuan Yiti Geju (The Unity of Diversity of the Chinese Nation)* (Beijing, Zhongyang Minzu Daxue Chubanshe).

Fei, X. (2004), 'Wenhua zhong Ren yu Ziran Guanxi de Zairenshi (Re-examining the Cultural Constructs of the Interrelationship between Humanity and Nature)', in his *Lun Renleixue yu Wenhua Zijue (On Anthropology and Self-Awareness of Culture)* (Beijing, Huaxia Chubanshe), 225–34.

Fei, X. (2009), 'Shitan Kuozhan Shehuixue de Chuantong Jiexian (On Extending the Frontiers of Traditional Sociology)', in his *Fei Xiaotong lun Wenhua Zijue (Fei Xiaotong on Self-awareness of Culture)* (Huhehaote, Neimenggu Renmin Chubanshe), 207–34.

Feng, S. (2007), *Zhongguo Tianwen Kaoguxue (Chinese Astro-archaeology)* (Beijing, Zhongguo Shehui Kexue Chubanshe).

Feuchtwang, S. (1989), 'The Problem of Superstition in the PRC', in G. Benavides & M. Daly (eds), *Religion and Political Power* (Albany, The State University of New York Press), 43–69.

Feuchtwang, S. & Wang, M. (2001), *Grassroots Charisma: Four Local Leaders in China* (London, Routledge).

FitzGerald, C. (1972), *The Southern Expansion of the Chinese People* (New York, Praeger Publishers).

Freedman, M. (1963), 'A Chinese Phase in Social Anthropology', *British Journal of Sociology*, 13: 1–19. https://doi.org/10.2307/587316

Fung, Y. (2011), *Zhongguo Zhexue Shi (History of Chinese Philosophy)*, 2 vols (Beijing, Shangwu Yinshuguan).

Gernet, J. & Vernant, J. (1990), 'Social History and the Evolution of Ideas in China and Greece from the Sixth to the Second centuries B.C.', in J.-P. Vernant *Myth and Society in Ancient Greece* (New York, Zone Books), 79–99.

Goody, J. (1996), *The East in the West* (Cambridge, Cambridge University Press). https://doi.org/10.1017/CBO9781139171052

Granet, M. (1930), *Chinese Civilization*, trans. K. Innes & M. Brailsford (London, Kegan Paul, Trench, Turner).

Granet, M. (1932), *Festival and Songs of Ancient China*, trans. E. D. Edwards (London, George Routledge).

Harrell, S. (ed.) (1995), *Cultural Encounters on China's Ethnic Frontiers* (Seattle, University of Washington Press).

Hegel, F. (1956), *The Philosophy of World History*, ed. and trans. J. Sibree (New York, Dover).

Helms, M. (1993), *Craft and the Kingly Ideal: Art, Trade, and Power* (Austin, University of Texas Press).

Holbraad, M. (2012), *Truth in Motion: The Recursive Anthropology of Cuban Divination* (Chicago, University of Chicago Press). https://doi.org/10.7208/chicago/9780226349220.001.0001

Hsu, F. (1963), *Clan, Caste, and Club* (Princeton, Van Nostrand).

Hubert, H. & Mauss, M. (1981), *Sacrifice: Its Nature and Function*, trans. W. D. Halls (Chicago, University of Chicago Press).

Ingold, T. (1986), *The Appropriation of Nature: Essays on Human Ecology and Social Relations* (Manchester, Manchester University Press).

Ingold, T. (2000), *The Perspection of the Environment: Essays in Livelihood, Dwelling and Skill* (London, Routledge). https://doi.org/10.4324/9780203466025

Jiang, S. (1928), *Fa, Xu, Zhua: Guanyu Tamen de Mixin (Hair, Whister, and Paw: Superstitions about Them)* (Beijing, Zhonghua Shuju, 2004).

Keightley, D. (2000), *The Ancestral Landscape: Time, Space, and Community in Late Shang China (ca. 1200–1045 B.C.)* (Berkeley, Institute of East Asian Studies).

Kohn, E. (2009), 'A Conversation with Philippe Descola', *Tipit'ı: Journal of the Society for the Anthropology of Lowland South America*, 7: 135–50.

La Fontaine, J. (1998), *Speak of the Devil: Tales of Satanic Abuse in Contemporary England* (Cambridge, Cambridge University Press). https://doi.org/10.1017/CBO9780511621758

Latour, B. (1993), *We Have Never Been Modern*, trans. C. Porter (Cambridge, MA, Harvard University Press).

Lattimore, O. (1967), *Inner Asia Frontiers of China* (Boston, Beacon Books).

Leach, E. (1954), *Political Systems of Highland Burma: A Study of Kachin Social Structure* (London, G. Bell).

Leach, E. (1961), *Rethinking Anthropology* (London, Athlone).

Leach, E. (1982), *Social Anthropology* (London, Fontana).

Lévi-Strauss, C. (1970), *The Raw and the Cooked: Introduction to a Science of Mythology, Vol.1*, trans. J. Weightman & D. Weightman (New York, Harper Torchbooks).

Lévi-Strauss, C. (1977), 'Do Dual Organizations Exist', in his *Structural Anthropology, Vol. 1* (London, Penguin Books), 132–66.

Lévi-Strauss, C. (1985), *The View from Afar*, trans. J. Neugroschel & P. Hoss (New York, Basic Books).

Lévi-Strauss, C. (1997), *Tristes Tropiques*, trans. J. Weightman & D. Weightman (New York, The Modern Library).
Lévi-Strauss, C. (2013), *Anthropology Confronts the Problems of the Modern World,* trans. J. Todd (Cambridge, MA, The Belknap of Harvard University Press).
Liang, Q. (1902), 'Lun Zhongguo Xueshu Sixiang Bianqian zhi Dashi (A Treatise on the Overall Tendencies of Chinese History of Ideas)', in his *Xin Shixue (New History)*, ed. with introd. X. Xia & Y. Lu (Beijing, Shangwu Yinshuguan, 2014), 125–252.
Liang, Y. (2005), *Diyu de Dengji: Yige Dali Cunzhen de Yishi yu Wenhua (The Hierarchies of Territories: Ritual and Culture in a Place in Dali)* (Beijing, Shehui Kexue Wenxian Chubanshe).
Liang, Y. (2010), 'Inalienable Narration: Nanzhao between China and Thailand', *Working Paper Series*, No.141 (Singapore, Asia Research Institute, National University of Singapore).
Lin, Y. (1936), 'Cong Renleixue de Guandian Kaocha Zhongguo Zongzu Xiangcun (Investigating Chinese Lineage Villages from Anthropological Perspectives)', *Shehuixuejie (Sociological Circle)*, 9: 125–42.
Ling, C. (1931), *Songhuajiang Xiayou de Hezhezu (The Hezhe in the Lower Songhuajiang Valley)*, 2 vols (Beijing, Minzu Chubanshe, 2004).
Liu, X. (2009), *Xinjiang Shiqian Zongjiao Yanjiu (A Study of the Prehistorical Religion in Xinjiang)* (Beijing, Minzu Chubanshe).
Macfarlane, A. (1978), *The Origin of English Individualism* (Oxford, Basil Blackwell).
Malinowski, B. (1948), *Magic, Science and Religion and Other Essays* (Glencoe, IL, The Free Press).
Marcus, G. & Fischer, M. (1986), *Anthropology as Cultural Critique: An Experimental Moment in the Human Sciences* (Chicago, University of Chicago Press).
Marriott, M. (ed.) (1956), *Village India: Studies in the Little Community* (Chicago: University of Chicago Press).
Mauss, M. (1990), *The Gift: Forms and Functions of Exchange in Archaic Societies* (London, Routledge).
Mauss, M. (2006), *Techniques, Technology and Civilisation*, trans. with introd. N. Schlanger (New York, Durkheim Press/Burghahn Books).
Müller, M. (1855), *The Languages of the Seat of War in the East: With a Survey of the Three Families of language, Semitic, Arian, and Turanian* (London, Williams and Norgate).
Müller, M. (2010), *Comparative Mythology: An Essay* (Whitefish, MN, Kessinger Publishing).
Overmyer, D. (1972), 'Folk-Buddhist Religion: Creation and Eschatology in Medieval China', *History of Religions*, 12: 42–70. https://doi.org/10.1086/462666
Pan, G. (1936), 'Jiazu Zhidu yu Zuanze Zuoyong (The Familial Institutions and the Function of Selection)', *Shehuixuejie (Sociological Circle)*, 9: 89–104.
Parkin, D. (2016), 'Can We Reconcile the Particular with the General in Anthropology?' lecture delivered at Daxuetang of Peking University, to be included in D. Parkin, *Shenchu Dangdai Shijie de Renleixue (Anthropology Situated in the Contemporary World)* (Beijing, Beijing Daxue Chubanshe, forthcoming).
Pedersen, M. (2001), 'Totemism, Animism, and North Asian Indigenous Ontologies', *Journal of Royal Anthropological Institute*, N.S, 7: 411–27. https://doi.org/10.1111/1467-9655.00070
Qian, M. (2004), *Linghun yu Xin (The Spirit and The Heart)* (Guilin, Guangxi Shifan Daxue Chubanshe).
Radcliffe-Brown [Bulang], A. (1936), 'Dui Zhongguo Xiangcun Shenghuo Shehuixue Diaocha de Jianyi (Suggestions for the Sociological Investigation of Rural Life in China)', trans. W. Wu, *Shehuixuejie (Sociological Circle)*, 9: 79–88.
Radcliffe-Brown, A. (1977a), 'The Comparative Method in Social Anthropology', in A. Kuper (ed.), *The Social Anthropology of Radcliffe-Brown* (London, Routledge and Kegan Paul), 53–72.
Radcliffe-Brown, A. (1977b), 'Religion and Society', in A. Kuper (ed.), *The Social Anthropology of Radcliffe-Brown* (London, Routledge and Kegan Paul), 103–30.

Redfield, R. (1973), *The Little Community/Peasant Society and Culture* (Chicago, University of Chicago Press).
Rowlands, M. (2014), 'Neolithicities: From Africa to Eurasia and Beyond', unpublished paper presented at the International Academic Workshop on Communication and Isolation, Quanzhou Maritime Museum, Quanzhou, Fujian Province, 22–24May.
Sahlins, M. (1988), 'Cosmologies of Capitalism: The Trans-pacific Sector of "the World System"', *Proceedings of the British Academy*, LXXIV: 1–51.
Sahlins, M. (1999), 'Two or Three Things that I Know about Culture', *The Journal of the Royal Anthropological Institute*, (N.S.) 5: 399–421. https://doi.org/10.2307/2661275
Sahlins, M. (2000), *Culture in Practice: Selected Essays* (New York, Zone Books).
Sahlins, M. (2003), *Stone Age Economics* (London, Routledge).
Sahlins, M. (2013), 'Foreword', to P. Descola, *Beyond Nature and Culture* (Chicago, University of Chicago Press), xi–xiv.
Said, E. (1978) *Orientalism* (London, Penguin Books).
Samuel, G. (1993), *Civilized Shamans: Buddhism in Tibetan Societies* (Washington, Smithsonian Institute Scholarly Press).
Smith, W. R. (1893), *Lectures on the Religion of the Semites* (New York, The Meridian Books, 1957).
Spengen, W. (2000), *Tibetan Borderlands: A Geohistorical Analysis of Trade and Traders* (London, Kegan Paul International).
Stein, R. (1972), *Tibetan Civilization*, trans. S. Driver (Stanford, Stanford University Press).
Stocking, G. (1987), *Victorian Anthropology* (New York, The Free Press).
Stocking, G. (1995), *After Tylor: British Social Anthropology, 1888–1951* (Madison, University of Wisconsin Press).
Strathern, M. (1988), *The Gender of the Gift: Problems with Women and Problems with Society in Melanesia* (Berkeley, University of California Press).
https://doi.org/10.1525/california/9780520064232.001.0001
Su, B. (1999), *Zhongguo Wenming de Qiyuan (The Origins of Chinese Civilisation)* (Beijing, Sanlian Shudian).
Tambiah, S. (1970), *Buddhism and the Spirit Cults in Northeast Thailand* (Cambridge, Cambridge University Press).
Tambiah, S. (1985), 'A Reformulation of Geertz's Conception of Theater State', in his *Culture, Thought, and Social Action: An Anthropological Perspective* (Cambridge, MA, Harvard University Press), 169–211. https://doi.org/10.4159/harvard.9780674433748
Thomas, K. (1973), *Religion and the Decline of Magic: Studies in Popular Beliefs in Sixteenth and Seventeenth Century England* (Harmondsworth, Middx, Penguin Books).
Tylor, E. B. (1871), *Primitive Culture*, 2 vols (London, John Murray).
Umesao, T. (2003), *An Ecological View of History: Japanese Civilization in the World Context* (Melbourne, Trans Pacific Press).
Vernant, J. (2006), *Myth and Thought among the Greeks*, trans. J. Lloyd (New York, Zone Books).
Vertovec, S. (2007), 'Super-diversity and its Implications', *Ethnic and Racial Studies* 30: 1024–54. https://doi.org/10.1080/01419870701599465
Viveiros de Castro, E. (1998), 'Cosmological Deixis and Amerindian Perspectivism', *Journal of Royal Anthropological Institute*, N.S., 4: 469–88. https://doi.org/10.2307/3034157
Viveiros de Castro, E. V. (2012), *Cosmological Perspectivism in Amazonia and Elsewhere: Four Lectures Given in the Department of Social Anthropology, Cambridge University, February–March 1998* (Hau, Masterclass Series, Vol. 1).
Wagner, R. (1981), *The Invention of Culture* (Chicago, University of Chicago Press).
Wang, G. (1908), 'Quzi Wenhua Jingshen (The Literary Spirit of Qu Yuan)', in his *Renjian Cihua (A Humanistic Discourse of Poetry)* (Beijing, Zhongguo Renmin Daxue Chubanshe, 2004), 130–4.

Wang, M. (2004), *Xicun Jiazu: Shequshi, Yishi, yu Difang Zhengzhi (The Lineage Village of Xicun: Community, Rituals, and Local Politics)* (Guiyang: Guizhou Renmin Chubanshe).
Wang, M. (2005), *Xin yu Wu You (Sensing-thinking with Things)* (Guilin, Guangxi Shifandaxue Chubanshe).
Wang, M. (2008), *Zhongjiangquan: 'Zangyi Zoulang' yu Renleixyue de Zaigousi (The Intermediaries: The 'Tibetan–Yi Corridor' and the Reformation of Anthropology)* (Beijing, Shehui Kexue Wenxian Chubanshe).
Wang, M. (2009), *Empire and Local Worlds: A Chinese Model for Long-term Historical Anthropology* (Walnut Creek, Left Coast Press).
Wang, M. (2010), *Renshengshi yu Renliexue (Histories of Lives and Anthropology)* (Beijing, Sanlian Shudian).
Wang, M. (2011), 'A Drama of the Concepts of Religion: Reflecting on Some of the Issues of "faith" in Contemporary China', *Working Paper Series*, No. 155 (Singapore, Asia Research Institute, National University of Singapore).
Wang, M. (2012), 'All Under Heaven (*tianxia*): Cosmological Perspectives and Political Ontologies in Pre-modern China', *Hau: Journal of Ethnographic Theory* 2(1): 337–383. https://doi.org/10.14318/hau2.1.015
Wang, M. (2014a), *The West as the Other: A Genealogy of Chinese Occidentalism* (Hong Kong, The Chinese University Press).
Wang, M. (2014b), 'Minzuzhi: Yizhong guangyi renwenxguanxixue de jieding (Ethnography: A Definition in the Broadened Terms of Human Relations)', *Xueshu Yuekan (Academic Monthly)* 47(3):129–40.
Wang, M. (2015), *Chaoshehui Tixi: Wenming yu Zhongguo (The Supra-societal Systems: Civilisations and China)* (Beijing, Sanlian Shudian).
Wang, M. (2016), 'Jubu zuowei Zhengti: Cong yige Anli Kan Shequ Yanjiu de Shiye Tuozhan (Parts as Wholes: The Extension of the Scope of Community Studies Seen from One Example)', *Shehuixue Yanjiu (Sociology Research)*, 30: 98–120.
Wang, M. & Shu, Y. (eds) (2015), *Wenhua Fuhexing: Xinandiqu de Yishi, Renwu yu Jiaohuan (Cultural Combinations: Ritual, Person, and Exhange in Southwest China)* (Beijing, Beijing Lianhe Chubanshe).
Weber, M. (1930) *The Protestant Ethic and the Spirit of Capitalism* trans T. Parsons (London, George Allen & Unwin, 1st English publication).
Wengrow, D. (2010), *What Makes Civilization? The Ancient Near East and the Future of the West* (Oxford, Oxford University Press).
Wilcox, C. (2004), *Robert Redefield and the Development of American Anthropology* (Lanham, Lexington Books).
Willerslev, R. (2007), *Soul Hunters: Hunting, Animism, and Personhood among the Siberian Yukaghirs* (Berkeley, University of California Press). https://doi.org/10.1525/california/9780520252165.001.0001
Wolf, E. (1982), *Europe and the People without History* (Berkeley, University of California Press).
Wu, H. (1956), 'Mingjiao yu Daming Diguo', in his *Dushi Daji* (Notes from Reading History) (Beijing, Sanlian Shudian), 235–70.
Wu, W. (1936), 'Bulang Jiaoshou de Sixiang Beijing yu Qi Zai Xueshushang de Gongxian (Professor Radcliffe-Brown's Intellectual Backgrounds and Academic Contributions)', *Shehuixuejie (Sociological Circle)*, 9: 1–42.
Wu, W. (1990), *Wu Wenzao Renleixue Shehuixue Yanjiu Wenji (Collection of Anthropological and Sociological Research Essays by Wu Wenzao)* (Beijing, Minzu Chubanshe).
Xiang, D. (1933), *Tangdai Changan yu Xiyu Wenming (Chang'an of Tang and the Civilizations from the Western Territories)* (Beiping, Harvard–Yenching Institute).

Xu, X. (1932), *Zhongguo Gushi de Chuanshuo Shidai* (Guilin, Guangxi Shifan Daxue Chubanshe, 2003).
Yang, B. (2005), *Wuyu zhi Guang (The Light of the Magiccal Jade)* (Shanghai, Shanghai Guji Chubanshe).
Yuan, K. (1991), *Zhongguo Shenhua Tonglun (A General Treatise of Chinese Mythology)* (Chengdu: Bashu Shushe).

Note on the author: Wang Mingming is one of the most prolific anthropologists in contemporary East Asia. He is Professor of Anthropology at Peking University. Among his numerous published works on anthropology, history, and cosmology (mostly in Chinese, a limited number in English), are *Social Anthropology and Sinology* (1997), *Beyond Rural China* (2003), *Subjects among Objects* (2006), *The Intermediary Circles* (2008), *Empire and Local Worlds* (2009), *Life-history and Anthropology* (2010), 'All Under Heaven (*tianxia*): Cosmological Perspectives and Political Ontologies in Pre-modern China' (2012), *Transcending the 'New Warring States'* (2012), and *The West as the Other: A Genealogy of Chinese Occidentalism* (2014), and *Supra-societal Systems: Civilizations and China* (2015).
wangmingming2006@163.com

To cite the article: Wang Mingming (2017), 'Some turns in a "journey to the West": Cosmological proliferation in an anthropology of Eurasia', *Journal of the British Academy*, 5: 201–250.
DOI https://doi.org/10.85871/jba/005.201

Journal of the British Academy (ISSN 2052–7217) is published by
The British Academy—the national academy for the humanities and social sciences.
10–11 Carlton House Terrace, London, SW1Y 5AH
www.britishacademy.ac.uk

Journal of the British Academy, **5**, 251–270. DOI https://doi.org/10.5871/jba/005.251
Posted 04 November 2017.

'Soliloquies of suffering and consolation': Fiction as elegy and refusal

Lecture on the Novel in English
read 23 May 2017

JOHN BURNSIDE
University of St Andrews

Abstract: Susan Stewart has said that in 'writing soliloquies of suffering and consolation … elegists have discovered … a powerful means of addressing the tensions between grief's inchoate emotion and social rituals of mourning.' Using work by Graham Swift, Adam Thorpe and Michael Bracewell, I will argue that such elegies have informed one important strand of British fiction over the last thirty years, where the growth of 'cultural totalitarianism' (cf. Jonathan Franzen) has engendered, on the one hand, a primal impulse to preserve individual integrity against societal control, and on the other, a profound grief for the consequent loss of communal and ritual life, as well as for the land itself, which has suffered significant degradation and damage over the same period, damage catalogued by a number of important eco-critical observers, with specific reference to Graham Harvey.

Keywords: British fiction, eco-criticism, grief, community, Graham Swift, Adam Thorpe, Michael Bracewell, Graham Harvey.

I

When Princess Diana died, on 31 August 1997, an astonishing and, initially at least, spontaneous outburst of public grief was unloosed in these islands. As the fatal crash occurred in the Pont de l'Alma tunnel, I was visiting friends in Orkney, and so began the week reasonably far from the madding crowd; the sad events of that Paris night did, of course, register in Stromness and Kirkwall but, overall, the public response was more respectful than excessive: measured, thoughtful, humane, considered. Six days on, however, when I flew in to Glasgow I found George Square literally carpeted with floral tributes and, as I continued my homeward journey to Fife, I was struck by an almost palpable, and near-universal sense of grief. Two days later, on a trip through

England ending in London, it became clear that, the denser the area of population in which I found myself, the more urgent, and the more puzzling, that grief became. By that time, of course, our politicians, not to mention the most narcissistic echelon of the celebrity class and, of course, The Media (it seems to have become accepted, or even de rigueur, to lump all of our press outlets together, good, bad and ugly) had jumped in to capitalise on the public mood, a mood at once powerful and lacking in focus, but even if these factors had not been present, the grief expressed in that massive, utterly sincere (though, in the end, short-lived) display—or, as I later came to see it, this *performance*—of communal, but not official, mourning could not be denied.

At the same time, that *public* grief was becoming denatured. In some quarters, it was even becoming muddled and tawdry and I, like many others, began to doubt that it was all about this woman who, as decent and kind as she surely was, did not seem sufficiently commanding, or sufficiently complex, as a public figure, to invoke such strong feelings amongst so many. At the same time, we could all see that this grief was genuine and, though nobody asked then and few ask now what its true roots might be, I was convinced that it had deep and authentic roots in *something*. A real loss, pertinent to all; a national tragedy for which the death of an English Rose[1] became symbolic and, at some private level, synchronous with the loss of a greater soul. The soul of the country, the soul of the land, some essential Britishness that, worn down by twenty years of a dog-eat-dog morality, was finally beginning to crumble, like our sea coasts, or the tilth of our over-farmed soil.

It is my contention, here, that we—all of us, whether we took part in that performance, or not—have long been afflicted by a keen sense of loss, but its nature is such that it does not allow for the kind of public performance that we need to heal it (as would be the case with a royal personage, or even a certain type of celebrity). For me, and many others, this sense of loss is predicated on the knowledge, both formal and experiential, that, since the Second World War and especially since an era of entirely cynical deregulation was initiated during the Thatcher era, this land—Britain, my home lands, my habitat—has been and continues to be ruthlessly degraded, denatured and even, in a meaningful sense, destroyed. I could say, simply, that I am grieving for the earth itself, and that this grief is exacerbated by being denied a communal performance of mourning worthy of its seriousness, mostly because it does not suit the politically powerful to admit that this degradation is going on and is, in some cases, permanent. There is even more to this, however, than the land alone. I, and

[1] Some of us may, perhaps, recall the new lyrics Bernie Taupin wrote for Elton John's 'Candle in the Wind', where Princess Diana is described as 'England's rose ... the grace that placed itself / where lives were torn apart' and (with a nod to William Blake) a near-Christ-like figure whose 'footsteps will always fall here, / among England's greenest hills.' The song concludes with a mourning cry from 'a country lost without your soul'.

many others, privately grieve for *us*—for a people that has become similarly denatured, greedier, more venial, less spontaneous and, at the same time, more anxious and hideously more susceptible to our machinery. According to the accepted environmental/climate change narrative, we are, moreover, supposed to accept that we are all equally guilty in the desecration of this land, just as all media outlets would seem to be equally guilty of degrading the quality of public debate. Thus we are both sinned against *and* sinning: though it goes without saying that those who sin most manage to persuade themselves that they are the least culpable of all. As one developer said to me a few years back, at a public meeting over a project that has now effectively destroyed the lone nature reserve in my nook of East Fife: 'I have no problem sleeping at night.' Well, of course he didn't.

If such men were more inclined to reflection, it might be useful to point out to them that this year marks the the twentieth anniversary of Graham Harvey's *The Killing of the Countryside*,[2] a book that, more than any other, catalogues the damage done to the land, and explains exactly how we in Britain lost our place in the world, whether it be the child's realm of birds and butterflies, or the grown-up's sense of belonging to the earth itself, or at least to some English garden, of no particular historical importance, that he or she stumbled upon during a day's outing. Harvey shows how that world was destroyed by a tragic combination of ill-considered subsidies, and the rapacious machinery of Big Finance,[3] pledged as it is (even bound by law) to make as much money for shareholders as can be squeezed from the system, no matter the consequences. Closely researched, elegantly written and passionate about the fabric of rural life, *The Killing of the Countryside* exposed the folly of a runaway subsidy system and the many harms it had caused, from environmental degradation to loss of habitat to rural unemployment—and, crucially, it reminded us that this approach was not a product of the EU, but had been introduced in Britain just after the war. It should have put us on track for a massive re-think about farming, but it didn't. What it did do was to remind us of just how much had been lost, all across the land. In this passage, Harvey is speaking of the chalk lands around Salisbury:

> [T]he farmers of the plain have transformed this landscape on a scale that would have seemed unthinkable even a generation ago. Without public consultation they have obliterated a living heritage thousands of years old. Nor is the destruction confined to chalk downland. Across the length and breadth of Britain the countryside has been reconstructed in the sole interests of intensive agriculture. The very essence of a nation is drained away, yet it seems scarcely a voice is raised in protest.

[2] Harvey (1997).

[3] This is shorthand, I know. But where would we be without some shorthand?

Why the silence? Partly, I think, it has to do with a continuing myth of progress. We have to use modern methods, they say, to feed the world (actually, a fair part of the crops produced in many of these areas went to waste, because of over-production of the most generously subsidised items or [on occasion] because it had to be declared unfit for human consumption. Meanwhile, much of the world remains hungry). Also, to complain about the modernisation of anything is to be seen as Luddite, anti-progress and a victim of *nostalgia*, a condition described repeatedly as a 'social disease', and ruthlessly treated as such, across the USA and Europe in the 19th century.[4] To be nostalgic is to become the grandmother who says she remembers the day when the gardens were full of butterflies, instead of just a few, or the old man who remembers peregrine falcons in the old quarry from which they have long disappeared (poisoned by the developer, perhaps, who wants to make the place into a waste-processing plant). For the technocrats, it was a smart move: destroy or steal the land we called home, then pathologise any and all objections. A similar step was taken when Nicholas Ridley, Baron Ridley of Liddesdale, popularised the term NIMBY (not in my back yard) to demonise the victims of 'developments' to which he was (mostly) immune.[5] Of course, nostalgia, like melancholy, is problematic. It tends to turn in upon itself, it can end up finding damage and degradation everywhere and it can obscure our critical faculties—but that is only the case when what is called nostalgia is *purely* nostalgia, just as it is only the case when melancholy is certifiably melancholy and not, say, justified mourning for an actual loss. At the root of the argument which follows I want to suggest that what we have been living through, privately, almost clandestinely, is a state of justifiable mourning for what has been destroyed or taken from us—from the land, from memory, from the best of our traditions, and from our sense of belonging—and we have been obliged to do so without the requisite public performance of communal grief for those losses. I believe that some novelists (and other artists, it goes without saying) have taken it upon themselves to create appropriate elegies that, while they do not, *cannot*, enact the necessary public ceremony, do offer us a model for consolation, and also, more importantly, for an informed refusal of the lies that we have been sold. Chief amongst these is the lie that production = progress. To produce, is not, of course, a sin, but 'production', here, actually means *profit* and everybody knows by now that profit is not shared. The third source of our grief is that we knew that this would be the case. I mean, surely, after all this time, do we really need to be told that only the rich get rich?

[4] Preferred treatments included stomach purging and leeching. In studies conducted on patients during the US Civil War, it was concluded that soldiers from the city, and/or men who had their own trades were less susceptible than those from the country. See Boym (2001).

[5] Though not entirely. See http://news.bbc.co.uk/2/hi/uk_news/2000000.stm. Such is our contempt for the land that even the privileged can be at risk.

II

These days, an expressed love of the land is de rigueur, in business as much as in literary circles, especially amongst the grant-seeking classes (developers, for example, talk the green and pleasant talk just as readily as any poet petitioning for a bursary). Yet I seem to recall a time when a stated interest in birds, or bees, or climate change for that matter, was less remunerative. When I started writing (putting out rather inept little poems with great big titles like 'Green' or even 'Dark Green'), the response of my peers, such as it was, couldn't help but bring back the experience of carrying a particularly beautiful or terrifying object to school for Miss Conway's legendary Nature Table: the extraordinary redness of an autumn leaf, the Jackson Pollock in-the-round of a cold plover's egg and even, on one occasion, a cow's eye (donated, I should say, by one of the slaughter-men at the abattoir I passed every day on my way to school). I bore them all to Miss Conway's classroom proudly, only to shrink back in self-rebuke and shame as my classmates crowded in to mock my find. Here, no doubt, lies the Ur-sentiment of that old phrase, pearls before swine, and any adult can tell you that it is unwise to let your enthusiasms show. To a solitary and proverbially sensitive child, however, the lesson that it is not done to express wonder *publicly*, or to find something beautiful *publicly*, whether 'in nature' or elsewhere, leaves something of a scar. These days, of course, now that some kind of stakes are involved, the mockery is not confined to children: let the wrong kind of person express native awe, or an appreciation of things green, and he (it seems males are the guiltier sex here) is soon treated to a moral homily on his intrusiveness as 'lone enraptured male'[6]—as if to be lone and enraptured were the property of a class, or a gender. Perhaps unabashed nature lovers might counter here with Seamus Heaney's more generous (and for me, more accurate) term, 'one of the venerators',[7] but the new territorialists of wonder aren't having it, and I am sure any *kleine Geschichten für Naturfreude* I might venture here will seem equally reprehensible to those who care to compete in such things.

And yet. There is a romance I cannot quite surrender, in spite of sniggering criticism and the vanishing of the land—a land that, for someone who flitted mid-boyhood from coal-town Scotland to steel-town Northamptonshire, must be called Britain, a romance of the given earth that, in extremis, I allow myself to recall as a garden, somewhere in the English West Midlands, a place I once found by purest chance. It was a long, hot summer. A friend and I parked her car at the end of a deep lane, where the woods opened out to grass and limestone, the only buildings immediately on the green a few houses and a recently abandoned Post Office, its windows

[6] Jamie (2008).
[7] Heaney (1984).

powdered with soot and dust. Opposite, set back a few metres from the square, the shipwreck of a church stood—is it only the English who know that whatever deity still subsists in our time, it only takes up residence when the church is disused or empty?—and a few metres further still, just off to one side along a narrow gravel path, there was a garden.

Needless to say, my friend and I spent the afternoon there, and it was one of the happiest afternoons I can recall; but I will not describe the place, or give directions, or name it. I am superstitious that way. Besides, though I go back to that place, in my mind's eye, at times of difficulty, it is a private matter, a story that speaks only to me, whereas what I am concerned with here is a more public, communal matter—or rather, with the substitution of private (or quasi-private) *enactments* for communal, fully *performed* ceremonies of mourning. One of our problems over the last fifty years, and certainly since the 1980s, is that we have withdrawn into our own places, our own personal tabernacles and gardens, to mourn alone. Nothing wrong with that in itself, maybe. But what we have lost, what we have had taken from us, is the ability to mourn together, as a community, as a society. To return to the Susan Stewart review that gives this essay its title:

> More often writing soliloquies of suffering and consolation than collective songs like the dirge, elegists have discovered that lyric sequences can provide a powerful means of addressing the tensions between grief's inchoate emotion and social rituals of mourning

adding that,

> How deeply we might comprehend formal expressions of grief, and whether such comprehension leads to understanding and sympathy, remain open questions. Recent prose memoirs … trace a mourner's growing self-knowledge as her life is changed and the dead come into clearer, often disconcerting, perspective. These narrative accounts of traumatic loss necessarily repeat and encompass it, acknowledging, if not an afterlife, at least an aftermath.

The outcome of this artistic process may be, not just a personal resolution of grief, but the public, or semi-public performance of 'the tension—famously explained by Freud—between melancholia, an endless process of painful repetition, and mourning, with its gradual movement toward closure.'[8] That last term comes more easily to North Americans than it does to us, perhaps, and I tend to replace it, for my own purposes, by an out-and-out commitment, not just to the idea of closure, but also to that difficult process, healing. I have, of course, wrenched Stewart's words from their origin as a poetry review into a somewhat alien context, but I think they more than

[8] Stewart (2011).

bear that. With all this in mind, I want to speak now, not of elegy for the individual, but for the land (or even, in a sense, for pastoral itself) and in prose moreover. I want to consider three novels, either published or conceived in the 1980s that, first, perform distinct elegies for the land (for the earth itself, for our sense of belonging, for history) and, second, carry us forward into the first stage of a healing process, that is, towards the the mourner's 'growing self-knowledge as her life is changed and the dead come into clearer, often disconcerting, perspective.' That self-knowledge implies, I think, a new sense of belonging, and with it, a refusal to collaborate further with the processes that undermined that sense of belonging, and vitally degraded what we had once considered home, whether by replacing the green and pleasant land with dark, Satanic mills, or redesigning the local pub (horse brasses, sepia photographs of peasant women, ornate pumps spewing out steely industrial lager, etc) to look and feel more 'authentic'.

III

First published in 1992, Adam Thorpe's *Ulverton*[9] is the kind of book that is impossible to summarise, without doing it real injustice. For my purposes, however, the publisher's description may suffice:

> At the heart of this novel lies the fictional village of Ulverton. It is the fixed point in a book that spans three hundred years. Different voices tell [its] story: one of Cromwell's soldiers staggers home to find his wife remarried, and promptly disappears, an eighteenth century farmer carries on an affair with a maid under his wife's nose, a mother writes to her imprisoned son, a 1980s property developer discovers a soldier's skeleton, dated to the time of Cromwell. ... Told through diaries, sermons, letters, drunken pub conversations and film scripts, this is a masterful novel that reconstructs the unrecorded history of England.

I would happily discuss the diverse narrative techniques of this book for hours (it is surprising, still, to remember that it was the fiction debut of a highly talented poet), but I want to concentrate, now, on the first chapter, in which the aforementioned 'Cromwell's soldier' (he is called Gabby by the supposed 'author' of this chapter, of which more later) returns to Ulverton to find his wife has married another man, one 'Thomas Walters' (please make a mental note of that surname). That none of these characters is 'real' is something we will not learn until the closing pages of the book but, as William, the old shepherd who is this chapter's purported narrator remarks, 'Whether a man has done a thing or no, I know when he believes he has, and that is all

[9] Thorpe (1992).

the same in the end.' In short order, Gabby disappears, and Willie suspects foul play, but says nothing.

A fine introduction to a novel in which, as time goes by, expressions of sincere belief trump any and all factual considerations (and an indication, from the start, of how prophetic *Ulverton* was, preceding as it did both Tony Blair's 'I am right because I am sincere' approach to truth, and Fox News' 'I am right because your facts, being yours and not mine, can have no possible validity', two stages in a process that, from the 1980s onward, has been both continuous and inevitable (I say inevitable, because the 1980s was a time, not only of financial and environmental, but also of dialogical deregulation). As Jürgen Habermas remarks:

> The concept of reaching an understanding suggests a rationally motivated agreement among participants that is measured against criticisable validity claims. The validity claims (propositional truth, normative rightness, and subjective truthfulness) characterise different categories of a knowledge embodied in symbolic expressions.[10]

However, what our politicians, PR-folks and some in the media have done, since the 1980s in particular, is to sacrifice both the 'propositional truth' and the 'normative rightness' elements of public discourse, so elevating 'subjective truthfulness' to the position of sole validity criterion—and, by extension, of decision making. The most obvious example: we went to war in Iraq, not because Saddam Hussein had WMD (weapons of mass destruction), and not because of any clear social or moral imperative, but because Blair and Bush sincerely believed we should do so and, in their sincere conviction, decided that to mislead the public about WMD and Iraq's involvement in international terrorism was justifiable, under the circumstances.

I digress, but only a little. For, having introduced not just the narrative seed, but also the main philosophical question of the novel, in this first chapter (that is, what is history, to whom does it belong and how do we use it), Thorpe offers us a powerful final section—written as a documentary TV script, entitled *A Year in the Life: Clive's Seasons*—in which sincere belief, manipulation of 'truth' and questions of authenticity and authorship combine to raise any number of thorny and urgent moral and political questions.

The chapter, innocently titled, 'Here: 1988', follows Clive Walters (we are not visibly led to the belief, but do assume, that he is a descendant of that Thomas Walters mentioned in the first chapter, a drunkard for certain, and possibly a murderer), as he pursues the second phase of a controversial property development in Ulverton, a place he claims to treasure, not only because (his first words on screen) his 'family came from round here' but also because 'it's beautiful and there's a history'. So beautiful, in fact, and so redolent of history, that he aims to destroy not only the character

[10] Habermas (1984).

of the village, but also of the local pub, (the 'New Inn', which has been at the centre of the novel throughout) bringing in bogus architectural styles and facsimile materiel, ('Romany Spartan, yep. For the en-suite. And Greensward for the lower toilet and Crinkle Tan for the upstairs.'). While conceding that 'you know, we developers have er, a little bit of a bad name', Clive relies on a 'subjective truthfulness' approach in his attempts to overcome opposition from the Ulverton Preservation Society and a sceptical planning sub-committee, mingling Blair-like sincerity of feeling, 'That's who I am. Sentimental I suppose', with sops to the politicos (the scheme will at least appear to include a few examples of that now notorious sub-category of semi-rural planning 'affordable housing'), and the usual developers' jargon that not only imposes false criteria of appropriateness and authenticity upon, but also derives as much as it can from, the very culture it is destroying. (At one point, local historian, Raymond Duckett, describes his home place in terms of local names and local knowledge, 'All the green fields had their em their own names you know. The Gore. Gumbledon Acres. Apple Dean. Whitesheet Haw. Brambleberry Piece. Top and er, Bottom Field. Little Hangy … old word for sticky. Not hanging. A whole—whole way of life. Knowledge … that's what is under threat! That old knowledge'—and we know he is right, just as we know that those delicious, rustic names will be preserved in the names of the streets and avenues and courts that paved them over.)

Time passes and, as the locals are effectively barred from the freshly renamed pub (it is now the 'Never Fear'), Clive Walters' victory seems assured—and if this were the case, it would make both novel and purported documentary depressingly realistic. However, in order to raise our hopes so that he can kick them back into touch on the final page, Adam Thorpe offers us a deus ex machina figure, one Adam (or possibly Alan) Thorpe, 'Local Author and Performer', the real and only begetter of Ulverton's first chapter, which turns out to be a complete fiction that he has placed in the the local paper, *The Wessex Nave* (a fine piece of wordplay, there), suggesting that the site of Clive Walters' second development, Little Hangy, is cursed (by the memory of poor Gabby's brutal murder at the hands of Clive's evil ancestor). It seems that Thorpe has come to believe that he can only fight fire with fire and, fortunately for Ulverton, this fictional 'author' has a gift for 'subjective truthfulness' all of his own:

> Yes, I've heard that Mr Walters isn't very pleased—I've received a … letter from him, saying so, in no uncertain terms. But, er, I don't regret using his name. The oldest stone in—in the graveyard here, that's legible. 1689. That's where I er, took it from. Er, I'm doing a whole series of stories on shepherds. I've done a lot of research, a lot of local research, and er, all my stories are based on fact and er, using local legends and so on.

This interview is, of course, more revealing in what it does not tell than what it does. Thorpe says he does not regret using Walters' name, but he says nothing about the effect his lie (and this fiction is a lie, though one might also argue that it is so in the way that Jean Cocteau claims all fictions to be: *un mensonge qui dit toujours la vérité*) on Clive's business and, of course, he is being amusingly disingenuous, tongue firmly in cheek, when he talks about 'based on fact' and the use of local legends. Yet how can we seriously debate any of these points? This is how all public relations is done now, up to and including the national level.[11] However, Clive is not done yet. He—and most of us—know that, for the developer, there is always another chance:

> bloody awful year. … For Clive. But there'll be another. Eh? Ups and downs. Another year. Yep. That's how, what you got—have to think. Another year. There's always that. Another year.

Some readers might see these remarks, at the fictional documentary's close, as Clive putting a brave face on a hopeless situation, but that seems to me a mistake. In reality (under the appeals system, and by other means, such as redrafting of existing proposals to look like new ones) the developer always gets another chance to pursue his or her schemes, while the preservation society, or the concerned environmental group, or the locals who just want to live in accord with their surroundings only get one. If they win, all they have achieved is a stay of execution; if they lose, they have lost. Not only that, the basis for individual objections in rural areas cannot be concern for a local bird species or a specific woodland, or for the loss of what various characters in the fictional documentary describe as 'wisdom', 'the old skills' or the wilful desecration of 'My bit of England, forever part of me …', it can only be predicated on 'loss of amenity' and similarly vague and selfish-seeming (NIMBY) concerns. Those who are sensitive to local beauty and history, those who love birds and woodlands, those who simply want their children to grow up in an area where they can see birds and trees and meet people who have 'the old skills' are doomed to fight an eternal rear-guard action, in which loss of habitat is more common than preservation—and this is one of the things that many of us mourn, as John Clare mourned Langley Bush and Cowper Green and Crossberry Way. In short, many of us have good cause to believe that Enclosure, supposedly a historical event, never ended and in fact continues today—and that is a cause for a grief which is not only not enacted publicly, but is also pretty much ignored. Why? Because it is nothing but nostalgia, a NIMBY rejection of progress and, in a society based on money and not much else, progress, (as 'development') is king. At the same time, because the field of battle is defined by those who favour 'development' over environment, the fight is always reduced to the level of

[11] Or, as Sharon Krossa, writer and academic technology consultant, remarked of the film Braveheart, 'The events aren't accurate, the dates aren't accurate, the characters aren't accurate, the names aren't accurate, the clothes aren't accurate—in short, just about nothing is accurate.' Wikipedia, http://en.wikipedia.org/wiki/Braveheart

petty squabbling. The most noble arguments are interdicted. The 'author', Adam (or possibly Alan) Thorpe, recognises this. Arguably, it takes a poet's gifts to write about the real world in a just way—and the greatest test of an elegy is its justness. *Ulverton* may conclude with a Pyrrhic victory—and for a writer, a victory based upon the sacrifice of truth, no matter how expedient, is still a Pyrrhic one—but it is also an elegy, not just for the land, but for the betrayal of communal life that any lie commits, even when that lie is part of a desperate stratagem to save something, at least, from those who would take it all.

IV

The element of soliloquy in the final chapter of *Ulverton* reveals the extent of the wider society's failure to take account of its citizens' views and of what is best for the land when big money is at stake, whether that money is in the hands of developers or agribusiness. Anyone who has fought for the environment in this country (through the official channels, at least) knows that the main so-called 'stakeholders' with regard to a planning decision are the developers, on one side, and anyone whose financial interests they might harm (along with a range of centrally controlled expert bodies whose remit is easily managed) on the other. In most cases, those who must live with the changes are ignored. True, the process now allows for a token period of 'public consultation', but those on the ground know that, barring a well-organised and *very* well-resourced oppositional force, any sufficiently connected developer is almost certain to get his or her way.

Thorpe exposes this beautifully in the tiny soliloquies delivered to camera by those who have no recognised stake in the future of *Ulverton*: the locals at the New Inn, for example, or an incoming mother—a Londoner, of course—seeking space and a different way of life for her children. The quality of these brief, often desultory soliloquies is either plaintive, or defensively dismissive. (The position of the less-deceived is easier to manage if, having recognised the enemy's unfair advantage, one gives up before the battle even starts: at least one salves a little pride from not being seen to fall for such scams as 'local consultation' or 'affordable housing'.) In both cases, however, they are deeply poignant. These asides express the despair, masked with wry and self-deprecating humour, of people who know that they haven't a chance—that, even if they were to win this time, history tells us that the enemy will keep coming back with a slightly altered plan and will eventually triumph.

To move from these soliloquies to Graham Swift's *Waterland*[12], in which one tragic historian offers up a book-length soliloquy of suffering, is like moving from a slow

[12] Swift (1983).

local drizzle into a downpour. In spite of its growing recognition as an English classic, there is still much to be said about this novel—not least the irony that it was a Londoner, whose only knowledge of East Anglia at that time came from a handful of short visits, who gave us this most beautifully rendered regional novel, a book that triumphantly fulfils Mary Austin's ideal:

> Art, considered as the expression of any people as a whole, is the response they make in various mediums to the impact that the totality of their experience makes upon them, and there is no sort of experience that works so constantly and subtly upon man as his regional environment. It orders and determines all the direct, practical ways of his getting up and lying down, of staying in and going out, of housing and clothing and food-getting; it arranges by its progressions of seed times and harvest, its rain and wind and burning suns, the rhythms of his work and amusements. It is the thing always before his eye, always at his ear, always underfoot. Slowly or sharply it forces upon him behaviour patterns such as earliest become the habit of his blood, the unconscious factor of adjustment in all his mechanisms. Of all the responses of his psyche, none pass so soon and surely as these into that field of consciousness from which all invention and creative effort of every sort proceed.[13]

I mention the regional novel because—though I am sure none of these authors would accept the mantle—the books I am considering here are, in their different ways, excellent examples of the genre. The trouble is that the word 'regional' has come to be seen as a limitation, a label for work that does not live up to the high demands of cosmopolitan fiction. Yet I would tend to argue that this is actually the opposite of the real situation; as Austin points out, the regional novel addresses the *totality* of our experience, something that the Hampstead adultery novel, or the latest slew of sly, fey or research-based *confezione* do not. It would be rewarding to consider the issue further in the light of Swift's masterpiece, but my concern here must be to focus in on one central strand of *Waterland*: that is, the question of history and its supposed opposite, progress.

For those unfamiliar with the book, *Waterland* concerns the history of two East Anglian families, the Cricks and the Atkinsons, separated by social class and wealth, but linked by a tragic secret. The narrator, a history teacher named Tom Crick, is about to be forced into retirement and, though he has personal grief of his own to contend with, we feel that, more than anything else, it is the age in which he lives, an age that denies history any place in the education system, that Crick grieves for most. For some reason, this novel's place as an English masterpiece didn't come overnight, perhaps because some readers were discombobulated by the suspicion that it was mainly about eel migration or, possibly, the nicer points of land drainage. In fact, it treated so many of art's 'major themes' that it is hard to look back and think of it as

[13] Austin (1996).

just one book. The tragic nature of childish curiosity, kinship, the play of water and land in East Anglia, the extremes—and the banal facts—of grief, all these and more are treated with astonishing skill in the pages of *Waterland*. However, I want to focus on Crick, and his view of history because, while the other losses this book deals with are familial or personal, the loss of history—the deliberate erasure of the subject from school syllabuses and from the communal consciousness—that became a hot topic in the Thatcher/Reagan era was, and continues to be, a matter for collective grief. The technocrats of the 1980s demanded that we sacrifice history so that progress could work more freely: history is bunk, they said, in a modern industrial society. Not only that, it might serve to temper our enthusiasm for the randomly new. As Crick points out:

> There's this thing called progress. But it doesn't progress, it doesn't go anywhere. Because as progress progresses the world can slip away. It's progress if you can stop the world slipping away. My humble model for progress is the reclamation of land. Which is repeatedly, never-endingly retrieving what is lost. A dogged, vigilant business. A dull yet valuable business. A hard, inglorious business. But you shouldn't go mistaking the reclamation of land for the building of empires.

Of course, *Waterland* is all about history—and specifically, the history of land reclamation, its temporary victories, and its return to the water. Reclamation, like maintenance, is work that is obliged to take the long view, and yields little or no quick profit, though it may pave the way for prosperity, as it does here for the great brewing family, the Atkinsons, who rise and fall, just as the water levels rise and fall, in what seems like a natural rhythm. (Their rise depends on the work of anonymous ditchers, meadmen and drainage workers, though, naturally, these workers will not share in the consequent wealth.) History, of course, teaches us how to understand, and even sometimes to predict Nature's rhythms, but Crick's boss, Lewis, and the one pupil the history teacher dangerously befriends, are both at pains to express their fashionable rejection of history's wise counsel and complexities. 'I want a future', the boy, Price, says. 'And you—you can stuff your past!' To have a future, in this boy's view, means to confine oneself to the here and now, not in the sense of Be (fully) Here (really) Now, but simply in that progressive sense of being prepared for whatever may come on the glorious journey into an ever-more prosperous and happy time ahead. Which never comes, of course, because as Crick says:

> [O]nly animals live entirely in the Here and Now. Only nature knows neither memory nor history. Man, man—let me offer you a definition—is the story-telling animal. Wherever he goes he wants to leave behind not a chaotic wake, not an empty space, but the comforting marker-buoys and trail-signs of stories. He has to go on telling stories. He has to keep on making them up. As long as there's a story, it's all right.

As with Clive Walters in *Ulverton*, what head-teacher Lewis and his ilk would do is to bulldoze those stories into the ground (for our own good, naturally) in the relentless and reckless onward pursuit of—what? It is difficult to tell in both these books what the antagonists *value*. Clive claims he doesn't think about money, that he doesn't see a piece of land and start calculating the profit—yet throughout his many soliloquies to the documentary maker's camera, money is *all* he ever talks about. Lewis, for his part, is an acolyte of an emergent school of thought for which looking back, taking stock or doubting are cardinal sins and the only permissible mental state is a prescribed optimism. He is, of course, right in thinking that any serious study of history precludes such silly optimism, and he is happy that it—and Crick—are to be scrubbed from the curriculum. What he forgets, however, is that humans need stories to live well, with others and with nature, and that, when the progressives bulldoze their way through what they think of as the redundant past, what they are really doing is stealing from others a set of narratives, and a way of life, that is, for them, the vivid present, that is: *tradition*. This is why progressives always get tradition so wrong: they think it pertains to the past; but in reality, tradition always operates in the present. How would it not? At the same time, what Lewis is concealing, or may not even be aware of in himself, is the proto-fascist tendency that guides mediocre people to take upon themselves extraordinary authority (a common sight in British society). For now, but not for much longer, Crick is there to question his intentions:

> Children, beware the paternal instinct whenever it appears in your officially approved and professionally trained mentors. In what direction is it working, whose welfare is it serving? This desire to protect and provide, this desire to point the way; this desire to hold sway amongst children.

He sounds, of course, like Cassandra. Soon, however, he—and his history—will be gone.[14]

[14] A recent study pointed out that, 'The view that too little British history is taught in secondary schools in England is a myth. Pupils in the schools visited studied a considerable amount of British history and knew a great deal about the particular topics covered.' However, the study went on to say that, 'Although pupils in primary schools generally had good knowledge of particular topics and episodes in history, their chronological understanding and their ability to make links across the knowledge they had gained were weaker.' It is not difficult to extrapolate from this and other studies a notion, at the very least, that history teaching has become ahistorical, in that it works with very specific topic areas, often cross-curricular, while failing to convey a sense of history as such, or to apply it to our own daily experiences. https://www.gov.uk/government/uploads/system/uploads/attachment_data/file/413714/History_for_all.pdf

V

I was in my early teens when I first began to experience the sense of loss that I am trying to characterise here, a complex set of emotions, full and partial memories and elements of fantasy, forensics, nightmare and homespun narrative that, for want of a better term, I have come to designate as grief for the land. I felt this grief, even then, not only for things that had vanished into the past, but for what was being discarded in my own lifetime, essential things that I could feel haemorrhaging away while we all went about the daily business of societal life, accompanied by the clamour of sales talk. As time passed, I felt more and more involved, more and more complicit, even as I suffered losses of place, of the other animals, of any accord on what was worthy of pursuit (art and philosophy had to be 'accessible' or it was deemed repugnantly elitist) and even of certain textures and subtleties of language. Beloved images, images that meant something to me and might have meant something to my children, lines of poetry and phrases of music, ideas in their richness and complexity (or breath-taking simplicity) were clouded by their appropriation into commerce, via advertising—the list goes on. I am not talking about a bourgeois aesthetic here, or of a class-based value system; I am talking about the essentials of a humanism. This wasn't a matter of fashion, shifting tastes or 'new thinking'; it was existential.

And the novel? I thought of the modern British novel, then, as too complicit with the social mainstream (a problem highlighted in 1994 during the controversy over James Kelman's Booker Prize victory for *How Late It Was, How Late*, when Rabbi Julia Neuberger complained: 'I'm really unhappy. Kelman is deeply inaccessible for a lot of people. I am implacably opposed to the book. I feel outmanoeuvred'[15] [my italics]) and much of what I encounter in today's soft-lit scene seems intent on continuing that trend. Yes, there is darkness in some of this work, but it's only film-noir, and there is social engagement, but not so much as to propose a new way of ordering the systems by which we operate day to day. Maybe I was just unlucky in my choices for too long, but I have to confess that I was lured away by the more daring and far more searching work of certain American writers (Andre Dubus, Shirley Jackson, the incomparable Don DeLillo, to begin with, then by writers like Keith Banner, say, or Steven Sherrill, whose present situation seems rather precarious, in the recent flood of clever, tricksy US fiction) and I took solace in European fiction, as well as the great Japanese masters: Natsume Sōseki, Jun'ichirō Tanizaki, Yukio Mishima, Kenzaburō Ōe and especially Yasunari Kawabata, whose mastery of the *mono no aware*—'beauty in sadness'—mode was not only very seductive to someone of my inclinations at that

[15] http://www.independent.co.uk/voices/highly-literary-and-deeply-vulgar-if-james-kelmans-booker-novel-is-rude-it-is-in-good-company-argues-1442639.html

time, but also seemed to reveal what I thought was a necessary truth: viz. that when a condition seems incurable, the artist's duty is to make of it a possible virtue. If Freud is right and melancholy is destined forever to repeat itself (and perhaps we could say the same for nostalgia) then might not the repetition become ever more precise, ever more beautiful, thus proposing a new way of proceeding?

But then—and I admit that I missed it at the time—I came to believe, by way of a surprising source, that *mono no aware* is the luxury of a certain class, available only to those who can afford, or are sufficiently dispossessed by the rise of mediocrity, to accept a consequent loss of community. In short, just as *mono no aware* emerged fully as aesthetic mode during a period when Japanese life was crashing into crass, 'Westernised' commercialisation, my own pose, built on this and other essentially defeatist ways of seeing, was a response to the rise, in Britain, of a twinned anti-intellectualism and reductionism fostered by American attitudes to money and culture, culminating in what Jonathan Franzen diagnoses as 'cultural totalitarianism'.[16] The source of this new position, if it can be called anything so grand, was a re-reading of the work of Michael Bracewell, who dedicated an astonishingly perceptive sensibility to the novel for some dozen or so years (*c.*1988 to *c.*2001) before moving—on?—to work in cultural criticism and art history. Perhaps, one day, the novelist will return, but for now, to my mind at least, Bracewell, in works like *Divine Concepts of Physical Beauty* (1989), *The Conclave*[17] (1992) and *Perfect Tense* (2001), has for some time been arguably the most under-appreciated of our living fiction writers.

His first novel, *Missing Margate*,[18] was published in 1988. Few works of fiction would be worse served by a brief précis, but it should be noted, for reference, that the plot revolves around an architect named Max de Winter, whose beloved wife, Rebecca, has recently left him.[19] As the book opens, Max is being courted by the editors of trendy new magazine, *Designate*, who want to use his acknowledged talent, his glamorous-couple lifestyle and his youth as a hook for a fashion feature. Max, however, has become deeply unhappy with his fame, and with the way life in London, a

[16] Franzen (2002).

[17] 'It's still one of my favourite pieces of work though because it's one of the only books from that period which was about its time rather than of its time. I still think it stands up as a kind of anatomy of a new middle class standpoint. There really were young people at that time thinking in terms of how near am I to somewhere where I can buy a bottle of Perrier water at eleven o'clock at night. I was interested in that state of banality. I was asking where the moral centre of that mind was.' (Michael Bracewell, interviewed by 3 *AM Magazine*, London 2001, http://www.3ammagazine.com/litarchives/sep2001_interview_bracewell.html).

[18] Bracewell (1988).

[19] References to Daphne du Maurier, British cinema and English culture pre WWII haunt the book throughout.

city he once loved, has become degraded at every level (a process in which his own feverishly-praised designs now seem to him to be implicated):

> For Max, the loss of each building was a defeat—he had wanted his buildings to glorify the financial centre of the UK. He had wanted them to be architectural jewels in the crown of England, their design offsetting the virtues of a green and pleasant land, their aesthetic references intended to echo a proud historic legacy of English tradition. He had wanted to stay at New Manderley, his garden palace, safe in the knowledge that London carried on in his absence growing prosperous and noble within the buildings that he had designed before his thirty-second birthday. How pitifully naïve. A sickness chilled him and a dread of the work he had done and the role that it played in New England as the kinky dungeon of London Style City and the Money Brothel of Britain where all the young executives smelled of stale fish and the sweat of progressive greed.

To distract himself from this sense, not only of having failed, but also of having unwittingly collaborated with a known enemy, Max recalls and reinvents scenes from old British, especially wartime, films, his fantasies populated by stereotypical 'Tommies', temporarily home from the front:

> He gave each of the Tommies a cold bottle of beer and he had one himself. 'Yes,' he said, with respectful warmth, 'there's a quality in England that will always shine, no matter what dirty tricks Johnny Banker may stoop to

and he remains convinced that what he has been complicit in losing, perhaps forever, is both irreplaceable and uniquely elegant:

> In his dreams Max knew an older England. The pictures of faded postcards brought tears to his eyes as he travelled up and down the lift in Heal's.

What Max is harking back to may well be a chimera—but it does belong to an age when English people could at least aspire to community, and to a sense of tradition and purpose—aspirations that the trolls at *Designate* do not even recognise and would only despise if they did. In many ways, *Missing Margate* foresees the crisis of identity and of confidence that gave the recent UKIP/BREXIT debacle its basic terms of reference. That the leaders were self-serving cynics might have been more obvious to more people had the feelings of loss and betrayal not run so deep; meanwhile, to argue that the sovereign England that seemed to be at risk had never existed was to miss the point (it is clear that England belongs, and has always belonged, to a very narrow class of persons whose historical and present ruthlessness is beyond question). It wasn't what existed that people saw as under threat, it was a myth to live by, an idea of England, a narrative. When asked, many English people, especially city and suburb dwellers, will describe England in terms of its rural features (as a garden, as a bluebell wood, as the 'wild' Lake District) in spite of the fact that, since World War II, rural

Britain has been savagely degraded, polluted and given away to corporate landowners and other interests, many from overseas, keen to mop up its most basic resources, including its privatised water and even the soil itself, while its definitive culture has been overwhelmed by the totalitarianism of Hollywood, Silicon Valley and McDonald's.

Yet what Max has lost is both more specific and more essential. As the 1980s grind on, what he sees disappearing is an English aesthetic and, as *Missing Margate* slides towards its inevitable denouement, fantasy is not enough. Max comes to feel that he owes an honour debt to himself, and to the London—the Britain—he finds himself complicit in betraying. From this point on, he sets out on a path that will be seen by some as terrorism, as he destroys all but one of the buildings he has designed. That he is also destroying his own legacy is clear. That to complete his task he must destroy himself is never much in question. This, he feels, is the only option that remains to him:

> There's a skip on every corner that I pass by and they're full of either builders' junk or *objets trouves*, depending on the postal district and my mood. Outside all the little houses and across all the waiting sites, beside dual carriageways and down dark alleys. Maybe they are the body bags of some authorised war, the collected dead of the mass gentrification of the future. Now that my war is finishing I can see the future as a city of catalogue design against a backdrop of ruins. *The strange thing is that after love there are fewer funnier topics than outraged dissent*. [my italics]

What is poignant here is that the losses Max is cataloguing are not funny at all. They are genuinely tragic, just as the desecration of the countryside in *Ulverton* and the loss of history in *Waterland* are tragic—not only because the damage done is probably irreversible, but also because the good men and women who witness the degradation are cast as the outsiders, the fogeys, the NIMBYs, who seem determined to stand, stubbornly in love with a mythical past, in the way of 'progress'—even though progress, for as long as anyone can remember, has simply been a synonym for profiteering.

It is clear, then, that Max is not victorious at the end of *Missing Margate*. To the general public, and to the authorities, he will be a madman; to the the staff of *Designate* he is an expensive inconvenience from which they are quick to move on. To the reader he has been, throughout, a kind of ghost, an escapee from a Daphne du Maurier world where such things still matter. Yet he is, nevertheless, strangely redeemed. He has eradicated the traces of his collaboration with a corrupted system and he has done so *as a performance*. Does 'society' care? Of course not. But then, 'society', that most ephemeral and inconstant of animals, has never really mattered—as Max realises, when he is finally reunited with Rebecca for his last act of vandalism:

> What would Society have made of this meeting? There was always someone ready to comment, some rattler in the *Tatler*, some maggot. The City slept around them. They did not know whether it was indifference that surrounded them or the massive silence of an artificial intelligence that they had become too tired, or too confused, to find stupid.

What matters is that notice has been served, that a public *non serviam* has been delivered. Whether it is witnessed by many, or only a few, is not the point; what matters is that it has happened, or even that has been imagined (in this case, in the pages of a novel called *Missing Margate*). What matters most, however, is its contribution to a mounting refusal of a system of profit and privilege that betrays our land, our history and our deepest values, whether for cash in plain brown envelopes, 'outside investment' or government subsidy, a refusal that, in its elegance and economy, recalls the farewell note that Billy Name left for Andy Warhol in 1970, when he left The Factory for good, words that serve as the poignant epigraph to *Missing Margate*:

I AM NOT HERE ANY MORE
BUT I AM FINE

REFERENCES

Austin, Mary (1996), *Beyond Borders: The Selected Essays of Mary Austin*, ed. Reuben J. Ellis, (Carbondale, Southern Illinois University Press).
Boym, Svetlana (2001), *The Future of Nostalgia* (New York, Basic Books).
Bracewell, Michael (1988), *Missing Margate* (London, Fourth Estate).
Bracewell, Michael (1989), *Divine Concepts of Physical Beauty* (London, Secker and Warburg).
Bracewell, Michael (1992), *The Conclave* (London, Secker and Warburg).
Bracewell, Michael (2001), *Perfect Tense* (London, Jonathan Cape).
Franzen, Jonathan (2002), *How to be Alone* (New York, Farrar, Straus and Giroux).
Habermas, Jürgen (1984), *Theory of Communicative Action, Volume One: Reason and the Rationalization of Society*, trans. Thomas A. McCarthy, (Boston, MA, Beacon Press).
Harvey, Graham (1997), *The Killing of the Countryside* (London, Jonathan Cape).
Heaney, Seamus (1984), *Station Island* (London, Faber and Faber).
Jamie, Kathleen (2008), 'A Lone Enraptured Male: The Cult of the Wild', *The London Review of Books*, 30(5): 25–27, 6 March. https://www.lrb.co.uk/v30/n05/kathleen-jamie/a-lone-enraptured-male
Kelman James (1994), *How Late It Was, How Late* (London, Secker and Warburg).
Stewart, Susan (2011), 'Discandied: On Women and Elegy: Learning to mourn with Susan Howe, Gertrude Schnackenberg, Anne Carson and C.D. Wright', *The Nation*, 24 August. https://www.thenation.com/article/discandied-women-and-elegy/
Swift, Graham (1983), *Waterland* (London, William Heinemann).
Thorpe, Adam (1992), *Ulverton* (London, Secker and Warburg).

Note on the author: John Burnside is currently working on a history of 20th-century poetry, with particular reference to politics, warfare and environmental degradation. He is Professor English at the University of St Andrews, with particular interests in eco-sophist and eco-critical writing, American poetry and the varieties and uses of creative non-fiction.
jb44@st-andrews.ac.uk

To cite the article: John Burnside (2017), '"Soliloquies of suffering and consolation": Fiction as elegy and refusal', *Journal of the British Academy*, 5: 251–270.
DOI https://doi.org/10.85871/jba/005.251

Journal of the British Academy (ISSN 2052–7217) is published by
The British Academy—the national academy for the humanities and social sciences.
10–11 Carlton House Terrace, London, SW1Y 5AH
www.britishacademy.ac.uk

Journal of the British Academy, **5**, 271–308. DOI https://doi.org/10.5871/jba/005.271
Posted 16 November 2017.

The determination of love

Warton Lecture on English Poetry
read 25 April 2017

ANDREA BRADY
Queen Mary University of London

Abstract: This essay explores love poetry in its most militant and perverse forms. It examines three 'determinations' of love: first, how love is defined (determined), given that true love always feels new and singular, but language is a repetition engine which can make these professions of love seem quotational; second, why love is fixated on ends, including catastrophe, the apocalypse and death, and how it might be released (de-termined) from that fixation; and third, how love can teach us to be resolute (determined) to close the gap between the world we experience and the one we desire. Love has been described by poets and philosophers as fullness, and as lack or hunger; as fusion, and as splitting; as original, and as serial or repetitive; as the end of time, or a return to its beginnings in the lost paradises of infantile or primitive experience. Love provokes an anamnesis of an archaic experience of the ideal. It is associated with creativity and fecundity. But it also prompts poets to anticipate the catastrophes of death or the destruction of everything that is. That destruction includes the end of poetry itself. Poets from Shakespeare and Marvell to Shelley or Robert Creeley have affirmed love only through risking its negation (and with the negation of love, the negation also of their own poetic practice). Why is love poetry so drawn to the fantasy of destruction? What is the use of love poetry in times of catastrophe? If artistic remembrance—as Herbert Marcuse puts it—'spurs the drive for the conquest of suffering and the permanence of joy', how can remembering love through poetry help us to address a new future, particularly one in which the traditional hierarchies that encumber lyric and love itself can be overturned?

Keywords: love poetry, catastrophe, death, lack, Shakespeare, Marvell.

PERVERSE AND MILITANT LOVE

Last year, when I began to consider the possible subjects for this lecture, we were beginning to recognise the crises of our historical moment: Brexit; Jo Cox; the Pulse nightclub; Obama's drones; Syria; the refugee crisis; Trump's unstoppable obscenity. Men with swastika neck tattoos declared their optimism on the nightly news. The world seemed even more than usual to be ruled by hate.

In such contexts, talking about love poetry feels embarrassing, even a little obscene. But the difficulty of reconciling the opposing urgencies of love and politics has always been a key topos of love poetry itself. It was powerfully articulated by Sorley Maclean, in a series of poems written in the context of the Spanish Civil War, here translated from Scottish Gaelic by Ian Crichton Smith:

> Girl of the yellow, heavy-yellow, gold-yellow hair,
> the tune of your lips and Europe's pain together.
> Lustrous, ringletted, joyful, beautiful lass,
> our time's shame would not infect your kiss.
>
> Can the music of your beauty hide from me
> the ominous discord in this harmony?
> The rampant thief and brute at Europe's head,
> the ancient songs, your lips so proud and red.
>
> … Can beauty and the mendacity of verse
> deceive the patient with its transient cures
> or hide the Spanish miner from his doom,
> his soul going down without delirium?
>
> … What is each ringlet of your golden hair
> when weighed against that poverty and fear
> which Europe's people bear and still must bear
> from the first slave-ship to slavery entire? (Maclean [1943] 1979: 20)

The poem is addressed to a generic 'Eimhir', the wife of Cuchulainn in Irish legend, though the identity of the subject of poem four has been identified as Nessa Ní Shéaghdha (later Nessa Doran), whom Maclean met in 1937 (Mackay 2010: 9, 11). The poem describes her beauty as a kind of music; but the poem's beauty is also a form of music, which does not seek to hide the discord of its times. Instead, it amplifies that discord, creating its particular harmonies by drawing together present violence and ancient songs.

Maclean's poem ends with its questions still open. He cannot pretend that there is an easy way of resolving the contradiction between personal desire and international catastrophe.[1] The poem holds that contradiction in the balance of its rhymes, without forcing its reconciliation, but also without surrendering to despair. And though I feel the intensity of that contradiction every day, I decided that in this lecture I wanted to affirm the value of poetry in times of catastrophe; and to recognise the work that all of us do to sustain each other and the world we make in a generous, critical understanding, which often takes the forms of love.

This is, for me, rather out of keeping. In my own poetic practice, and my critical writing, my usual instinct is to lodge with the negative. I have for several years now been working on a critical study about poetry and bondage, which considers not just formal but also physical constraints. Prison writing, slave songs, verse as chains or shackles, the sadomasochistic pleasures of bondage—thinking about these contexts has allowed me to think about how poets generate the image of freedom by imagining themselves in voluntary states of confinement; and how the occlusion from this image of the millions of people who do actually live, love, write and die in incarceration sets a limit to what we understand as lyric.

As part of that project, I was writing about the American poet Rob Halpern's book *Common Place*, which consists of erotic addresses to a Yemeni prisoner who died in Guantánamo Bay. Halpern's poems attempt to project love into a space of exception, a space where relation was banned. One of the questions his work poses is: 'What does it mean to love inside a system that has made love monstrous, to communize this eros' (Halpern 2015: 141). I also wanted an answer to this question. While I admire the ethical and formal audacity of his book, I was troubled in ways I could not fully explain by Halpern's proposition that erotic love might be a way of opposing militarised violence.

This opposition of love to war is an ancient fiction, most famously symbolised by the triste of Venus and Mars, caught in flagrante in Vulcan's net. Lisa Robertson imagines the scene in her glorious book *3 Summers*:

> I want a pause in vocation. Venus
> chatoyant in the formal dream
> please tranquilise efficient Mars and his
> efficient interests.
>
> The man's neck's flung back
> his man-shawl's agitated
> he has the soul of a mortal horse

[1] David Marriott's extraordinary short book *In Neuter* (2013) is another example of the difficult poetic task of integrating personal love with historical violence and crisis, a task which Marriott undertakes in an attitude of mourning but not reconciliation.

and his saliva's communal
flung supine beneath
the concept of a goddess
who unclasps the depth of his torso
with her skilled goddess mouth ... (2016: 43)

This interlude is another way of expressing the desire, which Robertson declares earlier in the book, to 'return to the sex of my thinking'; to bask in the luscious eroticism of maturity, stargazing and lying in stylish baths. Her sensual imagery suggests that love is one means by which queer or feminised subjects can overcome the masculinised violence that is associated with the American imperium elsewhere in her book.[2]

Robertson is imitating Lucretius here, who invokes Venus as muse in the beginning of his poem *De Rerum Natura*. In the translation by Lucy Hutchinson, a 17th-century republican whose own life was framed by war, Venus is implored:

Wherefore sweete language in my thoughts infuse
And lett not wars harsh sounds disturbe my muse;
Make sea and land a quiet calm possesse
For only thou with peace canst mortalls blesse,
Since Mars, the mighty God that rules in armes,
Lies in thy lap, bound with loves powerfull charmes,
And resting there his head in full delight,
On thy rich beautie feeds his greedie sight;
Hanging with amorous kisses on thy face,
Whilst thou (O Goddesse) doest this God embrace,
While he doth in thy sacred lap remaine,
Sweete peace for Rome by gentle prayers obteine,
For neither can we with a quiet mind
In time of warre, persue the worke design'd ... (1996: 30, ll. 27–40)

By binding and enchanting the god of war, the goddess of love frees the poet from the harsh sounds of violence, and allows him to write his magnificent thesis on how the world was made. It is important to note that this initiation of the work of imagining the world through love is repudiated in different ways, both by Lucretius—who goes on to say that the gods actually have no effect on human affairs, and to satirise romantic love in book IV—and by Hutchinson, who later rejects the profane and atheistical text she translated so lovingly in a moment of political catastrophe. These repudiations may have different motivations, but they are characteristic of the impulse to negation which often rides hard on the heels of the assertion of love, as I will argue later.

[2] Robertson writes, 'I feel ambivalent about adoring / The sex of Mars / Like America it basks / Exempt from dolorous stuff / The imperium's fucked up / How can we kiss and think?' (2016: 40).

The myth of Venus and Mars presents a tableau in which war is pacified by sensuality. But we know that militarised violence can be eroticised, often in very dangerous ways. Radical political movements have also asserted the inverse: that love can be militant. Martin Luther King's sermons, entitled *Strength to Love*, affirm that love is not 'some sentimental and weak response', but 'that force which all of the great religions have seen as the supreme unifying principle of life' ([1967] 1981: 8).[3] In Gwendolyn Brooks's poem, 'Black Love' is implored to:

> provide the adequate electric
> for what is lapsed and lenient in us now.
>
> Rouse us from blur, Call us.
>
> Call adequately the postponed corner brother.
> … Call to the shattered sister and repair her
> in her difficult hour, narrow her fever.
>
> Call to the Elders—
> our customary grace and further sun
> loved in the Long-ago, loathed in the Lately;
> a luxury of languish and of rust.
>
> … be
> the Alwayswonderful of this world. (1981: 29)

This language of love continues to infuse the Black Lives Matter movement, whose platform includes 'Loving Engagement': 'Guided by love, we continue to stand together for justice, human dignity and our share.'[4] Robin D. G. Kelley argued that 'M4BL's critique of U.S. militarism is driven by Love—not the uncritical love of flag and nation we saw exhibited at both major party conventions, but a love of global humanity' (2016: n.p.). This is a critical, deterritorialised love, a love that flows, rather than a love that solidifies around the stations of privilege.

Such love may bear a resemblance to Christian and socialist forms of belonging together, but it also recalls Franz Fanon's much-quoted testimony in *Black Skin, White Masks*: 'I believe in the possibility of love; that is why I endeavour to trace its imperfections, its perversions' ([1952] 1986: 42). Why perversions? Sigmund Freud described perversion as a detour in desire. He argued that 'the omnipotence of love is perhaps never more strongly proved than in such of its aberrations as these' ([1953]

[3] From his address to the anti-war group Clergy and Laity Concerned, King follows Nygren's classic work *Agape and Eros* (1953) in delineating the distinctions between eros, philia and agape in his sermon 'Loving Your Enemies' (52). He admits that people will find his recommendation to love the enemy 'idealistic and impractical'—an idea which could only work 'in some distant Utopia' (56).

[4] http://blacklivesmatter.com/guiding-principles/

2001: 161). A perversion is an overcoming by eros of the most deeply inscribed forms of socialisation that determine what we should honour and enjoy and when we should feel disgust or shame. In this sense, perversity is a radical way of recognising what we have been taught to love and hate.[5]

Fanon seeks to release the Black man from the nonbeing in which he is sealed up, unseen, unloved, unrecognised as human. White supremacy has fragmented and objectified him; it has presented his blackness to him as a sign of lack. His book is perverse, in that it works to reclaim the capacity to love and receive love that will restore the Black man to his full humanity and destroy the world as it now exists. This love is only perverse within the context of obscenely racialised institutions and ideologies that persuade the Black man that he is unlovable. To lay claim to love, Fanon must overcome the shame attributed to his historical position, and be free to love himself and others: 'As soon as I *desire* I am asking to be considered. I am not merely here-and-now, sealed into thingness. I am for somewhere else and for something else' ([1952] 1986: 218).

Sappho, the Greek and Latin elegists and the troubadours conspired to invent forms of erotic poetry based on the difficulty of loving supremely lovable objects. Dante, Petrarch and their imitators show us how hard it is to love beautiful, pious, chaste women. Fanon and Halpern are part of another tradition of love poetry, which—as the American poet Fred Moten describes it—expresses 'love for the unlovable'. In a recent interview, Moten cites a song by Snoop Dogg as an example of such love:

> There's this one moment in the song when he is speaking directly to men on death row and expresses love for them. 'All my dogs up against the life sentence.' For me, it was a totally important and beautiful moment in the song because he is expressing love for folks that are often conceived of as the very embodiment of the unlovable. That capacity to express love for those who are generally perceived of to be unlovable is important. On the most basic level, my work has been primarily structured by love of blackness and love of black people, both of which are often conceived of by what you called the mainstream media as 'unlovable.' (2016: n.p.)

Loving the unlovable is the paradoxical imperative at the heart of Moten's practice. The last poem in his book *B Jenkins*, an elegiac tribute to Moten's mother which invokes numerous friends and cultural heroes in a fused tribute to the endurance of Black culture, ends: 'this is the cluster song of our romance' (2010: 95). The book aggregates the destructive (cluster bombs, cluster fucks) and the creative, emancipatory value of song not around a single, conventionally lovable object, but around 'our

[5] On the relation of perversion to utopia in Marcuse, Janine Casseguet-Smirgel and Janet McDougall, see Whitebook (1995: 47–70).

romance': a collective work of love.

In different ways, Fanon, Moten and Halpern are seeking I think to unbind love from the conventions of the white, bourgeois, heterosexual family, and to encourage its redistribution, especially to people who are excluded from the protections which the state gives to particular forms of life and love. They also militate for the abolition of the ideology and institutions which declare those forms to be perverse. Poetry is one of those institutions. It has contributed immeasurably to our understanding of whom we ought to love, and why, and how, enforcing the romance plot of the heteronormative couple form which Lauren Berlant has described as 'a seductive desire, a fantasy of being emancipated into form's holding environment' (2012: 101). Berlant, like many feminist and queer critics, warns against regarding love as 'invulnerable to the instabilities of narrative or history', and particularly against ignoring the way that heterosexuality is enforced by institutions at the same time as it is represented simply as 'a relation of desire that expresses people's true feelings' (95).

But poetry is not solely a mechanism for enforcing erotic conformity. It extends an endless and often perverse capacity for love to the manifold, lovable and unlovable. All concepts, things, animals, people and relations can be the objects of poetic love, from the Brooklyn Bridge to the film industry in crisis; from a stupendous cat, to God, views of Eton College, a haggis, clouds, nations, babies, and even the product code for a replacement part for an obsolete Hotpoint tumble dryer. We could argue that poetry is an art of imagining the possible universality of love while preserving the particularity of its objects, without losing them in the fog of a concept which exceeds them.

I do not want to go on a Kantian detour here. I am still not even sure that militant poetic love is adequate to the challenge of confronting white supremacy, the judicial system or the war economy. I am reminded of the quote from Cornel West that I read on my friend Justin Katko's t-shirt at a poetry reading organised by Jessica Pujol this February for One Day Without Us, a day on which migrants staged the withdrawal of their labour in protest against xenophobic politics in the US and the UK. The quote was: 'Justice is what love looks like in public.' This beautiful equation might trigger some scepticism. It does not specify whether justice is like love because love is based on recognition before the other as justice is based on recognition before the law, or if it is because love can be ambivalent, bad, coercive or blistered by violence. Sara Ahmed has also shown that love can be deployed in the vocabulary of fascism (love of country, love of the Aryan race and so forth), just as easily as in the discourses of progressivism ([2004] 2014: 122–43).

The attempt to reconcile love and justice has come in for other forms of criticism as well. The philosopher Gillian Rose thought that the opposition between love and justice could not be mended. She argued that the diremption of the universal from the particular cannot be overcome 'with love, forced or fantasized into the state':

> If the dirempted terms of the ethical are set in opposition to each other, so that 'love'—discursive, friendly, saintly, agapic, aporetic, political—is opposed to 'the law'—the world, the city of man—and made into an unworldly culture—a city of God—this holy city will be infected with the same judgemental banality of opinion about good and evil it would repulse. (1992: 238)

Rose insists that acknowledging the incommensurability of love and justice in the 'broken heart' of modernity is the only ethical position we can maintain in this world. She calls this position the anxiety of the middle: staying in the fray, surrendering neither to despair not to hopes for transcendence.

And yet, poetry *is* an art of commensuration. It asserts itself as a common measure of all imaginable experiences, reconciling love with form, and unfolding the singularity where the universal and the particular meet. I am trying to do this right now. This lecture is really a celebration in miniature of the poems that give me life, the poems that—since I was a small girl, pulling at the frayed edges of the possible—have held me in the world. Tonight, in the pause which *is* vocation, I want to propose to you: to evoke my poetic loves as a way of imagining yours, and finding the measures we have in common.

But I also recognise a danger here. If love can be unrequited, so can poems. Alice Notley (2015: n.p.) describes love ever so tentatively, as an object:

> to kick as you walk on the blazing bare ground, where …
> sentimental, when what I love, I ... don't have that one
> word. This fire all there is ... to find ... I find it
> You have to find it. It isn't love, it's what?

Like a fire, love's radical uncertainty consumes you as you do the work of 'finding' your object. The coordinates of this uncertainty are different for everyone. The alchemical process by which poetry transforms the compacted experience of the individual into something other readers believe in does not always work; some love lyrics seem true and lovable, while others feel like a lump of rock you just want to kick out of the way. What makes the difference? Why do we love one poem and not another?

There are no easy answers to those questions. I am tempted to cite Montaigne's brilliantly simple response, in his essay 'On Friendship': 'If a man urge me to tell wherefore I loved him, I feele it cannot be expressed, but by answering; Because it was he, because it was my selfe' ([1603] 1965: 201). My own interest happens to be in those ways of loving in poems which are perverse or militant, and refuse to be reconciled to the way things are—even if that refusal takes the form of a fantasy of catastrophic destruction. The rest of this lecture will consider three aspects of love's determination: first, how love is defined (determined), given that true love always feels new and singular, but language is a repetition engine which can make these professions of love seem quotational—I will reflect on several influential definitions, and their consequences for poetics. Second, I will consider why love is fixated on ends, including catastrophe, the apocalypse and death, and how it might be released (de-termined) from that fixation. Third, I will argue that love can teach us to be resolute (determined) to close the gap between the world we experience and the one we desire.

To do this, I will have to admit that talking about love is embarrassing. Emmanuel Levinas, hardly the least sentimental of philosophers, backs away from the word: 'I don't very much like the word love, which is worn-out and debased. Let us speak instead of the taking upon oneself of the fate of the other' (2006: 88). Poets also admit the difficulty of professing love in ways that are meaningful and new: this difficulty is evident in the recurrence of defensiveness, negation, or shame as tropes in erotic poetry. But I also want to think about Levinas's resolution to 'take upon oneself of the fate of the other', in rather different terms, by considering how love can include the possibility of utopia—a possibility that cannot be addressed without further embarrassment. So much of the work of our profession involves transmuting love into rational accounts of cultural value, an approach to close reading driven—in Isobel Armstrong's memorable phrase—by 'the terrors of closeness' (2000: 102). I will have to overcome those terrors, in order to speak to you *from* the place love has made for me, and to speak *of* that place: to propose some theories of how, as Frank O'Hara said, we might 'live in the terrible western world // here where to love at all's to be a politician, as to love a poem / is pretention' (1995: 305).

DETERMINING THE MEANING OF LOVE

What do we talk about when we talk about love? The poets and philosophers are reluctant to say. Donne's lovers are 'by a love, so much refined, / That our selves know not what it is' ('A Valediction Forbidding Mourning', 1932: 37). David Hume, in his *A Treatise of Human Nature*, begins by averring that ' 'Tis altogether impossible to give any definition of the passions of LOVE and HATRED', but it is also 'unnecessary to attempt any description of them', 'because these passions of themselves are sufficiently known from our common feeling and experience' ([1739] 2000: 214). Too well-known to be defined, love—and its concomitant passion of hatred—can only be evaluated through a series of thought experiments which set out a hydraulics of impressions passing from the object to the subject. Though drawn by a very different animus, Shelley's 1818 'Essay on Love' shares Hume's scepticism about the definition of love: 'What is Love? Ask him who lives what is life; ask him who adores what is God' (Holmes 1996: 55). The true nature of love cannot be determined; it must simply be experienced.

Robert Creeley repeatedly returned to the challenge of writing in a new or true way about love. The attempt to speak 'For Love', in one of Creeley's most famous poems ([1966] 1978: 159), ends in deferral and dismay:

> Yesterday I wanted to
> speak of it, that sense above
> the others to me
> important because all
>
> that I know derives
> from what it teaches me.
> Today, what is it that
> is finally so helpless,
>
> different, despairs of its own
> statement, wants to
> turn away, endlessly
> to turn away.

To write about that which teaches me everything I know is of course impossible; but in turning away from the task of speaking of it, the task which defines my vocation, I seem to turn away from love itself. The poem enacts that 'despair of its own / statement', falling, faltering, stopping:

> If the moon did not ...
> no, if you did not
> I wouldn't either, but
> what would I not
>
> do, what prevention, what
> thing so quickly stopped.
> That is love yesterday
> or tomorrow, not
>
> now.

Yesterday I wanted to speak of it; today the mood is different—petty, irritable, tedious. The speaker has not written the poem he meant to write: 'Love, what do I think / to say. I cannot say it.' He cannot articulate his wish, cannot make a verbal image of his object. The inability to speak of love undermines not only the feeling, it seems, but also the poet's trust in his own practice, and so the poem leaves us with a commemoration not of love or of the beloved Bobbie, but of failure.

Shakespeare's sonnet 116, one of the most famous definitions of love, also climbs over a series of negations to the rim of failure:

Let me not to the marriage of true minds
Admit impediment; love is not love
Which alters when it alteration finds,
Or bends with the remover to remove:
O no; it is an ever-fixéd mark,
That looks on tempests and is never shaken;
It is the star to every wand'ring bark,
Whose worth's unknown, although his highth be taken.
Love's not Time's fool, though rosy lips and cheeks
Within his bending sickle's compass come;
Love alters not with his brief hours and weeks,
But bears it out even to the edge of doom.
  If this be error and upon me proved,
  I never writ, nor no man ever loved. ([1609] 1997: 1864)

The poem defines love by telling us everything it is not: love is *not* something which bends or alters; it is *not* becoming.[6] Oh no. It is Being, unmoved by the tempest of suffering or lack. It is the star fixed in a superior heaven which looks down on catastrophe; it is constant, and in that magnificent phrase, 'bears it out even to the edge of doom'. As in Creeley's poem, the sonnet uses apophasis to make something out of negation; but Shakespeare draws that rhetoric towards a brilliantly witty and self-cancelling conclusion: the potential for failure in determining love could erase my writing and the whole history of love. Such obliteration is never really a risk, because the reader affirms his vision of love simply by reading his poem: reversing the logic of the couplet, if this poem was ever written, then its claims cannot be in error. Nonetheless, the poem's lingering negativity points to the difficulty of affirming love, a difficulty that takes us to the edge of doom.

These qualities of negation and impossibility are also apparent in Andrew Marvell's poem 'The Definition of Love' (probably written in the 1650s), which attributes qualities to love—it is rare, strange, high. But none of these tell us what love actually is. Instead, Marvell launches into a complicated complaint against fate. He says that the 'iron wedges' of fate prise the lovers apart:

[6] Helen Vendler reads this sonnet, rather unnecessarily, as rebuttals of the youth's assertions that love is transitory, and changes when the lovers change. She argues that the second half of the sonnet is a 'reinscription', which moves from 'a love first described in transcendent vertical terms as a secular Petrarchan fixed star' to 'the immanent horizontal Christian Pauline form of stoic fidelity in endurance.' (1999: 488–9, 491).

IV
For Fate with jealous eye does see
Two perfect loves, nor lets them close;
Their union would her ruin be,
And her tyrannic power depose.

V
And therefore her decrees of steel
Us as the distant poles have placed,
(Though Love's whole world on us doth wheel)
Not by themselves to be embraced;

VI
Unless the giddy heaven fall,
And earth some new convulsion tear;
And, us to join, the world should all
Be cramped into a planisphere.

VII
As lines so loves oblique may well
Themselves in every angle greet;
But ours so truly parallel,
Though infinite, can never meet. (2003: 110–11)

The lovers are like parallel lines, or like the poles—never to meet, and yet the axis on which the world turns. Their union would require the radical reorganisation of the universe, the unmaking of geometry, which might also collapse the Earth itself: this is the cost of their love, total catastrophe, the destruction of the conditions of life. The definition of love looks like impossibility.[7] Yet that impossibility is productive:

II
Magnanimous Despair alone
Could show me so divine a thing
Where feeble Hope could ne'er have flown
But vainly flapped its tinsel wing. (109)

Catastrophic love is, in its way, more powerful than happy love; it raises us up to glimpse astral truths, while hope cannot get off the ground. I will come back to the attractions of catastrophe shortly.

Marvell's poem is indebted to Plato in a number of ways, one of which is its contention that the lovers are being punished by Fate because their union could depose Fate's 'tyrannic power'. This recalls Aristophanes's fable in the *Symposium*,

[7] B. J. Sokol (1988: 169–70) argues that the poem reverses the genealogy of Love from Plato's *Symposium*, making Love here the child of Despair and Impossibility.

which says that humans were originally joined together in units of two, with a complete set of organs on each side. These spherical conjoined lovers 'were terrible in their strength and vigour; they had great ambitions and made an attack on the gods', and tried to roll up to heaven, so the gods cut them in two 'like a flatfish' (Plato 1999: 23). This is the story that most people remember when they think of the *Symposium*. Socrates's more philosophical proposition, which he has learned from the absent Diotima, is that love is an action which can only be known by its object—all love is love of something. He defines love as 'the desire to have the good forever' (43). But that good does not exist in this world—it can only be imitated by the particular, flawed bodies we see in front of us. So love is a sublimation, which carries us away from the material world which changes and decays to another, better one which 'always is, and doesn't come into being or cease; it doesn't increase or diminish' (49). According to this deeply influential theory, love mediates between the real and the ideal, exalting those who experience it properly and illuminating the limits of the perceptible world. But sublimation also risks a negation of what is, the material world discarded as the empty shell of a truth content that cannot exist here.

Love as creativity

Socrates also compares love to reproduction, but not the kind we might expect: love, he says, gives birth to beauty. Plato is drawing on a vast and expansive tradition that associates love with creation, both the creation of living beings, and of the natural world itself. This tradition reaches back to the very first known love poem, the Sumerian 'Love Song of Shu-Sin', written around 2000 BCE (Black 1998: 88–9), which commemorates the union of the king with Inanna, the goddess of love and procreation, in a ceremony that maintained the fertility of the Earth and its people.

Lucretius, as we have seen, invokes Venus as a metonymy for nature's fecundity; in Stephen Rodefer's version she is:

> Mother of heroes, mover of hearts of men and of gods,
> Delicious Venus, everyone's voluptuary,
> Under skies of shooting stars you till our seas
> And fertile earth with signal visitations,
> For every living gene is organised by your sight—
> Beholding you we rise, like the spring to the sun.
> The sky is clear for you, the weather quiet,
> For you the artful earth comes up with sweetest flowers,
> The ocean waves with laughter, the calmer heaven glows
> With larger light for you. At the vernal equinox,
> When the southwind swells its belly,

> First the birds feeling the vibration
> Soar on your coming, then the cows go wild,
> Bolt their fields and swim the streams for love,
> They are so driven by your desire!
> Everywhere through seas, through mountains, and in the air
> All creatures are moved to love's blandishments
> And overnight you populate the earth with love. ('After Lucretius', 2008: 28–9).

Lucretius is drawing on the cosmologies of Heraclitus and Empedocles, in which the universe is born from the flux of love and strife (Smith 1985: 3). In Hesiod's *Theogony*, Love and the 'broad-breasted Earth' are born immediately after Chaos (2006: 13–14, ll. 116–22). Spenser's 'Hymn to Love' draws on these ancient theories, depicting a newborn Eros moving through 'The world that was not till he did it make', arranging the elements and quelling their contentions ('Hymn to Love', 1999: 454–5). The Modernist poet Mina Loy draws on similar images for her *Songs to Joannes* (100 years old this April):

> When we lifted
> Our eye-lids on Love
> A cosmos
> Of coloured voices
> And laughing honey
>
> And spermatozoa
> At the core of Nothing
> In the milk of the Moon (1997: 56)

Echoing the affiliation of the mother with 'cosmic reproductivity' in her poem 'Parturition' (1997: 7), Loy imagines a dynamic and combative force of love creating the lovers' world, just as the pre-Socratics believed it built the cosmos, from 'the impact of lighted bodies / Knocking sparks off each other / In chaos' (1997: 59). But at the heart of this cosmic process of reproduction is 'nothing': empty space, failure or lack rather than plenitude and form (Pozorski 2005: 62–4).

The belief that love drives the forces of life to combine into more complex units also lies behind the psychoanalytic account of the opposition between Eros and Thanatos, love and the death drive. One such account, by Jonathan Lear, even claims that 'the world exists because we love it' (1998: 140). That is, the mother's milk keeps the infant alive, but the infant projects his desires onto the mother's breast, imagining that he has created it spontaneously out of his hunger for it; similarly, we imagine that the world that sustains us takes its particular form in response to our need for it. Lear extends Donald Winnicott's description of the 'good enough' mother to the whole world[8]; the world's loving form reflects the infant's libidinal investment in it. But Lear underemphasises the importance for Winnicott of the survival, by mother or world, of the infant's attempts to destroy them. Jessica Benjamin has argued that this survival is the very foundation of the erotic: the survival of the object of desire shows that the object is distinct from the subject's desires for it, and produces a space of intersubjectivity where subject and object can exist in a relation of mutuality.

> Without successful destruction there can be no escape from the realm of idealization and fantasy, and hence no sexuality that is not literal and concrete, in its own way captive to the symbolic equation as much as pornography; no sexuality that includes recognition, and so no confrontation with difference and outsideness that is not violent and traumatic. (1995: 209)

By attempting to destroy the other, the subject changes his object. This change is experienced by the subject as the recognition he craves, but also allows the subject to share his destructive desires and watch them be transmuted by the other, rather than having to internalise them and cope with them entirely on his own in a fantasy of omnipotence and singularity. Love may create the world, but the world's ability to survive the lover's attempt to destroy it is what makes love bearable. The relation of creation to destruction as a way of negotiating such fantasies will become clearer when I come to speak about the importance of catastrophe in love poetry later in this lecture.

The contemporary philosopher Alain Badiou also defines love as a process of world-making. Love, he says, is 'always the possibility of being present at the birth of the world' (2012: 26). Badiou describes love as an event, a moment of origin which reveals a universal truth. He emphasises the revolutionary nature of the lover's perspective: lovers view the world not through two singular and separate identities, but 'through the prism of our difference, so this world can be conceived, be born, and not simply represent what fills my own individual gaze' (26), united as in Aristophanes's fable. This new perspective is the foundation of love's 'minimal communism' (90), a fusion of identities brought together through a chance encounter. Badiou's emphasis on chance recalls both Lucretius and Sartre, for whom the random nature of the encounter is a source of grief; the lover, Sartre argues, realises that his love is 'one love among others and is limited by the beloved's facticity as well as by the contingency of encounters. It becomes love in the world, an object which presupposes the world and which in turn can exist for others' ([1943] 1993: 370). The Sartrean lover wants to defeat this contingency, and to extract a form of self-determination from a chance encounter. But for Badiou, the beauty of love is precisely its 'unique trust placed in chance' (17). Through their effortful commitment, the lovers transform chance into a

[8] Winnicott coined this phrase in a 1953 essay ('Transitional Objects and Transitional Phenomena'), but it runs throughout his work; see also *Playing and Reality* ([1971] 1991).

world, an act of creative investment which Badiou compares to writing poetry. 'Mallarmé', he says:

> saw a poem as 'chance defeated word by word'. In love, fidelity signifies this extended victory: the randomness of an encounter defeated day by day through the invention of what will endure, through the birth of a world. (45)

When we write a poem, or declare our love, we utter a word 'the effects of which, in existence, can be almost infinite. That is also the desire driving a poem. ... To make a declaration of love is to move on from the event-encounter to embark on a construction of truth', Badiou argues (42). 'I love you' is thus not a redundant cliché, but the initiation of a philosophical project which renews the world.

Badiou's association of love with poetry as forms of making is not uncommon. Like love, poetry is often described as a form of world-making: among many examples is Sir Philip Sidney's claim in his *Defence of Poesy* that Nature's 'world is brasen, the Poets only deliver a golden' one (2004: 9). Writing or reading poetry, in turn, is also experienced by some as a kind of love-making. Looking 'upon fine Phrases' from Shakespeare and Milton made Keats feel 'like a Lover' (Letter to Bailey, 14 August 1819; 1970: 655–6).[9] For Gertrude Stein, 'that is poetry really loving the name of anything' ([1935] 1985: 231–2).[10] Her essay 'Poetry and Grammar' is a sensual declaration of love for language: poetry is:

> concerned with using with abusing, with losing with wanting, with denying with avoiding with adoring with replacing the noun. It is doing that always doing that, doing that and doing nothing but that. Poetry is doing nothing but using losing refusing and pleasing and betraying and caressing nouns.

Lisa Robertson, again drawing on the scene of Venus and Mars trapped in the net of Vulcan, also writes of reading as a feeling of being 'caught, as if in a venal snare': 'Overwhelmingly in my submission to reading's supple snare, I feel love' (2012: 33, 39).

Jeanne Heuving has argued that for a number of poets writing in the Olsonian tradition of open field poetics, their 'most important and defining poetry is significantly derived through their discovery of how to engage sexual love and its energies' (2016: 9): love is not merely their theme, but an emancipatory force which drives their experiments with form and language. For one of those poets, Robert Duncan, love is

[9] Marjorie Levinson (1988: 172) describes Keats as taking Milton as his ego-ideal: 'Keats doesn't want to *have* Milton, originally. He wants to *be* Milton, but the only way to do that, given Keats's circumstances, is to make of Milton the introjected erotic object: the possessed otherness that is inalienable because always already alien.'

[10] On the centrality of love for Stein's notion of composition in the 1920s and 1930s, see Abraham (1996: 87) and Chessman (1989: esp. 79–111).

similar to poetry, in that each provokes a deepening of experience which outsiders might regard as perverse:

> Just as Love going deeper into the matter of love, being in love with being in love, altho this is what makes men lovers, is viewd as a disorder of feeling by men who are not lovers, so Poetry going deeper into the nature of poetry is not only in literature departments but in certain schools of poetry and among certain critics and leaders of the art, attackt as a disorder of art. (Duncan, 'Notes to Ground Work', quoted in Fredman, 2009: 28)

The notion of love and poetic experimentation as related 'disorders' has a particular context for Duncan, whose 1944 essay on 'The Homosexual in Society' associated sexual love and experimental poetics with the demand for human freedom articulated by the civil rights and gay rights movements. Reflecting on that essay's militancy fifteen years later, Duncan wrote that:

> I was, I think, at the threshold of a critical concept: sexual love wherever it was taught and practiced was a single adventure, that troubadours sang in romance, that poets have kept as a traditional adherence, and that novelists have given scope. Love is dishonored where sexual love between those of the same sex is despised; and where love is dishonored there is no public trust. (1944: n.p.)

Duncan described the voice of his earlier essay as a guilty one, whose view of society as sinister and repressive was inflected by 'the dawning realization that we are all exiles from paradise'. For him, love is a form of creativity which nonetheless reminds us of all that we have lost: poetry, similarly, becomes the song of lamentation for an irrecoverable past rooted in a fabled and idealised time before the repressions of adult love.

Love as repetition

I have been alluding to just some of the many writers who think of poetry as an art of sensuality in language. The most famous example of this sensuality of poetic language is Roland Barthes's ecstatic elicitation of the pleasure of the text, which he says offers 'the pledge of continuous jubilation, the moment when by its very excess verbal pleasure chokes and reels into bliss' (1975: 8). The plenitude of the text, in Barthes's deeply psychoanalytic account, is like the mother's overflowing milk; reading is therefore a kind of return to the lost paradise of infantile fulfilment. This image brings us to the second mode of determining love, which also extends from both Plato and Freud: as repetition. This tradition represents love as anamnesis, or the unforgetting of an archaic experience, whether of the ideal, or of infancy. As Shelley's 'Essay on Love' puts it, love is a form of 'thirsting after our likeness': 'It is probably in correspondence with this law that the infant drains milk from the bosom of its mother'

(Holmes 1996: 55–6). Freud takes up this image in his essay on 'Infant Sexuality', where he says that just as the satisfaction the baby feels 'must have been previously experienced in order to have left behind a need for its repetition', so the pleasures of adult love recollect an infantile pleasure: 'There are … good reasons why a child sucking at his mother's breast has become the prototype of every relation of love. The finding of an object is in fact a refinding of it' ('Three Essays on Sexuality', [1953] 2001: 184, 222).

Nonetheless, the serial nature of love is often represented by poets as a problem. Kierkegaard satirised the erotic poets for claiming that 'there is but one and only one beloved in the whole world, and this one and only one time of erotic love is love, is everything; the second time is nothing', and for suggesting that 'to love a second time is not also to love but, to poetry, is an abomination' ([1847] 1995: 49). Shakespeare does not represent second love as abomination, but he does admit, in sonnet 110, that:

> Alas, 'tis true, I have gone here and there
> And made myself a motley to the view,
> Gor'd mine own thoughts, sold cheap what is most dear,
> Made old offences of affections new;
> Most true it is that I have look'd on truth
> Askance and strangely: but by all above,
> These blenches gave my heart another youth,
> And worse essays prov'd thee my best of love.
> Now all is done, have what shall have no end,
> Mine appetite I never more will grind
> On newer proof, to try an older friend,
> A god in love, to whom I am confin'd.
> Then give me welcome, next my heaven the best,
> Even to thy pure and most most loving breast. ([1609] 1997: 1863)

This sonnet turns from repetition to singularity: from the 'motley' of a mixed, foolish promiscuity to perpetual confinement with 'a god in love'. Its new promise of constancy is articulated most precisely in the poem's ninth line: 'Now all is done, have what shall have no end'. This line is exquisitely balanced: now against the past (all I have done) and the future (what shall be endless); all against none (no end); what is against what will be; what is done, against what is endless; what you have, and what you shall not have (an end). This balance signifies a monumental transition. The speaker is determined that change (his changing affections) is finished. Indeed, 'all is done': change has changed to changelessness; the sublunary world of mutability is the scene for something eternal. It is this ending which makes way for that which has no end. But the endlessness of commitment is literally predicated on everything being 'done', accomplished, finished—an endlessness dependent on an end. The fragility of this resolution is also signified earlier by the paradoxical wish to be confined to a god—to be bound by something boundless—and by the repetition of 'most' in the final line. This is a poor way of intensifying the poem's conclusion and filling out the metre, and we might feel simply that Shakespeare should have done better; but it produces a paradox which unravels the assurance of the poem as a whole. The sonnet ends with repetition, when it had promised the end of repetition.

Perhaps Kierkegaard is right. There are very few good poems about late, mature, or long love: William Cowper's 'To Mary' (1905: 427–8) and W. S. Graham's 'To My Wife at Midnight' (2004: 262–5), might qualify; but even those poems get their energy from the anticipation of death. Perhaps this is why love poems tend to dwell on what Badiou called the event of love rather than on the way love persists. Enduring love is the incremental result of small, undramatic acts of generosity and understanding, repeated over time. Catastrophes, on the other hand, are singular and individualising. Shakespeare's sonnets, like love poetry more generally, are full of catastrophes. Sonnet 55 sings your praises 'Even in the eyes of all posterity / That wear this world out to the ending doom' ([1609 1997: 1853); in sonnet 107, true love will never be 'forfeit to a confin'd doom' ([1609] 1997: 1862); the Rockies may tumble, Gibraltar may crumble, they're only made of clay. There is undoubtedly a latent aggression in these predictions, which would destroy the world in order to prove the speaker's fidelity. There is also perhaps a fear: if love made the world, the loss of love might unmake it. Love arrived after Chaos, and gave Chaos a structure; and when I love her not, Chaos is come again.

Judging from the poems, it is much easier to celebrate the event of first love than enduring love. Three years into his sonnet sequence, Shakespeare wondered:

> Why is my verse so barren of new pride?
> So far from variation or quick change?
> Why with the time do I not glance aside
> To new-found methods and to compounds strange?
> Why write I still all one, ever the same,
> And keep invention in a noted weed,
> That every word doth almost [tell] my name,
> Showing their birth, and where they did proceed?
> O, know, sweet love, I always write of you,
> And you and love are still my argument;
> So all my best is dressing old words new,
> Spending again what is already spent:
>   For as the sun is daily new and old,
>   So is my love still telling what is told. (Sonnet 76, [1609] 1997: 1857)

How, Shakespeare asks, can I write more than one poem about my singular beloved, without copying myself and the whole history of erotic verse? Why can I not innovate, but just keep dressing up my old fictions and repeating myself? One answer might be that the sonnet is, like love, inherently repetitive. Great sonnets can reveal the passionate emergence of a singularity from the predictable recurrence of soundings and tropes, but this is particularly difficult to achieve in a sonnet sequence, each individual poem of which strives to be both new and authentic, and a coherent part of an extended narrative.

If love is repetitive and common, so is the language in which it is expressed. 'I love you' is 'the very sentence of indigence' (Nancy 2003: 264), a clichéd formulation which John Keats mocked as a banality or a lie:

> And what is love? It is a doll dressed up
> For idleness to cosset, nurse, and dandle.
> A thing of soft misnomers, so divine
> That silly youth doth think to make itself
> Divine by loving, and so goes on
> Yawning and doting a whole summer long … (1970: 394)

Even after he fell in love with Fanny Brawne, Keats wrote to his brother and sister-in-law, 'Nothing strikes me so forcibly with a sense of the rediculous as love. A Man in love I do think cuts the sorryest figure in the world' (Letter 156, to George and Georgiana Keats, 27 September 1819; 1935: 401). And yet, as often happens, true love made him into a believer: 'I never knew before, what such a love as you have made me feel, was; I did not believe it; my Fancy was afraid of it, lest it should burn me up' (Letter 136, to Fanny, 8 July 1819; 1935: 356). Finding the language to describe this unique experience of love presented a particular challenge. 'For myself I know not how to express my devotion to so fair a form: I want a brighter word than bright, a fairer word than fair' (Letter 134, To Fanny Brawne, 1 July 1819; 1935: 353). He wished to distinguish his love from the endless clichés he had parodied, but this would require a new language, made of words never before used—a language which could serve no purpose as communication.

Denise Riley descries the drive for originality, in writing about love, as futile; she echoes Kierkegaard in her poem 'Two Ambitions to Remember': 'Some words you may use only once. / Repeat them to some newer heart / and all your accuracy is gone' (1985: 56). 'I love you' is always a repetition or a quotation. Riley extends this argument in her book *Words of Selves*:

> This hopeless drive for originality resembles the problem of writing an original love letter (or, rather, a convincing love letter, since any emotional originality here is impossible: the truer the love, the more unapologetically ordinary its language)—a letter that could convince its author of its constancy and of hers, when inevitably she finds herself echoing the same expressions used to others before. It is a linguistic humiliation when the apparent rarity and singularity of feeling announces itself as, after all,

> condemned to verbal repetition, yet it seems cheapskate to reiterate the phrases written in all sincerity over the decades. (2000: 61)

'I love you' is simultaneously the most powerful and direct expression of love, and its most inadequate shadow; it is necessary, singular, and powerful, but also repetitive—not only of all the times you've said it yourself, to different people, in different situations, but also of the whole history of human love. As the young Shelley wrote:

> One word is too often profaned
>   For me to profane it,
> One feeling too falsely disdain'd
>   For thee to disdain it. (Holmes 1996: 246)

'I can give not what men call love'; he asks instead for the beloved to accept worship and devotion, or seek out a new language which remains undefiled by repetition.

Love as lack

The theories I have been discussing suggest that the repetitive nature of love recalls a memory of the ideal uncorrupted by materiality, and an infantile experience of satiety, profusion and world-making omnipotence. But that satisfaction is also accompanied by the painful memory of lack or hunger. Laplanche also argued that the plenitude of the mother's breast can never be rediscovered in any form of adult sexual love; the original object of love is irrecoverable.[11] Although he depicted the baby, flushed with feeding, as an image of post-coital bliss, Freud observed that there is 'something in the nature of the sexual drive [which] itself is unfavourable to the realisation of complete satisfaction' ('On the Universal Tendency to Debasement in the Sphere of Love,' [1957] 2001: 188–9). In ancient myth this dissatisfaction is dramatised as starvation. Aristophanes says that when the separated lovers find each other they fuse together so desperately that they neglect all their other needs and starve to death (Palto 1999: 24). In his *Amoretti*, Edmund Spenser describes himself as succumbing to rapturous admiration for his beloved while 'I starue my body and mine eyes doe blynd' ('Amoretti' 87, 1999: 431). Love, in these myths, is not a source of plenitude and creativity, but a threat to the subsistence of the organism whenever it becomes too obsessively fixated on the object; sexual desire is not a fountain of nourishment, but of hunger and lack.

[11] Catherine Belsey (1994: 52) cites Laplanche's argument that 'there is no primordial, original, founding sexual object at all, but only an object subsequently sexually cathected, and invested with sexual meanings initially learned from others' through care received in infancy.' For Laplanche, the lost object of desire portrayed in Aristophanes's fable is actually the object of self-preservation, and cannot ever be rediscovered, because the object which has been lost is not the same as that which is sought (Laplanche, 1976: 20).

We have already encountered this notion of love as lack in Loy's image of the 'nothing' which is at the heart of cosmic reproductivity, and the missing detainee who is the object of Halpern's poetic eros. Lack is also the form of love we are perhaps most familiar with from love poetry, with its endlessly unrequited, moaning lovers, pining for their absent, cruel or unyielding objects. Some poets go so far as to allege that there can be no desire without lack: 'Whoever desires what is not gone? No one. The Greeks were clear on this. They invented eros to express it' (1998: 11), Anne Carson argues. This invention can also be traced to Plato's *Symposium*. Socrates tells a story in which Poenia (or poverty) waits outside Aphrodite's birthday party; when Poros (or plenty) emerges and collapses in a drunken stupor, she seduces him, and becomes pregnant with Eros. Eros is thus the child of lack and resourcefulness, and the resources he has are always 'draining away' (39–40).

In his 1961 seminar on the transference which begins with an extended reading of the *Symposium*, Jacques Lacan fixates on Poenia's destitution: 'poor Aporia [*Penía*], by definition and structure, has nothing to give above and beyond her constitutive lack or aporia' ([1961] 2015: 121). Lacan finds in Plato the expression that love is 'giving what you don't have' (ibid.), which he refines in his 1965 seminar to specify that 'loving is to give what one does not have … to someone who does not want it' (1965: 165). I do not want to get mired in a lot of Lacanian technicalities here, particularly regarding his controversial association of lack with femininity. Instead, we can subvert his dictum, and notice that giving a lack is also a way of giving a space in which possibility infuses the impoverishment of the present. This may sound like futility, but it could be construed as a form of utopian thought: the gift of what we do not have, what we can scarcely imagine, the child of our resourcefulness and our failure, to a world too drunk on its riches to know it needs it.

Søren Kierkegaard follows a different route but also arrives at a definition of (Christian) love as lack: as infinite debt to the beloved. Kierkegaard argues that

> Love has been called a want, but, note well, such a want that the lover continually wants what he actually possesses … for his own sake the lover wishes to remain in debt; he does not wish exemption from any sacrifice, far from it. Ready, indescribably ready, as love's prompting is, he wants to do everything and fears only one thing, that he could do everything in such a way that he would get out of debt. ([1847] 1995: 178)

It is a joy to be in debt, and a disaster to repay. Kierkegaard describes this condition of indebtedness as 'the crowning garland on the festivity' (187). For me, this infinite and festive debt describes the 'fail again, fail better' experience of writing verse much more accurately than any Platonic theory of sublimation. The impossibility of speaking truly and completely about love leads not to the end of writing, but to its infinitude. I cannot pay you, my beloved, back with a poem which fully represents your singularity; no poem is ever enough for you, and this gives me joy, because I am determined to remain in a debt, to you and to poetry, which I cannot exhaust, however long I live.

The exquisite torture of love as lack is writ large in the Petrarchan tradition. One of Henry Howard, the Earl of Surrey's translations of Petrarch represents the lover as completely out of step with the quiet world: the night is serene, the sea calm—but the lover suffers.

> Alas! so all things now do hold their peace!
>   Heaven and earth disturbed in no thing;
>   The beasts, the air, the birds their song do cease,
>   The nightès car the stars about doth bring.

'So am not I, whom love, alas! doth wring,' and though my 'sweet thoughts' of the beloved sometimes bring pleasure, they are immediately also a source of pain: 'When that I think what grief it is again, / To live and lack the thing should rid my pain' (1965: 20). That curative thing which is lacking is the beloved, but the poem also gives pleasure—it is the form in which 'I weep and sing', modulating between the joy and fellowship of a conventional sonnet form, and the isolated woe which is its conventional content. The poem is both the evidence of lack, and its compensation. It reveals a lover set apart by what he lacks, who is also inscribed into a companionate history of human love by his ability to model that desire within the sonnet's repetitive form.

The writer whom I associate most intensely with this idea of love as lack and the poem as compensation, of the seduction of a drunken resourcefulness by the figure of poverty who waits outside the party, is John Wieners. Many of his poems commemorate the loss or absence of his lovers, but also grant a magical restitution: Wieners repeatedly asserts that poetry itself has the power to 'cure the / hurts of wanting the impossible / through this suspended vacuum' ('Supplication', 1998: 125). His poems show how desire can move across this vacuum, towards the missing beloved or the reader. Poems can cure the hurt of wanting the impossible because nothing is impossible to poems; they are magical instruments that ensure that 'no man dies loveless', that 'I shall never be lonely again, because of the love that dwells within poetry's mouth' ('The Lanterns Along the Wall', 1988: 106). In his 'Poem for Painters', Wieners describes love as Surrey did, as lack:

> I look for love.
>   My lips stand out
> dry and cracked with want
>   of it.
>   Oh it is well.
> My poem shall show the need for it. (1998: 29)

The poem offers an illusion of control over the force of love, making absent love appear in the space where it is desired. He goes on to echo Marvell's geometrical conceit:

> No circles
> but that two parallels do cross
> And carry our souls and bodies
> together as the planets,
> Showing light on the surface
> of our skin, knowing
> that so much of it flows through
> the veins underneath. (1998: 29)

Souls and bodies travel across the vacuum of space not on circular orbits but parallel lines which somehow manage to cross. This is an imaginative consolation, but one which—as in Marvell's poem—requires the defeat of gravity and geometry and the reorganisation of the universe.

Wieners's love poems reveal the lack and need of the abandoned lover, a subject position familiar from the Petrarchan tradition; but they also show how love creates a world. One of the most moving portraits of catastrophic love is his poem 'Cocaine':

> For I have seen love
> and his face is choice Heart of Hearts,
> a flesh of pure fire, fusing from the center
> where all Motion is one.
>
> And I have known
> despair that the Face has ceased to stare
> at me with the Rose of the world
> but lies furled
>
> in an artificial paradise it is Hell to get into.
> If I knew you were there
> I would fall upon my knees and plead to God
> to deliver you in my arms once again.
>
> But it is senseless to try.
> One can only take means to reduce misery,
> confuse the sensations so that this Face,
> what aches in the heart and makes each new
>
> start less close to the source of desire,
> fade from the flesh that fires the night,
> with dreams and infinite longing. (1998: 76)

This extraordinary poem imagines love as both hell and paradise, the suffering of lack and the experience of profusion. Love is the pure, creative fire at the centre of the cosmos, an ethereal centre where (if we were to read this as a reference to Aristotelian physics) all motion is 'one'—unchanging, constant. The Face of love gives and withholds its divine, life-giving gaze, withdrawing from the world it creates and returning to the 'artificial paradise' which we might also associate—through Baudelaire, and Wieners's own history—with narcotic derangement. The poem shifts momentarily to a more local 'you', whose location is undiscoverable, before confessing the futility of any prayer for restitution. But the poem is itself such a prayer, and thus engages in a version of apophasis: it denies the worth of pleading as it pleads. It wishes to dull the senses and make the image of desire fade, and at the same time sharpens the senses and conjures an unforgettable image of desire. It stokes a cosmic fire while fantasising about the relief of routinisation; and—like Shakespeare's sonnet 110—it exercises the discipline of ending with a profession of endless longing.

Is it true that 'only recollection's love is happy', as Kierkegaard's aesthete argues in *Either/Or*, or must these recollections of lost love always take the form of grief ([1843] 1987: 41), as they do throughout Wieners's writing? Memory, Herbert Marcuse argued, can be a source of joy, and a means of resisting the tyranny of fate and time, particularly the time of alienated labour. Marcuse was criticising the way that civilisation represses pleasure, and prohibits us from accessing the fulfilment we once enjoyed either as infants or as a species. He proposed that one way of overcoming this repression is through memory, which allows us to retrieve those archaic experience of gratification, from a time before the pleasure principle was supplanted by the 'order of renunciation'. Our utopian hopes are not fictional; we are not just imagining another world, we can remember it. However, this makes happiness:

> essentially a thing of the *past*. The terrible sentence which states that only the lost paradises are the true ones judges and at the same time rescues the *temps perdu*. The lost paradises are the only true ones not because, in retrospect, the past joy seems more beautiful than it really was, but because remembrance alone provides the joy without the anxiety over its passing and thus gives it an otherwise impossible duration. Time loses its power when remembrance redeems the past ([1955] 1972: 163–4).

This argument resonates with Wieners's poems, in which the 'artificial paradise' of lost love can only be entered through suffering and returned to in dreams. But that remembered paradise endures forever, unlike the fleeting present in which desire is realised and then lost. Past love can seem like the only happy love because its fate, to use Marvell's term, is already determined; poems seal that moment of consummation in their amber.

Hunger and fusion

In 'Cocaine', Wieners imagines love as a centre where flesh of pure fire is 'fused' and all motion becomes 'one'. Like Marvell, he uses cosmic imagery to represent a wish for bodily and psychic conjunction—the desire, as Freud put it, 'to make the I and the love object one, to abolish all spatial barriers between them' ([1926] 2001: 122). Freud saw that 'at the height of being in love, the boundary between I and object threatens to melt away' ([1929] 2001: 66). This loss of boundary between self and other is embraced in many accounts of love, from Aristophanes's fable of the conjoined lovers in the *Symposium*, to John Donne's poem 'The Ecstasy', to Freud's 'oceanic feeling', or Badiou's 'Two Scene'. Max Weber argues that:

> the erotic relation seems to offer the unsurpassable peak of the fulfilment of the request for love in the direct fusion of the souls of one to the other. This boundless giving of oneself is as radical as possible in its opposition to all functionality, rationality, and generality ([1948] 1991: 347).

Fusion is not just a way of describing a desire for sexual intercourse or the recollected unity of the mother–infant dyad, but a form of radical generosity which opposes Enlightenment rationality and returns humans to their charismatic animal natures. However, if the fantasy of fusion is a way of returning to the materiality of the body, the body is also the limit of that fantasy, whether it be chaste bodies which resist penetration, absent bodies which can only be remembered and not touched, or mortal bodies which must succumb to death.

The fantasy of fusion also forms part of Hegel's elusive fragment 'On Love', in which love arrives late to a world filled with dead things. In Hegel's argument, the subject first loves the objects which surround him. These objects are dead and regard him with indifference, or not at all; the lover, unrequited in his desire for these things, lives on in a necrophiliac despair, unable to bear thinking 'of himself as this nullity' (1970: 304), unable really to live. He can only return to life, recognise himself as living, through love's pedagogy, which teaches him to treat a living being as something other than an instrument or an object. Hegel says that lovers relinquish the love of things to come together as mortal beings and form 'a living whole'. The lovers free themselves from the fetters of materiality and fuse psychically and sexually in an attempt to overcome the separation of their finite, bounded bodies, and to negate their mortality. Love strives to annul the possibility of death 'as a mere abstract possibility, to unite even the mortal element and to make it immortal' (1970: 305–6). The lovers learned about their finitude from living in a world of dead things, and they rebel against that finitude through reproduction—the making of a living being in which they are fused, in the form of a child. Leaving aside the bias towards reproductive heterosexuality in Hegel's account, we can read in this strange little text a clear indication of the necessity of an encounter with death to the determination of the subject which is so important to Hegel's philosophy. I will return to this theme in a moment.

It may seem paradoxical that love is imagined as constituted by lack, and at the same time inspires endless fantasies of fusion, which almost convey an excess of presence: two beings so closely locked together that there is no internal or external space where they are not mixed. But these two tropes are linked, I think, by hunger. Love poems are full of the regressive impulse to try to reclaim the lost paradise of (literal) fulfilment. Come live with me and be my love; withdraw with me into a fantastic paradise of plenitude. But the ancient pleasures we remember are elusive and cannot be recaptured. Love always entails a yearning and feeling of incompletion or hunger, even starvation. No one can survive in a private world of uninterrupted erotic fusion with the beloved. Withdrawing into such a world not only deprives the self of nourishment; it also jeopardises our participation in the making of the world. Jonathan Lear's remark, cited earlier, suggests that 'the world exists because we love it'. If we withdraw our world-constituting love and give it to a single person, then the world might cease to exist. Such love is potentially catastrophic.

DE-TERMINING LOVE: LOVE POETRY AND THE CATASTROPHE OF DEATH

The specific world-ending catastrophe that haunts many love poems is death.[12] Shakespeare says about the idea 'That Time will come and take my love away': 'This thought is as a death' (sonnet 64, [1609] 1997: 1855). Death is the black hole of thought; it powerfully draws all thoughts toward it, and puts out their lights. Death is the absolute singularity, the cancellation of the debt. It is the opposite of festivity and of the banality of repetition. It is the ultimate rebuke to the infantile fantasy of omnipotence. But these are not its functions in love poetry. Oh no. For poets, death is the recurrent emblem *of* omnipotence, the occasion of their triumph over time and decay. The catastrophe of death is what the poem alone can outlast. Think of the troubadours pining for death as a release from the anguish of love; of the way Petrarch's *Rime Sparse* and Dante's *Vita Nuova* meditate on death as a means of transcending the limits of the body; of the repeated invocation of death in Shakespeare's sonnets as the threat against which the poems are raised; or W. S. Graham's late poem,

[12] The most interesting exploration of this topic is still by Denis Rougemont ([1939] 1983).

'To My Wife at Midnight' (2004: 262–5), in which the poet's thoughts as he sleeps beside his wife Nessie Dunsmuir turn to death and desire.

Graham's powerful poem compiles many of the themes of this lecture: the two are alone and separate, but also fused—'where we each reach / Sleeping alone together, / Nobody can touch' (263). Her sleeping, present absence creates the space which enables him to compose this poem to her: neither out of hearing, nor truly in it, she is both his interlocutor, and turned away from him; she does not speak to him directly, though her heart answers 'my dear my dear // My dear for all it's worth' (264). The poem regresses, in a way which was quite common in Graham's work, first to childhood ('coming out to play'; 'to play the games of Greenock / Beside the sugar-house quays', 264, 265), then historically—to the field at Culloden (265), where the Hanoverians finally defeated the Jacobite uprising. This site brings a surprising note of war into a poem of night, restfulness, the cat going through its flap, and the Coleridgean meditation echoed in its title. We learn that the speaker has acquired a wound, and that he is begging Nessie 'to help me now to go', to 'buckle me for the war' and 'kiss me and fasten my drowsy armour tight' (265). Nessie is like Venus, consorting with Mars; and the poem could be read as a witty Donnean innuendo about the desire to 'go' or come:

> Is the cat's window open?
> Shall I turn into your back?
> And what is to happen?

However, Graham strikes a more melancholic note; instead of disarming him, Nessie prepares him for the fight as he 'goes under'—into the unconsciousness of sleep or death. With his going he imagines sleep as a little death, his soul watching from the stoure at Culloden as Nessie, untroubled by time, sleeps here too, still living but in a 'lonely place' in his absence. Her love empowers him to stand and fight, but not to survive. The poem is a lonely address to the warm body beside him, imagining the scene changed into death. It is Nessie's beating heart which keeps his soul from skipping and missing a beat, the rhythms of her body which keep the poem's tercets anchored in the darkness. The image of death spoils the pleasure of lying warmly with the beloved; the poem shows how that paradise is always already lost, and even the paradise of childhood is cultivated on the ruins of historical premises. Put a different way, it shows how the bliss of loving intimacy can be claimed amid those ruins. Like many love poems, Graham's constructs in its forever present declaration of love, a way of forestalling the catastrophe of death to come which it cannot stop repeating.

Marcuse argued that memory can even overcomes the most repressive force of all: death itself. He suggested that 'in a repressive civilisation, death itself becomes an instrument of repression.' Nonetheless, the biological necessity of death:

> does not refute the possibility of final liberation. … Men can die without anxiety if they know that what they love is protected from misery and oblivion. After a fulfilled life, they may take it upon themselves to die—at a moment of their own choosing. ([1955] 1972: 165)

This hope—that we can imagine a world in which we could die whenever we choose, without anxiety, knowing that what we have worked to make will last—is outrageously utopian. But it is also a central theme of many of the poems I am discussing: that they can overcome death through love. Love induces fears of mortality, which the poem's immortality can assuage; the poem is the articulation of a demand which speaks forward to future readers, and backwards, to the lost paradises of infantile experience.

Keats was of course both half in love with easeful Death, and plagued by fears of ceasing to be. He wrote to Fanny Brawne that he broods over 'two luxuries' as he walks:

> your Loveliness and the hour of my death. O that I could have possession of them both in the same minute. I hate the world: it batters too much the wings of my self-will, and would I could take a sweet poison from your lips to send me out of it. From no others would I take it (Letter 139, to Fanny, 25 July 1819; 1935: 362).[13]

Love makes him wish for death, but also for endless life: 'I shall never be able to bid you an entire farewell. If I am destined to be happy with you here—how short is the longest Life. I wish to believe in immortality—I wish to live with you for ever.' (Letter 223, July 1820; 1935: 500). And when his death was actually approaching, as his health failed and he planned his journey to Italy, he asked his friend Charles Brown to look after Fanny. 'The thought of leaving Miss Brawne is beyond every thing horrible—the sense of darkness coming over me—I eternally see her figure eternally vanishing' (Letter 238, To Charles Brown, 30 September 1820; 1935: 520). It is this figure which makes him fear the death he longed for, and which he sees, and cannot bring himself to regard, in the pain of their misunderstandings and separation.

Those fears fed off and into his fantasies of withdrawing from the world into a private space of erotic monopolisation of the other, and his hopes for poetic immortality. He begged Fanny Brawne:

[13] Levinson offers an interesting reading of Keats's relationship to Brawne, whom she says 'was pretty unanimously judged to be cool, vain, and self-involved': she argues that Keats typically loved narcissistic women because he himself was 'seeking after object-love' (quoting Freud, 'On Narcissism'); and that in the presence of such women he felt at ease because 'I forget myself entirely' (letter to George Keats, 14–31 October 1818; Levinson 1988: 180–1, n. 15).

> Do not think of any thing but me. Do not live as if I was not existing—Do not forget me … for you to love me as I do you, you must think of no one but me. (Letter 216, to Fanny, May 1820; 1935: 490).

It is a sentiment he echoes in his poem 'To Fanny', where he makes his life contingent on total possession of her:

> O! let me have thee whole, —all—all—be mine!
> That shape, that fairness, that sweet minor zest
> Of love, your kiss, —those hands, those eyes divine,
> That warm, white, lucent, million-pleasured breast, —
> Yourself —your soul —in pity give me all,
> Withhold no atom's atom or I die … (1970: 689)

At such moments, Keats acts the part of the obsessional lover that Sartre identifies. He wants to be the one 'whose function is to make trees and water exist, to make cities and fields and other men exist, in order to give them later to the Other who arranges them into a world.' By giving her the world, he becomes 'the unsurpassable', the 'absolute end', not a means but the anchor and foundation of all values ([1943] 1993: 369). In such a case, world-making is not a generous and creative endeavour, but a way of shrinking the actual in order to constrain the beloved and ensure her dependency. Sequestered by illness, Keats accuses Fanny of flirtation, of not taking their love as seriously as he does:

> My love has made me selfish. I cannot exist without you—I am forgetful of everything but seeing you again—my Life seems to stop there—I see no further. You have absorb'd me. I have a sensation at the present moment as though I was dissolving. (Letter 220, to Fanny, 5 July? 1820; 1935: 496)

He is already withdrawn, dying, destroying his world and himself in order to live wholly in a love which makes him feel as if he were 'dissolving'—as he wished, in his 'Ode to a Nightingale', to 'Fade far away, dissolve, and quite forget / What thou among the leaves hast never known': age, sickness and death. He wants the beloved to withdraw with him, into the world he has made to exist, a world beyond common values: the world his poetry constitutes. But as we have already seen, such a withdrawal is catastrophic, and threatens to obliterate the shared world and starve those who practise it.

Keats's attempts to control his beloved remind us that there is an excess which can never be accounted for by the demand for love. This excess is the beloved object, that figure who engenders the poem, and who constantly escapes its constraints. The beloved is always more than the poem can be, a real person whose speech, dreams, manners and body exceed the poem's frame. What the poem preserves for eternity is, as John Donne put it, a 'relic', not the fullness of the irrecoverable object for which the poem is perpetually hungry. The fugitive nature of that object installs a lack at the centre of the love poem which threatens the poem's claim to be the foundation of value. But the excess is also the irrecoverable plenitude of feeling and language which any single poem cannot contain, the fantastic ideal which casts a shadow over the existing text and which we could identify with the nightingale's high requiem. Hegel argued that 'a pure heart is not ashamed of love; but it is ashamed if its love is incomplete' (1970: 306), if some part of the subject remains separate or exclusive, not given over to love. This, Judith Butler says, is Hegel at his most Kleinian, a recognition 'of the hostility in love that keeps love from ever being absolute' (2012: 15): 'on the one hand, the individuality of the other precludes the union, and yet to rage against that individuality is to strike at the other whom one loves' (13). The poet is particularly at risk of the shame of incompletion, the inability to contain the excess of language and desire even in the purest of hearts or most capacious of poems.

Perhaps this is what gives the lie to the poem's claims to omnipotence and world-making: love cannot impose its structure on that excess which is the beloved, the poem's own beginning. And so chaos is come again. I have argued, following Jessica Benjamin, that the object's survival is the basis of erotic mutuality. The attempt to destroy the beloved object or world that object constitutes and inhabits is proof that the object really does exist, independent of the subject's fantasies. The icy beloved of the Petrarchan tradition is a caricature, an outline which masks an actual, various person whom the poem cannot contain. The unrequited lover's bitterness tells us that this object actually exists, and that she resists both his fantastic idealisation and his violence. The fantasy of destroying the other, or indeed the world, is part of the dream of omnipotent possession. But rather than proving the unity of the couple, it leaves the lover alone. At least then the lover knows he is not repeating: the poem comes to stand in for the singularity of feeling and utterance which love, common, repetitive love, prohibits. But the problem for poets, of course, is that they are never alone. Their endurance depends on another kind of loving repetition: by readers.

THE DETERMINATION OF LOVE

So at the terminus of this lecture, we have arrived at a point of intense ambivalence. Love can be a figure for the making of the world—and for its destruction. It can remind us of the blissful fullness of infancy and fusion with the mother—and the pain of emptiness or lack. It is singular and new; it is repetitive and ordinary. It is a gift of something we do not have but can only imagine, a communisation of eros which is embedded in the language that never lets us forget that we are not the first to feel the intensities of passion for a singular individual. But it also causes us to imagine withdrawing from or destroying the world; it skirts the edge of doom, and draws us inexorably towards the catastrophe of our mortality. It is perhaps inevitable, in this historic moment, and in the intellectual traditions that dominate our culture, that it is the latter vision which determines our perspective on love—though I hope everyone reading this essay has had a chance to feel otherwise.

Our tendency when thinking about love, in other words, is to give in to what the late Mark Fisher described as 'capitalist realism': the belief that only catastrophe is inevitable. Now that 'capitalism seamlessly occupies the horizon of the thinkable', Fisher argues, 'poverty, famine and war can be presented as an inevitable part of reality, while the hope that these forms of suffering could be eliminated [is] easily pained as naïve utopianism (2009: 8, 16). I want in this final moment to turn away from capitalism's realistic scoffing at the possibility of the end of suffering, and argue that by making us contemplate death and the annihilation of the existing world, love poems help us to survive the catastrophes which are already here. This is the opening of Sophie Robinson's poem 'where the heart is streaming':

> there are places in which the mind thrives like plankton, where jobs
> are easy to come by & every apartment overlooks the park, where
> the funeral has barely started & the heart is a mist that rises & clears
> like a browser & streaming faster — a gapless surface of fake solids
>
> & there are places in which love reproduces itself like a lizard's tail, heeds
> to no alarm or database. places where the sun raises like a fat cunt
> glowing in the sky. places where the rats don't race but rat out
> their days in a waterlogged stupor. places you can dive into from a height.
>
> there are places where a heart is megashared & its kitchens always full
> of foods. where babies name themselves. a place you cannot unknow …
>
> (2014: n.p.)

The world Robinson imagines is not wholly free of violence or fear. These are places where 'nobody dies', and 'in which the lives of happy & boring people unfold / day after day, where nobody writes anything down & nobody suffers'. The production of this world is not divorced from the production of our own: 'like a hybrid tea rose sewn / together in a factory in bangladesh & sold for eight hundred times its worth'. It is a utopia, but a perverse one, a world made not just for impossibly sublime objects, but for the unlovable, and everyone in between. It crosses the parallel lines of the real and the ideal, its desire moving across that gap which separates the world we live in from the one we can imagine, and which we can only speak about stupidly, repetitively, and therefore truly. But in order to really imagine such a world, we also have to find a way to overcome the obsession both with the event and with catastrophe which characterises so much love poetry and revolutionary thinking. A poetics of enduring love might help us to understand how worlds are built and not just destroyed; but such a poetics entails the surrender of the fantasy of omnipotence and singularity which redeems poets from their dependence on the objects that they cannot contain, and therefore seek to destroy.

What might such a poetics look like? As I have said, there are precious few examples of it: of mature love which is also infantile in its hopefulness. Robinson's poem echoes the refrain from Frank O'Hara's 'Ode to Joy', which has been looping in my head repeatedly over the past year. 'We shall have everything we want and there will be no more dying' (1995: 281). This is the most beautiful expression of an infantile wish for omnipotence and bliss that I can imagine. It reminds me of Spenser's characterisation in his 'Hymn to Love' of Eros as both a baby, and 'the eldest of the heavenly Peers'. Love is an ancient child who delights in play and presence, communicates through touch, hungers for fullness and experiences absence as pain. Infinitely old, and infinitely young, the figure of Eros—and O'Hara's refrain—urge us to believe that these desires are not immature, but love's final and interminable condition.

Keston Sutherland has described writing poetry in a similar spirit, as a response to the wish 'to break out from infinite emptiness, to escape from the absolute, fearful, disgusting and extinct identity of a dot lost in alien infinity' (2016: 109–10). He writes:

> There is no escape at last from that form of the subject for so long as we are in reality crushed, wasted and emptied out by capital, and not worked out by our own really free exertions of thinking, feeling and love, just as in reality there is no escape from death. But the work of struggling to explode that form and to produce an infinite and ineradicable act of defiance against it is somehow obscurely essential to poetic expression. … Poetry makes resound right now and in this world the promise of whatever we would risk this crushed life for. (110)

I started this lecture by admitting my scepticism about communised eros—a melancholic scepticism which picks through such statements with its long nails. But thinking about love poetry over the past year has helped me to understand Keston's wish, which is also O'Hara's. Love is the determination to make a world, which requires us also to risk destroying one. It is the belief that we *can* make love real on the edge of doom, can create a loving world that will sustain us. Behind us is the irrecoverable paradise of total fulfilment. Ahead of us is catastrophe. We are bound together in the present by all the things we lack, and by repetition: each time we profess our loves, we stand in the light of our particularity and all those whose gestures and care have kept us alive, and which we repeat and extend, bearing it out to the edge of doom. Love is the name for this desire to make a world, a world we must defend with all our wit, strength and festivity against the powers of death. As O'Hara puts it in his 'Ode: Salute to the French Negro Poets', 'the only truth is face to face, the poem whose words become your mouth / and dying in black and white we fight for what we love, not are' (1995: 305).

Bright star, would I were steadfast as thou art.

Standing—with militant love—against the killing by police of Alton Sterling (photo by Jonathan Bachman of Ieshia Evans in Baton Rouge).

Acknowledgements: I would like to thank Amy De'Ath, Sam Ladkin and John Wilkinson for their comments on an earlier draft of this lecture, and Isobel Armstrong for her generous response to my work. I am also grateful to Marlene Dumas for permission to use her fierce painting 'Hierarchy' in the publicity for this event.

REFERENCES

Abraham, Julie (1996), *Are Girls Necessary? Lesbian Writing and Modern Histories* (New York & London, Routledge).

Ahmed, Sara ([2004] 2014), 'In the Name of Love', in *The Cultural Politics of Emotion* (Edinburgh, Edinburgh University Press), 122–43.

Armstrong, Isobel (2000), *The Radical Aesthetic* (Oxford, Blackwell).

Badiou, Alain (2012), *In Praise of Love*, with Nicolas Truong, trans. Peter Bush (London, Serpent's Tail).
Barthes, Roland (1975), *The Pleasure of the Text*, trans. Richard Miller (New York, Farrar, Straus and Giroux); first published 1973.
Belsey, Catherine (1994), *Desire: Love Stories in Western Culture* (Oxford, Blackwell).
Benjamin, Jessica (1995), *Like Subjects, Love Objects: Essays on Recognition and Sexual Difference* (New Haven, CT & London, Yale University Press).
Berlant, Lauren (2012), *Desire/Love* (Brooklyn, Punctum).
Black, Jeremy (1998), *Reading Sumerian Poetry* (Ithaca, NY, Cornell University Press).
Brooks, Gwendolyn (1981), 'Black Love', *Ebony* (August): 29.
Butler, Judith (2012), *To Sense What is Living in the Other: Hegel's Early Love*, 100 Notes—100 Thoughts no. 66 (Kassel, Documenta 13).
Carson, Anne (1998), *Eros the Bittersweet* (Champaign, IL, Dalkey Archive Press).
Chessman, Harriet Scott (1989), *The Public is Invited to Dance: Representation, the Body, and Dialogue in Gertrude Stein* (Stanford, CA, Stanford University Press).
Cowper, William (1905), *The Complete Poetical Works of William Cowper*, ed. H. S. Milford (London, Henry Frowde).
Creeley, Robert ([1966], 1978), *Poems 1950–1965* (London, Marion Boyars), 159–60.
Donne, John (1932), *Complete Poetry and Selected Prose*, ed. John Hayward (London, Nonesuch).
Duncan, Robert (1944), 'The Homosexual in Society', *Politics* 1.7 (August); revised and expanded version, *Jimmy & Lucy's House of "K"* 3 (January 1985).
Fanon, Franz ([1952] 1986), *Black Skin, White Masks*, trans. Charles Lam Markmann (London, Pluto Press).
Fisher, Mark (2009), *Capitalist Realism, Is There No Alternative?* (Winchester, MA, Zer0 Books).
Fredman, Stephen (2009), *Contextual Practice: Assemblage and the Erotic in Postwar Poetry and Art* (Stanford, CA, Stanford University Press).
Freud, Sigmund ([1926] 2001), 'Inhibitions, Symptoms and Anxiety', in *The Standard Edition of the Complete Psychological Works*, vol. XX (1925–1926): An Autobiographical Study, Inhibitions, Symptoms and Anxiety, The Question of Lay Analysis and Other Works (London, Vintage).
Freud, Sigmund ([1929] 2001), 'Civilisation and its Discontents', in *The Standard Edition of the Complete Psychological Works*, vol. XXI: The Future of an Illusion, Civilization and Its Discontents, and Other Works (1927–1931) (London, Vintage).
Freud, Sigmund ([1953] 2001), *The Standard Edition of the Complete Psychological Works*, vol. VII: A Case of Hysteria, Three Essays on Sexuality, and Other Works, 1901–1905, ed. James Strachey (London, Vintage).
Freud, Sigmund ([1957] 2001), *The Standard Edition of the Complete Psychological Works*, vol. XI: Five Lectures on Psycho-Analysis, Leonardo Da Vinci and Other Works, 1910 (London, Vintage).
Graham, W. S. (2004), *New Collected Poems*, ed. Matthew Francis (London, Faber).
Halpern, Rob (2015), *Common Place* (New York, Ugly Duckling Presse).
Hegel, G. W. F. (1970), 'On Love', in *On Christianity: Early Theological Writings*, trans. T. M. Knox (Gloucester, MA, Peter Smith), 302–8.
Hesiod (2006 edn), *Theogony, Works and Days, Testimonia*, ed. Glenn W. Most (London & Cambridge, MA, Harvard University Press).
Heuving, Jeanne (2016), *The Transmutation of Love and Avant-Garde Poetics* (Tuscaloosa, AL, University of Alabama Press).
Holmes, Richard (ed.) (1996), *Shelley on Love: Selected Writings* (London, Flamingo for Harper Collins).
Howard, Henry Earl of Surrey & Thomas Wyatt (1965), *The Works*, ed. George Nott, 2 vols, vol. 1 (New York, AMS Press).
Hume, David ([1739] 2000), *A Treatise of Human Nature*, ed. David Fate Norton & Mary J. Norton (Oxford, Oxford University Press).

Hutchinson, Lucy (1996 edn), *Lucy Hutchinson's Translation of Lucretius, De Rerum Natura*, ed. Hugh de Quehen (London, Duckworth).
Keats, John (1935), *The Letters*, ed. Maurice Buxton Forman, rev. ed. (Oxford, Oxford University Press).
Keats, John (1970), *The Complete Poems*, ed. Miriam Allott (London, Longman).
Kelley, Robin D. G. (2016), 'What Does Black Lives Matter Want?', *Boston Review*, 17 August, http://bostonreview.net/books-ideas/robin-d-g-kelley-movement-black-lives-vision
Kierkegaard, Søren ([1843] 1987), *Either/Or*, Part I, ed. and trans. Howard V. Hong & Edna H. Hong (Princeton, NJ, Princeton University Press).
Kierkegaard, Søren ([1847] 1995), *Works of Love*, Kierkegaard's Writings Vol. XVI, ed. and trans. Howard V. Hong & Edna H. Hong (Princeton, NJ, Princeton University Press).
King, Martin Luther Jr. ([1967] 1981), *Strength to Love* (Philadelphia, PA, Fortress Press).
Lacan, Jacques ([1961] 2015), *Transference: The Seminar of Jacques Lacan, Book VIII*, ed. Jacques-Alain Miller, trans. Bruce Fink (Cambridge, Polity).
Lacan, Jacques (1965), 'Crucial Problems for Psychoanalysis', Seminar XII, in *Jacques Lacan in Ireland*, trans. Cormac Gallagher, http://www.lacaninireland.com/web/wp-content/uploads/2010/06/12-Crucial-problems-for-psychoanalysis.pdf
Laplanche, Jean (1976), *Life and Death in Psychoanalysis*, trans. Jeffrey Mehlman (Baltimore, MD, Johns Hopkins University Press).
Lear, Jonathan (1998), *Love and Its Place in Nature, A Philosophical Interpretation of Freudian Psychoanalysis* (New Haven, CT & London, Yale University Press).
Levinas, Emmanuel (2006), *Entre Nous: Thinking-of-the-Other*, trans. Michael B. Smith & Barbara Harshav (London & New York, Continuum).
Levinson, Marjorie (1988), *Keats's Life of Allegory; The Origins of A Style* (Oxford, Blackwell).
Loy, Mina (1997), *The Lost Lunar Baedeker* (Manchester, Carcanet).
Mackay, Peter (2010), *Sorley Maclean* (Aberdeen, AHRC Centre for Irish and Scottish Studies).
Maclean, Sorley ([1943] 1979), *Poems to Eimhir*, trans. Iain Crichton Smith (Newcastle, Northern House).
Marcuse, Herbert ([1955] 1972), *Eros and Civilisation* (London, Abacus).
Marriott, David (2013), *In Neuter* (Cambridge, Equipage).
Marvell, Andrew (2003 edn), *The Poems*, ed. Nigel Smith (London, Longman).
Montaigne, Michel de ([1603] 1965), 'Of Friendship', in *Essays*, trans. John Florio, 3 vols., vol. 1 (Dutton & New York, Dent).
Moten, Fred (2010), *B Jenkins* (Durham, NC, Duke University Press).
Moten, Fred (2016), 'Interview', *Lunch Ticket*, http://lunchticket.org/fred-moten-poet/
Nancy, Jean-Luc (2003), 'Shattered Love', in *A Finite Thinking*, ed. Simon Sparks (Stanford, CA, Stanford University Press).
Notley, Alice. (2015), 'This Fire', *Poetry* (July/August), https://www.poetryfoundation.org/poetrymagazine/poems/58234/this-fire
Nygren, Anders ([1930/36] 1953) *Agape and Eros*, trans. Philip S. Watson (SPCK, Westminster).
O'Hara, Frank (1995), *The Collected Poems*, ed. Donald Allen (Berkeley & Los Angeles, CA, University of California Press).
Plato (1999 edn), *The Symposium*, trans. Christopher Gill (London, Penguin).
Pozorski, Aimee L. (2005), 'Eugenicist Mistress & Ethnic Mother: Mina Loy and Futurism, 1913–1917', *Melus*, 30.3 (Fall): 41–69 https://doi.org/10.1093/melus/30.3.41
Riley, Denise (1985), *Dry Air* (London, Virago).
Riley, Denise (2000), *Words of Selves, Identification, Solidarity, Irony* (Stanford, CA, Stanford University Press).

Robertson, Lisa (2012), *Nilling: Prose Essays on Noise, Pornography, the Codex, Melancholy, Lucretius, Folds, Cities and Related Aporias* (Toronto, Bookthug).
Robertson, Lisa (2016), *3 Summers* (Toronto, Coach House).
Robinson, Sophie (2014), 'where the heart is streaming', *Morning Star*, (8 July), https://www.morningstaronline.co.uk/a-899d-Two-poems-by-Sophie-Robinson#.WQNWctLyvIU
Rodefer, Stephen (2008), *Call It Thought* (Manchester, Carcanet).
Rose, Gillian (1992), *The Broken Middle* (Oxford, Blackwell).
Rougemont, Denis (1983), *Love in the Western World* (Princeton, NJ, Princeton University Press); first published 1939.
Sartre, Jean-Paul ([1943] 1993), *Being and Nothingness*, trans. Hazel E. Barnes (London, Routledge).
Shakespeare, William ([1609] 1997), *The Riverside Shakespeare*, ed. G. Blakemore Evans, J. J. M. Tobin *et al.*, 2nd ed. (Boston, MA & New York, Houghton Mifflin).
Sidney, Philip (2004 edn), *Sidney's 'The Defence of Poesy' and Selected Renaissance Criticism*, ed. Gavin Alexander (London, Penguin).
Smith, A. J. (1985), *The Metaphysics of Love, Studies in Renaissance Love Poetry from Dante to Milton* (Cambridge, Cambridge University Press).
Sokol, B. J. (1988), 'The Symposium, Two Kinds of "Definition", and Marvell's "The Definition of Love"', *Notes and Queries*, n.s. 35, 169–70.
Spenser, Edmund (1999 edn), *The Shorter Poems*, ed. Richard A. McCabe (London, Penguin).
Stein, Gertrude ([1935] 1985), 'Poetry and Grammar', in *Lectures In America* (Boston, MA Beacon Press).
Sutherland, Keston (2016), 'Infinite Exhaustion', in *Brittle Land*, ed. Alexandra Navratil (Rome, Roma Publications & Berlin, Dan Gunn), 83–110.
Vendler, Helen (1999), *The Art of Shakespeare's Sonnets* (Cambridge, MA, Harvard University Press).
Weber, Max ([1948] 1991), *From Max Weber, Essays in Sociology*, ed. H. H. Gerth & C. Wright Mills (London, Routledge).
Whitebook, Joel (1995), *Perversion and Utopia: A Study in Psychoanalysis and Critical Theory* (Cambridge, MA, MIT Press).
Wieners, John (1988), *Cultural Affairs in Boston, Poetry and Prose 1956–1985*, ed. Raymond Foye (Santa Rosa, CA, Black Sparrow).
Wieners, John (1998), *Selected Poems 1958–1984*, ed. Raymond Foye (Santa Rosa, CA, Black Sparrow).
Winnicott, Donald W. (1953), 'Transitional Objects and Transitional Phenomena: A Study of the First Not-me Possession', *International Journal of Psychoanalysis*, 34(2): 89–97.
Winnicott, Donald W. (1971, 1991), *Playing and Reality* (London & New York, Routledge).

Note on the author: Andrea Brady's books of poetry include *The Strong Room* (Crater Press, 2016), *Dompteuse* (2014), *Cut from the Rushes* (Reality Street, 2013), *Mutability: Scripts for Infancy* (Seagull Books, 2012), and *Wildfire: A Verse Essay on Obscurity and Illumination* (Krupskaya, 2010). She is Professor of Poetry at Queen Mary University of London, where she runs the Centre for Poetry and the Archive of the Now. She is also co-publisher of Barque Press.
a.brady@qmul.ac.uk

To cite the article: Andrea Brady (2017), 'The determination of love', *Journal of the British Academy*, 5: 271–308.
DOI https://doi.org/10.85871/jba/005.271

Journal of the British Academy (ISSN 2052–7217) is published by
The British Academy—the national academy for the humanities and social sciences.
10–11 Carlton House Terrace, London, SW1Y 5AH
www.britishacademy.ac.uk

Journal of the British Academy, **5**, 309–329. DOI https://doi.org/10.5871/jba/005.309
Posted 16 November 2017.

We don't torture: Moral resolutions, temptation, and the doctrine of double effect[1]

Philosophical Lecture
read 3 June 2015

RICHARD HOLTON
University of Cambridge

Abstract: 'We don't torture', announced both Bush and Obama. But what Bush meant as a statement of fact, Obama meant as a statement of resolve. Exploring this example, this article examines how moral resolutions work to overcome the rationalisations that temptation engenders. This in turn sheds light on the the nature of our moral concepts. Resolutions are typically framed using intentional notions (torture, murder, theft). Reflection on the reasons for this provides a new perspective on what is right, and what is wrong, about the doctrine of double effect.

Keywords: resolution, resolve, torture, doctrine of double effect, intentional, rationalisation.

'We don't torture', said George W. Bush in November 2005.[2] His statement was a simple statement of fact, and it was false. The US had been torturing detainees, with the express permission of Donald Rumsfeld, the Secretary of Defense, since late 2002.[3]

In January 2009, on his second day as president, Barack Obama used the same words. It is possible that some torture was still then going on. But even if it was, Obama's words would not have been straightforwardly false, for he was using them in a different way, as the full quotation makes clear:

[1] Material from this paper was also presented to audiences at MIT, Cambridge, Sheffield, Southampton, Yale and LMU. I am very grateful for the comments received on those occasions, and to Rae Langton and Judy Thomson for comments on the written version.
[2] At a news conference in Panama City, 7 November 2005. For a further statement nearly two years later to much the same effect see *The New York Times* 6 October 2007: 'This government does not torture'.
[3] According to *ABC News*, 11 April 2008, Bush admitted that he was aware that his National Security Team had discussed 'enhanced interrogation techniques' including waterboarding. So it seems likely that he was not simply speaking falsely; he was lying.

> We believe we can abide by a rule that says, We don't torture, but we can effectively obtain the intelligence we need.[4]

The pragmatics here are complicated. In part Obama was reporting his conviction that torture was not required to obtain the intelligence that the US thought it needed. Beyond that, though, speaking as Commander in Chief, Obama's words had the force of a command not to torture, a command that was more clearly expressed in an executive order signed on the same day.[5] But they also had the force of a commitment, a first-person-plural version of the kind of thing that is more normally expressed in the singular: I don't lie, I don't steal, I don't cheat, I don't torture.

My focus in this paper is on this last idea, on the idea, as I shall call it, of the *moral resolution*. Resolutions are familiar enough in other domains. Temptation tends to corrupt judgement: under its lure our view of what is best will often shift. Resolutions help to prevent this. By committing, in advance, to a certain course of action, we remove the need for deliberation under temptation, and so reduce the risk of succumbing. Much the same happens, I will argue, with moral resolutions. In the heat of the moment—a provocation, a war, a major terrorist attack—judgements may be corrupted, so that some may be tempted to pursue policies—such as torture—that in a cool hour would have been seen to be wrong. It is by forming moral resolutions we can resist such slippage.

Moral resolutions are worthy of study in themselves, and part of my interest is in looking at how they work. I want, though, to do something more. I want to use moral resolutions to shed some light on the doctrine of double effect—on the doctrine that the intention with which an action is done can have some impact on that action's permissibility. In recent years that doctrine has come under sustained criticism from Judith Jarvis Thomson and Thomas Scanlon. The thrust of their criticism stems from the initially compelling idea that in deliberating whether an action is permissible, we should look outward, to the action and its consequences, rather than inward, to the actor's intentions. Thomson asks you to imagine that you are a doctor, deciding whether it is permissible to give a dying patient the fatal dose of morphine that he requests. She says:

> Suppose that, pursuant to the hospital's rules, you ask me—I am the appropriate hospital official—whether it is legally permissible for you to inject the lethal dose. I reply: 'Well, I don't know. I can't tell unless you tell me what your intention would be in injecting the drug. If you would be injecting to cause death, either as means or end, then no. But if you would be injecting only to cause relief from pain, then yes.' This is

[4] *The New York Times* 23 January 2009.

[5] The executive order required all interrogation to follow the *Army Field Manual,* a document that had forbidden torture for many years.

> an absurdity. How on earth could it be thought proper for the legal permissibility of acceding to turn on what the doctor intends to bring about by acceding? Surely it should turn on the patient's condition and wishes.[6]

In many cases asking after an agent's intention in such circumstances would indeed be absurd, and I will endeavour to give some explanation of why. Nevertheless, I think that understanding the role of moral resolutions shows that a purely outward focus—in this case on the patient's condition and wishes—is inadequate. When an agent is in a morally tempting situation that corrupts their judgement, focusing just on the merits of the case will often lead to moral disaster. Instead, they will need to go back to the resolutions they formed earlier. This will involve a focus on their intentions twice over: first, because their resolutions are themselves intentions; and second, because, since those resolutions will themselves typically be formed in terms of intentional actions, they will need to understand their current motivations if they are to decide whether they are sticking with them or not.

If it is right that effective moral actors will often need to look in to their own intentions rather than out to the world, that rather undercuts the Thomson/Scanlon argument against the doctrine of double effect. However, it does not by itself do anything to re-establish that doctrine. Even if it is true that, in situations of temptation, actors will often need to look to their intentions, it does not follow that we assess the rightness of their actions by whether or not they do so. If actors behave well without recourse to their resolutions, that is fine; we do not think that there is something missing. And even if they do look to their resolutions, why should we think that the content of those resolutions will need to allude to intentions? So if an account of moral resolutions is to underpin a defence of something like the doctrine of double effect, more will have to be said.

The final idea I explore here is that, if they are to be effective, resolutions must indeed make reference to agents' intentional actions; so they point us towards an account in which intentional actions provide the primitive bedrock upon which our moral judgements are built. Such an account does not support a literal-minded doctrine of double effect, since, in central cases, it denies that the same action can be performed with different intentions: change the intention and one changes the intentional action. But it captures what I take to be the truth in the doctrine: namely, that intention matters.

That, in outline, is my path. I start by looking at resolutions.

[6] Thomson (1997).

MORAL RESOLUTIONS

Why do we need resolutions even in simple non-moral cases? Why try to bind ourselves in advance? After all, it is surely rational to make a decision using all of the available information, including that which will only be available later. If we abstractly resolve at New Year to give up chocolate, that fails to take into account the information about just how attractive the chocolate will be each time it is actually offered, information that would be available if we were just to wait to decide each case on its merits. So wouldn't it be more rational to avoid resolutions altogether?

Most of us have enough self-knowledge to realise that there is something wrong with this line of thought. We know that the chocolate can *tempt* us: it can lead us to eat it when in prospect we didn't want to, and when in retrospect we will regret what we have done. One way to understand that is in terms of a shift in *desires*. The proximity of the chocolate, whether temporal or spatial, leads us to desire it more than we do when it is not close. But that is only part of what is going on. In addition, the presence of the chocolate influences our *beliefs*. If we start to think about it, we will convince ourselves that it will give us more pleasure than we had anticipated, or that the reasons for abstaining are not really so strong, at least not on this occasion. We can, after all, always give up chocolate tomorrow.[7] The rules governing our behaviour are almost never absolute—almost any rule will admit of exceptions. So, with a little ingenuity, we can almost always find the room for rationalisation and self-deception.

This means that resolutions have two complementary roles to play. They serve to enshrine our earlier desires and our earlier reasoning against the competition of the *desires* that arise in the moment of temptation. But, in addition, they serve to enshrine our earlier reasoning against the competition of the *reasoning* that we would do in the moment of temptation. That is why we should not open our resolutions up to reconsideration when the temptation is upon us. The empirical evidence bears this out. Dieters who form implementation intentions to see them through tempting moments—intentions such as 'If there are left-overs, I will freeze them immediately'—are more successful at losing weight than those who simply form the goal of losing weight. When they arrive at the tempting moment, their plan carries them though—more precisely, the presence of the left-overs serves as a cue to trigger the implementation of the action, and so the food goes into the freezer with scarcely a second thought. But if they add to the implementation intention a *because*-clause—'If there are left-overs, I will freeze them immediately *because I want to remain slim*'—all of the benefits are lost. Now the presence of the left-overs serves as cue to trigger not just an action but

[7] See my *Willing, Wanting, Waiting* (Holton 2009: Ch. 5) for a discussion of the empirical evidence on this.

also an awareness of the reason for that action. That in turn leads the dieters to reconsider that intention, and then to find a reason not to act on it.[8] Again, it is because the rules governing our behaviour are not absolute that we have the leeway to rationalise.

I suggest that much the same structure applies in the weightier cases of moral temptation, although admittedly here the empirical evidence is rather thin. Here too there is temptation to do the wrong thing, and since abstract moral principles invariably admit of plausible exceptions—that is something particularists are right about—there is room to rationalise. Resolutions are what stand in the way of such rationalisation. It is precisely because of the vulnerability of moral principles to exceptions that personal moral rules are so important.[9]

Some forms of moral temptation are obvious. People want things even though they know that they are not entitled to them—to take them would be stealing, or would involve cheating, or fraud or the like. In such situations normally morally upright people will sometimes rationalise modestly immoral actions, but the room to do so is limited, and so the misbehaviour is correspondingly limited. People will, for instance, take a can of Coca-Cola from a communal refrigerator—that is hardly stealing—but not the less valuable dollar bill that has been left there on a plate.[10]

Other cases of moral temptation are rather harder to spot, whether by actor or spectator. The temptation may not be driven by desire for personal gain. It may be driven by the desire to benefit others, or simply by the desire to be effectual, to get something done when one feels powerless. Such motivations bring us back to the dismal story of the authorisation of torture by the Bush administration.

Some think that torture is *never* morally justified. But, as anyone who has taught a first-year class on the subject knows, it is far from obvious that that is the case. It is easy to construct a story in which it looks as though torture may be permissible, or even required. A staple is the 'ticking bomb' case: a bomb has been planted that will kill millions of innocents; the only hope is to defuse it. The terrorist who planted it has been captured, but refuses to say where it is. Time is short.

Should the terrorist be tortured in an effort to find the bomb? Opinions differ, but many think that torture here may well be morally justified; and for those who resist such a conclusion, it is easy to increase the numbers at risk from the bomb (What if it

[8] Wieber *et al.* (2011).

[9] Particularists standardly go further and say that moral principles invariably admit of genuine, rather than merely apparent, exceptions; I am sympathetic, but remain neutral on the issue here. For the canonical statement see Dancy (1983). Clearly I am not inclined to conclude from this that moral principles have no useful role.

[10] Ariely (2012). He presents a vivid set of empirical studies on the role of self-deception in maintaining a morally justifiable self-image, and on the constraints on it—the extent of the moral wiggle room.

were half the world?) and the nastiness of the terrorist (What if he is gloats over the destructiveness of the bomb, which he designed to cause maximum suffering?).

Nevertheless, if such a 'ticking bomb' had been planted by a combatant in wartime, torture would be legally prohibited. The Third Geneva Convention allows for no exceptions. Is this because the framers of the conventions never considered ticking-bomb cases or their like? Or because, whilst the framers were aware of them, they thought it clear that torture in any such case would be morally wrong? Either is possible, but it seems unlikely that such substantial moral claims would have been built into conventions that were designed to be universally adopted. More likely the framers of the conventions thought that, although ticking-bomb cases and their ilk could arise, the chance of them actually occurring, and moreover of the people involved correctly identifying them, is small. In contrast, once exceptions that allow for torture are in place legally, the likelihood that they will be unjustifiably exploited is large. Just as dieters do better if they do not reconsider their diet at the moment they are tempted to eat, so, in time of war, combatants do better if their personal rules forbid torture. Likewise legal policies do better by blocking torture in all cases, since, if it is allowed in exceptional cases it is all too easy to come up with a story that in this case things really were exceptional. Policy on torture needs to be made in times of peace, and then adhered to in times of war.[11]

This is certainly the view of many who have been involved in conflict. Two former Marine Generals, Charles Krulak and Joseph Hoar, wrote in *The Washington Post* that 'Complex situational ethics cannot be applied during the stress of combat. The rules must be firm and absolute; if torture is broached as a possibility it will become an actuality.'[12] A failure to see this seems to be part of what happened during the Bush 'war on terror'; or at least, that is the most charitable gloss that can be placed on those events. Let us recall what happened. The US had fought two world wars, and then wars in Korea and Vietnam, in many cases against armies that were systematically

[11] It is striking that all of the four of the treaties that constitute the Geneva conventions were drafted in response to war. The first, which laid down rules to govern the treatment of the wounded and sick, was drafted in 1869 after the Crimean War and the Battle of Solferino. The second, which extended the rules to cover war at sea, was drafted in 1907 as the tenth Hague Convention, after the Russo–Japanese war. The third, which dealt with the treatment of prisoners of war, was drafted in 1929 after the First World War. And the fourth, which dealt with the treatment of civilians during war was drafted in 1949 after the Second World War, a time at which the three earlier treaties were all extensively revised. In each case the treaties tried to make good the shortcomings that the wars had revealed in earlier agreements.

[12] Krulak & Hoar (2007). Jeff McMahan (2008) also makes the point that the theoretical possibility of cases in which torture may be justified should not lead us to put into place institutional policies that ever allow torture (see pp. 124ff). What I am adding to this institutional claim is the idea that this reflects a general feature of resolutions, applicable even in the personal case.

using torture, without itself using torture as an officially sanctioned policy.[13] This changed in 2002 when, under the direction of Donald Rumsfeld, it became explicit policy to reconsider the practice of interrogation, in particular to investigate the use of so-called 'enhanced' techniques.[14] The result was the endorsement of a set of methods of interrogation—including throwing people against walls, facial slaps, stress positions, cramped confinement, sleep deprivation and, most notoriously, waterboarding—that most certainly counted as torture by international standards.[15]

The level of self-deception that occurred once the question of whether to torture was opened up is striking: The Office of Legal Counsel (OLC), whose role it is to give legal advice to the executive, came up with a bizarrely restrictive account of what would constitute torture. If physical it would require pain 'of an intensity akin to that which accompanies serious physical injury such as death or organ failure'; if mental it would require suffering bringing 'lasting psychological harm, such as seen in mental disorders like post-traumatic stress disorder'. As it stands, such a definition is scarcely coherent: death is not a form of serious physical injury; it is rather something that may result from such injury; and neither death nor organ failure need be painful. More substantially, even if something along these lines were properly formulated, it would have no precedent in US or international law, as the OLC could surely have seen. Other features of the OLC advice on the legality of torture were equally deluded: an attempt to defend it via an application of the doctrine of self-defence that was clearly legally hopeless, and an insistence, later overturned by the Supreme Court, that detainees at Guantánamo fell outside the scope of the Geneva Conventions.[16]

[13] That is not, of course, to say that US personnel never tortured in those wars; but it was never official policy. For extensive documentation of the role of the UK, France, and the US in developing and deploying 'clean', i.e. non-marking, torture, see Rejali (2007).

[14] For an account of how Rumsfeld put in place a team of interrogators and lawyers who would open these questions see Sands (2008). Rumsfeld's task was doubtless made easier by the writings of theorists—Alan Dershowitz (2002) being the most prominent—who advocated the legalising of torture in ticking-bomb-style cases. For a more recent example, see Allhoff (2012). What is striking about this latter work is that an author whose basic motivation is consequentialist seems so utterly unconcerned about the consequences that his writing might have for those who are likely to torture in circumstances in which even he would think them unjustified.

[15] See Sands (2008). For a compelling first-person account of how awful waterboarding is, see Hitchens (2008).

[16] For discussion, see Sands (2008). Again, for the purposes of this article I give the most charitable diagnosis, the one that makes those involved least culpable. I am not sure that we should be so charitable, but many do see it this way. Thus Deputy Attorney General Joseph Margolis in his decision that John Yoo, one of the OLC team, should not face disciplinary action from the Pennsylvania Bar, wrote that 'loyalty to his own ideology and convictions clouded his view of his obligation to his client and led him to author opinions that reflected his own extreme, albeit sincerely held, views of executive power while speaking for an institutional client'. Margolis, 'Memorandum for the Attorney General', 5 January 2010, available at: judiciary.house.gov/issues/issues_OPRReport.html.

The connection between the official authorisation of torture and the general treatment of US detainees, most centrally at Abu Ghraib, remains controversial. But there is much evidence that there was influence, so that, as Krulak and Hoar put it:

> As has happened with every other nation that has tried to engage in a little bit of torture—only for the toughest cases, only when nothing else works—the abuse spread like wildfire, and every captured prisoner became the key to defusing a potential ticking time bomb … any degree of 'flexibility' about torture at the top drops down the chain of command like a stone—the rare exception fast becoming the rule. [17]

Those who advocate rules that permit torture in ticking-bomb cases and the like are keen to insist that it will be carefully regulated; but that assumes that the regulators will be immune to self-deception in the face of temptation, something that the behaviour of the OLC during the Bush presidency should make us doubt.

Why did this happen? Why did the Bush administration endorse torture during the 'War on Terror' after a century of conflict in which it was prohibited? There may be many factors in play. I suggest a central one was that the administration succeeded in convincing itself that things were sufficiently different that any prior resolutions—whether encapsulated in legal rules or in less formal moral thinking—simply did not apply. This was a new world, with a new kind of enemy, one to be treated in a completely different way. In retrospect, that looks absurd. But that was not how things seemed to some at the time, or, indeed, how they still seem to some now.

The approach I have been developing bears some similarities to rule utilitarianism, so let me conclude this section by stressing some differences. Rule utilitarianism insists that we sometimes have utilitarian reasons to abide by rules even if the immediate result looks to be a reduction in utility: overall, we increase pleasure if we stick to a rule of always telling the truth, even if we can find particular cases in which lying brings more pleasure. An obvious difference in the approach I am advocating is that it need not be utilitarian: resolutions can serve to protect moral thinking of any kind. A prohibition on torture can be grounded in both utilitarian and non-utilitarian considerations. But, second, and most relevant here, rule utilitarianism is typically presented as a response to the difficulties involved in calculating what action is best, and this often leads to the thought that it is a policy patronisingly enforced upon the less able by the more able. In Bernard Williams's memorable phrase, it brings with it a whiff of Government House.[18] In contrast, self-deception in the face of temptation is

[17] Krulak & Hoar (2007). Henry Shue (1978) made a similar point about the likely spread of torture a long time ago. For discussion of the links between the torture policy authorised by Rumsfeld and the treatment of detainees at Abu Ghraib see Sands (2008) and Jeremy Waldron (2005). Waldron develops the idea of anti-torture law as an 'archetype', that fits well with the account presented here.

[18] Williams (1985: Ch. 6).

something to which we are all vulnerable. While we might hope that regulators will suffer from it less than most, they are far from immune, as the Bush White House shows. They needed the framework provided by prior resolutions; but they turned their back on them.

There is a further charge that is often levelled against utilitarianism, which is that it may well be a self-effacing policy: to be an effective utilitarian agent, one would need to believe that utilitarianism is false. Here again what I am advocating is different. To refuse to reconsider a resolution in times of temptation is not to turn against the use of reason; it is merely to turn against its use under those circumstances, exactly because those are circumstances in which it cannot be exercised well. It may be that simply trying to decide whether or not these are tempting circumstances will be enough to trigger reconsideration, in which case the disposition to stick to one's resolutions cannot itself involve the exercise of reason. But even that does not entail a rejection of reason.

My argument has been premised on the idea that ticking-bomb cases are rare, and that those that can at the time be identified as such are much rarer still. But what should happen if one really were to occur? What should an interrogator do if it was clear that very many lives were at risk, and that torture was the only likely way of saving them? I have no easy answer, just as I have no easy answer for what in general one should do if it seems that breaking one's resolutions, or breaking the law, would be best. In trivial cases, like dieting or exercise, there is always a trade-off between the resoluteness needed to avoid judgement shift, and the risk of becoming inflexibly bound to a policy that should in some circumstances be broken. The real problem in such cases is the descriptive one of explaining how we can generally succeed in not reopening a question, while at the same time remaining vigilant for those cases where we should—a phenomenon which I suspect is best explained by positing two somewhat independent systems, a conscious system of deliberation, and a second unconscious alarm system, which can trigger the first when a threshold is crossed (compare the fuel gauge on a car with the warning light that signals a nearly empty tank). In many such cases it does not matter if the alarm system goes off too readily, causing an unwarranted re-evaluation: the odd indulgence is not going to cause any harm.

In cases of potentially justified torture we cannot be so glib. If a ticking-bomb case really arose, those confronted with it would have to decide what to do, and then the judiciary and the community would have to decide how to treat them in the light of what they had done. I think that they should certainly be liable to criminal prosecution, even if we conclude that what they did was justified, although of course this should be recognised in sentencing. We can only hope that such a case will not arise, since pre-emptively building provision for it into the law will make things much worse. This is one area in which we can embrace the maxim that hard cases—hard hypothetical cases—make bad law.

So much, for now, for moral resolutions. Let us change direction for a while, and examine some recent work on the doctrine of double effect.

THOMSON AND SCANLON ON DOUBLE EFFECT

In its classical form, the doctrine of double effect is the claim that the moral standing of an action, most centrally its moral permissibility, can turn on the intentions of the agent. More specifically, it is that claim that there are certain acts with two effects (the 'double effect'), where acting with the intention of achieving one of them is permissible, while acting with the intention of achieving the other is not. Many discussions of the doctrine have focused on reactions to particular cases. So, for instance, some have argued that dropping a bomb with the intention of destroying a legitimate military target may be permissible, even if it is known that civilians will be killed (the war is just, the target important, there is no other way of destroying it, etc); whereas dropping the bomb in exactly the same place with the intention of killing those civilians is not. Others have disagreed. Stalemate looms.

Clearly we cannot rest with simple intuitions at this level. Judith Jarvis Thomson and Thomas Scanlon have tried to undercut the doctrine of double effect more fundamentally while explaining its apparent appeal. Their arguments are my concern here. I start with Thomson.

Thomson

Thomson makes use of a distinction between the evaluation of agents, and the determination of what is permissible: 'the question whether it is morally permissible to do a thing is just not the same as the question whether the person who does it is thereby shown to be a good person.'[19] When it comes to evaluating agents—to deciding whether they are kind, or generous or principled—it is quite right to take into account their mental states, including the intentions under which they act. In contrast, when we determine the permissibility of an action we should not, as a matter of course, look to the intention of the agent who performs it. Sometimes intentions will be relevant—they may be relevant, for instance, in determining whether someone has made a promise, and that will be important in determining what is subsequently permissible. Less directly, intentions may give information about how wholeheartedly or carefully the agent will pursue the action, and that too might be relevant to its permissibility. But in the absence of special features like these, the proper evaluation of the

[19] Thomson (1997: 517).

permissibility of an action will proceed without reference to intentions. Proponents of the doctrine of double effect, who think that intentions will in general affect the permissibility of an action, have thus run together two very different things.

Thomson gives examples to support her argument. One case: suppose we had found out that Eisenhower was sending US troops onto the beaches of occupied France, not with the intention of liberating Europe, but with the intention of getting many of them killed. Would that have been a reason for trying to get the invasion cancelled? It might have been indirectly—a general with these intentions would hardly be a reliable military planner. But suppose we could be assured that the plan would be in no way compromised. Then, argues Thomson, we would have no reason cancel the invasion.[20] The permissibility of the action rests on what will happen, not on the intentions with which it is performed.

Thomson's second example we have already encountered. Consider a dying patient whose agony can only be relieved by a dose of morphine so strong that it will kill him. Does the permissibility of giving the dose depend on the intentions of the doctor? As we saw, Thomson argues that it does not. In thinking that it does, we conflate the evaluation of the agent with that of the action:

> If a doctor will inject her patient intending his death as an end and, moreover, wants his death only because his death will constitute revenge, then that does matter morally. But we have to be careful about how it matters. I suggest that it has no bearing on whether it is morally permissible for her to act. Whatever her intention may be, the patient, we are supposing, desperately wants her to inject the drug.[21]

We should agree with Thomson that there is an important distinction between evaluating the agent and evaluating the action, and that intentions may be relevant to the former when they are not relevant to the latter. And I am also inclined to agree that it is hard to see much moral difference between intending to end the patient's pain with the knowledge that this will kill him, and intending to end his pain by killing him. However, that in itself does not show that intentions will *never* make the difference between the permissibility and impermissibility of an action. If Thomson wants to extend her argument to cover *all* cases, it has to encompass, as she accepts, the case where the doctor is motivated solely by desire for revenge. Should we accept what Thomson says there?

Suppose that, rather than being a hospital official, you are the local prosecutor, and you come across compelling evidence that the doctor's sole motivation in giving the injection was revenge. Would you be justified in instigating a murder prosecution against her? It strikes me that you would; indeed, you would be failing in your job if

[20] Thomson (1997: 516, n.19).
[21] Thomson (1997: 516).

you did not. Of course, in doing so you would almost certainly be making some assessment of the doctor's character. But I take it that that would not be the ground of the prosecution. We prosecute on the basis of the wrongness of the action, not on the defectiveness of the character. Killing from revenge is murder, and that is about as wrong an action as you can get.

Things might look somewhat different from the perspective of the hospital official, though not, I think, fundamentally so. It is a little difficult to fill out the case, since it is hard to imagine that any doctor would go to an official to ask if it is permissible to kill a patient from revenge: it is rather obvious what the answer would be. Suppose then that the official independently knows of the doctor's motivation, and is faced with the question of whether to let her go ahead. If the official's primary concern is the good of the patient, and this can only be achieved by allowing the doctor to give the injection despite her vengeful motivation, then perhaps this is the course that the official should approve. But it is hard to imagine that such advice could be given without qualm, even putting aside any concerns the official might have about becoming an accomplice. If there were any other way of achieving the good end—changing the roster of doctors, for instance, so that a compassionate one would be in charge of the patient—then surely that would be the course to take.

There would, I think, be fewer qualms in the imaginary Eisenhower case: Thomson is surely right it would have been unthinkable to call off the invasion on discovering the nature of Eisenhower's intentions. A sufficient explanation of the difference may simply be that the outcome of the invasion was so much more important than any question of Eisenhower's misdeeds. A second factor is that, whilst Eisenhower was at the centre of planning the invasion, it wasn't just his project. If it turned out that everyone involved in its organisation, from Roosevelt and Churchill down, was motivated primarily by a desire to kill Allied troops, then we might find some pressure to think rather differently; but to imagine that is to imagine a situation so bizarre that it is hard to know what to think.

This is a further difference. The vengeful doctor presents us with a clear case of murder. During a war, in contrast, it is much harder to say what is and is not murder. Of course there are murders committed by combatants during wars, on non-combatants, on combatants who have surrendered and the like. But once killing becomes morally acceptable, as it does in a legitimate war, our conception of murder becomes much harder to apply. Even a killing that is parallel to the doctor case, motivated entirely by considerations of personal revenge, is less obviously murder when the two protagonists are combatants in a legitimate war: the war provides a justification that the individual would lack. We might describe Eisenhower's motives as murderous in the envisioned circumstances, but this is more of a rhetorical move than a substantial one.

Is it important whether we can see an act as an instance of murder? I think it is—just as it was important in our earlier discussion whether an act was an instance of torture. We will return to this issue a little later. But first I want to introduce Thomas Scanlon's considerations on the topic, and to say some more about the general idea that questions of permissibility of action should look outward and not inward.

Scanlon

In a generally very sympathetic discussion of Thomson's approach, Scanlon objects that the crucial distinction is not between the evaluation of an action and the evaluation of an agent: his worry is that when we are concerned with particular actions, we can recognise that an agent is good, and that their motivation is good, but still think that they have made a morally bad decision. So in place of Thomson's distinction, Scanlon wants to draw a new one between the role of principles as *guides to deliberation* and their role as *standards of criticism*; or, in short, between the *deliberative* stance and the *critical* stance.[22]

The basic idea is this: when we assess the moral standing of a possible action there are two different things that we might be doing. The first, taking the deliberative stance, involves us in looking, as if from the point of view of the actor, at the considerations for and against that action. That is what actors themselves do, but it is not limited to them; it is also what we do when we give them advice. The second, taking the critical stance, involves assessing the way that an agent goes about deciding on a particular action. Scanlon's contention is that when we take the critical stance in this latter way, intentions are relevant. But when we take the deliberative stance, they are not. When an agent deliberates what to do, they cannot look to their own intentions as relevant factors, and nor can we cite their intentions in giving them advice. (We put aside cases where the intention makes a difference to the obligations that the agent is under: for instance, where they have made a promise.)

Furthermore, according to Scanlon, the issue of permissibility concerns only the first, deliberative, question. Putting these two contentions together then takes him, via a somewhat different route, to much the same conclusion as Thomson's. For while we may take their intentions into account in *criticising* an agent, Scanlon holds that the proponent of the doctrine of double effect makes a mistake in saying that intention is relevant to the *permissibility* of the agent's action.[23]

[22] Scanlon (2008: 20–5).

[23] At times Scanlon seems to *identify* the deliberative question with the question of what is permissible: 'As guides to deliberation, moral principles answer a question of permissibility: "May one do X?"' (2008: 22). I am not happy with phrasing this entirely in terms of permissibility, which I think has a firmer place in a legal setting than in much ordinary moral thought. We might think, from the deliberative position,

There is something plausible in this, an insight that Scanlon's account shares with Thomson's. Surely agents cannot make actions permissible just by forming the right intention: they cannot bootstrap them into permissibility. Returning to our earlier example, the bomber pilot who wanted the civilians dead could surely not think 'It is impermissible to drop the bomb intending the deaths of civilians, but it is permissible to drop a bomb with the intention of destroying the military target, so that's what I'll intend' and thereby make the action permissible. But then equally, we might think, having formed a certain intention in the past should not make any difference. If an action is permissible this is something that is determined by how the world stands, independent of the mental life of the actor (again we put to one side special cases like having made a promise). The focus of moral deliberators should be outward, towards the world, and not inward, towards their own states of mind. We might think worse of the bomber pilot who intends the death of the civilians, but in answering the deliberative question of whether it is permissible to drop the bomb, this is beside the point.

LOOKING OUTWARD AND MORAL RESOLUTION

Despite the plausibility of these considerations, in the light of what I said earlier about moral resolutions, I do not think that this way of putting the point can be right. It cannot be the case that in deliberating about how to act, or in advising others on how to act, we should always look out to the world, rather than in to the agent's intentions. Very often, if I am to act well, I will need to deliberate by looking to my moral resolutions. Similarly, when we ask someone for moral advice, it may be that the best they can give is to point us back to our resolutions. 'We don't torture' may have been the best thing that the Bush administration could have been told. But resolutions are just a special sort of intention. It follows that we will need to look to our intentions.

It might be objected to this that the content of the resolution is just the moral rule, and not the intention to follow that rule, so that morally resolute agents are not really looking to their resolutions, but to the rules beyond them. On this approach, in resolving not to torture, an agent comes to believe that torture is wrong; the resolution just serves to preserve that belief. That, however, is to misunderstand the role that resolutions need to play. I suggested that the agent who resolves not to torture may well think that there could be situations in which torture would be morally justified. So

that it would be better not to perform some selfish act, without thinking it actually impermissible to do so. Scanlon suggests that talk of the good is only apt for evaluation and not for deliberation (24–5); again, I do not see why. But I will stick mainly with talk of 'permissible', together with its its dual, 'not permissible not', i.e. obligatory, and their negations.

reminding themselves of a moral rule that might admit of exceptions would not do the work that is required; on the contrary, it may well make things worse, since it would encourage further deliberation about whether the rule should apply in this case, deliberation that might well culminate in the conclusion that it should not: that was what we saw in the dieting case. What the agent needs is the resolution, which is essentially self-regarding: *I* do not torture; or, perhaps better, since it gives the individual commitment the backing of group solidarity: *We, the members of this community,* do not torture, which was the idea I attributed to Obama.

This provides an important corrective to the idea that moral deliberation should only look out to the world. In itself, though, it provides no support to the doctrine of double effect. For the advantages given by resolutions that we have considered so far are merely pragmatic: they enable us to avoid temptation. Perhaps they also confer an epistemic advantage: they enable us to keep in touch with the moral truth. But from what we have seen so far, they do not make any difference to the permissibility of an action: their existence does not make an action permissible or impermissible.[24]

There is, however, a further consideration. How should we understand the content of resolutions? They do not, by their nature, have to make reference to intentional actions. While I might resolve not to murder or to torture, it seems that I could equally resolve not to kill, or resolve not to cause suffering. My suggestion, though, is that to be effective resolutions will need intentional contents. Recall that, in Thomson's hospital case, things seemed to change once we raised the possibility that the doctor was in the business, not just of killing the patient, but of murdering him. Murder is an intentional notion. Let us turn once again to that.

INTENTIONAL CONCEPTS

When Thomson and Scanlon insist that permissibility of an action is independent of the actor's intention, I take it that they are committed to thinking that the action can be identified independently of that intention. But can we identify actions independently of intentions? Many verbs, especially those that are used in moral assessment, build in intentions: 'to murder'; 'to steal'; 'to rape'; 'to defraud'; 'to mock'; 'to cheat'; 'to torture'; 'to humiliate'. The contrast is with non-intentional verbs like 'to drop' or 'to kill'. As a first approximation, we can think of the non-intentional verbs as those that we can prefix with modifiers like 'unintentionally' or 'inadvertently' without causing bafflement. We can straightforwardly say that someone unintentionally

[24] Scanlon sometimes talks this way; e.g. 'what *made* the action wrong was not that I have acted for a bad (selfish) reason' (2008: 24; his emphasis).

killed, but it would be rather odd to say that they unintentionally murdered. Conversely, adding the modifier 'intentionally' to a non-intentional verb adds content. To say that someone intentionally killed is to say more than that they killed; whereas to say that they intentionally murdered is to say no more than that they murdered. Exactly which intentions are needed for the application of any of these verbs is often a matter of debate: does murder require that one is trying to kill, or that one is reckless about whether one will? Such debates have echoed around both legal and informal usage. But there is no serious debate that there is some intentional requirement built into the very notion of murder.

Empirical psychological findings show that moral assessment and the use of intentional descriptions are intimately tied up: people tend to use 'higher level', intentional descriptions when a good thing is done by someone they like ('tipping generously'), but 'lower level' non-intentional descriptions when the same thing is done by people they don't like ('adding extra money to the bill'); the tendency is reversed if it is a bad thing done.[25] Moving away from intentional descriptions is a way of moving away from moral attribution altogether.

If opponents of the doctrine of double effect think that intention is not relevant to permissibility, then presumably they must think that even if we naturally characterise actions using intentional concepts when we morally evaluate them, if we want to properly evaluate their permissibility we should strip them down to a corresponding thin non-intentional concept. That assumes that we can do so: it assumes that where we have an intentional action, to φ, there will be a equivalent description, to intentionally ψ, where 'ψ' is a non-intentional verb; and it is the permissibility of ψ-ing that we need to assess. But can we strip concepts down in this way?

It may be possible in any *particular* case to give a non-intentional description of a bad action in such a way that it is clear what is wrong with it. But can we give a *general* characterisation that would serve to feature in a resolution? Consider how we might try to formulate a non-intentional resolution that would do the work done by a resolution against torture. It will not do just to formulate it as 'We will treat our detainees as well as circumstances permit', since clearly those who are inclined to torture will argue that these circumstances do require it. So we might go to the other extreme of specificity and say: 'We do not inflict waterboarding on detainees', 'We do not deprive detainees of sleep', etc. But, whilst admirably clear, and hence well proofed against the attempt to provide exceptions, that would be much too limited; it would just be an

[25] Kozak *et al.* (2006). To be clear: the authors do not identify 'higher level' descriptions with the intentional; they rather think of them in terms of a by-construction: one does a relatively higher level action by doing an appropriate lower level one. Nevertheless, in the examples that they give, the higher level actions are typically intentional, the lower level ones typically not ('She tipped generously by adding extra money to the bill').

invitation to invent new tortures. Or we might try to characterise actions in terms of their effects: 'We do not cause pain or humiliation to our detainees', etc. But that is too broad. Mere capture will be humiliating to many, and a certain amount of pain may be the unavoidable result of keeping people secure, and of providing the medical care that they need. The natural response at this point is to say that they should not be hurt or humiliated *on purpose*; but with which purpose? People should not be hurt or humiliated, one might say, with the purpose of torturing them, which takes us back to where we started. If it is to be effective, the resolution needs to strike a balance between being too open ended, which will lead to too much reconsideration, with all of the risks of self-deluded rationalisation, and too specific, which will get the extension wrong. It will need to be, as we might say, *sufficiently predictive* of moral wrong-doing. My claim is that only the intentional notion of torture can play the needed role here.

There is nothing, apart, perhaps, from its awfulness, that is special about torture. Though I will not argue the case here, I suggest that much the same account can be given of the other core intentional notions that feature in our moral and legal thinking: to murder, to steal, to rape, to defraud and the like. These too are intentional for a reason; and we can get an insight into that reason by looking at their role in resolutions. If they are to feature in resolutions that have the right kind of force, they will need to be intentional.

Note that I am not saying that being intentional is good enough for a concept to play this role. We can create intentional notions by simple prefixing 'intentionally' onto non-intentional ones. From 'to drop' we can create 'to intentionally drop'; from 'to kill' we can create 'to intentionally kill'. That will not do the work. Return to Thomson's case of the doctor and the dying patient. In that case, I argued, it made all the difference if we saw the doctor's act as an act of murder. So one resolution that we might expect people to have—one that we might hope would go without remark in any decent person—is a resolution not to murder. Is that the same as a resolution not to kill? Absolutely not. The compassionate doctor who is prepared to use euthanasia sometimes has a resolution not to murder but no resolution not to kill. Her critic might, of course, argue that euthanasia is murder; but that is a substantial moral claim, and one that such a doctor will reject.

I have argued elsewhere that these intentional concepts are prime, in the sense that they cannot be factored into a mental element—the *mens rea*—and an outcome—the *actus reus*.[26] I will not repeat that argument, which is modelled on Williamson's argument about knowledge.[27] Let me just distinguish it from a rather more familiar claim

[26] Holton (2015); revised version forthcoming in Gardner *et al.*
[27] Williamson (2000).

with which it might be confused. It is sometimes claimed that concepts like murder are morally 'thick' in that they combine both descriptive and evaluative content: describing something as a murder (rather than just a killing) is to express one's moral disapproval.[28] About that I have my doubts. It seems to me that a sufficiently perverse god might make it morally right for me to murder, by, say, hanging the fate of the rest of the human race on whether I will do so. Indeed, if something like moral particularism is correct, it will be possible to arrive at such cases for any concept. At most there may be some *prima facie* disapproval, but even there it does not seem incoherent (rather than utterly morally perverse) for someone to argue that murder is in general a good thing. In contrast, my claim is that we cannot deny the intentionality of murder—the idea that it has a *mens rea*—although we might, of course, dispute exactly how that is to be understood.

DOUBLE EFFECT RECONCEIVED

If this is on the right lines, then the debate around the doctrine of double effect looks rather different. As we saw, the standard move in trying to assess it is to take apparently identical actions, and then to vary the intention with which they are performed: the actor does the same thing, but with a different intent. Then a judgement is made about whether the two cases differ in their permissibility. The defender of the doctrine says that sometimes the permissibility does differ; the opponent says that it does not. My contention has been that this approach is methodologically flawed. If actions are to be characterised in intentional terms, holding the action fixed whilst varying the intention is not in general possible. To that extent, then, both supporters and critics of the doctrine have been working with a false presupposition when describing such cases.

The picture that we have in its place is of numerous different intentional concepts that we invoke when we make moral judgements. Intentions matter because these concepts matter, and they are intentional. To that extent, the defender of the doctrine of double effect has got something right. This is not to say that we have a fixed number of such intentional concepts, and that moral reasoning simply consists of applying them. The process of moral reasoning has involved refining the ideas we have (so that a killing may be a murder if it is done inadvertently but recklessly, but will not be if done in necessary self-defence; or an act of theft is not blameworthy, though it is still

[28] For a set of recent essays on the idea, see Kirchen (2013). Note that neither Ryle (1968, 2009), who is often taken as the originator of this approach, nor Geertz (1973), who has done so much to develop in within anthropology, thought of thick concepts as exclusively moral in this way. Plausibly, though, they did both think of them as intentional.

an act of theft, if it is done under sufficient duress). Sometimes mere refinement is not enough: the concept of sexual harassment simply was not around fifty years ago, but we have it now. Having it has enabled us to gain moral insight that was formerly obscured, and to form resolutions—how to act, but also how to respond to others' acts—in consequence.[29] Other concepts that once figured large in our moral thinking have now largely dropped out: for instance, the idea of honour. Just as with science so with ethics: progress requires us to get our conceptual vocabulary right.

There is thus no guarantee that every case will be covered by some relevant intentional concepts; and even if it is, there is no guarantee that our corresponding moral evaluations will be right. Much of the controversy concerning permissibility concerns exactly the cases that are not so covered: cases, for instance, around euthanasia, or the ethics of war, where much of the debate about double effect has taken place. It could be that we have yet to develop the relevant intentional vocabulary here: advances in medical technology make that not implausible in the former case at least; perhaps the same can be said of warfare, although there, while the methods have become way more efficient, the basic issues look largely unchanged. If no such development is forthcoming, we have to do the best we can using the standard combination of intuitive responses and general-purpose principles.

My surmise will be that in such cases intentions will turn out to matter little to permissibility; those are the cases to which Thomson and Scanlon devote much of their discussion, and that loom large in discussions of double effect more generally. But we will fail to see what was right about the doctrine of double effect if we fail to see that the categories we apply in more familiar terrain are shot through with intentionality.

CONCLUDING COMMENTS

I have taken a rather winding path: from the role of resolutions, to the nature of the actions in terms of which those resolutions should be framed, to the role of intentions in moral permissibility. I am sure that that is not the only path that I could have taken to any of these conclusions. Rather than looking at intentional notions through the lens of resolutions, I could have looked at them more directly in terms of moral evaluation. There is something, I hope, to be gained, though, in looking at a topic from a slightly less familiar direction. Thomson and Scanlon have greatly improved our discussion of double effect by focusing on deliberation and advice; my contention has been that here too intention, and resolution, have a central role to play.

[29] For a philosophical discussion, see Fricker (2007).

REFERENCES

Allhoff, Fritz (2012), *Terrorism, Ticking Time-bombs and Torture* (Chicago, IL, University of Chicago Press).

Ariely, Dan (2012), *The Honest Truth about Dishonesty* (New York, Harper).

Dancy, Jonathan (1983), 'Ethical Particularism and Morally Relevant Properties', *Mind*, 92: 530–47. https://doi.org/10.1093/mind/XCII.368.530

Dershowitz, Alan (2002), 'Want to Torture? Get a Warrant', *The San Francisco Chronicle*, 22 January.

Fricker, Miranda (2007), *Epistemic Injustice: Power and the Ethics of Knowing* (Oxford, Oxford University Press).

Gardner, J., Green, L. & Leiter, B. (eds) (forthcoming), *Oxford Studies in Philosophy of Law*, Vol 3. (Oxford, Oxford University Press).

Geertz, Clifford, (1973), 'Thick Description: Toward an Interpretive Theory of Culture', in *The Interpretation of Cultures: Selected Essays* (New York, Basic Books), 3–30.

Hitchens, Christopher (2008), 'Believe Me, It's Torture', *Vanity Fair*, August, http://www.vanityfair.com/politics/features/2008/08/hitchens200808

Holton, Richard (2009), *Willing, Wanting, Waiting* (Oxford, Oxford University Press).

Holton, Richard (2015), 'Crime as Prime', *Law and Ethics of Human Rights*, 9: 181–93.

Kirchen, Simon (ed.) (2013), *Thick Concepts* (Oxford, Oxford University Press).

Kozak, M., Marsh, A. A., & Wegner, D. M. (2006), 'What Do I Think You're Doing? Action Identification and Mind Attribution', *Journal of Personality & Social Psychology*, 90: 543–55. https://doi.org/10.1037/0022-3514.90.4.543

Krulak, Charles & Hoar, Joseph (2007), 'It's Our Cage Too: Torture Betrays Us and Breeds New Enemies', *The Washington Post*, 17 May.

McMahan, Jeff (2008), 'Torture in Principle and Practice', *Public Affairs Quarterly* 22: 111–28.

Rejali, Darius (2007), *Torture and Democracy* (Princeton, NJ, Princeton University Press).

Ryle, Gilbert (1968), 'The Thinking of Thoughts', *University Lecture* 18 (Saskatoon, University of Saskatchewan, 1968); reprinted in his *Collected Essays 1929–1968* (London, Routledge, 2009), 494–510.

Sands, Philippe (2008), *Torture Team* (New York, Palgrave Macmillan).

Scanlon, Thomas (2008), *Moral Dimensions* (Cambridge, MA, Harvard University Press).

Shue, Henry (1978), 'Torture', *Philosophy and Public Affairs*, 7(2): 124–43.

Thomson, Judith Jarvis (1997), 'Physician-assisted Suicide: Two Moral Arguments', *Ethics,* 109: 514–15.

Waldron, Jeremy (2005), 'Torture and Positive Law: Jurisprudence for the White House', *Columbia Law Review*, 105: 1681–750.

Wieber, Frank, Gollwitzer, Peter M., Gawrilow, Caterina & Oettingen, Gabriele (2011), 'Intending to Lose Weight: Benefits of Why Reasoning and Implementation Intentions', ms.

Williams, Bernard (1985), *Ethics and the Limits of Philosophy* (London, Fontana Press).

Williamson, Timothy (2000), *Knowledge and Its Limits* (Oxford, Clarendon Press).

Note on the author: Richard Holton is a Professor of Philosophy at the University of Cambridge, and a Fellow of Peterhouse. He works primarily on moral psychology, ethics, philosophy of law and philosophy of language. Recent publications include *Willing, Wanting, Waiting* (OUP 2009). He is currently working on a book on moral kinds.
rjh221@cam.ac.uk

To cite the article: Richard Holton (2017), 'We don't torture: Moral resolutions, temptation, and the doctrine of double effect', *Journal of the British Academy*, 5: 309–329.
DOI https://doi.org/10.85871/jba/005.309

Journal of the British Academy (ISSN 2052–7217) is published by
The British Academy—the national academy for the humanities and social sciences.
10–11 Carlton House Terrace, London, SW1Y 5AH
www.britishacademy.ac.uk

Journal of the British Academy, **5**, 331–355. DOI https://doi.org/10.5871/jba/005.331
Posted 29 November 2017.

Burial mounds of Scythian elites in the Eurasian steppe: New discoveries

Albert Reckitt Archaeological Lecture
read 1 December 2016

HERMANN PARZINGER
Fellow of the Academy

Abstract: This article is dedicated to the phenomena called 'kurgans', the monumental burial mounds of riding nomads of the Scythian period. Kurgans were first investigated in southern Ukraine and southern Russia, the core area of Scythian tribes according to Herodotus. East of the Ural Mountains, however, the kurgans are less known, as only very few of these monumental burial mounds have been decently excavated. In the last 20 years, however, several Russian–German projects under the author's leadership have been dedicated to a better understanding of monumental kurgans in the steppe belt of Eurasia—Kazakhstan, southern Siberia, the Ural region and the northern Caucasus—contributing an enormous amount of new information about the complexity of these burial monuments. It has become clear that these elite burial monuments are not only important for rich funerary goods but also for the complex structure of the kurgans themselves, which only can be fully understood if they are considered as rituals which became architecture.

Keywords: Eurasia, steppe belt, Scythians, kurgans, monumentality, elites, riding nomads.

The relics of ancient rider-nomads of the 8th–3rd centuries BC, the older Iron Age, hold a special position in the study of the cultural development of the Eurasian steppe belt, for in them a clear social stratification can be recognised for the first time in the history of this area. The power and rank of individual members of the ruling class are manifested above all in their burial customs and monumental grave structures, as well as in the incredibly rich grave goods. These innumerable golden objects and valuable imported goods leave no question about the high standing accorded these elites by their communities. This phenomenon appeared first during the Scythian period; there were no true forerunners in preceding Bronze Age cultures in this area.

SCYTHIAN ROYAL GRAVES IN THE NORTH PONTIC STEPPE

Royal graves of the Scythians first became known in the steppe area north of the Black Sea.

Since the late 19th century, archaeological research in this area has been engaged in excavating dozens of magnificently furnished large grave mounds, known as 'kurgans'. Although many kurgans were plundered in antiquity and in later times, exceptional objects buried with the deceased and discovered again and again are indicative of the presence of resplendent graves. Quite often the earth heaped up to build a kurgan reaches a height of 12–15 m, for which reason such mounds can be seen as an enormous communal achievement: a large number of people had to be assembled, organised for work, and provided with accommodation and food.

The kurgans were built on the grass sod of the steppe, and most were stabilised with an additional stone circle at the base. The slopes were often finished with mud packing and a stone mantle. It is estimated that in Chertomlyk on the Lower Dnieper River, one of the largest kurgans, the grass sod had to be cut over a surface area of more than 75 ha in circumference in preparation for construction. This also relays an impression of the actual aim of kurgan structures: the prince symbolically took his pasture with him into death, or into life after death. The pasture was thus a personal possession of the prince, just like his personal objects, followers and horses (Rolle 1979, Grakov 1980: 60 ff., Rolle *et al.* 1998: 28 ff.).

The Scythians in the northern Black Sea region buried their dead in catacombs underneath the kurgans, which could be entered through a passageway—a *dromos*. In large kurgans this could be very complex and varied. Not infrequently, the *dromos* led to a catacomb that was 10 to 18 m deep and connected to further side chambers in which components of the grave furnishings, graves of the followers or horses were deposited.

The grave chambers of these exceptionally large kurgans seldom corresponded entirely with one another with regard to their structure and arrangement. In the famous kurgan at Solokha, which was almost 18 m in height, the main grave was in the centre, and had been plundered over the course of time. To the right and left of the entrance shaft were two catacombs: in one were the remains of the deceased, clothed in a garment ornamented with sewn-on gold platelets; in the other were some of the funerary furnishings, including bronze cauldrons, gold-covered wood cups, silver *kylikes* (wine cups) and Greek amphorae. A further, even more intricately built, catacomb, located in the southwest of this kurgan, had not been robbed. A long passage ran from the entry shaft towards the north to the grave chamber, which was 'guarded' by two youthful warriors. On the north wall of this main chamber, in a side niche just before the royal interment, was a further warrior, equipped with a sword, spears and quiver (*goryt*), perhaps the arms bearer or bodyguard of the royal interred. This person, buried in a side niche in the east, was laid to rest with all of the status symbols of a Scythian leader: a golden neckring, golden bracelets, a gold-sheathed *akinakes* (dagger), a sceptre shaft in the right hand, numerous decorated gold platelets sewn onto the clothing, bronze and silver tableware, Greek drinking vessels and much more. Another side chamber contained even more wine amphorae (Grakov 1980: 57 ff.).

The heaped earthen construction of the kurgan in Chertomlyk had similar dimensions to the mound in Solokha. Both are dated to the 4th century BC. In the centre of this kurgan was an entry shaft that led 10 m downwards (Figure 1), onto which clover-leaf-shaped, elongated rounded catacombs opened in all four corners. In the southeast were wine amphorae and a bronze cauldron and garments decorated with gold platelets; in the northeast were six more amphorae and a skeleton with a quiver and clothes garnished with gold appliqués. Two skeletons lay next to each other in the southwest catacomb (probably servants or guards), their clothing and weapons likewise decorated with gold. Finally, in the northwest was the skeleton of a female (probably the wife of the king), whose garment was studded with sheet-gold bearing figural decoration. Although the interments had been plundered, numerous gold objects remained behind, among them the gold appliqués on the clothing, the golden sheath of a quiver displaying a scene from the Achilles myth, and two swords with golden hilts. Three further pits containing a total of eleven horses with gold and silver bridles were discovered to the west of the main chamber (Grakov 1980: 60 ff.; Rolle *et al.* 1998: 28 ff.).

Large kurgans with large grave inventories rich in gold objects are no rarity in the lower Dnieper region and may be deemed characteristic of the Scythian elite in this area. Such monuments include the Tolstaya Mogila, Soboleva Mogila, Babina Mogila,

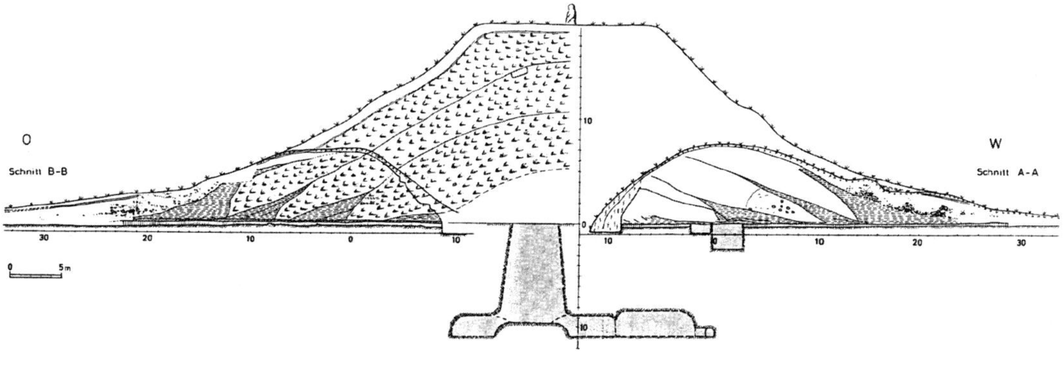

Figure 1. Reconstruction of the kurgan at Chertomlyk, combining historical drawings and results of modern excavations (Rolle *et al.* 1998).

and the Oguz kurgans, as well as complexes in Aleksandropol, Melgunov, Ryzhanovka and many more places. All date mainly to the 4th century BC (Rolle 1979; Grakov 1980: 53 ff.; Mozolevskiy & Polin. 2005). These royal Scythian kurgans, listed here as representative of many others, demonstrate, on the one hand, that in all parts of the Eurasian steppe the leading class of rider-nomads received special treatment upon their death, while, on the other hand, the particularities of grave construction and funerary equipment could follow quite different traditions. The status of the ruling class was likely the same everywhere, yet the symbols that expressed this status differed considerably in the various regions. This is underlined by the results of the research projects that we began in the late 1990s in various parts of southern Siberia; these were especially concerned with the architecture of these monuments.

THE GREAT KURGAN OF BAIKARA IN NORTHERN KAZAKHSTAN

This kurgan is located in the north Kazakhstan steppe, far to the east of the Ural Mountains. It stood in the middle of an expansive Scythian cemetery of kurgans. As the excavation results show, this complex was not a real kurgan but, far more, a sanctuary, in which a complex ritual had taken place, leaving behind archaeologically discernible traces (Parzinger *et al.* 2003).

The erection of the Baikara kurgan in the 5th/4th century began with the preparation of the surface for the later mound (phase 1). An approximately circular ditch was dug that surrounded an area cleared of steppe grass and topsoil, and with the subsurface clay exposed everywhere. An entrance in the southeast led from above to the kurgan's interior. It extended into a *dromos*, which led downwards like a ramp, then ran for a few metres as an underground, tunnel-like, passage only large enough to crawl through, and finally to two steps at the end, near the centre of the mound and the former earthen surface. There the passage was adjoined to a short plank walkway that ended in front of 27 stone net-weights in the centre of the mound's original surface. The weights were from a fishing net that had been deposited there. To the north of the weights was a rather shallow oval pit, laid out with bast mats. Eleven postholes were found in the western half of the kurgan's surface. Apparently eleven wooden posts had been positioned there, onto which perhaps objects had been attached that were of significance for cultic activities (Parzinger *et al.* 2013: 12 ff.).

At a later time the dromos and the pits were filled and closed, and the wooden posts in the west removed (phase 2). The complex had now fulfilled its purpose. Finally, the entire inner surface of the kurgan was covered with several layers of birch bark, giving it a yellowish-white appearance. This surface was surrounded by a stone wall, which opened in the southeast, where the passage through the circular ditch was also located (Parzinger *et al.* 2013: 36 ff.).

The erection of the actual kurgan likely followed directly at this time (phase 3). The structure consisted of grass sod and was covered with a massive layer of clay, upon which a stone mantle was laid, whose edges adjoined the stone wall. Thereby, the kurgan was not a wholly symmetrical complex: it was somewhat higher and steeper in the west half than in the east half. Hence, the east side was better suited for ascending the kurgan, which, in turn, underscores that access to the kurgan must have occurred from this direction. It is noteworthy that there were cavities and hollow spaces in the interior of the kurgan. Three passages—a larger one from the south and two somewhat narrower ones from the north—led to the centre of the mound and were passable only in a crouched position. They must have originally joined in a central room; however, this space was completely destroyed by a later Sarmatian grave shaft. The passages were built of a post framework together with wattle on the walls and ceiling and with birch bark on the ground (Parzinger *et al.* 2003: 50 ff.).

When the passageways and the central room were no longer of significance, the supporting posts were removed, causing them to collapse; the depressions that gradually appeared on the surface of the kurgan were evened out (phase 4). The kurgan regained its original form, yet with a somewhat higher and steeper half in the west (Figure 2, see over). Directly west of the mound's centre, a stone platform, almost rectangular in form, was erected, which served as the basis for a structure built of a reddish, fired clay–sand mixture. Possibly, this conical form was meant to be like that found in the two smaller pits of phase 1. It can be assumed, perhaps, that cultic activities were performed in the surroundings of this stone platform with its reddish conical crown. Yet, due to later disturbance and restructuring of this area in Sarmatian times, no remains have been preserved (Parzinger *et al.* 2003: 36 ff.).

With phase 4, the Scythian-period form of this kurgan, which is dated to the 5th/4th century BC, was complete. The temporal interval between phases 1 and 4 was probably quite brief, but it cannot be determined precisely. The fact that the individual phases in the building work related to one another and therefore stood in conjunction supports the argument that they were planned as such from the very beginning and that lengthy intervals between the phases were unlikely.

Accordingly, we can conclude that at the very beginning of kurgan construction a burial ceremony was enacted with a dromos and symbolic grave pit, which were then closed off, before the actual building of the kurgan commenced. The kurgan had three passages and one central room in the interior, which had no practical function and can only be understood as part of cult ceremonies, but which can no longer be reconstructed. In the final phase 4 of the kurgan, the stone platform and conical mound upon it, the latter of a reddish clay–sand mixture, were visible from afar in the green

Figure 2. Baikara, Phase 4 (Parzinger *et al.* 2003).

steppe, as described by Herodotus. He wrote of mounds in honour of the war god, on which an iron short sword stood upon a platform made of twigs, which symbolised this deity. Herodotus further emphasised the asymmetrical form of the mounds: one side was easier to access. This corresponds with the sanctuary of Baikara. Even though Herodotus' description cannot explain the find context at Baikara, unique among kurgans of Scythian times, it does show that such complexes could have played an important role not only in funerary ceremonies but also as sanctuaries.

THE ROYAL MOUND OF ARZHAN IN TUVA

These observations, which were indeed new, made it necessary to investigate large kurgans in other sub-regions of southern Siberia in order to learn more about their architectural development, attendant rituals and related symbolism. It was decided to study the kurgans in Tuva, the most southeasterly area in Siberia to be reached by rider-nomads bearing a marked Scythian material culture. The core questions were: at what point in time and under what influences did groups of rider-nomads with their characteristic way of life and economic forms, their new techniques in warfare, special artistic forms of expression and hitherto unknown social differentiation, as displayed in their monumental grave mounds, appear? Within the Eurasian steppe belt we can trace this process of change, which substantially reformed Bronze Age traditions that had developed over centuries, at the earliest in Tuva on the upper course of the river Yenissei. The cemetery of Arzhan is located in northern Tuva, one of the largest and most important cemeteries in southern Siberia, with countless monumental grave mounds.

The first large kurgan there, Arzhan 1, was excavated by M. P. Griaznov in the 1970s. This monumental burial complex comprised a platform built of stone, almost 100 m in diameter and only 3–5 m in height. Revealed underneath this platform was a wooden construction (Figure 3), still unique today, which consisted of numerous rectangular to slightly trapezoidal chambers arranged radially in several rows around the centre. The timber grave chamber in the centre was surrounded by eight wooden

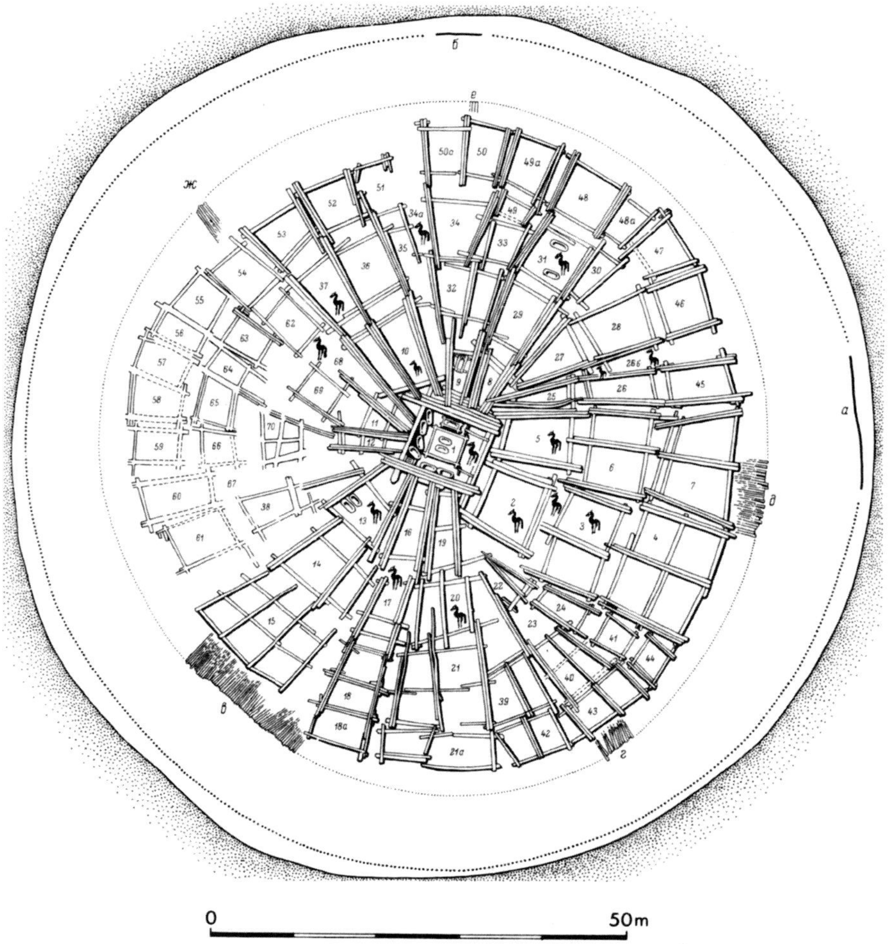

Figure 3. Arzhan 1, reconstruction of the looted kurgan (Griaznov 1984).

coffins, which evidently contained the interred entourage, which upon the death of the ruler was slain and placed with him in the grave, as described by Herodotus in his writings about the Black Sea Scythians. Buried in various chambers grouped around the central grave were more than 200 horses, which likewise counted as possessions of the royal pair or were sacrificed during the burial ceremony in their honour (Griaznov 1984).

The burial place for the prince and his wife in the centre of the kurgan was found in an almost completely plundered state. Nevertheless, indications of splendid furnishings were discovered: remnants of marvellous garments made of sable fur, various coloured woollen textiles as clothes, bags and belts, and also gold jewellery, hundreds of gold appliqués sewn onto the clothing and a myriad of turquoise inlays that likely originally enhanced massive gold objects that were taken when the grave was plundered. Of special note are the remaining bits of weaponry: bronze daggers and arrowheads made of bronze and bone, whose forms directly follow in the tradition of Late Bronze Age forerunners and which must therefore stem from the very beginning of the Scythian period. This is supported by the observation that the handle ends of the daggers already bear ornamentation in the so-called animal style. For example, one representation is of a boar in 'tip-toe' gait, a motif that is characteristic of the very beginning of the Scytho–Siberian animal style, whose earliest phase is recorded only in southern Siberia (Griaznov 1984). Dendrochronological analyses on the beams in the grave chamber enable a reliable dating of Arzhan 1 kurgan to the end of the 9th and early-8th century BC.

Research on this burial place thus brought forth the hitherto oldest, firmly dated, early Scythian material known in the Eurasian steppe. Tuva and bordering parts of southern Siberia are therefore likely to have played a decisive role in the emergence of the material culture of the rider-nomads of the older Iron Age. All of the features that characterise Scythian culture farther west emerged here first. This applies to the material culture and the typical animal style, as well as to the burial customs typifying special treatment of the ruling class, the erection of monumental kurgans, the practice of family members and attendants following the leader into death, and the splendid grave inventories of gold and other prestigious objects.

Members of this rider-nomad ruling class were buried in Arzhan over a longer time span; perhaps the beginnings of dynasties even developed there. It is noteworthy, for example, that among the hundreds of grave mounds only four kurgans were built with stone platforms, each at a distance of 3–4 km from one another and arranged in a line from west to east. Kurgan Arzhan 1, farthest to the west, is the oldest mound, while Arzhan 2 kurgan in the far east was the last mound to be erected and apparently the youngest, dated to the close of the 7th century BC.

During the excavation of Arzhan 2 kurgan, between 2000 and 2003, we did not find the grave of the royal ruler in the centre but, instead, on the northwest periphery of the mound (burial 5). The fill and the stone covering of the 5 × 5 m large shaft were found in an undisturbed state, already signalling an untouched grave (Figure 4). At a depth of about 4 m the beam cover of the grave chamber came to light. It was in an undisturbed state as well; only the end in the south had collapsed slightly, due to the weight of the fill. Exposure of the chamber showed that under the first beam cover was a second beam cover, built of even sturdier trunks, which lay transversely to the upper ones. Inside the outer chamber was a further inner chamber. Very little earth lay in the area of the head and chest. The four interior walls of the inner chamber were originally draped with coloured textiles, of which only sparse remnants were still preserved. Upon the carefully finished wooden floor lay a double burial: a male in the northeast and a female in the southwest. Originally the floor was covered with a black felt carpet. The bones of the interred were not very well preserved. The heads of both the deceased had shifted backwards at an angle; evidently they had originally been laid upon cushions, which had long since decomposed (Čugunov *et al.* 2003, 2006, Parzinger 2006: 613).

The man wore a massive neckring of gold, which was decorated all round in the animal style. Soldered to the widened square-view side of the ring were countless small figures of panthers. The upper garment, presumably a cloak with a short upright

Figure 4. Arzhan 2, elite grave 5 after the first cleaning.

collar, was ornamented with thousands of small panther figures. They were sewn onto the chest and back of the garment as well as the sleeves in curvilinear arrangement, thereby rendering the impression of a winged-like ornament. Although the man's leggings were not preserved, he obviously wore long trousers made of felt or leather, decorated with thousands of tiny golden beads (diameter ca. 1 mm). The trouser ends were inserted in knee-high boots that ended in broad gold cuffs. Behind and underneath the man's head were five flat animal figures made of gold with drop-like enamel inlays (four winged horses and one stag), which were fastened to his hat. His weaponry comprised an iron dagger, worn on the right hip. Restoration of the dagger revealed that its handle and blade were decorated with remarkable gold inlays that represented animal figures (tigers, panthers and ungulates). The dagger was attached with a cord to a belt; the belt and the cord also bore numerous ornaments of cast gold with the animal-style decoration.

Next to the left-hand side of the interred body lay a golden quiver (Figure 5). The wooden arrowshafts were painted in alternating blue and red bands. The severely corroded three-winged arrowheads were made of iron, and—as revealed during restoration—traces of gold can be recognised and they were decorated with animal images. The carrying straps of the quiver were likewise rich in gold mountings. Finally, the remains of the bow were found underneath the quiver. Between the quiver and the northeast chamber wall lay an iron battle pickaxe with a wooden shaft. The shaft was almost completely covered with spiral gold incrustations. Deposited to the left of the man's head and above the quiver was a small round bronze mirror (Čugunov *et al.* 2003, 2006, Parzinger 2006: 613).

The grave furnishings of the woman also included a bronze mirror, placed to the left of the head. It was somewhat larger than the man's mirror and had an organic handle decorated with gold. In the area of her head, as part of a headdress, three gold plates

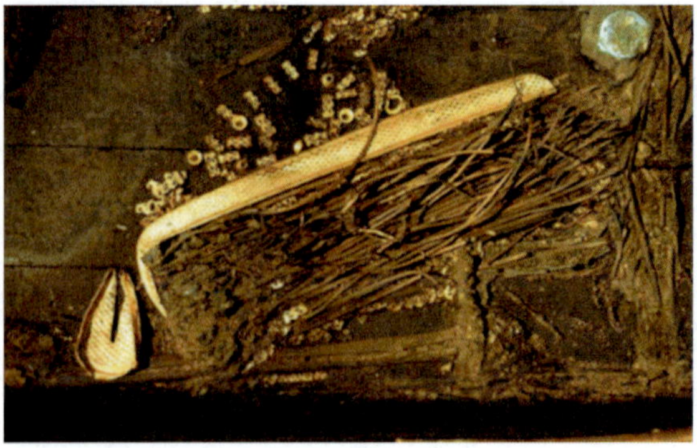

Figure 5. Arzhan 2, detail from the northeastern corner of grave 5 with the man's weaponry.

were found, in openwork and decorated in animal style. The same designs are seen in a pair of gold pins, two masterpieces: the shafts are completely decorated in animal style and crowned, in one case, with an exquisitely worked figure of an animal and, in the other, with a stylised winged creature. The woman's upper garment resembled that of the man, with thousands of small panther figures arranged to form a winged-like ornament. Unlike the man's upper garment (with cast gold panther figures), chased gold panther figures were sewn onto the woman's garment. Lying in the chest area were innumerable beads made of garnet, malachite, gold and paste, and, in addition, two gold earrings with granulation. The lower clothing of the woman was not preserved, only a few beads were present that indicate a skirt that likely reached over the knees. Thousands of millimetre-sized gold beads were concentrated in the area of the feet together with two gold bands with granulation and enamel inlays, which suggest boots made of leather or felt. Like the man, the woman had an iron dagger, worn on the right hip. Its blade was incrusted with gold, and its handle was of solid gold with representations of animals (panthers). Suspended from the woman's belt on a finely worked fox-tail chain was a gold, miniature cauldron, also with animal-style decoration. To the right and above the woman, near the west chamber corner was a wooden cup with a golden handle, the woman's golden comb with wooden teeth, and her gold pectoral decorated in animal style; several leather sacks held the remains of food that had originally been packed in them (Čugunov *et al.* 2003, 2006).

The royal grave in Arzhan 2 kurgan, with almost 9000 objects, ca. 5600 of which are made of gold, is one of the richest grave inventories found in Siberia and in the Eurasian steppe as a whole. The double burial of the man and woman contained, aside from thousands of golden panthers attached to clothing, gold-ornamented hats and boots, a gold neckring, a golden pectoral, gilded weapons and much more. Many of these objects may be considered masterpieces of the early animal-style art. Yet, these pieces are especially interesting, because they do not display any influences from other cultural spheres outside this region. Indeed, they represent local creations from the early Scythian period in Tuva (Čugunov *et al.* 2003, 2006).

Furthermore, Arzhan 2 kurgan yielded numerous graves of the Scythian period, which can be viewed as those of the violently slain followers and attendants of the ruler (so-called '*Totenfolge*'), as well as one grave with fourteen horses. Moreover, located in the centre of the kurgan were two graves that were completely empty. To their south was a rectangular sacrificial fireplace encircled by stones, and standing in its vicinity were two extremely schematic warrior stelae (so-called 'deer-stones or '*Hirschsteine*'). The southeast periphery of the kurgan also has a gallery made of stone slabs that display different representations (animals, parts of armament, a chariot, etc). Doubtless the kurgan was not solely a place for burial, but also a place of cult, a sanctuary, in which the interment of the royal pair and the violent slaying of their followers, in connection with different cultic activities, were 'staged' (Čugunov *et al.* 2003, 2006).

THE LARGE KURGAN OF BARSUCHIY LOG IN KHAKASSIA

Following the Yenissei River downstream from its source in Tuva and crossing the western Sayan Mountains to the north, we reach a totally different kind of landscape —the Minusinsk Basin, most of which today belongs to Khakassia with a small part in the Krasnoyarsk region. Throughout time the fertile valleys and plains in this region, with their relatively mild climate, have been densely settled. During the Scythian period the concentration of population in the area is especially noticeable, as attested by the thousands of 'corner kurgans' of the Tagar culture (8th–3rd century BC). Whether with or without a heaped earthen mound, with or without graves of the upper class or of ordinary people, these burial grounds consistently display stone slabs and tall stone stelae in the corners and along the sides.

Our knowledge of the Tagar culture in the Minusinsk Basin is based primarily on graves. Evidently, the monumental kurgans, in which members of the upper class were interred, were not erected until the late Tagar culture (5th–3rd century BC). In the preceding centuries—that is during the early Scythian period—they are found in Tuva adjoining to the south, but as far as represented in the present state of research they are absent from the Minusinsk Basin. The rulers of this region were buried in the expansive necropolis of Salbyk, a steppe landscape on the left banks of the Yenissei River and north of Abakan, the present-day capital of Khakassia. Located in this landscape are the largest kurgans in the entire Minusinsk Basin—more than a dozen monumental mounds made of sods and with a square ground plan, and enclosed by megalithic-like stone settings consisting of horizontal slabs alternating with standing stones and large stelae of several metres' height.

One of the large kurgans in Salbyk was excavated in the 1950s; the grave, however, had been robbed. Underneath the corners of the monumental stone enclosure a human 'foundation deposit' was discovered: the bones of adults and children. Sunken into the ground in the western half of the kurgan was a beamed chamber with a pyramidal wooden roof structure as a cover, which had evidently been accessible for further burials over a longer timespan—a tunnel-like passage led from the west through the sod kurgan to the chamber. It was later brought to collapse, when the grave chamber was permanently sealed. Unfortunately, due to insufficient documentation, few details are known about the kurgan's structure. The total plunder of the grave chamber thwarts closer insight into the burial equipment of a royal grave in the Minusinsk Basin.

In order to fill the gaps in research on this important region of finds in southern Siberia, a project was undertaken in 2004, dedicated to the comprehensive study of the Barsuchiy Log kurgan, located 35 km north of Abakan and not far from Salbyk. Although excavations have been conducted in the Minusinsk Basin for almost 300 years, this was the first time that one of the monumental burial complexes of the Tagar culture of the Scythian period was investigated with modern excavation and documentation materials. The Barsuchiy Log kurgan, still ca. 10 m in height, is a peculiarity among Eurasian large kurgans due to its pyramidal shape. In addition, it has a ca. 55 × 55 m large enclosure with an entrance in the east, built of massive stone slabs, a characteristic feature of the Tagar culture in this region. Investigations revealed that the kurgan was built of grass sod, as was likely the case with the large mound in Salbyk. However, the outer mantle of the Barsuchiy Log kurgan consisted of orange-red clay blocks; thus, it was visible from afar in the steppe as a red pyramid (Figure 6).

However, before this pyramid was built, two wall-like platforms were erected upon the original surface of grass sod with an access (*dromos*) to the grave chamber in between. This dromos was built of massive larch beams insulated with birch bark. Due to its excellent state of preservation, many building details can be documented. The passage led from the west to the grave chamber, likewise built with massive beams

Figure 6. Barsuchiy Log, sections through the kurgan.

Figure 7. Barsuchiy Log, the intentionally burnt burial chamber.

and covered with birch bark. The chamber was ca. 7 × 7 m in area and almost 5 m deep in the west half of the kurgan's inner surface. After the deceased had been laid upon the floor of the grave pit, at a depth of more than 4 m, the wood grave chamber was set alight (Figure 7) and allowed to collapse into the pit. After that the actual kurgan was constructed.

The construction of the kurgan was not accomplished in one course of building work, but—similar to the kurgan in Baikara—in several stages. Accordingly, in the west half of the complex the two aforementioned platforms were first built on both sides of the dromos, while from the east, at about the same height, a stone pavement led to the grave chamber. Several wooden columns, 6 m in height, were set up north of the construction, their bases initially inserted in colossal birch drums like column bases. After the cultic rituals connected with the installation in Barsuchiy Log had ended, the wooden columns were dismantled, laid next to their bases and together with the entire kurgan covered with red clay blocks in a single phase of work.

All of the large kurgans in the steppe north of Abakan between Salbyk and Barsuchiy Log display huge, funnel-shaped, looting pits west of the mound's centre.

Through investigations in Salbyk and Barsuchiy Log, we know that the burials were located precisely in this area. The grave robbers knew this as well, and they undertook enormous earth-moving activities. This extreme effort is actually quite unusual for looting activities in recent centuries and perhaps Barsuchiy Log provides an explanation for this: the grave place in Barsuchiy Log was completely ravaged, numerous skeletal components were missing, and the few that remained were scattered about in disorder. At the end of this destruction, the robbers deposited the head of a dog in the pit, dating into the 1st century BC (on the basis of radiocarbon dates) and therefore belonging to a period immediately after the Tagar culture. This deposition of dogs or their heads in plundered Tagar burials can be deemed characteristic of the Tes culture, which came after Tagar culture, and which is linked with the Hsiung-nu. In any case, the Tes people represent another population group that entered the Minusinsk Basin from the southeast from 200 BC. Evidently, the pillage of these large kurgans occurred at a considerably earlier time than was previously thought. Several factors suggest that the intent of these new intruding groups was to open and rob the royal graves of earlier rulers in the region and, in the sense of a *damnatio memoriae*, to desecrate the graves, and with that to break the sacred power of the former lords before the eyes of their people and then implant their own. When so much energy is invested in the destruction of kurgans and the annihilation of their significance, then this underscores all the more impressively the profound meaning that these burial monuments must have had for the population who built them.

ROYAL KURGANS OF THE SAKA AND THE SAUROMATIANS

Another important province for finds of Scythian rider-nomads in the Eurasian steppe belt is the steppe region west of the Altai Mountains, which extends as far as the Irtysh River. One extraordinary grave, rich in gold furnishings, is known from this region: the royal grave of Issyk, located ca. 50 km east of Almaty, in the southeast of Kazakhstan, in an area ascribed to the Saka. The earthen mound of this kurgan reaches 60 m in diameter and 6 m in height. Located underneath was the central burial, which had been completely looted, but next to it was a further grave complex that had remained undisturbed. This was the grave of a Sakan prince dated to the end of the 6th/early-5th century BC. In the north a young man of Europoid type had been laid to rest in a rectangular chamber built of carefully carpentered larch beams. He lay in an extended supine position, as is typical for nearly all Scythian graves found between the Dniester and Yenissei rivers. The south and west part of the chamber was furnished with tables and trays made of wood, as well as vessels and various containers made of wood, bronze, silver and clay. The deceased wore a tall, pointed head covering,

Figure 8. Reconstruction of the so-called Golden Man from Issyk.

a kaftan-like sleeved jacket, trousers and half-length boots. All of the clothes were apparently made of red felt and adorned with ca. 4000 platelets of gold with figural motifs. Even his weapons (dagger and sword) were incrusted with gold, which led to his epithet: 'the golden man of Issyk' (Figure 8) (Akišev 1978).

Further investigations of the Sakan period in the so-called 'Seven Rivers Country' in southeast Kazakhstan were conducted within the framework of the Berlin Excellence Cluster TOPOI between 2008 and 2011. Investigators here were concerned with the distribution of kurgan cemeteries in steppe landscapes, which generally were not settled in the Late Bronze Age until the beginning of the 1st millennium BC. With the change to a more humid and cooler climate came a change in the vegetation cover, and so a steppe vegetation gradually emerged that was excellently suited for stock-raising. At the same time, the intensive use of steppe areas by Sakan rider-nomads can be noted; among other things they left behind their cemeteries in this vast landscape. The positioning and distribution of these burial places obviously imply a division and marking of the area. In addition, the structure of the cemeteries is quite regional—solely local regularities are recognisable. The kurgans are consistently arranged in rows (Figure 9); although it has also been noticed that in the area east of Almaty one kurgan in each row is built in rectangular form, whereas all the others are round.

Figure 9. Monumental elite kurgans from Semirechye in southeastern Kazakhstan.

The largest grave mounds there reach truly monumental dimensions; they are always surrounded by a wall-like or street-like enclosure, which apparently marked a sacred sphere around the kurgans in which ritual pits and further burials were found (Gass 2014, 2016, Parzinger 2014).

Other groups of rider-nomads settled farther in the northwest, south of the Ural Mountains. Written sources mention the presence of the Sauromatians there, who were related to the Scythians and had a comparable way of life and similar economic forms and social structure. Located there as well are a considerable number of large kurgans. Among them is the royal burial of Filippovka, near the flow of the Ilek River into the Ural River. It is dated to the time of transition from the Sauromatian to early Sarmatian period, and was without question the burial place of a tribal prince. This burial is assigned to the 4th century BC and is therefore coeval with most of the royal graves of the Black Sea Scythians farther west. In Filippova a long, narrow dromos with a step leads to a spacious round grave pit, in which an apparently tent-like wooden construction was originally erected over the grave. Although the burial had been plundered, excavations brought to light a rich grave inventory: sword and dagger made of iron with a golden handle and gold-incrusted blade, golden straps of a horse bridle, gold and silver vessels, many theriomorphic gold appliqués for wooden vessels, stag figures in gold sheet over a wooden core, and much more. The representations of stags, predatory animals, birds of prey and riders deviate slightly in their style from those on Scythian works in the northern Black Sea area. The latter were essentially marked to a large degree by motifs in Greek art and iconography (*Oro* 2001). In addition, there were massive gold and silver vessels, clearly of Achaemenid provenance, which probably reached Sauromatian territory in the north via the Khorezm region south of the Aral Sea, which was already part of the Persian Empire.

The kurgan cemeteries in the Sauromatian territory also display a defined construction, in that all of the mounds are consistently ordered in rows. With the aid of geophysical prospecting methods, we wanted to learn more about the structure of the kurgans' immediate surroundings. During work at the cemetery of Tört Oba, in the area of Aktiube in outermost northwest Kazakhstan, we came across numerous Sauromatian and also older Bronze Age graves, which were not recognisable on the surface, as well as pits, presumably of cultic use (Parzinger *et al.* 2015). Of particular note were the elongated, narrow rectangular ditch squares, which extended in front of the kurgans towards the southeast (Figure 10). They measured up to 50 m in length and 20 m in width. Excavations revealed that these ditches were completely filled with horse bones (partly calcined). This provided evidence that they must have been places of cult activities in association with the kurgans. These ditch squares were connected with extensive offerings of horses, made in honour of the deceased at the relevant kurgan.

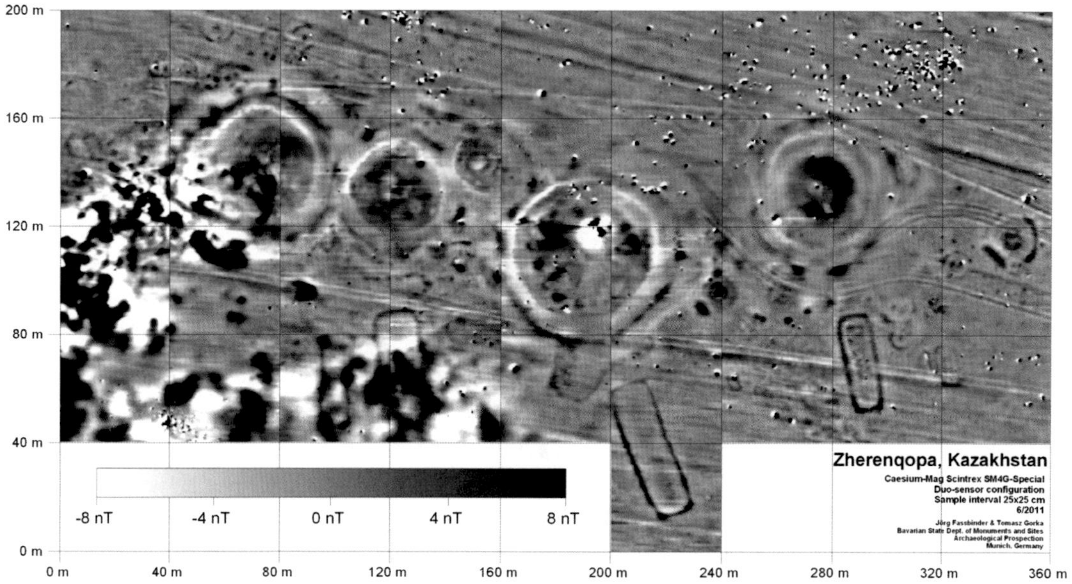

Figure 10. Geophysical prospection in Tört Oba, Aktiube province, south of the Ural mountains.

SCYTHIAN KURGANS IN THE NORTHERN CAUCASUS

Opposite the north Black Sea area and the regions east of the Ural Mountains as far as southern Siberia, the steppe areas north of the Great Caucasus, between the Sea of Azov in the west and the Caspian Sea in the east, are, on the whole, still uninvestigated with regard to cultural relationships during the Scythian period. The number of large kurgans and extensive fields of burial mounds of that time is remarkably large and thus the potential for their investigation is of great significance. Nonetheless, this vast sphere is a blank area on the archaeological map of monuments of Scythian rider-nomads. Geomagnetic surveys have attested numerous find complexes in the surroundings, especially of larger kurgans, which should be investigated archaeologically more closely (Figure 11, see over) (Fassbinder *et al.* 2015, Parzinger *et al.* 2016). Excavations there in the late 19th century were carried out solely in the area east of Stavropol, in the Sultan (Bryk) kurgan. This site was situated upon a high plateau and dominated the entire surrounding landscape. However, the published reports provide little useful information; apparently the grave chamber had been plundered. Yet we do know that the kurgan was built of quality ashlar masonry, otherwise known only among the kurgans in the eastern Crimea (Kerch) that showed strong Greek influence. Under the Sultan (Bryk) kurgan was a passage hewn into the natural clay subsoil, which could be passed only by bending double, and which divided into two passages farther along. Both of these passages ended approximately underneath the centre of the kurgan.

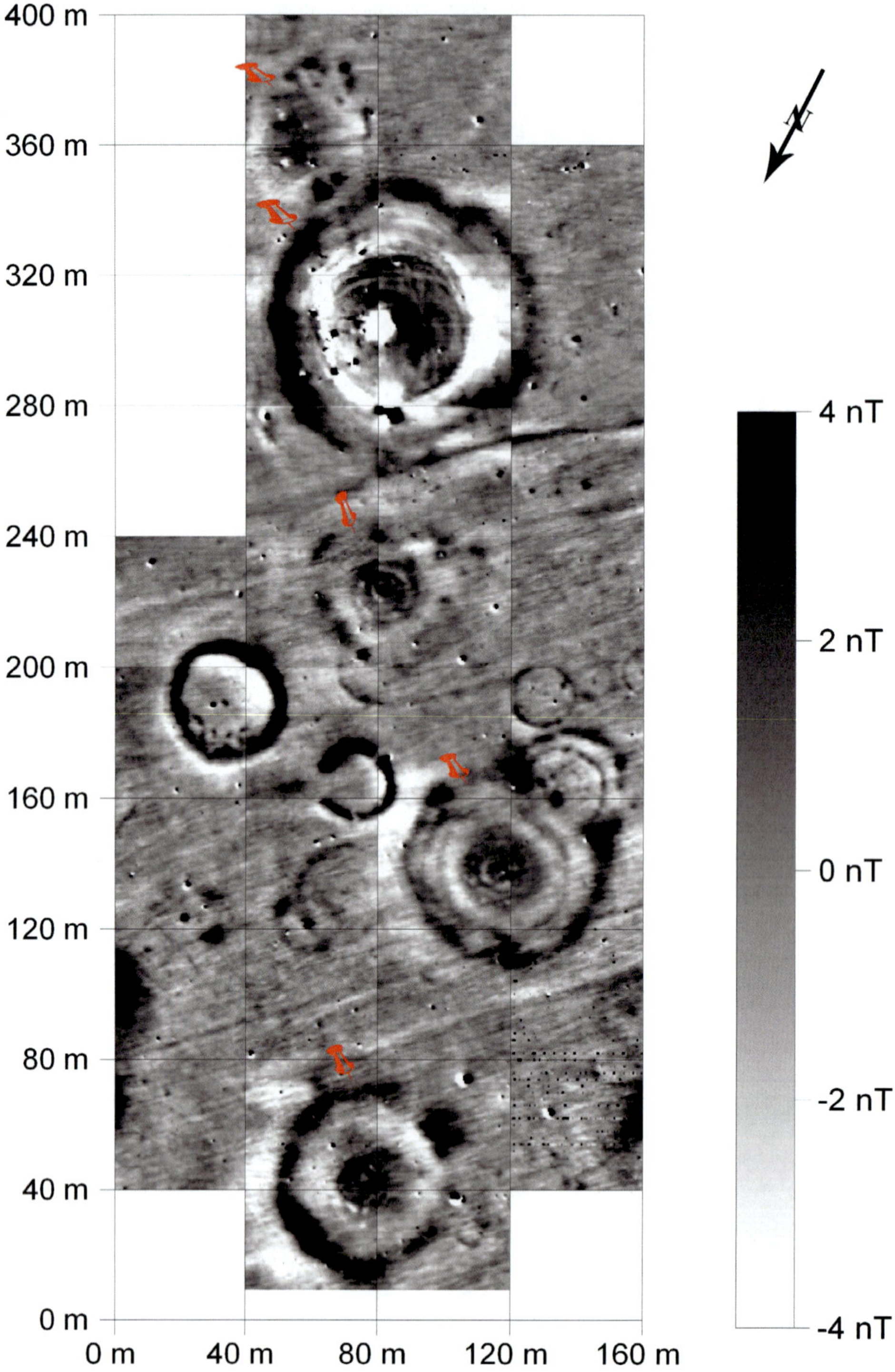

Figure 11. Geophysical prospecting around kurgans at Vinogradnyi in the northern Caucasus.

Clearly they did not lead to the grave itself, but ended underneath the grave chamber. This unusual situation brings to mind the three passageways that led into the grass-sod kurgan in Baikara in northern Kazakhstan. There too, practical reasons for these structures are lacking. The situation might have served ritual purposes, although given the lack of significant find contexts, we cannot go into more detail.

Comparably more is known about the Kuban region farther west in the Caucasus foreland than the area of Stavropol. Excavations were conducted in the Kuban region in the late-19th century and also repeatedly in the 20th century. Among the most famous kurgans investigated are those in Kelermes, Kostromskaya, Maikop and Ul (Grakov 1980: 104 ff., Galanina 1997). The central grave shaft underneath the monumental kurgan in Kelermes and in Kostromskaya was built over by a construction of wooden posts, resembling a hut. Around the grave pit, arranged in a row on two sides or on all four sides, were up to 24 horses lying on their sides (Figure 12). Many gold

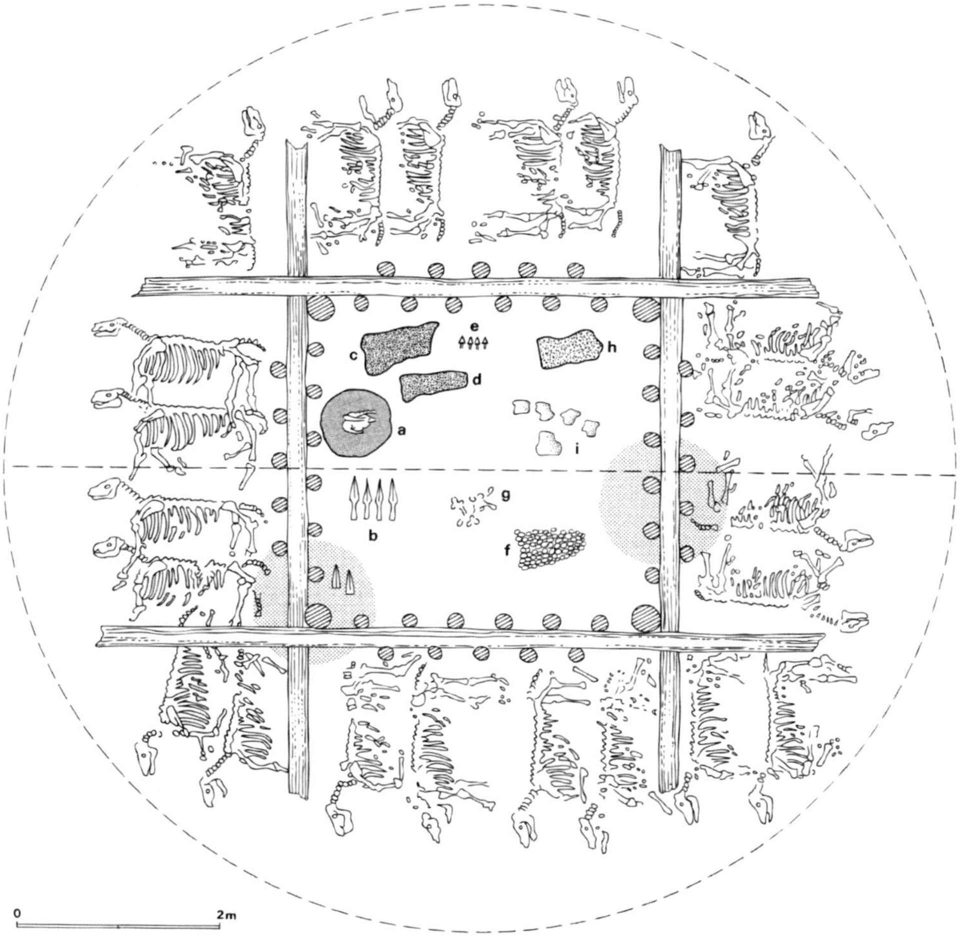

Figure 12. Plan of the burial chamber from Kelermes, excavations in late 19th century (Galanina 1997).

objects dated to early Scythian times in Kelermes show distinct parallels with the treasure of Ziwiyeh, northwest Iran. Both find complexes date to the 7th century BC. Moreover, objects made of sheet gold with figural decoration from Ziwiyeh and Kelermes possess motifs adapted from the Assyrian–Median artistic sphere and integrated in the animal style. The Old Oriental heritage is no longer recognisable in this form in the animal-style works of later Scythian times (Ghirshman 1979).

The mounds of the 4th century BC in Ul are not particularly high and are located at a short distance from Kelermes. Burials were apparently re-enacted, for the mound held wooden grave structures and an unusually rich grave inventory consisting of gold, silver and bronze vessels, imported Greek ceramics, gold jewellery and much more, but no remains of the deceased were present. Perhaps here we have a symbolic grave (cenotaph) for a leader of a Scythian–Maiotian group in the Kuban area, who fell in battle in a foreign land, and whose corpse could not be brought back for burial (Parzinger 2004: 119).

CONCLUDING REMARKS

Despite the sometimes considerable differences in structure and design of monumental large kurgans in various cultural spheres of the Eurasian steppe between the Dnieper in the west and the upper Yenissei in the east, certain basic principles are apparent: underneath the monumental mounds, erected with an enormous effort of labour, are subterranean grave chambers with luxurious furnishings. As described by Herodotus (IV 71), a Scythian prince had to be accompanied to the grave by his wife, his attendants, his horses, his weaponry, his jewellery and his costly clothes, as well as his most important and valuable possessions. Thereby, gold objects played a special role.

Funerary customs were of profound importance for the Scythians, particularly when the ruling class was concerned. This is demonstrated by excavation find contexts and also by a story told by Herodotus, relating to the campaign of Darius. When the Persian king invaded Scythian territory (starting from the lower Danube), the Scythian army withdrew constantly, devastating the land behind and always avoiding battle, yet not surrendering. It thus forced the enemy into a tiresome pursuit. The Scythian King Idanthrysos declared that he would be prepared to fight if the Persians approached the burial places of the ancestors and threatened to destroy them. The tombs of the Scythian kings were located—according to Herodotus—in the landscape of Gerrhos (Herodotus IV 71), through which the Borysthenes (Dnieper River) flowed. Indeed, many richly furnished Scythian large kurgans are known in the lower Dnieper region, which was the background to this story.

Since the first opening of Scythian 'kings' kurgans' in the north Pontic steppes in the 19th century, we have known that rider-nomads of the earlier Iron Age of the 1st millennium BC went to considerable effort to demonstrate the high status of their leaders, even after their death. Monumental burial complexes and legendary luxurious grave furnishings played a central role. Despite—or perhaps due to—the magnificent grave gifts, research on the kurgan structures themselves has not had proper attention until now. Recent excavations at selected sites in northern Kazakhstan (Baikara), Tuva (Arzhan) and the Minusinsk Basin (Barsuchiy Log), augmented by geophysical surveys and supplementary excavations in the surroundings of kurgans in southeast Kazakhstan, in the southern Urals and in the northern Caucasus, have contributed new insights and at the same time broadened our knowledge about funerary customs of the Scythian elites in the Eurasian steppe.

This research has shown that the raising of the mounds proceeded in stages, each connected with cultic and ritual activities. These activities were firm components of the performance of a royal Scythian burial, and were full of symbolism that we are only now beginning to understand. The diligent investigation of the kurgans of Baikara, Arzhan und Barsuchiy Log had made us vividly aware that there were considerable differences between the areas of the Eurasian steppe ruled by individual rider-nomads. There was, however, a common idea, probably connecting together various religious beliefs, as already shown by the animal-style decorations and other details in kurgan construction. However, in their local transformation these ideas were marked differently, and local traditions are perceptible. This became particularly noticeable in our surveys in southeast Kazakhstan, in the southern Urals and in northern Caucasus, which were focused exclusively on the structure of cemeteries and cultic complexes located in the immediate vicinity of large kurgans, without investigating the individual mounds, as the find contexts from kurgan surroundings hold a high information value for interpreting the burial structures themselves.

The finding that in Arzhan the royal burial in a large kurgan is still preserved has fundamentally changed our picture of the treatment of the deceased rider-nomad elites in southern Siberia. It was hitherto assumed that furnishings rich in gold did not characterise graves of the elites, but Arzhan shows that we must reckon with magnificent burials farther east in the Eurasian steppe belt, not at all inferior to those in the north Pontic regions. Without doubt, Arzhan is only the tip of the iceberg! That 300 years of excavation activities had to elapse before research benefited from a discovery like that in Arzhan is unquestionably due to the extensive looting, especially of large kurgans. Yet the find contexts in Barsuchiy Log have taught us that this was not only a result of modern plunder, but apparently to an even stronger degree part of a historical–political development, which occurred towards the end of the Scythian period in the steppe. New groups intruded into areas held until then by Scythian rider-nomads, where they encountered tribes with a marked social structure and a firmly established elite. The deceased members of the ruling class were honoured and commemorated in their monumental burial complexes even after death, which is demonstrated in many sites. If the new rulers wished to put an end to the continuing power of earlier elites, the ravage and despoil of their burial complexes was an effective means, as shown by the extraordinary finds from Barsuchiy Log. The gold found there was not robbed because of its material value but because of its enduring symbolical significance.

Note on the author: Professor Dr. Hermann Parzinger, former Director and later President of the German Archaeological Institute and actual President of the Prussian Cultural Heritage Organisation in Berlin, Corresponding Member of the British Academy and of other German and international Academies of Sciences, dedicated the last two decades to the investigation of Scythian monumental kurgans throughout the Eurasian steppe belt. Among his most important publications are: *Die Skythen* (C. H. Beck, Munich, 2004) and *Die frühen Völker Eurasiens. Vom Neolithikum bis zu Mittelalter* (C. H. Beck, Munich, 2006), offering a broad overview on the prehistory of Eurasia.
Professor Dr. Hermann Parzinger
Stiftung Preussischer Kulturbesitz
von-der-Heydt-Str. 16-18
D-10785 Berlin
parzinger@hv.spk-berlin.de
htpp://www.preussischer-kulturbesitz.de

REFERENCES

Akišev, K. A. (1978), *Kurgan Issyk. Iskusstvo sakov Kazachstana* (Moscow, Nauka).
Čugunov, K. V., Parzinger, H. & Nagler, A. (2003), 'Der skythische Fürstengrabhügel von Aržan 2 in Tuva. Vorbericht der russisch-deutschen Ausgrabungen 2000–2002', *Eurasia Antiqua*, 9: 113–62.
Čugunov, K. V., Parzinger, H. & Nagler, A. (2006), *Der Goldschatz von Aržan. Ein Fürstengrab der Skythenzeit in der südsibirischen Steppe* (München, Hirmer).
Fassbinder, J., Gass, A., Hofmann, I., Belinskij, A. & Parzinger, H. (2015), 'Early Iron Age Kurgans from the North Caucasus', *Archaeologia Polona*, 53: 280–4.
Galanina, L. K. (1997), *Die Kurgane von Kelermes. 'Königsgräber' der frühskythischen Zeit*, Steppenvölker Eurasiens I (Moscow, Palaeograf).
Gass, A. (2014), 'Das Land der sieben Flüsse im 2. bis 1. Jahrtausend v. Chr.', *eTopoi. Journal for Ancient Studies*, 3: 87–106.
Gass, A. (2016), *Das Siebenstromland zwischen Bronze- und Früheisenzeit. Eine Regionalstudie* (Berlin, de Gruyter).
Ghirshman, R. (1979), *Tombe princière de Ziwiyé et le début de l'art animalier scythe* (Paris, Gallimard).

Grakov, B. N. (1980), *Die Skythen* (Berlin, VEB).
Griaznov, M. P. (1984), *Der Großkurgan von Aržan in Tuva, Südsibirien*, Materialien zur Allgemeinen und Vergleichenden Archäologie 23 (München, C. H. Beck).
Mozolevskiy, B. N. & Polin, S. V. (2005), *Kurgany skifskogo Gerrosa IV v. do n. e.* (Kiev, Akademija).
Oro. Il mistero dei Sarmati e degli Sciti (2001), exhibition catalogue (Milan, Mondo Mostre).
Parzinger, H. (2004), *Die Skythen* (Munich, C. H. Beck).
Parzinger, H. (2006), *Die frühen Völker Eurasiens. Vom Neolithikum bis zu Mittelalter* (Munich, C. H. Beck).
Parzinger, H. (2014), 'Central Asia Before the Silk Road', in C. Renfrew & P. Bahn (eds) *The Cambridge World Prehistory.* Volume 3: West and Central Asia and Europe (Cambridge, Cambridge University Press), 1617–37.https://doi.org/10.1017/CHO9781139017831.098
Parzinger, H., Zajbert, V., Nagler, A. & Plešakov, A. (2003), *Der große Kurgan von Bajkara. Studien zu einem skythischen Heiligtum*, Archäologie in Eurasien 13 (Mainz, Philipp von Zabern).
Parzinger, H., Gass, A. & Fassbinder, J. (2015), 'Geophysical Research Findings in Early Iron Age Cemeteries with Large Burial Mounds in Kazakhstan and Northern Caucasus', in V. Molodin & S. Hansen (eds) *International Symposium 'Multidisciplinary methods in Archaeology: Latest Updates and Outlook'. 22–26 June 2015 Novosibirsk* (Novosibirsk, Nauka), 62–9.
Parzinger, H., Gass, A. & Fassbinder, J. (2016), 'At the Foot of Royal Kurgans. The Latest Geoarchaeological and Geophysical Studies', *Science First Hand Novosibirsk*, 1(43): 74–89.
Rolle, R. (1979), *Totenkult der Skythen. Teil I, Das Steppengebiet*, Vorgeschichtliche Forschungen 18 (Berlin & New York, de Gruyter).
Rolle, R., Murzin, V. & Alekseev, A. (1998), *Königskurgan Čertomlyk. Ein skythischer Grabhügel des 4. vorchristlichen Jahrhunderts*, Hamburger Forschungen zur Archäologie 1 (Mainz, Philipp von Zabern).

To cite the article: Hermann Parzinger (2017), 'Burial mounds of Scythian elites in the Eurasian steppe: New discoveries', *Journal of the British Academy*, 5: 331–355.
DOI https://doi.org/10.85871/jba/005.331

Journal of the British Academy (ISSN 2052–7217) is published by
The British Academy—the national academy for the humanities and social sciences.
10–11 Carlton House Terrace, London, SW1Y 5AH
www.britishacademy.ac.uk

Oxford University Press, Great Clarendon Street, Oxford OX2 6DP

Articles first published online in the *Journal of the British Academy* in 2017
This print collection first published 2018

British Library Cataloguing in Publication Data
Data available

Library of Congress Cataloging in Publication Data
Data available

ISBN 978-0-19-726623-6

Typeset by New Leaf Design, Scarborough, North Yorkshire
Pod

This print publication reproduces articles that have been published in the online open-access *Journal of the British Academy* (ISSN 2052-7217). More information about the *Journal* is available at www.britishacademy.ac.uk/journal

Articles published in the online *Journal* may include colour versions of illustrations (including additional plates not printed here) and may be supported by supplementary audio-visual or data content.

Printed and bound by CPI Group (UK) Ltd, Croydon, CR0 4YY